ACCP AMBULATORY CARE NEW PRACTITIONER SURVIVAL GUIDE/RESOURCE MANUAL

SECOND EDITION

For order information or questions, contact:
ACCP Ambulatory Care New Practitioner Survival Guide/Resource Manual
American College of Clinical Pharmacy
13000 West 87th Street Parkway
Suite 100
Lenexa, Kansas 66215
(913) 492-3311
(913) 492-0088 (fax)
www.accp.com

Director of Publications: Nancy M. Perrin
Publications Project Manager: Janel Mosley
Copy Editors: Kimma Sheldon, Donna diNatale
Desktop Publisher/Graphic Designer: Jen DeYoe

Copyright © 2008 by the American College of Clinical Pharmacy. All rights reserved. This book is protected by copyright. No part of this publication may be reproduced, stored in a retrieval system, or transmitted, in any form or by any means, electronic or mechanical, including photocopy, without prior written permission of the American College of Clinical Pharmacy.

Printed in the United States of America.

Library of Congress Control Number: 2007929146
ISBN: 978-1-932658-58-3

Editor

Melissa M. Blair, Pharm.D., FCCP, FASHP, BCPS, CDE
PGY1 Residency Program Director
New Hanover Regional Medical Center
Wilmington, North Carolina

Assistant Editors

Sara Klockars, Pharm.D., BCPS
Clinical Pharmacy Specialist, Primary Care
Kaiser Permanente–Colorado
Denver, Colorado

Mitzi Wasik, Pharm.D., BCPS
Clinical Assistant Professor
University of Illinois at Chicago College of Pharmacy
Chicago, Illinois

Jennifer Askew, Pharm.D., CPP
Manager, Outpatient Pharmacy Services
New Hanover Regional Medical Center
Wilmington, North Carolina

Anthony Ishak, Pharm.D., BCPS
Primary Care Clinical Specialist
Boston Medical Center
Boston, Massachusetts

Kathleen Lindauer, Pharm.D., CACP
Clinical Pharmacy Manager, Outpatient Services
WT Anderson Health Center
Macon, Georgia

Many thanks to the following individuals for helpful contributions

Melissa Blair
New Hanover Regional Medical Center

Betsy Blake
South Carolina College of Pharmacy

Mark Britton
University of Oklahoma College of Pharmacy

Amie Brooks
St. Louis College of Pharmacy

Jennifer D'Souza
Midwestern University Chicago College of Pharmacy

Lori Dickerson
Medical University of South Carolina Family Medicine

Lisa Edgerton
New Hanover Regional Medical Center Family Medicine

Michael Ernst
University of Iowa Colleges of Pharmacy and Medicine

Francine Farnsworth
Salem Veterans Affairs Medical Center

Kristen Felice
University of Illinois at Chicago College of Pharmacy

Kathy Fit
Midwestern University—Chicago College of Pharmacy

David Hachey
Idaho State University Family Medicine

Ila Harris
University of Minnesota Colleges of Pharmacy and Medicine

Eric Jackson
University of Connecticut School of Medicine

Sheila Kasten
Kaiser Permanente of Colorado

Teresa Klepser
Ferris State University College of Pharmacy

Sara Klockars
Kaiser Permanente of Colorado

Christopher Lamer
Cherokee Indian Hospital

Sunny Linnebur
University of Colorado School of Pharmacy

Debra Lopez
University of Texas at Austin College of Pharmacy

Deanna McDanel
University of Iowa College of Pharmacy

Candis Morello
University of California, San Diego
Skaggs School of Pharmacy

Erin Newkirk
University of Iowa College of Pharmacy

Rosalyn Padiyara
Midwestern University Chicago College of Pharmacy

Karen Steinmetz Pater
University of Pittsburgh School of Pharmacy

Beth Bryles Phillips
University of Georgia College of Pharmacy

Kelly Ragucci
South Carolina College of Pharmacy

Rami Rihani
Dreyer Medical Clinic

Melissa Rice
Kaiser Permanente of Colorado

Brian Sandhoff
Kaiser Permanente of Colorado

Amy Schwartz
University of Texas—Pan Am College of Pharmacy

Allen Shek
University of the Pacific School of Pharmacy

Renu Singh
University of California, San Diego
Skaggs School of Pharmacy

Steven Smith
Toledo Hospital Family Practice Residency

Pamela Stamm
Auburn University School of Pharmacy

Jessica Starr
Auburn University, Harrison School of Pharmacy

Amy Stump
University of Wyoming School of Pharmacy

Ryan Suemoto
Naval Medical Center, San Diego

Andrea Wessell
South Carolina College of Pharmacy

Sarah Westberg
University of Minnesota College of Pharmacy

Lori Wilken
University of Illinois at Chicago

Thanks to the following individuals for their peer review comments

Jacintha S. Cauffield, Pharm.D., BCPS
Southwest Washington Medical Center, Family Medicine of Southwest Washington

Christina E. DeRemer, Pharm.D., BCPS
Medical College of Georgia Health System

Disclosure of Potential Conflicts of Interest

Honoraria (Speaker): Amie Brooks (Sanofi-Aventis); Debra Lopez (Eli Lilly); Lori Wilken (Pfizer)
Grants: Amie Brooks (GlaxoSmithKline); Allen Shek (GlaxoSmithKline, Schering-Plough); Lori Wilken (GlaxoSmithKline)

CONTENTS

FOREWORD	v

CLINICAL SERVICES

HOW TO INITIATE PHARMACY INVOLVEMENT IN AN AMBULATORY CLINIC	1
MULTIPLE ROLES OF THE CLINICAL PHARMACIST IN THE FAMILY PRACTICE RESIDENCY PROGRAM	4
PHYSICIAN SURVEYS	8
COLLABORATIVE PRACTICE POLICY/PROCEDURE	14
COLLABORATIVE PRACTICE AGREEMENT	20
CLINICAL PHARMACISTS SCOPE OF PRACTICE	22
SUBURBAN HEIGHTS MEDICAL CENTER PHARMACOTHERAPY CLINIC POLICIES AND PROCEDURES	23
PHARMACOTHERAPY CLINIC REFERRAL FORM	26
CLINICAL PHARMACIST SCOPE OF PRACTICE	27
CLINICAL PHARMACY REFERRAL FORM	28
BILLING FOR PHARMACY SERVICES IN AMBULATORY CARE	29
ANTICOAGULATION SERVICE	31
ANTICOAGULATION SERVICE— POLICY/PROCEDURE	41
ANTICOAGULATION SERVICE POLICY—CHEROKEE INDIAN HOSPITAL	43
ANTICOAGULATION SERVICE PROCEDURE	47
PRIVILEGE REQUEST—PHARMACY	49
CHEROKEE INDIAN HOSPITAL	50
ANTICOAGULATION DRUG THERAPY MANAGEMENT PROTOCOL	51
ADULT ANTICOAGULATION PROTOCOL—CDTM	55
COUMADIN CLINIC DISMISSAL LETTER	59
REMINDER OF MISSED APPOINTMENTS	60
ACUTE DEEP VEIN THROMBOSIS TREATMENT WITH LOW-MOLECULAR-WEIGHT HEPARIN PROTOCOL	61
PHYSICIAN'S PROTOCOL	62
PRIMARY CARE AND CHOLESTEROL MANAGEMENT GROUP SERVICE AGREEMENT, NOTE TEMPLATES, LETTERS, EVALUATION, AND CONSULT	65
CHOLESTEROL GROUP PATIENT INTRODUCTION LETTER	69
CHOLESTEROL MANAGEMENT GROUP—PROVIDER CONSULT	71
CARDIOVASCULAR RISK EDUCATION AND MANAGEMENT PROGRAM PROTOCOL	72
CLINICAL PHARMACY CARDIAC RISK SERVICE	77
CORONARY ARTERY DISEASE SERVICE POLICY AND PROCEDURE	90
HEART FAILURE CLINIC	100
AMBULATORY BLOOD PRESSURE MONITORING REFERRAL SERVICE	109
HYPERTENSION CLINIC	111
ADULT HYPERTENSION PROTOCOL	113
SMOKING CESSATION PROGRAM PROTOCOL	121
SMOKING CESSATION CLINIC POLICY AND PROCEDURE	131
SMOKING CESSATION PROGRAM COLLABORATIVE PRACTICE AGREEMENT	134
ADULT TOBACCO CESSATION PROTOCOL	141
PHARMACY ASTHMA PROGRAM	147
METERED-DOSE INHALER SPACER PROTOCOL—POLICY AND PROCEDURE	153
ASTHMA SHARED MEDICAL APPOINTMENT	158
ADULT TYPE 2 DIABETES PROTOCOL	161
ENDOCRINOLOGY DIABETES CARE CLINIC	168

DIABETES CARE CLINIC IN ENDOCRINOLOGY	169
DIABETES DRUG THERAPY MANAGEMENT PROTOCOL	172
DIABETES DISEASE MANAGEMENT PROTOCOL	174
DEPO-PROVERA CONTRACEPTION PROTOCOL	181
DEPO-PROVERA INJECTION PROTOCOL	184
EMERGENCY CONTRACEPTION POLICY	186
GERIATRIC ASSESSMENT CLINIC	189
OUTPATIENT GERIATRIC CARE	190
SENIORS CLINIC REFILL PROTOCOL	194
FAMILY MEDICINE REFILL PROTOCOL	196
REFILL CLINIC POLICIES AND PROCEDURES	199
DRUG REFILLS POLICY	
IMMUNIZATION PROTOCOL AND SURVEYS	208
HEALTH FAIR SCREENING FORM	212
INDIGENT CARE PROGRAM	213
PHARMACEUTICAL REPRESENTATIVE POLICY AND PROCEDURE	218
INTERACTIONS WITH PHARMACEUTICAL AND PROPRIETARY COMPANIES—POLICY AND PROCEDURE	219
POLICY STATEMENT ON MEDICAL SERVICE REPRESENTATIVES	221

EDUCATION

THERAPEUTICS FOR FAMILY PRACTICE RESIDENTS	227
PHARMACOTHERAPY ROTATION FOR FAMILY PRACTICE RESIDENTS	228
DRUG FOCUSED HOME VISIT—GOALS AND OBJECTIVES	229
JOURNAL CLUB PRESENTATION—GOALS AND OBJECTIVES	230
FAMILY PRACTICE RESIDENCY PROGRAM JOURNAL CLUB	231
JOURNAL CLUB PREPARATION EVALUATION	232
JOURNAL CLUB SESSION EVALUATION	233
THERE'S NO SUCH THING AS A FREE LUNCH	234
ADVANCED PRACTICE EXPERIENCE IN PRIMARY CARE/FAMILY PRACTICE	235
FAMILY MEDICINE INPATIENT ROTATION	241
DIABETES FOR A DAY EXERCISE	243
INSULIN PRACTICE QUESTIONS AND KEY	244
PATTERN MANAGEMENT PROBLEMS AND KEY	245
AMBULATORY CARE CLERKSHIP ROTATION PRE- AND POST-TEST AND ANSWER KEY	247
ANTICOAGULATION PHARMACIST CREDENTIALING EXAMINATION AND CERTIFICATION	249
PHARMACIST COMPETENCIES—ANTICOAGULATION	254
WRITTEN COMPETENCY ASSESSMENT	255
PHARMACIST COMPETENCIES— SMOKING CESSATION	261
SELECTED REFERENCES	267

FOREWORD

Welcome to what we hope will be a useful tool for you. The *ACCP Ambulatory Care New Practitioner Survival Guide/Resource Manual,* Second Edition, was created to provide assistance for new pharmacy practitioners in ambulatory care or for those already practicing who would like to expand their present role. This guide, in its second edition, is an update of a project coordinated by Ila Harris several years ago. The original guide was started to provide a reference for practitioners in Family Medicine, but it has been greatly expanded during the years to include pertinent resources for all ambulatory care practitioners.

The second edition of the survival guide is divided into three parts: clinical services, education, and references. Examples of what other practitioners have developed are included for your perusal. Feel free to use any of the information provided because that is the purpose of this guide. Please remember to acknowledge the original author if you directly download pieces of this guide. Also, this survival guide has been peer reviewed in a limited fashion. Please verify all information before incorporating it into your practice.

The development of this guide would not have been possible without the support of the American College of Clinical Pharmacy Ambulatory Care Practice and Research Network. The material contained within these pages was voluntarily submitted entirely by members of the Practice and Research Network. We thank those of you who participated in making this an invaluable resource.

Melissa Blair, Pharm.D., FCCP, FASHP, BCPS, CDE
Editor

CLINICAL SERVICES

HOW TO INITIATE PHARMACY INVOLVEMENT IN AN AMBULATORY CLINIC

Submitted by: Renu F. Singh

Revised: February 2007

TYPES OF AMBULATORY CLINICS/PRACTICES

Collaborative vs. pharmacist-managed
- **General:** Internal Medicine, Family Practice, General Drug Refill, Drug Therapy Management (DTM)
- **Specialty:** Anticoagulation, Diabetes, Hypertension (HTN), Asthma, Human Immunodeficiency Virus (HIV) (Virology), Thyroid, Lipid, Congestive Heart Failure (CHF), Compliance, Neurology, Oncology, *Helicobacter pylori,* Women's Health, Psychiatry, Preventive Care, Transplant, Pain
- **Consultant:** Nursing homes
- **Private:** Collaboration with private physician practices

INITIATING A SERVICE

Find a need and fill it.
- May be pharmacist-managed or collaborative (e.g., anticoagulation vs. asthma/HIV/diabetes clinic)
- Choose an area of priority needs.
- Choose an area that interests you.
- Identify practitioners who are interested in your service or collaboration.
- Allow time for staff to become familiar with you and to trust you.
- Private group physician practices—send letters to local practices (e.g., asthma)

Proposal
- Write down ideas and present them to a small group of key practitioners first for feedback.
- Key components of written proposal:

Introduction/Background
- Current clinic situation
- Current problems

Benefits of your service
- Improved patient care
- Reduction of health care costs (e.g., hospital admissions, emergency department visits, drug costs)
- Cite references of similar pharmacist-managed services and their outcomes.
- Increased time for physicians to see more acute patients
- Availability of pharmacist to physicians/practitioners
- Collaborative research opportunities on health outcomes

Proposed service
- Outline your services.
- How many patients do you expect to see per clinic session (e.g., new patients vs. follow-ups vs. telephone follow-ups)?
- Who can refer patients (local service vs. hospital-wide)?
- Be aware of some clinics that expand rapidly (e.g., anticoagulation).
- Ensure that you have adequate staff to cover heavy patient load and allow you time for vacation, illness, conference attendance, etc.

Resources required
- Clinic rooms
- Office
- Computer or laptop
- Filing cabinet
- Equipment (e.g., computer, office supplies, telephone)
- Scheduling clerk
- Billing assistance

Budget
- Who pays for your salary?
- Equipment (e.g., computer, laptop, stationery)

Timeline
- When do you anticipate starting this service?
- How many days/sessions per week (best to start with one or two half-days per week initially and increase gradually, if needed)?

○ Proposal should be signed by pharmacist and supportive practitioners.

Prescriptive Authority
- State-specific
- Michigan Pharmacy Law: Prescriber is any licensed health professional acting under delegation of a licensed physician.
- Pharmacist must record name of delegating physician on the prescription.
- All drugs can be prescribed except CII (Schedule II controlled substance) drugs and anabolic steroids.
- Veterans Administration (VA) hospitals
- In 1995, guidelines were established for drug prescribing authority for clinical pharmacy specialists, clinical nurse specialists, nurse practitioners, and physician assistants.
- Scope of practice for each type of practitioner is determined by the practice site.
- Authorized practitioners do not require physician co-signatures.

Protocols
- Try to be nonspecific; this allows greater clinical flexibility.
- Scope of practice: what will you do, laboratory ordering, etc.
- Documentation procedures
- Review process for nurses and physicians
- Know when to refer
- Billing
- How will follow-up be done?
- Should revise at least every two years (or as new guidelines are published)

Skills
- Good patient interactive skills
- Good communication skills with other clinic health care professionals
- Physical assessment skills
- Patient assessment requires both subjective and objective evaluation.
- May be focused or broad
- Some states require physical assessment skills for prescriptive authority.
- Practice critical
- Use skills of other team members.

Documentation
- Legal document
- Develop guidelines to ensure consistent format
- New patient versus established patient versus telephone follow-up

Legal Ramifications
- State pharmacy law
- Institutional guidelines
- Strongly consider additional liability insurance.

Time Commitment
- Anticipate patient load will increase.
- Start slow, go slow. Iron out early problems before expanding and increasing numbers of patients.
- Vacation/sick days: Who will cover (train other pharmacists—evaluation process)?

Training Other Pharmacists
- Define credentials/knowledge required
- Develop standardized training program.
- Goals of service
- Review of required skills
- Clinic procedures
- Experiential training
- Examination

Funding/Reimbursement
- Get to know your billing personnel.
- Identify payer groups for patients.
- Reimbursement is tricky if clinic is within hospital.
- Capitated health care plans
- Consider joint funding from medical department and pharmacy.
- Outcome research on pilot project may provide justification for funding.
- Research grants

Advertising/Promoting Visibility
- Goal: Increase the visibility and awareness of your clinic
- Target key practitioners from whom you will be getting referrals.
- Promote your services by giving a talk at their weekly conference.
- Use brochures, flyers, and business cards.
- Attend and give Grand Rounds.

Teaching
- Pharmacy students: Wait six months or longer until better established in clinic
- Pharmacy residents (may be a residency project; may assist you with protocols, etc.)
- Other pharmacists (who may be interested in your service—potential clinical pharmacists for you)
- Research

- Outcomes (health care resources vs. disease-specific parameters, patient satisfaction, and questionnaires)

Others: Establishing yourself in a new area in a hospital or clinic
- Be visible and available.
- Attend conferences that your practitioners do.
- Keep up with key literature in your area.

Networking
- American College of Clinical Pharmacy (ACCP) Practice and Research Network
- Join their active Listserve.
- American Society of Health-System Pharmacists
- Ambulatory care Listserve
- Create your own networking group with other ambulatory care practitioners in your local area.

MULTIPLE ROLES OF THE CLINICAL PHARMACIST IN THE FAMILY PRACTICE RESIDENCY PROGRAM

Submitted by: Lori Dickerson

Created: June 2001

Presented at the Association of Family Practice Residency Directors Workshop for Directors of Family Practice Residencies. June 2001, Kansas City, Missouri

Goals

This workshop will focus on ways to use and integrate the clinical pharmacist in the Family Practice residency program from the perspective of the clinical pharmacist and the program director. In addition, methods of funding and collaboration for such a position will be discussed.

Background

- The value of pharmacists in the training of family physicians was first described in the 1980s. Since then, there has been increased involvement of clinical pharmacists as teachers within Family Practice residency programs.
- Studies have demonstrated an association between clinical pharmacists in family practice programs and improved drug prescribing, patient satisfaction, and patient outcomes.
- Studies in other ambulatory care settings have demonstrated that clinical pharmacists improve patient outcomes in anticoagulation, asthma, diabetes mellitus (DM), heart failure (HF), and HTN.
- These studies have helped support the role of clinical pharmacists as teachers in Family Practice residency programs.

State of Clinical Pharmacy in Family Practice Residency Programs in the United States

- Recent survey of 579 Family Practice residency programs to evaluate the involvement of clinical pharmacists
- One hundred fifty-five residency programs indicated a clinical pharmacist on the faculty (27%).
- 56% in community-based programs, 44% in university-based programs
- One hundred thirty pharmacists responded to a thirty-item Web-based survey.
- 89% with a Pharm.D. degree; 69% with clinical pharmacy residency training; 12% with fellowship training
- 80% with a faculty appointment in College of Pharmacy
- 52% with a faculty appointment in College of Medicine
- Sources of salary support include College of Pharmacy, Family Practice residency program, Hospital Pharmacy Department, grants, and Area Health Education Consortium.
- Average salary was $66,000 (range: $46,000–$125,000)
- Allocation of time and activities
 43% teaching
 37% patient care
 12% research
 12% administration
 Less than 5% drug distribution

Clinical Pharmacist Roles at Medical University of South Carolina (MUSC) Family Medicine Residency Program

- Clinical pharmacists have been involved in the Department of Family Medicine (DFM) since 1975.
- Positions funded by the College of Pharmacy and Department of Hospital Pharmacy
- Primary role as preceptors of Pharm.D. students
- Clinical pharmacy services for family medicine residents/faculty
- Educational activities with family medicine residents/medical students
- Full-time position funded in 1997 in conjunction with the residency program transitioning to a community hospital
- Expanded role/responsibilities for the clinical pharmacist
- Primary responsibility to coordinate and deliver pharmacotherapy curriculum in the residency program
- Other clinical, scholarly, and administrative responsibilities evolved.
- Pharmacists are evaluated by residents, as are other faculty members.

- Serves as a drug therapy resource to current faculty and residents, former residents, and many community physicians
- Goal was to shift appropriate responsibilities from other faculty to the clinical pharmacist, allowing other faculty to spend time doing more productive activities (i.e., patient care)

Teaching Responsibilities

The longitudinal pharmacotherapy curriculum is delivered on a 24-month cycle as part of the Skills Seminar Series for Family Practice residents. The skills seminars are mandatory educational sessions (2 hours/week) for second- (PGY2) and third-year (PGY3) residents; topic areas include pharmacotherapy, behavioral science, practice management, and procedures. The pharmacotherapy curriculum reflects the most common problems managed in the office setting:

HTN
Coronary artery disease (CAD)
Atrial fibrillation
CHF
DM
Asthma and chronic obstructive pulmonary disease
Menopause
Contraception
Sexually transmitted diseases
Drug use in pregnancy and lactation
Dermatology (skin infections and rashes)
Depression, anxiety, and psychosis
Thyroid disorders
Acquired immune deficiency syndrome (AIDS) and opportunistic infections
Osteoarthritis, rheumatoid arthritis, and gout
Pain management
Peptic ulcer disease and GERD
Respiratory tract infections
Urinary tract infections

The pharmacotherapy curriculum is introduced in an intensive orientation month each July. Orientation is primarily for interns, but it is attended by many PGY2 and PGY3 residents as well. Topics presented during this month reflect the acute management of common problems encountered in the hospital setting:

Stage III HTN and hypertensive crisis
CHF
Asthma and/or chronic obstructive pulmonary disease
Hyperglycemia and hypoglycemia in type 1 and 2 DM
Thromboembolism
Cerebrovascular accident and stroke prevention in atrial fibrillation
Infectious diseases

Drug therapy education is also provided in the nursing home on a weekly basis (one-half hour per week for PGY2 and PGY3 residents). Topics presented reflect the management of chronic problems in nursing home patients:

Principles of drug use/polypharmacy
Incontinence
Pain management
Fever and infection
Falls and fall prevention
Behavioral disorders and dementia
Depression, anxiety, and psychosis

Finally, information on new drugs, regimens, formulations, and herbal product preparations is presented during ten-minute "pearls" during Monday morning reports.

Goals
The general goals and objectives for the pharmacotherapy curriculum are to

- Write appropriate prescriptions and drug orders by hand and using the computerized patient records (CPR), based on individual patient needs and in accordance with selected insurance policies and South Carolina law.
- Use different sources of drug information, including (but not limited to) the pharmacist, medical texts, primary literature, drug information centers, poison control centers, the Internet, online information sources, and pharmaceutical representatives.
- Choose appropriate over-the-counter (OTC) preparations for common ailments in various patient populations.
- Evaluate whether a new drug or different drug should be added to the prescribing armamentarium.
- Understand and apply pharmacokinetic principles for specific drugs and drug dosing in particular patient populations.
- Limit the number of drugs per patient to decrease the opportunity for drug interactions and adverse drug reactions (ADRs) and to increase compliance.
- Identify and prevent common adverse effects and drug interactions.
- Select specific cost-effective choices from a group of pharmacotherapeutic alternatives.
- Set specific end points for each management plan, and monitor the outcomes of pharmacotherapeutic interventions.
- Limit prescriptions for controlled substances and other substances with abuse potential.
- Prescribe generically when possible, except in the small number of instances when there is documented brand superiority.

- Obtain a detailed drug history, including the use of OTC products and herbal remedies, known drug and food allergies, and potential areas for noncompliance.

Delivery of pharmacotherapy curriculum is through the following methods

- Case-based interactive discussions
- Skills stations (e.g., asthma and DM self-management)
- Drug "Stumpers" (Jeopardy)
- Self-audit and group feedback

Delivering a successful pharmacotherapy curriculum

- Information must be practical and relevant.
- Delivery should be in conjunction with a family physician and/or behavioral scientist.
- Didactics must be reinforced at the point of care.

Point-of-care pharmacotherapy education (precepting)

To complement didactic teaching activities, the clinical pharmacist is involved in point-of-care education of family medicine residents. The pharmacist works with the family physician to review and reinforce important drug therapy issues during

- Inpatient rounds (three times/week)
- Nursing home rounds (once/week)

Point-of-care education in the office setting is done on request. Residents page the clinical pharmacist for assistance with drug therapy issues during clinic hours. Some clinical pharmacists formally participate in office precepting with

- Scheduled precepting in conjunction with the family physician
- Formal chart reviews with verbal and/or written feedback
- Video monitoring
- Duplicate (carbon copy) prescription review programs

Pharmaceutical industry curriculum

This portion of the curriculum is designed to teach residents how to appropriately interact with pharmaceutical representatives and how to manage a drug sample closet. Residents are taught how to ask appropriate questions of the pharmaceutical representative to obtain useful information (based on the work from Shaughnessy and Slawson [1999]).

The drug sample closet has been maintained to provide an educational opportunity for residents. Because most family physicians will distribute sample drugs, residents should learn to appropriately use drug samples. The sample closet is maintained on the basis of JCAHO (Joint Commission on Accreditation of Healthcare Organizations) policies and is stocked according to a "Sample Formulary." The Sample Formulary is reviewed quarterly by the residents and residency program faculty during a monthly business meeting, and new drugs are considered for addition to the formulary and the sample closet.

Elective pharmacotherapy rotations

Residents (three or four per year) are offered elective months (PGY2 and PGY3) in pharmacotherapy and evidence-based medicine.

Other educational responsibilities

Medical student, nurse practitioner/physician's assistant education during family practice rotations

Scholarly Responsibilities

The clinical pharmacist is involved in scholarly works in the Family Practice residency program, including clinical research, continuous quality improvement, research programs for residents, and publications.

Collaborative research activities

Collaborate with family physicians on grant submissions for randomized control trials, residency training grants, etc. Some pharmacists coordinate and participate in drug company–sponsored clinical trials.

Continuous Quality Improvement

Serve on the Continuous Quality Improvement committee and participate in drug-related quality improvement activities with other members of the team.

Clinical Scholars Program

Research curriculum for the PGY2 and PGY3 residents coordinated by the clinical pharmacist, program director, and another faculty member in the research division. Residents form teams to do quality improvement work and traditional research projects, and they present their work during Research Day each June.

Publications

The clinical pharmacist collaborates with family physicians and residents on scholarly publications for the family medicine and pharmacy literature.

Many clinical pharmacists publish a monthly newsletter about new drug information for the residency program. Some provide a "drug handbook" of important drug information for all residents.

Administrative Responsibilities

The clinical pharmacist serves as the Assistant Residency Program Director, coordinating the didactic and evaluative components of the residency program. The clinical pharmacist, in conjunction with the program director, coordinates the orientation month, morning reports, noon conferences, skills seminars, and Clinical Scholars Program. The activities are often reviewed with the program director to ensure that important issues in Family Practice are adequately covered.

The clinical pharmacist is involved in resident recruitment, setting policies and procedures, maintaining the core curriculum guide, overseeing residency committees, etc.

The pharmacist interacts with the pharmaceutical representatives and maintains all sample-related policies and procedures in the Family Practice office.

The pharmacist maintains a pharmacotherapy library (references) for use by all members of the program.

Clinical Responsibilities

The Family Medicine residency program must choose a practice model for the clinical pharmacist: direct patient care versus education and consult. At the MUSC Family Medicine residency program, the model is education and consult, rather than direct patient care. However, many clinical pharmacists participate in direct patient care activities. Often, direct patient care activities are provided only for the faculty practice, and the pharmacists provide education and consultation for the residency practice.

Direct patient care activities often include anticoagulation (i.e., warfarin) services, chronic disease management services (e.g., DM, HTN, HF, and hyperlipidemia), prevention services (e.g., smoking cessation, contraception), polypharmacy management services, drug refill services, and patient education services. Some pharmacists provide these services in conjunction with a family physician and bill an entry-level charge for the service.

Often, the clinical pharmacy "clinics" provide the teaching service structure for Pharm.D. students and pharmacy residents. Some pharmacists have Family Medicine residents do rotations with the clinical pharmacist to teach drug therapy principles.

Many pharmacists coordinate the drug assistance programs provided by the pharmaceutical industry. These programs provide drugs to patients without medical insurance, and they are an alternative to providing chronic drug samples.

Integrating Clinical Pharmacotherapy Education in Your Residency Program

- Incorporated in existing educational activities and provided by a current member of your faculty (e.g., physician, nurse practitioner, behavioral scientist, pharmacist)

What can the Society for Teachers of Family Medicine (STFM) Group on Pharmacotherapy do to help your program?

- Collaborating with a local College of Pharmacy to jointly fund a position
  Advantages: shared funding (sometimes fully funded) with College of Pharmacy; provides faculty member and affiliated students/residents on clinical rotations and allows a lot of time for resident, student, and patient education
  Disadvantages: shared funding equals many responsibilities to both institutions; faculty member often pulled away from patient care with pharmacy student/resident responsibilities; pharmacy may want pharmacist to perform direct patient care (may be conflicting viewpoints)
- Collaborating with the affiliated Hospital Department of Pharmacy Services to fund a position
  Advantages: shared funding (sometimes fully funded) with Hospital Pharmacy; may be as simple as having someone come and give didactic lectures to someone rounding with the inpatient team.
  Disadvantages: pharmacist often pulled back to the Hospital Pharmacy for dispensing activities; agenda for education may be primarily inpatient based; time may be constrained by other hospital-related activities (e.g., JCAHO and ADR reporting)
- Fully funding a position through the Family Medicine Residency Program
  Advantages: the residency program can design the position to fulfill its needs; the pharmacist can take on additional administrative responsibilities to allow other providers more productive patient care time; pressures to provide direct patient care and bill for services are reduced
  Disadvantage: Funding
- Other opportunities for funding a position
  - Nurse Practitioner/Physician's Assistant Program
  - Health maintenance organization
  - Pharmaceutical industry (?)

Reference

1. Dickerson LM, Denham A, Lynch T. The state of clinical pharmacy practice in Family Practice residency programs. Fam Med 2002;34:653–7.

PHYSICIAN SURVEY
Submitted by: Mark Britton

Created: 1996

Which of the following describes your current status within the organization (check all that apply)?
- _____ Emergency Medicine
- _____ Family Medicine
- _____ Internal Medicine
- _____ Obstetrics/Gynecology
- _____ Surgery
- _____ Faculty Physician
- _____ Resident
- _____ Intern

Before August 1996, had you ever worked with a clinical pharmacist (one with a Pharm.D. degree and residency or fellowship training in ambulatory care or primary care pharmacy practice)?
- _____ Yes
- _____ No

Please indicate your level of receptivity for the following patient care functions that may be provided by pharmacists.

Drug Therapy Decision-Making

	Very Unreceptive	Unreceptive	Neither Receptive nor Unreceptive	Receptive	Very Receptive
Selecting drug therapy by a protocol for a patient with a predefined medical problem	1	2	3	4	5
Independently selecting drug therapy for a patient with a predefined medical problem	1	2	3	4	5
Authorizing continuation of current drug	1	2	3	4	5
Planning an appropriate interval for follow-up to assess effectiveness of current drug therapy	1	2	3	4	5

Assessing Responses to Drug Therapy

	Very Unreceptive	Unreceptive	Neither Receptive nor Unreceptive	Receptive	Very Receptive
Taking a drug history	1	2	3	4	5
Ordering laboratory tests by a protocol to assess for effectiveness or potential toxicity of drug therapy for a patient with a predefined medical problem	1	2	3	4	5
Independently ordering laboratory tests to assess for effectiveness or potential toxicity of drug therapy	1	2	3	4	5
Providing limited physical assessment (e.g., blood pressure (BP), pulse rate, weight)	1	2	3	4	5
Responding to telephone inquiries from patients about their drug therapy	1	2	3	4	5

Preventive Health

	Very Unreceptive	Unreceptive	Neither Receptive nor Unreceptive	Receptive	Very Receptive
Recommending screening tests for DM, dyslipidemia, and HTN	1	2	3	4	5
Performing screening tests for DM, dyslipidemia, or HTN	1	2	3	4	5
Interpreting the results of screening tests for DM, dyslipidemia, and HTN	1	2	3	4	5

Documentation

	Very Unreceptive	Unreceptive	Neither Receptive nor Unreceptive	Receptive	Very Receptive
Documenting patient care activities in the medical record	1	2	3	4	5
Documenting drug therapy recommendations for a patient's primary care physician (PCP) when solicited by that provider	1	2	3	4	5
Documenting drug therapy recommendations for a patient's PCP when not solicited by that provider	1	2	3	4	5

Patient Education

	Very Unreceptive	Unreceptive	Neither Receptive nor Unreceptive	Receptive	Very Receptive
Teaching a patient how to assess drug therapy using devices such as glucometers and peak expiratory flow meters	1	2	3	4	5
Teaching a patient how to inject insulin	1	2	3	4	5
Teaching a patient the best times to use prescribed drugs	1	2	3	4	5
Teaching a patient the likely outcomes they should expect from each prescribed drug	1	2	3	4	5

Please select in order of importance five of the following conditions for which you feel your patients could obtain an improved therapeutic response if you could create more time for education about their drug therapy. (1 = most important, 2 = next most important, etc.)

_____ Angina
_____ Asthma
_____ Chronic Pain
_____ CHF
_____ Chronic Obstructive Pulmonary Disease (COPD)
_____ Diabetes
_____ Dyslipidemia
_____ Hypertension
_____ Nicotine Addiction
_____ Seizure Disorder
_____ Thromboembolic Disorder
_____ Other_____

Please select, in order of importance, five of the following conditions for which you feel your patients could obtain an improved therapeutic response if you could create more time for drug initiation and titration. (1 = most important, 2 = next most important, etc.)

    _____Angina
    _____Asthma
    _____Chronic Pain
    _____CHF
    _____COPD
    _____Diabetes
    _____Dyslipidemia
    _____Hypertension
    _____Nicotine Addiction
    _____Seizure Disorder
    _____Thromboembolic Disorder
    _____Other_____

Please select, in order of importance, five of the following drugs for which you feel your patients could obtain an improved therapeutic response if outpatient pharmacokinetic dosing services were available. (1 = most important, 2 = next most important, etc.)

    _____Carbamazepine (Tegretol®)
    _____Digoxin
    _____Gentamicin
    _____Lithium
    _____Phenobarbital
    _____Phenytoin (Dilantin®)
    _____Primidone (Mysoline®)
    _____Procainamide
    _____Quinidine
    _____Theophylline
    _____Tobramycin
    _____Valproic acid (Depakote®)
    _____Vancomycin
    _____Warfarin (Coumadin®)
    _____Other_____

FAMILY MEDICINE CLINICAL PHARMACY SERVICES—PHYSICIAN SURVEY

Submitted by: Melissa Blair

Created: October 2001

The Family Medicine clinical pharmacists are trying to determine areas where we can formally standardize services (for example, through case management or consultation). If you would please take five to ten minutes to answer the following questions, we would greatly appreciate it! Thank you.

1. What pharmacy services do you *currently use* in the clinic? Please rank the services you use in order, with 1 being the most used.

   _____ Asthma   _____ Headaches   _____ Nutrition
   _____ Anticoagulation   _____ Hyperlipidemia   _____ Osteoporosis
   _____ CHF   _____ Hypertension   _____ Pain management
   _____ Depression   _____ Drug administration   _____ Peptic ulcer disease
   _____ Diabetes   _____ Drug education   _____ Smoking cessation
   _____ Financial assistance   _____ Drug management   _____ Women's health
   _____ Gastroesophageal reflux disease (GERD)   _____ Other (please specify)

2. Please rate on a scale of 1 (least) to 5 (most) how helpful pharmacists have been in providing the above services.

       1   2   3   4   5

3. What pharmacy services *would you consider using* in the clinic? (Please check all that apply.)

   _____ Asthma   _____ Headaches   _____ Nutrition
   _____ Anticoagulation   _____ Hyperlipidemia   _____ Osteoporosis
   _____ CHF   _____ Hypertension   _____ Pain management
   _____ Depression   _____ Drug administration   _____ Peptic ulcer disease
   _____ Diabetes   _____ Drug education   _____ Smoking cessation
   _____ Financial assistance   _____ Drug management   _____ Women's health
   _____ GERD   _____ Other (please specify)

4. Are there any other areas where you feel clinical pharmacists would be beneficial?

5. Are there any areas where you feel clinical pharmacists are not necessary?

Thank you for your time.

AMBULATORY CLINICAL PHARMACY SERVICES—PHYSICIAN SURVEY

Submitted by: Melissa Blair

Created: August 2002

The Family Medicine clinical pharmacists are trying to determine areas where we can formally standardize services to all providers in the MUSC system on a referral basis. Please assist us in the development of this service by answering the following questions and returning the survey in the enclosed envelope.

1. **Which of the following describes your current department within MUSC?** (Please check all that apply.)

    - ❑ Medicine (please list subspecialty)_____
    - ❑ Orthopedics
    - ❑ Neurology
    - ❑ Pediatrics
    - ❑ Neurosurgery
    - ❑ Surgery (please list subspecialty)_____
    - ❑ OB/Gyn
    - ❑ Other (please list)_____

2. **Have you ever worked with a clinical pharmacist?**

    - ❑ Yes   If yes, please describe _____
    - ❑ No

3. **The following are roles a clinical pharmacist may perform in a collaborative practice agreement with a physician. Which of the following roles do you think are important for pharmacists to provide after a patient referral to the Pharmacotherapy Clinic?** (Please check all that apply.)

    - ❑ Selecting drug therapy for a patient with a predefined medical problem (e.g., asthma, DM, HTN, lipids)
    - ❑ Initiating drug therapy for a patient with a predefined medical problem (e.g., asthma, DM, HTN, lipids)
    - ❑ Monitoring drug therapy through assessment of efficacy and toxicity
    - ❑ Continuing drugs based on efficacy and toxicity profiles in accordance with established end points
    - ❑ Modifying drug therapy based on efficacy and toxicity profiles in accordance with established end points
    - ❑ Initiating requests for, or performing, and interpreting results from appropriate laboratory and other diagnostic studies needed to assess drug therapy
    - ❑ Teaching a patient to assess drug therapy through the use of devices (e.g., glucometers, peak flow meters)
    - ❑ Providing patient education about disease states and drug therapy
    - ❑ Administering drugs
    - ❑ Other (please specify)_____

4. **The following are common education and drug management services offered by ambulatory clinical pharmacists. In which of these situations do you feel your patients would benefit from a referral to the Pharmacotherapy Clinic?** (Please check all that apply.)

    - ❑ Asthma
    - ❑ Anticoagulation
    - ❑ CHF
    - ❑ DM
    - ❑ Dyslipidemia
    - ❑ Financial assistance
    - ❑ General drug education
    - ❑ General drug management
    - ❑ Hypertension
    - ❑ Immunization/drug administration
    - ❑ Nutrition
    - ❑ Osteoporosis
    - ❑ Pain management
    - ❑ Smoking cessation
    - ❑ Therapeutic drug monitoring
    - ❑ Other (please specify)
    _____
    _____

5. **Of the above services, please list the top three you would most likely use.** (Please rank in order of importance.)
    1. _____
    2. _____
    3. _____

6. **Are there any other areas where you feel a referral to a clinical pharmacist would be beneficial?**

7. **If you would not use this service, please state why.**

COLLABORATIVE PRACTICE POLICY/PROCEDURE

Submitted by: Melissa Blair

Revised: 2004

Definitions

Collaborative Drug Therapy Management (CDTM) Agreement

A voluntary written agreement between a pharmacist and prescriber that permits expanded responsibilities for the pharmacist, such as initiating, modifying, and monitoring drug therapy; ordering and performing laboratory tests; assessing response to therapy; performing limited physical assessment; educating and counseling patients; and administering drugs. CDTM agreements are based on protocols and/or practice guidelines and are intended to optimize patient care outcomes.

Pharmacy Credentials Committee

A committee appointed by the Director of Pharmacy Services charged with reviewing and making recommendations on applications for CDTM, CDTM agreements, and protocols. Expected actions include approval, denial, or deferment for further information.

Policy

This policy describes CDTM policy and associated procedures. The purpose of a CDTM agreement between a pharmacist and physician is to optimize drug therapy regimens, provide drug and disease state education to the patient, decrease drug complications, and improve quality of life and overall patient well-being. CDTM is defined and supported by the state of South Carolina Pharmacy Practice Act. The following policy establishes the mechanism for the appropriate use of CDTM within the MUSC.

The Director of Pharmacy Services is charged with administration of this program. The CDTM is authorized for MUSC patients only in accordance with the parameters dictated by the CDTM agreements developed and approved through this procedure. CDTM agreements must be reviewed and updated or else discontinued at least every two years.

Procedure

Application for CDTM

Pharmacists wishing to enter into a CDTM agreement shall complete the Application for CDTM (Appendix A) and submit both the application and required supporting documentation to their supervisor. The request is reviewed and approved by the applicant's supervisor, the Pharmacy Credentials Committee, and Director of the Department of Pharmacy Services (and Chair of Pharmacy Practice for College of Pharmacy Faculty applicants).

Collaborative Drug Therapy Agreement

After the application is approved, the applicant may initiate a discussion with a physician known to him or her. A description of the type of DTM the pharmacist would like to collaborate on is presented to the physician for discussion of feasibility, etc. A protocol is then developed to clearly define roles and responsibilities of each party—the physician's role in diagnosis and the pharmacist's responsibility for monitoring or initiating therapy and modifying it as necessary. The format of the *Model Collaborative Drug Therapy Management Agreement* (Appendix B) should be followed.

The written protocol represents the formal agreement between the physician and pharmacist. It should represent the voluntary participation of each party and be written carefully and succinctly, defining the role of each. It should describe the specific responsibilities authorized by the physician, the method of documentation to be used, the types of initiation and modification of drug therapy that the pharmacist can perform, and the procedures and plans the pharmacist should follow. Algorithms may be included in the protocol to aid in drug therapy modification in response to blood values, patient response, adverse effects, etc. The protocol should facilitate frequent quality communication between the physician and pharmacist and provide oversight and quality assurance activities.

Approval of the CDTM Agreement

1. Pharmacy Services Approvals—The draft CDTM agreement is submitted to the applicant's coordinator, manager, and Pharmacy Credentials Committee for review and approval.
2. Medical Approvals—After approval by the Pharmacy Credentials Committee, the CDTM agreement is approved by the Chair of the collaborating physician's department.
3. Administrative Approval—The CDTM agreement is reviewed and approved by the Director of Pharmacy Services (and Chair of Pharmacy Practice for College of Pharmacy Faculty applicants).
4. Physician and Pharmacist signatures

The physician and pharmacist consummate the agreement by their signature and the recording of their respective license numbers.

Location of Application and Collaborative Drug Therapy Management Agreements

The original signed documents are maintained on file in the office of the Director of Pharmacy Services. CDTM protocols are posted on the Department of Pharmacy Services Collaborative Drug Therapy Management Web page.

Appendix A

APPLICATION FOR COLLABORATIVE DRUG THERAPY MANAGEMENT

1. PERSONAL DATA:

Name:_____
       (last)   *(first)*   *(middle)*

Office Telephone _____ Pager # _____ Email_____

2. EDUCATION

College/University	Graduation Date	Degree Awarded

Attach copy of diploma(s).

3. POSTGRADUATE TRAINING

Program	Institution	Date Completed
Residency		
Specialized Residency		
Fellowship		

Attach copy of residency certificate(s).

4. QUALIFICATIONS—Indicate (✓) which of the following requirements are met:

Met	Verified	The minimum requirements to apply for Collaborative Drug Therapy Management privileges are:
		A. Graduation from a pharmacy program accredited by the American Council on Pharmaceutical Education (ACPE) or an alternative educational program accepted by the Board of Pharmaceutical Specialties (e.g., pharmacy school outside the United States)
		B. Current, active license to practice pharmacy in the state of South Carolina
		C. Must meet one of the following two requirements:
		1. Bachelor of Science in Pharmacy degree (or equivalent) plus a, b, c, or d below:
		a. Five (5) years of practice with substantial component (> 50%) of patient care activities in pharmacotherapy **OR**
		b. Completion of a Pharmacy Practice or Specialty Residency and three additional years of practice with a substantial component (> 50%) of patient care activities in pharmacotherapy **OR**
		c. Completion of BOTH a Pharmacy Practice Residency and a Specialty Residency with a substantial component (> 50%) of patient care activities in pharmacotherapy **OR**
		d. Certified in an area applying for collaborative practice
		2. Doctor of Pharmacy degree plus a, b, or c below
		a. Three (3) years of experience with a substantial component (> 50%) of patient care activities in pharmacotherapy **OR**
		b. Completion of a Pharmacy Practice or Specialty Residency with a substantial component (> 50%) of patient care activities in pharmacotherapy **OR**
		c. Certified in an area applying for collaborative practice

COLLABORATIVE DRUG THERAPY MANAGEMENT

Requested	Approved	CDTM privileges may encompass the following activities executed within established protocols or approved guidelines by a CDTM agreement with a physician of the MUSC Medical Staff:
		A. Perform limited physical assessment evaluation as indicated
		B. Initiate drug therapy as necessary
		C. Modify or discontinue ongoing drug therapy
		D. Order appropriate tests necessary to determine a baseline level or to monitor the efficacy or toxicity of newly initiated or concurrent drug therapy management
		E. Perform point-of-care testing to monitor the efficacy or toxicity of drug therapy
		F. Administer drugs per protocol
		G. Refer patients by consult to other health care providers
		H. Conduct and coordinate clinical drug investigations and research under established regulations

PRIVILEGES REQUESTED

The applicant indicates which of the following activities are requested using the following codes: (1) Perform unsupervised, (2) Perform with supervision, or (3) Not requested or approved

Requested by:

_____   _____
Pharmacist   Date

Approved by:

_____   _____   _____
Printed Name   Signature   Date
Coordinator

_____   _____   _____
Printed Name   Signature   Date
Manager

_____   _____   _____
Printed Name   Signature   Date
Chair, Pharmacy Credentials Committee

_____   _____   _____
Printed Name   Signature   Date
Chair, Pharmacy Practice
(when applicable)

_____   _____   _____
Printed Name   Signature   Date
Director, Pharmacy Services

Appendix B

MODEL COLLABORATIVE DRUG THERAPY MANAGEMENT AGREEMENT

Pharmacist:

Practice Location:

Protocols/Guidelines/References:

Delegated DTM Activities:
- A. Perform limited physical assessment evaluation as indicated within established protocols or approved guidelines
  Specifics if required for this physician
- B. Initiated drug therapy as necessary within established protocols or approved guidelines
  Specifics if required for this physician
- C. Modify or discontinue ongoing drug therapy within established protocols or approved guidelines
  Specifics if required for this physician
- D. Order appropriate tests necessary to determine a baseline level or to monitor the efficacy or toxicity of newly initiated or concurrent drug therapy management
  Specifics if required for this physician
- E. Perform point-of-care testing to monitor the efficacy or toxicity of drug therapy
  Specifics if required for this physician
- F. Administer drugs within established protocols or approved guidelines
  Specifics if required for this physician
- G. Refer patients by consult to other health care providers within established protocols or approved guidelines
  Specifics if required for this physician
- H. Conduct and coordinate clinical drug investigations and research under established regulations
  Specifics if required for this physician

Pharmacy Services Approvals

Printed Name	Signature	Date
Coordinator		

Printed Name	Signature	Date
Manager		

Printed Name	Signature	Date
Chair, Pharmacy Credentials Committee		

Medical Staff Approval

_____ _____ _____
Printed Name   Signature   Date
Medical Department Chair

Administrative Approvals

_____ _____ _____
Printed Name   Signature   Date
Chair, Pharmacy Practice
(when applicable)

_____ _____ _____
Printed Name   Signature   Date
Director, Pharmacy Services

This Collaborative Drug Therapy Management Agreement is entered into this
_____ day of the month of _____ in the year _____, by and between:

_____ _____ _____
Pharmacist Printed Name   Signature   License Number

_____ _____ _____
Physician Printed Name   Signature   License Number

_____ _____ _____
Physician Printed Name   Signature   License Number

_____ _____ _____
Physician Printed Name   Signature   License Number

COLLABORATIVE PRACTICE AGREEMENT

Submitted by: Amie Brooks, Rosalyn Padiyara, Jennifer D'Souza, and Rami Rihani

Revised: 2006

DREYER MISSION

"Dreyer Medical Clinic is dedicated to providing or making available the most progressive and cost-effective health care in the greater Fox Valley area. This includes an expression of concern for each of our patients as an individual member of the human family."

AUTHORITY

As a physician of the Dreyer Medical Clinic I, *Physician's Name*, authorize *Pharmacist Name*, Pharm.D., a clinical pharmacist who holds an active license from the Illinois Board of Pharmacy, to manage patients of the Dreyer Medical Clinic, pursuant to a written referral from other practitioners or from me.

SCOPE OF PRACTICE

In managing the patients, the clinical pharmacists may modify or discontinue drug therapy, may order laboratory tests, and may exercise other pharmaceutical care management related to monitoring or improving the outcomes of drug therapy.

The pharmacists will have the authority to manage patients with diabetes as outlined in the Diabetes Management Clinic Protocol and American Diabetes Association (ADA) Clinical Practice Recommendations.

The pharmacists will have authority to manage lipid therapy according to the National Cholesterol Education Program (NCEP) Adult Treatment Panel III guidelines and as outlined in the Lipid Disease Management Protocol in defining therapeutic goals and managing therapy.

The pharmacists will have authority to manage adjunctive therapy, such as hypertension, as required to support the achievement of therapeutic goals for other therapies authorized in this section.

The pharmacists will have the authority to assess a patient's drug therapy. This will involve laboratory and clinical monitoring for response and toxicity, assessing drug compliance issues and/or barriers, using the most clinically efficient therapy, and providing education to the patients.

The pharmacist will see the patient only if the patient has been seen by the primary care physician at least once in the previous year. If a patient does not show up for a *scheduled* primary care physician visit, that patient will be seen only once by the clinical pharmacists until he or she is able to attend a visit with the PCP.

DOCUMENTATION

Progress notes on specific patient visits as well as general patient information taken on entry into the Lipid Disease Management Clinic and Diabetes Disease Management Clinic will be documented by the electronic medical record.

AGREEMENT REVIEW AND DURATION

This agreement shall be valid for a period not to exceed **two years** from the effective date of the original agreement or **two years** from the date of signed subsequent amendments. However, it may be reviewed and revised at any time at the request of any of the physicians. The physician may list any exclusions or specific instructions in the area provided below:

Special Instructions/Exceptions:

_____
_____
_____

RECORD RETENTION

1. Each physician who agreed to sign this agreement shall keep a copy of this agreement on file at his or her primary place of practice.
2. A copy of the patient's referral shall be maintained in the patient's electronic medical record and kept on file by the clinic pharmacists.

Prepared by Dreyer Medical Clinic
Aurora, Illinois

WITHDRAWAL OR ALTERATION OF AGREEMENT

The physician may withdraw from the agreement at any time or may override this agreement whenever he or she deems such action necessary or appropriate for a specific patient.

AGREEMENT SIGNATURES

Date_____
Signatures:

_____
Physician (print)   Signature   License #

_____
Medical Director (print)   Signature   License #

_____
Director of Pharmacy (print)   Signature   License #

_____
Clinical Pharmacist (print)   Signature   License #

CLINICAL PHARMACISTS' SCOPE OF PRACTICE

Submitted by: Amy Schwartz

Revised: 2000

The following describes the privileges allocated to the Clinical Pharmacists practicing within Suburban Heights Medical Center

- Access to the medical records (hard copy and computerized)
- Document pertinent findings and recommendations in the medical records
- Order laboratory and noninvasive tests (e.g., EKG, x-rays) to facilitate therapeutic monitoring. Applies only to tests directly related to the condition(s) necessitating clinical pharmacist referral
- Request consultations from other health care practitioners (e.g., professional referrals)
- Interview patients and perform minor physical assessments to determine patient response to therapy
- Evaluate patient response to pharmacological interventions and adjust dosages as clinically indicated. Drugs affected will include those related to the condition(s) necessitating clinical pharmacist referral
- Order prescription refills in accordance with existing clinic protocol. Initiate new prescriptions after conferring with the referring physician (excluding dose adjustments as noted above)
- Initiate, coordinate, and participate in research projects and/or quality assurance assessments

The above items may be reviewed periodically and modified as deemed necessary. Additions/subtractions to the Scope of Practice can occur after obtaining approval from the individuals listed below.

Approved by:

_____
Medical Director
Suburban Heights Medical Center

_____
Director of Pharmacy
Suburban Heights Medical Center

_____
Amy Schwartz, Pharm.D.
Clinical Pharmacist
Assistant Professor Pharmacy Practice
Midwestern University

_____
Janet Ritter, Pharm.D.
Clinical Pharmacist
Assistant Professor Pharmacy Practice
Midwestern University

SUBURBAN HEIGHTS MEDICAL CENTER PHARMACOTHERAPY CLINIC POLICIES AND PROCEDURES

The purpose of this document is to state the policies and procedures that will govern daily clinical activities within the Suburban Heights Medical Center (SHMC) Pharmacotherapy Clinic (PC).

Goals

- To provide proficient and reliable pharmacotherapy management services
- To improve outcomes (clinical, humanistic, and economic)

Objectives

- To use a multidisciplinary approach to the delivery of patient care
- To provide consultative and interim services
- To provide educational services for patients (and/or caregivers)
- To provide educational services for SHMC clinical staff
- To provide an educational training site for pharmacy (and other health-related professions) students and residents
- To provide a template for research and quality assurance projects

Guidelines For Referral

- Only SHMC patients may be referred to the PC. Referrals will be accepted during regular clinic hours.
- The information provided on the referral form should be comprehensive. Any health care practitioner (e.g., nurses, nurse practitioners, physician assistants) may complete the forms, but the patient's physician <u>must</u> sign all forms.
- Physicians must indicate the service(s) requested and whether recommendations and/or management is preferred.
  - **Only short-term follow-up will be provided**.
- Patient acceptance requires:
  - The patient to be reliable, capable, and cognizant, **or**
  - The availability of a reliable, capable, and cognizant caregiver, **and**
  - Consistent medical follow-up
- *The clinical pharmacists reserve the right to decline referrals that are deemed inappropriate. An explanation will be documented in the patient's medical record.*
- New referrals will be scheduled either through a representative of the referring physician or the SHMC receptionists.
- Completed referral forms should be placed in the Clinical Pharmacists' mailbox (in Family/Internal Medicine, located behind the receptionists).
- Office telephone numbers:
  - The clinical pharmacists are also available by pager. The SHMC operators should be contacted for all paging purposes.
- The referral process for inpatients is identical to that for ambulatory patients (e.g., hospitalized patients who are referred for outpatient assistance at the time of discharge).

Scheduling Appointments

- Consultations with the clinical pharmacists are <u>only</u> available by scheduled appointments.
- As previously mentioned, either a representative of the referring physician or the SHMC receptionists will schedule new referrals. The SHMC receptionists will handle all scheduling thereafter. Attempts will be made to conveniently schedule patients; coordination of appointments will be encouraged. The clinical pharmacists will notify SHMC receptionists of all scheduling changes.
- The interval between visits will be determined on a case-by-case basis (i.e., patient-dependent).
- The SHMC receptionist will verify all appointments on the preceding day. It will be the responsibility of the patient to inform the SHMC receptionists of his or her continued availability for an appointment. A fee may be applied to the accounts of patients who repeatedly fail to show up for scheduled appointments.
- Patients who arrive more than fifteen minutes late will be rescheduled. Permission for late patients to be seen on arrival will be at the discretion of the clinical pharmacist.

Clinic Visits

Medical records will be made available for each visit (per SHMC policy). Shadow files will be developed and maintained for all PC patients and kept within the clinical pharmacy office. Shadow files serve to document the activities of the clinical pharmacists; provide information when the medical record is unavailable; and facilitate data collection for research interests. The information contained within the files includes (but is not limited to) the following: copies of visit notes, laboratory results, and flow sheets. SHMC clinical personnel are able to review individual shadow files on request.

The clinical pharmacists will be responsible for disseminating the information obtained during personal interviews (in accordance with the SHMC Clinical Pharmacists Scope of Practice document). Because the PC is a pharmacy practice teaching model, students or residents, under the direct supervision of a clinical pharmacist, may perform patient interviews.

Laboratory tests will be requested in accordance with the SHMC Clinical Pharmacists' Scope of Practice document. Before their scheduled appointment, patients will be instructed to contact the clinical pharmacists so that laboratory orders can be placed. The appropriate time frames (for laboratory draw and receipt of results) will be relayed to patients. Inappropriate acquisition of laboratory tests may necessitate appointment rescheduling. Authorized personnel will draw laboratory tests, with results forwarded to the clinical pharmacists.

Noninvasive tests (e.g., EKG, x-rays, etc.) may be ordered as necessary to assist with patient assessment (in accordance with the SHMC Clinical Pharmacists' Scope of Practice document).

Treatment regimen modifications will be handled in accordance with the SHMC Clinical Pharmacists' Scope of Practice document. All visit notes will be delivered to the referring physician for review and co-signature. All interchanges between physicians and clinical pharmacists will be clearly documented in the medical records.

The ordering of prescription drugs (new or refills) will be handled in accordance with the SHMC Clinical Pharmacists' Scope of Practice document.

The clinical pharmacists will be responsible for contacting the referring physician with any acute medical problems observed during a clinic visit, new onset or exacerbation, requiring immediate attention. The same policy will apply to the receipt of critical laboratory results.

Patients will be encouraged to maintain routine medical follow-up. When applicable, the clinical pharmacists may help facilitate the scheduling process.

Medical Emergencies

Occasionally during PC visits, a patient may be identified as experiencing an acute medical emergency. In such instances, the referring physician will be contacted as soon as possible. If the referring physician is not available, the physician's partner and/or the on-call physician will be contacted. Patients will be continuously monitored while awaiting response. The clinical pharmacists will maintain active CPR certification.

Patients who are at home at the time of an acute medical emergency and who contact the clinical pharmacy office for assistance will be instructed to call their physician and/or 911 (depending on the situation).

Patients may call the clinical pharmacy office with non-emergency concerns or questions. If, on questioning, the complaint is determined to be an emergency, the preceding policy will apply.

Education

Patient education will be a continuous process. To facilitate individual cognizance, patient-pharmacist partnerships will be developed during initial visits. Periodically, the clinical pharmacists may provide patient education programs related to general medical topics for the entire SHMC population. Pharmacy students and residents will be involved in these undertakings as part of their training requirements.

Staff development and education will be facilitated through inservice training and/or newsletter. As above, pharmacy students and residents will be involved with these undertakings as part of their training requirements.

Discharging Patients from Clinic

The PC clinic offers short-term disease state management and assistance with drug-related issues. Similar to other referral services, when stability and/or target goal(s) are attained, patient follow-up will be discontinued. Definitions for stability and/or target goal(s) will be individualized and clearly described in the patient's medical record. If stability is lost at a future date, patients may be referred back to the PC for further assistance.

Patients who fail to schedule follow-up appointments after being notified by mail on three successive occasions will be discharged from the clinic. A copy of the third/final letter will be placed in the patient's medical record to serve as notification to other health care providers.

Patients who fail to show up for three consecutive scheduled appointments will be discharged from the clinic. Similar to the above, before discontinuation, the patients will have received notification in the mail to reschedule after each failed appointment. A copy of the third/final notification will be placed in the patient's medical record.

The ability of patients to comprehend and comply with their treatment regimen(s) will be assessed periodically. The clinical pharmacists reserve the right to discontinue the follow-up of patients who become inappropriate. Examples of such instances include, but are not limited to, deterioration in the functional status or the loss of an acceptable caretaker. The explanation for discontinuation will be placed in the patient's medical record. Patients will receive in writing an explanation of the reason(s) for termination, together with encouragement to maintain normal follow-ups with their physician(s).

Patients may request PC follow-up discontinuation. Patients must inform the clinical pharmacist of their plans, after which the clinical pharmacist will discuss the pros and cons of the decision. The request and reason(s) for discontinuation will be documented in the patient's medical record. On discharge, patients will be encouraged to maintain normal follow-ups with their physician(s).

Patients may request reinstitution of PC services after follow-up has been discontinued. Reinstitution will use the referral process previously outlined. Consistent with this policy, the clinical pharmacists reserve the right to decline said referral if the patient is deemed inappropriate.

PHARMACOTHERAPY CLINIC REFERRAL FORM

The Pharmacotherapy Clinic offers <u>short-term</u> disease state management and assistance with drug-related issues. Please provide the following information:

From Dr._____   Office Extension _____
          please print

Patient Name_____   Chart # _____

Phone #_____   Gender ❑ female   ❑ male

DOB _____ / _____ / _____

Please select the service(s) of interest

❑ Diabetes   ❑ Anticoagulation
❑ Asthma   ❑ Congestive Heart Failure
❑ Hypertension   ❑ Smoking Cessation
❑ Hyperlipidemia   ❑ Psychiatry
❑ Pain Management   ❑ Gastrointestinal Issues
❑ Drug Profile Review

❑ Other:_____
_____

Please provide
❑ Recommendations only
❑ Recommendations together with modifications

Additional comments or other pertinent information
_____
_____
_____

❑ New patients <u>will not</u> be scheduled during the same week that they are referred (so that the Clinical Pharmacists have an opportunity to perform chart review). *Please check this box if the patient requires more immediate attention.*

I consider this referral to the Pharmacotherapy Clinic a necessary part of this patient's medical care:

Physician Signature_____ ; Date _____ / _____ / _____

Once the patient has been scheduled, please return the completed form to the Clinical Pharmacy office. Thank you.

For Internal Use Only:

Received by_____ ; Date _____ / _____ / _____

CLINICAL PHARMACIST SCOPE OF PRACTICE

Submitted by: Kathy Fit

Revised: November 2005

The following outline describes the privileges allotted to the Clinical Pharmacist practicing at WellGroup HealthPartners:

1. Review patient charts.
2. Interview patients and perform minor physical assessments as deemed necessary to assess patient's response (or lack thereof) to therapy.
3. Record pertinent findings, patient education, and recommendations in the medical records.
4. Order appropriate laboratory tests to aid in monitoring drug therapy according to an established protocol or in consultation with the primary physician(s).
5. Identify and provide verbal and/or written recommendations for drug-related problems.
6. Identify and provide verbal and/or written recommendations pertaining to cost-effective therapy and/or professionally recognized treatment guidelines.
7. Evaluate patient response to pharmacological interventions and adjust doses as clinically indicated for six to twelve months between physician visits. Drugs affected will include those directly related to the condition necessitating referral to the clinical pharmacist from the primary physician.
8. Authority to verbally order or renew prescriptions for patients being monitored by the clinical pharmacist according to an established protocol or in consultation with the primary physician(s).
9. Provide patient education.
10. Provide staff education and development.
11. Coordinate and conduct clinic drug investigations/research and quality assurance assessments.
12. Evaluate drug information resources and update as necessary.
13. Precept pharmacy residents and pharmacy students.

The items listed above may be reviewed periodically for any necessary alterations. Additions or deletions to this list may occur after approval by the names listed below.

Approved by (sign and date):

_____
Medical Director
WellGroup HealthPartners

_____
Assistant Administrator
Ancillary and Support Services
WellGroup HealthPartners

_____
Clinical Pharmacist
WellGroup HealthPartners

Prepared by WellGroup HealthPartners, Chicago, Illinois

CLINICAL PHARMACY REFERRAL FORM

Submitted by: Kathy Fit

Revised: March 2006

This is the form for all the services that are available from the clinical pharmacy program at WellGroup HealthPartners.

Referring Physician: _____ Office Ext:_____

Patient Name:_____ Chart #:_____

Patient's Phone #_____ Gender: female male

DOB: _____/_____/_____

Please select the service(s) of interest
- ❑ Hypertension (modifications implemented only after physician review)
- ❑ Hyperlipidemia (modifications implemented only after physician review)
- ❑ Drug Profile Review/Herbal Product Review (modifications implemented only after physician review)
- ❑ Smoking Cessation—Please answer the two questions below if requesting smoking cessation services.

Additional Smoking Cessation Information

1. Additional Diagnosis Code:_____
   (Some providers will only reimburse smoking cessation if the patient has a medical condition that is negatively affected by smoking.)

2. *Please indicate how you would like the clinical pharmacist to initiate drug therapy for smoking cessation*
   - ❑ *Initiate drug therapy based on the protocol. No need to consult physician.*
   - ❑ Recommend drug therapy and consult physician prior to initiating drug therapy.

I consider this referral to the Pharmacotherapy Clinic a necessary part of this patient's medical care:

Physician Signature_____; Date _____/_____/_____

Prepared by WellGroup HealthPartners, Chicago, Illinois

BILLING FOR PHARMACY SERVICES IN AMBULATORY CARE

Submitted by: Amy Stump

Created: November 2006

Definitions

Common Terms Used in Medical Billing
- Evaluation and Management (E/M) Code: Numeric code used to describe services such as office visits, hospital visits, and consultations
- Current Procedural Terminology (CPT): Codes published by the American Medical Association that are the standard for reporting health care–related procedures performed in addition or subsequent to E/M services
- International Classification of Disease Ninth revision (ICD-9) Codes: Numeric codes used to identify a disease state when submitting charges
- Superbill: Billing and routing slip used to communicate charges for a patient visit
- National Provider Number: Number unique to each provider that is used when submitting charges from that provider to a third-party payer

Services That May Be Billed For

Drug therapy management services, in which a face-to-face patient encounter occurs that is separate from dispensing/counseling functions provided by the pharmacist. Components of DTM services may include, but are not limited to, assessment of patient drugs, order and/or interpretation of pertinent laboratory values, intervention to improve drug therapy, and disease state or other patient education to improve patient outcomes with regard to obtaining evidence-based goals.

Types of Billing Practices for Pharmacy Services

Incident-to physician referral: Billing practice that uses E/M codes and ICD-9 codes to communicate complexity of visit. Charges are based on two of the following three components: complexity of decision-making, amount of history reviewed, and physical examination performed. Because pharmacists may be limited in the amount of physical examinations performed, charges are usually decided on the basis of decision-making and history, and ICD-9 codes are used to support the reason for the patient visit. Patients must already be established with a physician in the practice and referred to the pharmacist. This method is submitted to a third-party payer, and the practice is reimbursed either as a percentage of the standard Medicare rate or on a contractual rate/fee basis. Controversy surrounds this type of billing because pharmacists are not listed as providers under Medicare Part B. Some pharmacists believe that billing using the 99211 level is the appropriate way to use this method, whereas others bill at the 99212–99214 levels. See Table 1 for an explanation of established patient E/M codes.

- **Pharmacist CPT Codes:** Newly created codes for pharmacist use. Charges are based on the length of time spent with the patient. Charges are submitted to a third-party payer and reimbursed on the basis of prenegotiated contract rates. A contract is negotiated with each insurance payer the pharmacist submits to, because the codes are classified in category III (experimental) and currently have no the standard dollar amount attached. See Table 2 for an explanation of pharmacist CPT codes.

- **Facility Fee:** The practice charges a flat fee for a patient visit. Insurance is not billed, and the patient pays the fee out-of-pocket at each visit. The fee is charged for the use of the facility space and equipment. The facility fee may not be created just to bill for pharmacy services. If implemented, each patient visit to any provider in the clinic must be charged the facility fee to maintain fair business practices.

- **Fee-for-Service:** In this billing system, a service, such as counseling on the use of a glucometer, is associated with a fee that the patient pays out-of-pocket. Insurance is not billed. Fee schedules are created at the individual site, and many items are factored in, such as time spent with the patient and cost of any point-of-service laboratory tests performed.

Table 1: Explanation of E/M Codes

E/M Code	Complexity of Decision-making	History Obtained	Approximate Length of Visit (minutes)
99211	Minimal	Minimal	5
99212	Straightforward	Problem focused	10
99213	Low complexity	Expanded problem focused	15
99214	Moderate complexity	Detailed	25
99215[a]	High complexity	Comprehensive	40

[a]To bill at the 99215 level, a review of systems involving at least 10 organ systems must be performed; thus, a pharmacist would typically not bill at this level.

Table 2: CPT Codes Used for Pharmacist Billing

CPT Code	Description	Approximate Length of Visit (minutes)
99605	Initial patient visit	15
99606	Established/subsequent patient visit	15
99607	Additional time during either initial or subsequent patient visit	Additional 15

Steps to Initiate Billing for Pharmacy Services

1. Speak to the person at your facility who is in charge of the billing office, the clinic manager, and the medical director to educate these key positions on pharmacy billing practices and begin the process of deciding which billing method is most appropriate for your site.
2. Have the billing office call several of the most common medical insurance plans accepted by your clinic to learn their views on pharmacist billing.
3. Have the billing office contact the local Centers for Medicaid/Medicare Services (CMS) representative to learn how billing for pharmacist services in your area is viewed.
4. Obtain a National Provider Number through the National Plan & Provider Enumeration System at the following Web site: *https://nppes.cms.hhs.gov;* then click on National Provider Identifier.
5. Begin the billing rate negotiation process with individual insurers if using the pharmacist CPT codes. Rates can be negotiated on an amount per minute basis or a rate based on the code charged.
6. If using a fee-for-service or facility fee model, create the fee schedule that will be implemented.
7. Consideration for low-income, uninsured patients may result in the creation of a sliding fee schedule based on patient financial status. A sliding fee schedule may be implemented in addition to the listed billing practices to serve this patient population. If implemented, patient visits to any provider at the site must be eligible for the sliding fee schedule to maintain fair business practices.

Documentation Required to Support Billing Practices

1. Both incident-to and CPT code billing practices may be audited by payers; therefore, documentation must be rigorously maintained and support the charges submitted to the payer.
2. Incident-to-physician referral: The complexity of decision-making and amount of history reviewed with the patient must be documented in SOAP (subjective, objective, assessment, and plan) note format. In addition, the superbill must be completed using correct E/M and ICD-9 coding for the diagnoses addressed at the visit. Having the patient sign the superbill helps document that the patient was present at the appointment and agrees to the charges.
3. Pharmacist CPT codes: Length of time spent with patient must be documented as well as enough supporting data from the visit to justify the length of the visit. Supporting data include education provided, interpretation of laboratory data, and amount of history gathered and should be documented in SOAP note format. In addition, the superbill must be completed using the correct CPT code and possibly ICD-9 codes to communicate what was addressed at the visit.
4. Facility fee and fee-for-service billing practices do not require the same intensity of documentation as other billing practices for use in audits. When using these practices, documentation may be determined in a more site-specific manner. SOAP note format is encouraged because this is the standard documentation format for providing patient care.

Where to Learn More

1. Speak with the clinic coders, office manager, and others in the billing office. They can provide a wealth of knowledge regarding medical billing in general.
2. ICD-9-CM Expert for Physicians—Volumes 1 and 2 International Classification of Diseases Ninth Revision Clinical Modification, Seventh Edition
3. CPT Expert, Sixth Edition

ANTICOAGULATION SERVICE

Submitted by: Ila Harris

Revised: 2006

Under Minnesota law, the Pharmacy Practice Act allows pharmacists to practice under a Collaborative Practice Agreement with individual physicians. Pharmacists may participate in the practice of managing and modifying drug therapy on a case-by-case basis according to a written protocol between the specific pharmacist and the individual physician/physicians who is/are responsible for the patient's care and authorized to prescribe drugs.

By signing this document, the named physicians agree that the named pharmacist may enter into a Collaborative Practice with them for the management of anticoagulation in patients receiving warfarin according to the attached protocol for the Anticoagulation Service. By signing this document, the physician agrees with the anticoagulation management outlined in the attached protocol. Resident physicians are supervised by the faculty physicians listed; therefore, the signatures approve the referral of resident physician's patients to the ACC.

Anticoagulation service protocol and collaborative agreement approved by:

PHARMACIST CLINICIAN

_____ _____
Name   Date
License #:

FACULTY PHYSICIANS

_____ _____   _____ _____
M.D.   Date   M.D.   Date
License #:   License #:

DATE OF IMPLEMENTATION: _____

DATES ANNUAL REVIEW COMPLETED: _____

Under Minnesota law, the Pharmacy Practice Act allows pharmacists to practice under a Collaborative Practice Agreement with individual physicians. Pharmacists may participate in the practice of managing and modifying drug therapy on a case-by-case basis according to a written protocol between the specific pharmacist and the individual physician/physicians who is/are responsible for the patient's care and authorized to prescribe drugs.

The named pharmacy residents below may enter into a Collaborative Practice with the physicians for the management of anticoagulation in patients receiving warfarin according to the attached protocol for the ACC.

Anticoagulation Service Protocol and Collaborative Agreement

PHARMACY RESIDENTS:_____
STAFF:_____
Medical director:_____
Primary clinician: _____
Nursing staff: _____

Purpose/Background

A formal protocol at Bethesda Clinic for the management of patients receiving anticoagulation was believed necessary. When international normalized ratio (INR) results were available the following day, it was often difficult or impossible to contact the patient in a timely manner to make a dosage adjustment. In addition, results of laboratory tests that were drawn on Fridays were being called in to the doctor on call, who did not have access to the medical chart. Doses were often adjusted without talking to the patient to ask for information such as his or her dose, diet, and other drugs. A point-of-care testing instrument (Coagu-Check®) was obtained for use in the laboratory, which provides results within minutes. This provided an opportunity to develop an anticoagulation protocol that is coordinated by the clinical pharmacist. This protocol provides more consistent care for patients and allows an exchange of important information between the patient and the health care provider when the INR results are in and the dose is adjusted. Data are available that a pharmacist-run anticoagulation service (ACC) can improve care, reduce complications, reduce hospitalizations and emergency department visits, and reduce overall costs.[1,2] The American College of Chest Physicians consensus conference on antithrombotic therapy ("Chest guidelines") recommends that clinicians have a systematic process of managing oral anticoagulation dosing that includes a knowledgeable provider, organized system of follow-up, and patient communication and education.[3]

Qualifications of Pharmacists

Ila M. Harris is a clinical pharmacist who has both her bachelor of science degree in pharmacy (B.S. Pharm.) and doctor of pharmacy (Pharm.D.). She completed a one-year specialty pharmacy residency in Family Medicine. She has been in practice after completing her residency since 1994 and is a registered pharmacist. She is also a Board Certified Pharmacotherapy Specialist (BCPS). Previously, she was in charge of an ACC in another clinic. Pharmacy residents involved in this protocol have their Pharm.D. degrees and are registered pharmacists.

Policy

The clinical pharmacist and pharmacy residents will follow this written protocol. Pharmacy students who see patients will do so under the supervision of the clinical pharmacist, pharmacy resident, or physician. If the primary physician, acute care doctor, or faculty preceptor is seeing the patient or reviewing the INR, he or she should also follow the written protocol. Slight deviations from the dose adjustment protocol may occur per clinical judgment. The only patients seen under this protocol are those under the care of physicians at Bethesda Clinic.

Organization

The clinical pharmacist will coordinate the ACC. Pharmacy residents will also see patients. Pharmacy students who see patients will do so under the supervision of the clinical pharmacist, pharmacy resident, or physician. The clinical pharmacist or pharmacy resident will see patients to evaluate out-of-range INRs, follow their warfarin therapy, and make dosage adjustments per protocol if necessary. When they are not available, the primary physician (if available), the acute care doctor, or the faculty preceptor will see the patient. If the INR is drawn when the patient is in the clinic being seen by a physician, then the result will be reported to the physician and the physician will adjust the warfarin dose, if necessary.

When outlined by the protocol, or at any time an unusual or unexpected situation arises, the clinical pharmacist may consult the primary physician or faculty preceptor for medical guidance. If oral vitamin K is necessary, this will only be initiated after discussion with a physician. If the patient has a critically high INR or serious bleeding, the patient will be seen by the faculty preceptor or another physician seeing patients in the clinic. If the patient has an unrelated serious complaint during the visit (e.g., chest pain), the patient will be seen by the faculty preceptor or another physician seeing patients in the clinic.

When the clinical pharmacist or pharmacy resident is not available, the primary physician (if in clinic), the acute care doctor, or the faculty preceptor will evaluate the INR, see the patient, and adjust the warfarin dosage, if necessary.

Procedures

Warfarin will be initiated and discontinued only by a physician. The protocol outlines procedures for monitoring and adjusting warfarin doses only. Slight deviations from the protocol per clinical judgment may be warranted.

Guidelines for Referral

Under Minnesota law for Collaborative Practice Agreements, all patients must be referred to the pharmacist on a case-by-case basis. When an INR is drawn and the results are reported to the clinical pharmacist, he or she will page the primary physician or the supervising faculty preceptor (if the physician is a resident physician under the supervision of a faculty preceptor) and ask if he/she would like his/her patient to be followed under the ACC, under the direction of the clinical pharmacist. If yes, the clinical pharmacist will document on the INR shingle (Appendix A) and the Coumadin flow sheet the date and the physician by which the patient was referred to the ACC. It will be understood that the patients will be monitored by the ACC while they are receiving warfarin. When the physician (either resident or faculty) signs the INR shingle stating that the patient was referred to the ACC, they are confirming that the patient was referred.

Clinic Visits

Patients are seen by the clinical pharmacist, pharmacy resident, or physician when their INR is out of range and it has been determined that they need to be seen. The patient will be placed in an examination room by the nursing staff, and vital signs will be checked. The clinical pharmacist or pharmacy resident will evaluate patients for out-of-range INRs, monitor their warfarin therapy, and make dosage adjustments per protocol, if necessary. When they are not available, the primary physician (if available), the acute care physician, or the faculty preceptor will see the patient. If the INR is drawn when the patient is in the clinic being seen by a physician, then the result will be reported to the physician, and the physician will adjust the warfarin dose, if necessary.

Information from the protocol (Appendix C) will be discussed with the patient, and the dose will be adjusted, if necessary, per protocol. The patient will be educated on the dose change and when to return for an INR. Written instructions will be provided by giving the patient a copy of the INR shingle. Clinic visits will usually be fifteen minutes or less, unless extensive education is deemed necessary. If the patient needs extensive education and he/she is not able to stay, then he/she will be asked to return for an appointment for warfarin education.

Fingerstick INRs greater than 3.5 will always be repeated intravenously with drawn blood and sent to Health East laboratories to be run for confirmation.

Clinical Activities Provided by the Clinical Pharmacist and Pharmacy Resident

Under this protocol, the clinical pharmacist and pharmacy resident are authorized to make warfarin dosage adjustments without prior physician consultation as long as the dosage adjustment follows the protocol. Slight alterations to the protocol may be warranted as seen fit by clinical judgment.

The protocol also authorizes the clinical pharmacist and pharmacy resident to order INR laboratory and hemoglobin tests, if necessary. The names of both the faculty preceptor and clinical pharmacist/pharmacy resident will be used, as authorized by this protocol.

This protocol also authorizes the clinical pharmacist/pharmacy resident to write or call in new prescriptions for warfarin if the adjusted dose requires a new strength. The clinical pharmacist/pharmacy resident is also authorized to write or call in refill prescriptions if the patient needs refills. The names of both the faculty preceptor and the clinical pharmacist/pharmacy resident will be used, as authorized by this protocol.

Documentation

The patient visit and dosage change will be documented on the INR shingle (Appendix A) and in the flow sheet in the patient's chart. If the clinical pharmacist/pharmacy resident sees the patient, the information will be communicated to the primary physician by placing the chart with the shingle, laboratory result sheet, and flow sheet in the primary physician's box for review and co-signature.

Billing

If the patient must be seen for an out-of-range INR, the procedure for any office visit will be followed. If the patient usually has a co-pay, he or she must pay it.

When the clinical pharmacist/pharmacy resident sees the patient, a level 1 visit will be billed as an incident-to service. The service was performed under the direct supervision of the faculty preceptor, who is present at the clinic at the time of the visit. When the primary physician, faculty physician, or acute care doctor sees the patient, the visit will be billed as deemed appropriate by the physician.

If the patient is in an alternate environment such as a nursing home or when the laboratory tests are drawn outside the clinic, the patient will be managed by a telephone call and will not be billed. If the patient is in the clinic for a visit with his/her physician, the patient will not be billed extra for the INR; however, the level of the visit may be higher.

Termination of Care

A patient will be discontinued from the ACC if he or she is no longer receiving warfarin. If the patient repeatedly fails to come for INR visits, continuation in the ACC will be discussed with the primary physician.

Quality Improvement

The protocol will be reviewed yearly by the clinical pharmacist and faculty physicians and revised as needed.

```
┌─────────────────────────────────────────────────────────────────────────────┐
│ Patient presents for laboratory appointment between 9:00 and 11:30 A.M. and │
│ 1:30 and 4:00 P.M. for INR using Coagu-Check.® Patient fills out            │
│ questionnaire on INR shingle (Appendix A) while waiting for result. Patient │
│ is instructed to wait in upstairs waiting room. Chart will have been pulled │
│ when patient is scheduled for laboratory work.                              │
└─────────────────────────────────────────────────────────────────────────────┘
                                      │
                                      ▼
┌─────────────────────────────────────────────────────────────────────────────┐
│ INR goal range (on flow sheet in chart) checked by laboratory technician,   │
│ and INR determined to be "in goal range" or "out of goal range." If no goal │
│ INR in chart, follow "out-of-goal range."                                   │
└─────────────────────────────────────────────────────────────────────────────┘
                    ↙                                    ↘
        ┌──────────────────────┐              ┌──────────────────────┐
        │ INR "out of goal     │              │ INR "in goal range"  │
        │ range"               │              │                      │
        └──────────────────────┘              └──────────────────────┘
                    │                                    │
                    ▼                                    ▼
    ┌──────────────────────────────┐      ┌──────────────────────────────┐
    │ Chart with shingle to Nicole │      │ Chart with shingle to Nicole │
    │ or Jen (by dumb waiter) to   │      │ or Jen (by dumb waiter) to   │
    │ determine when INR should be │      │ determine if patient needs   │
    │ rechecked.                   │      │ to be seen and, if not, when │
    │                              │      │ INR should be rechecked.     │
    └──────────────────────────────┘      └──────────────────────────────┘
                    │                                    │
                    ▼                                    ▼
    ┌──────────────────────────────┐      ┌──────────────────────────────┐
    │ Dr. Harris, pharmacy         │      │ Dr. Harris, pharmacy         │
    │ resident, primary physician  │      │ resident, primary physician  │
    │ (if in clinic), acute care   │      │ (if in clinic), acute care   │
    │ physician, or faculty        │      │ doctor, or faculty preceptor │
    │ preceptor (in that order)ᵃ   │      │ (in that order)ᵃ will        │
    │ will review chart and        │      │ determine if patient needs   │
    │ determine when INR should be │      │ to be seen and, if not, when │
    │ rechecked.                   │      │ INR should be rechecked.     │
    │                              │      │ Patient will usually need to │
    │                              │      │ be seen (unless holding for  │
    │                              │      │ surgery or INR is within 0.1 │
    │                              │      │ of goal, etc.). (See         │
    │                              │      │ Appendix B.)                 │
    └──────────────────────────────┘      └──────────────────────────────┘
                    │                           ↙            ↘
                    │               ┌────────────────┐  ┌────────────────┐
                    │               │ Patient does   │  │ Patient needs  │
                    │               │ not need to be │  │ to be seen.    │
                    │               │ seen           │  │ Nicole or Jen  │
                    │               │                │  │ notified       │
                    │               └────────────────┘  └────────────────┘
                    ▼                       │                   │
    ┌──────────────────────────────┐◄───────┘                   │
    │ INR shingle and flow sheet   │                            │
    │ are completed. Nicole or Jen │                            │
    │ notified                     │                            │
    └──────────────────────────────┘                            │
                    │                                           ▼
                    ▼                       ┌──────────────────────────────┐
    ┌──────────────────────────────┐        │ Nicole or Jen notifies       │
    │ Nicole or Jen inform patient │        │ patient that he/she needs to │
    │ of INR result and instruct   │        │ be seen. Patient is roomed   │
    │ patient to continue same     │        │ and BP/HR is done.           │
    │ dose and when to recheck     │        └──────────────────────────────┘
    │ INR. Copy of INR shingle     │                            │
    │ given to patient             │                            ▼
    └──────────────────────────────┘        ┌──────────────────────────────┐
                    │                       │ Dr. Harris, pharmacy         │
                    ▼                       │ resident, primary physician  │
    ┌──────────────────────────────┐        │ (if in clinic), acute care   │
    │ Patient instructed to make   │        │ doctor, or faculty preceptor │
    │ appointment before leaving.  │        │ (in that order)ᵃ will see    │
    │ If patient unable to make    │◄───────│ patient, hold or make        │
    │ appointment, copy of INR     │        │ adjustment in warfarin dose  │
    │ shingle is given to patient, │        │ or give vitamin K (if        │
    │ which includes date for      │        │ necessary), and inform       │
    │ follow-up INR. Patient       │        │ patient when to return for   │
    │ instructed to call and       │        │ next INR. Protocol will be   │
    │ schedule INR.                │        │ followed (see Appendix C).   │
    └──────────────────────────────┘        │ INR shingle and flow sheet   │
                    │                       │ are completed. Copy of INR   │
                    ▼                       │ shingle is given to patient. │
        ┌──────────────────────┐            └──────────────────────────────┘
        │ Patient leaves.      │
        └──────────────────────┘
```

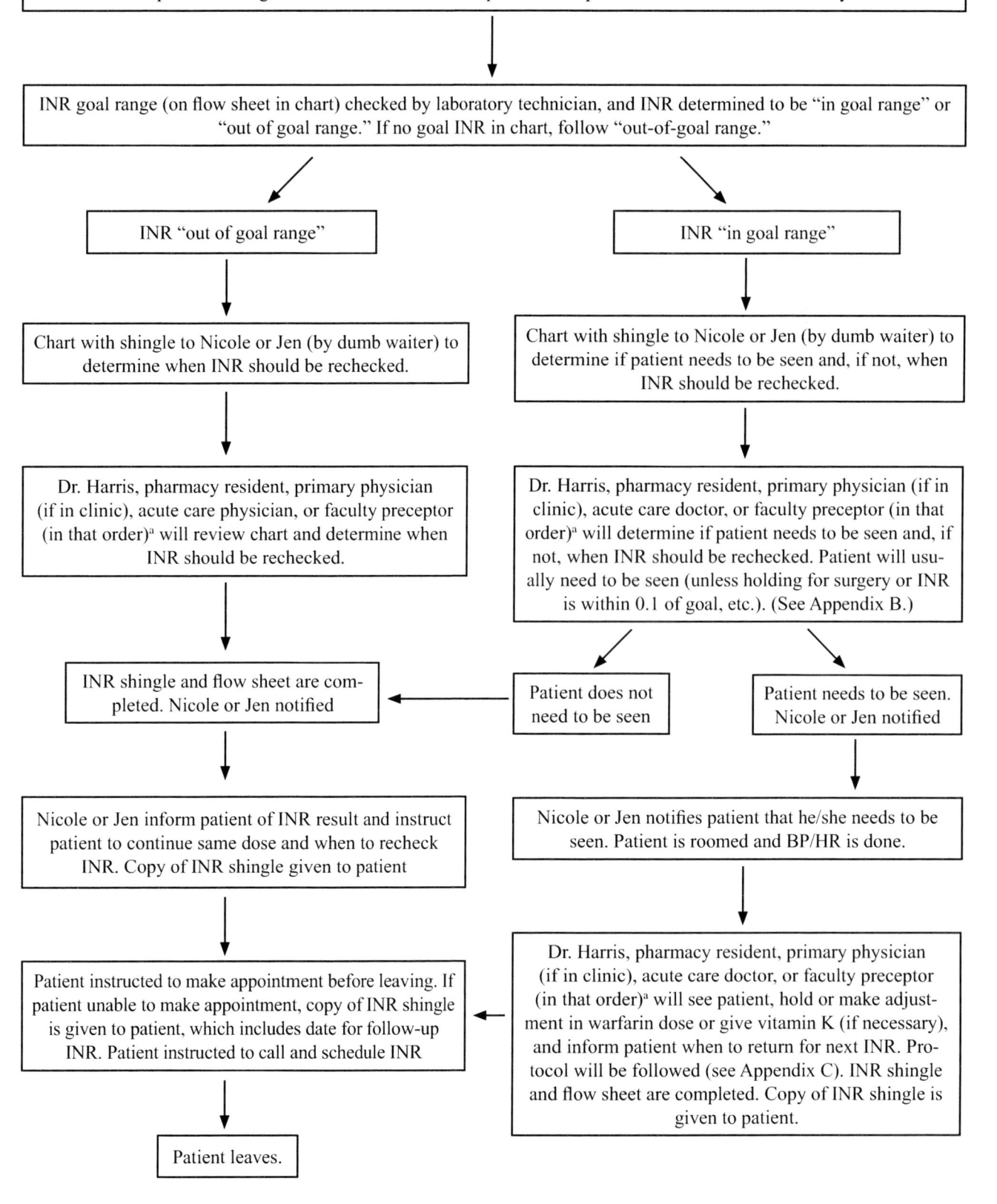

ᵃFirst, Dr. Harris or the pharmacy resident will be contacted. If unavailable, the primary physician will be contacted if he/she is in clinic. If the primary physician is unavailable, the acute care doctor faculty preceptor will be contacted.

Appendix A

(1) What dose of Coumadin are you currently taking? _____

(2) What strength Coumadin tablet(s) do you have at home (list all)? _____

(3) Have you missed any doses in the past WEEK?   ❏ YES   ❏ NO
   If yes, how many doses and when? _____

(4) Have you taken any extra doses in the past week?   ❏ YES   ❏ NO
   If yes, how many extra doses and when? _____

(5) Have you eaten more or less salads and/or green leafy vegetables and/or broccoli in the past two weeks?
   ❏ YES   ❏ NO
   If yes, please describe: _____

(6) Have you started or stopped any other drugs (including over-the-counter or herbals) in the past few weeks?
   ❏ YES   ❏ NO
   If yes, please explain: _____

(7) In the past one to two weeks, have you noticed any problems with bleeding that are DIFFERENT from any usual problems (e.g., nose bleeds, gums bleeding when brushing teeth, easy bruising, excessive bleeding if you cut yourself, blood in urine, blood in stool)?
   ❏ YES   ❏ NO
   If yes, please describe: _____

(8) Do you have any other concerns or problems about your Coumadin therapy?
   ❏ YES   ❏ NO
   If yes, please explain: _____

(9) Do you need a refill of your Coumadin?
   ❏ YES   ❏ NO

(10) What is your current phone number? _____

INR Shingle

Date:_____ INR (Coagu-Check®):_____ Goal INR (from flow sheet):_____

New warfarin (Coumadin) dose: _____

Recheck INR: _____

Comments:_____
_____
_____

Appendix B

If INR is out of range, the dose will be adjusted UNLESS any of the following apply:

- The INR is within 0.1 of the goal INR.
- The patient missed one or more doses in the past week.
- The patient took one or more extra doses in the past week.
- The patient took an interacting drug that has now been discontinued.
- The patient recently started an interacting drug and the INR is expected to change.
- The patient had a significant change in dietary vitamin K intake.
- The patient had a significant change in alcohol intake (if concurrent liver disease).
- The INR is being checked before a procedure and is currently being held.
- The warfarin is being held because of a recent supratherapeutic INR.
- The warfarin was started or adjusted less than five days ago.
- Any other reason based on the clinical judgment of the clinical pharmacist or physician.

Appendix C

Protocol for out-of-range INR visits

- If the clinical pharmacist or pharmacy resident is available, he or she will see the patient. After the patient has been seen, the dose of warfarin will be adjusted, if necessary, according to the protocol below, and the INR shingle will be filled out and signed (Appendix A) and the flow sheet will be updated. If the clinical pharmacist is not available, the primary physician (if available), the acute care doctor, or the faculty preceptor will see the patient. This protocol addresses what procedure will be followed regardless of who sees the patient, with information added on how the clinical pharmacist/pharmacy resident should handle certain situations.
- If the INR is drawn when the patient is in the clinic being seen by a physician, then the result will be reported to the physician on the anticoagulation shingle. The patient will be asked to fill in the INR shingle, and the physician should address the answers; discuss them with the patient; adjust the warfarin dose, if necessary, per the protocol; inform the patient of his or her new dose and return INR; and give the patient the yellow copy of the shingle.
- If patients are in alternative environments (e.g., home care, nursing home, hospice) and normally have their INR drawn elsewhere, the triage nurse will take the telephone call. In general, the INR shingle will not be filled out in these circumstances. The documentation will occur on the telephone shingle and the flow sheet. The triage nurse will give the chart and telephone shingle to the clinical pharmacist, the pharmacy resident, the primary physician, the acute care doctor, or the faculty preceptor (in that order), who will make the dosage adjustment (if necessary) and record it on the shingle and flow sheet. The dose instructions will be provided back to the nurse or patient by a telephone call, either from the triage nurse or the clinician who adjusted the warfarin dose.
- The INR, goal INR, and INR shingle (Appendix A) will be reviewed with the patient.
- The goal INR will be determined by the indication for warfarin and the goal stated in the CHEST guidelines. (Table 1).
- Drug interactions will be evaluated.
- The duration of anticoagulation will be reviewed per the CHEST guidelines (Table 1), and if the duration of therapy is complete, discontinuation of warfarin may be discussed with the primary physician.
- If the INR is high, the patient will be asked more specifically about any bleeding symptoms and if anything else is going on (e.g., sick, drinking alcohol).
- If the INR is low, the patient will be asked about symptoms of <u>venous thromboembolism</u> (VTE), depending on their indication.
- If the INR is more than 5 or bleeding is present (excluding minor bleeding), the ACCP guidelines in Table 2 will be followed. Because these recommendations are only grade 2C (e.g., unclear clarity of risk/benefit, observational studies; only very weak recommendations; other alternatives may be equally reasonable), some alterations to these guidelines will be allowed as seen fit by clinical judgment.
- If the INR is out of the goal range but 5 or less, the dosage of warfarin will be adjusted as follows:
  ◦ The weekly dose will be calculated.
  ◦ The weekly dose will be adjusted by 5–20%.
- If the INR is very high (e.g., more than 9–10), the dose may be lowered by more than 20%.
- One or two doses of warfarin may be held, depending on the bleeding risk of the patient and the VTE risk.
- Every effort will be made to maintain a simple regimen for the patient, using the available warfarin strengths and what they have at home (Table 3). However, new dosage strengths may need to be started.
- Patients will be informed about their new warfarin dose and when to return for their next INR. Patients will receive written information in the form of a copy of the INR shingle. This protocol allows the clinical pharmacist/pharmacy resident to order the INR. The names of both the clinical pharmacist and the faculty physician will be provided, as authorized by this protocol.
- The new dose and date of the return INR will be provided for them in writing.
- Frequency of INR monitoring will depend on patient's INR stability on current dose of warfarin (Table 4).
- Hemoglobin should be checked once yearly while on warfarin. The chart will be checked to ensure this has been checked in the past year; if not, a hemoglobin concentration will be ordered.
- If a new strength or refill of warfarin is needed, a written prescription will be given, or it will be called in to their pharmacy. The clinical pharmacist is authorized to write or call in these prescriptions, and the names of both the faculty physician and the clinical pharmacist will be provided.
- The information will be recorded on the INR shingle and on the Coumadin flow sheet in the patient's medical record.
- In the case of any questionable indication, contraindication, need for temporary discontinuation (e.g., surgery, dental procedure), or issue that arises, the clinical pharmacist/pharmacy resident will consult the primary physician or faculty preceptor.
- In the case of a critical value (e.g., INR is more than 9) or if the patient has bleeding (other than minor bleeding) or if anything unusual or complicated arises, the clinical pharmacist/pharmacy resident will consult the faculty preceptor. The faculty preceptor will see the patient if necessary.
- If the patient appears not to have previously received education about his/her anticoagulation therapy or he/she is a new patient, he/she will receive one-on-one education concerning the following, and written materials will be provided:
  ◦ Indication for warfarin
  ◦ Complications and management of complications
  ◦ Need for blood tests (monitoring)
  ◦ Drug interactions (especially OTC drugs and herbal products)
  ◦ Dosing and importance of compliance
  ◦ Dietary considerations
  ◦ Special precautions (e.g., aggressive contact sports, caution when using knives or machinery)
  ◦ Goal INR
  ◦ Therapy duration

The chart will be placed in the primary physician's box for review and signature.

Table 1: Recommendations for Long-Term Warfarin Therapy

Thromboembolic Disorder	INR	Duration	Evidence	Comments
VTE: Deep vein thrombosis (DVT) or pulmonary embolism (PE)				
DVT/PE with reversible or time-limited risk factor	2–3	At least 3 months	Strong	Time-limited risk factors: surgery, immobilization, estrogen
First idiopathic PE or proximal DVT	2–3	At least 6–12 months	Strong	Treat recurrence or continuing risk factor for cancer, anticardiolipin antibody syndrome [AAS]) for ≥ 12 months, some data for long-term therapy
First DVT or PE with deficiency of anti-thrombin, protein C or S, factor V Leiden, or prothrombin 20210	2–3	6–12 months	Strong	Some weak data for long-term therapy
First DVT or PE with AAS or ≥ 2 thrombophilic conditions (factor V Leiden and prothrombin 20210)	2–3	12 months	Fairly strong	Some weak data for long-term therapy
Isolated symptomatic calf DVT	2–3	At least 6–12 weeks	Strong	
CAD/Acute MI				
Alternative to aspirin alone for primary prevention in men at very high risk of cardiovascular (CV) events	1.5		Fairly strong	For moderate-risk patients, only aspirin (ASA) is recommended
High-risk patients with MI, including large anterior MI or acute MI with severe left ventricular (LV) dysfunction/CHF, previous emboli, or evidence of mural thrombosis	2–3 plus ASA 81 mg	3 months	Strong	In low- to moderate-risk MI patients, ASA is recommended over warfarin
Any patients post-MI (low to high risk)	See comment	Up to 4 years	Fair	Warfarin IF meticulous INR monitoring and adjustment is standard and accessible. INR 3–4 without ASA or 2–3 with ASA
Atrial fibrillation (including paroxysmal/intermittent)				
< 65 years old without risk factors		Long-term	Fairly strong	Use ASA 325 mg/day
65–75 years old without risk factors	2–3	Long-term	Strong	Either warfarin or ASA 325 mg/day as an acceptable alternative
> 75 years old OR any one or more of the risk factors listed	2–3	Long-term	Strong	Risk factors: prior ischemic stroke, transient ischemic attack (TIA), systemic embolism, moderate to severe LV systolic dysfunction and/or CHF, HTN, DM
Atrial flutter	2–3	Long-term	Weak	The same recommendations as for atrial fibrillation should be followed
Conversion of atrial fibrillation				
Elective direct current (DC) cardioversion of atrial fibrillation	2–3	7 weeks	Fairly strong	3 weeks before and at least 4 weeks after
Valvular heart disease				
Rheumatic mitral valve disease with history of systemic embolism or AF	2–3	Long-term	Fairly strong	Do not use concomitant ASA. If recurrent systemic embolism occurs despite warfarin, target INR should be increased to 2.5–3.5 or ASA 81 mg/day added
Rheumatic mitral valve disease in sinus rhythm if left atrial diameter is > 5.5 cm	2–3	Long-term	Weak	
Mitral valve prolapse (MVP) with documented systemic embolism or recurrent TIAs despite ASA therapy	2–3	Long-term	Weak	
Mechanical and bioprosthetic heart valves				
Bioprosthetic heart valve	2–3	3 months; then ASA 81 mg/day	Variable	Alternative for aortic valve: ASA
Bioprosthetic heart valve with left atrial thrombus at surgery or h/o systemic embolism	2–3	3–12 months	Weak	Duration is for embolism; uncertain duration for left atrial thrombus
Mechanical prosthetic heart valve: aortic	2–3	Long-term	Variable	If normal left atrial size and in sinus rhythm. Valves: St. Jude bileaflet, Carbomedics bileaflet, Medtronic tilting disk. 2.5–3.5 if atrial fibrillation
Mechanical prosthetic heart valve: mitral	2.5–3.5	Long-term	Fairly strong	An alternate is 2–3 plus ASA 81 mg/day
Mechanical caged ball or caged disk valve OR any mechanical valve plus other risk factors OR any mechanical valve with systemic embolism with therapeutic INR	2.5–3.5	Long-term	Weak	PLUS ASA 81 mg/day, Risk factors: Atrial fibrillation, MI, left atrial enlargement, low EF, endocardial damage

Table 2: Management of Increased INR (Grade 1 and 2C recommendations; use as general guide only)

INR		Patient Situation	Action
< 5	and	No significant bleeding or need for rapid reversal	Lower dose OR omit dose; monitor more often and restart at lower dose when INR approaches 3. If INR is only minimally above the therapeutic range, then no dose reduction may be required
< 9	and	In need of rapid reversal (e.g., before surgery)	Give oral vitamin K_1 (2–4 mg) with the expectation that a reduction of the INR will occur within 24 hours. If the INR remains high at 24 hours, an additional dose of 1–2 mg of oral vitamin K_1 can be given
≥ 5 and < 9	and	No bleeding and no risk factors	Omit 1–2 doses of warfarin; monitor INR more often. Restart warfarin at a lower dose when the INR falls into the therapeutic range
		No bleeding, but at risk of bleeding	Omit 1 dose of warfarin and give oral vitamin K_1 (≤ 5 mg; generally 2.5 mg)
≥ 9	and	No clinically significant bleeding	Omit next several warfarin doses, and give oral vitamin K_1 (5–10 mg), with the expectation that the INR will be reduced substantially after about 24–48 hours. Monitor INR closely and repeat vitamin K_1, if necessary. Resume warfarin at a lower dose when INR is in the desired range
		Serious bleeding at any INR elevation or warfarin overdosage	Hold warfarin, give vitamin K_1 10 mg by slow intravenous infusion for 20–30 minutes and supplement with fresh frozen plasma or prothrombin complex concentrate (alternative: recombinant factor VIIa) (depending on urgency); if needed, repeat vitamin K_1 injection every 12 hours; if continuing warfarin therapy is indicated after high doses of vitamin K_1, then give heparin until the patient is responsive to warfarin
		Life-threatening bleeding or warfarin overdose	Hold warfarin and give prothrombin complex concentrate supplemented with vitamin K (10 mg by slow intravenous infusion); recombinant factor VIIa may be considered an alternative to prothrombin complex concentrate; repeat, if necessary, depending on INR

Table 3

Available tablet strengths (in milligrams) and colors of Coumadin®	
1	Pink
2	Lavender
2.5	Light green
3	Beige
4	Blue
5	Peach/orange
6	Kelly green
7.5	Yellow
10	White

Table 4: Frequency of INR Monitoring

- Within 1 week of therapeutic INR after warfarin initiated
- Within 2 weeks (1 week preferred, if possible) after change in warfarin dose or potentially interacting drug, or medical status
- Every 2 weeks until stable (e.g., 2–3 consecutive therapeutic INRs); then every 4 weeks[a]

[a]Every attempt will be made to ensure that patients do not go beyond 6 weeks without INR monitoring.

References

1. Chiquette E, Amato MG, Bussey HI. Comparison of an anticoagulation clinic with usual medical care: anticoagulation control, patient outcomes, and health care costs. Arch Intern Med 1998;158:1641–7.
2. Wilt VM, Gums JG, Ahmed OI, Moore LM. Outcome analysis of a pharmacist-managed anticoagulation service. Pharmacotherapy 1995;15:732–9.
3. 6th Consensus Conference on Antithrombotic Therapy; Chest supplement. January 2001.
4. Norton JLW, Gibson DL. Establishing an outpatient anticoagulation clinic in a community hospital. Am J Health Syst Pharm 1996;53:1151–7.
5. Foss MT, Schoch PH, Sintek CD. Efficient operation of a high-volume anticoagulation clinic. Am J Health Syst Pharm 1999;56:443–9.
6. Institute for Clinical Systems Improvement; Anticoagulation Therapy Supplement.
7. Seventh Consensus Conference on Antithrombotic Therapy; Chest supplement. September 2004.

ANTICOAGULATION SERVICE—POLICY/PROCEDURE

Submitted by: Melissa Blair

Created: September 2000

Purpose

To establish guidelines for monitoring anticoagulation therapy in patients at the family medicine center. The purpose of the service is to provide continuity of care to patients who require anticoagulation; enhance patient care through education, monitoring, and close follow-up; and reduce adverse events associated with anticoagulation therapy.

Policy

Refer to Department of Family Medicine (DFM) Clinical Pharmacy Service.

Procedure

Guidelines for referral

Refer to DFM Clinical Pharmacy Service.

Clinic visits

Time and Place:
- Refer to DFM Clinical Pharmacy Service.

Procedure

All patients will be instructed to report to the laboratory for a prothrombin time (PT) or INR laboratory test on a specific day. Laboratory order forms will be completed in advance by the pharmacy faculty, resident, or student.

The initial visit may require up to one hour at the Family Medicine Center and will include extensive education (see Patient Education). Follow-up visits will be scheduled according to INR values. Patients initiating warfarin therapy may require frequent follow-up during the first month. Face-to-face or telephone follow-up will be used for patients. Compliance, complications of therapy, adverse effects, drugs, and diet will be assessed during follow-up.

Therapeutic and Nontherapeutic Values

After evaluation and consideration of all contributing factors, including missed/extra doses, drug changes, dietary changes, illness, and potential bleeding problems, dosage adjustments will be made according to the flow sheets in Figure 1. A change in dosage is not necessary if reasons are identified for a nontherapeutic INR. A Clinical Pharmacy note will be written in the electronic medical record (EMR) and sent to the appropriate provider for co-signature. Patients will be scheduled for a PT/INR and follow-up appointment by the clinical pharmacist. These appointments may be in the clinic or by telephone depending on specific patient variables.

Figure 1. Dosage adjustment protocols.

Low Intensity INR (Goal 2-3)

INR < 1.5	INR 1.5 - 1.9	INR 2.0-3.0	INR 3.1-4.0	INR 4.1-5.0	INR > 5.0
Extra dose(s) and/or increase weekly dose by 10-20% RTC 1-2 weeks	Extra dose and/or increase weekly dose by 5-15% RTC 2-4 weeks*	No Change RTC 4-6 weeks	Hold dose and/or decrease weekly dose by 5-15% RTC 2-4 weeks*	Hold dose(s) and/or decrease weekly dose by 15-20% RTC 1-2 weeks	Contact MD Hold dose(s) and/or decrease weekly dose by 15-20% RTC within 1 week

High Intensity INR (Goal 2.5 - 3.5)

INR < 2.0	INR 2.0 - 2.4	INR 2.5 - 3.5	INR 3.6 - 4.0	INR 4.1 - 5.0	INR > 5.0
Extra dose(s) and/or increase weekly dose by 10-20% RTC 1-2 weeks	Extra dose and/or increase weekly dose by 5-15% RTC 2-4 weeks*	No Change RTC 4-6 weeks	Hold dose and/or decrease dose by 5-15% RTC 2-4 weeks*	Hold dose(s) and/or decrease dose by 10-20% RTC 2-4 weeks	Contact MD Hold dose(s) and/or decrease dose by 10-20% RTC 1-2 weeks

*Dosage adjustment may not be necessary.
**Dose should be increased or decreased after two consecutive super- or subtherapeutic INR values.
RTC = return to clinic.

Patient Education

An extensive longitudinal program of patient education will be provided. Patients and family members/caretakers will be provided the following information.
- Purpose of the ACC and follow-up procedures
  - Indication for warfarin therapy
  - Goal INR
  - Signs and symptoms of bleeding
  - Complications of anticoagulation therapy
  - Instructions on how to take the warfarin
  - What to do if a dose is missed
  - What to do if bleeding occurs
  - Identification of warfarin dose by color
  - Drug–Diet interactions (foods containing vitamin K)
  - Drug–Drug interactions (prescription, OTC, and herbal products)
  - Importance of compliance

Planned Surgeries and Procedures

Patients will be instructed to inform all health care providers about warfarin therapy. On notification of planned procedures, the clinical pharmacist will contact the primary DFM provider. Plans for the interruption of therapy will be made and forwarded to the appropriate surgeon/physician. The patient will follow up for PT/INR laboratory values within seven to ten days of restarting warfarin therapy.

Missed Appointments

Refer to DFM Clinical Pharmacy Service.

Documentation

All patient encounters, including telephone follow-up, will be documented in the EMR using the clinical pharmacy warfarin flow chart. Information provided will include reason for therapy, duration of therapy, goal INR, current INR, drugs, present dose, new dose, next appointment, and provider. All notes will be co-signed by the attending pharmacy faculty and primary care provider.

ANTICOAGULATION SERVICE POLICY—CHEROKEE INDIAN HOSPITAL

Submitted by: Chris Lamer

Revised: February 2007

Purpose

The ACC is designed to allow pharmacists to clinically manage selected patients receiving oral anticoagulant therapy through a pharmacy-based protocol. Purposes of this pharmacy-based point-of-service program are to provide appropriate and safe use of a potentially toxic drug, warfarin (Coumadin®). Methods used to accomplish this objective include obtaining subjective and objective clinical data, educating patients, ordering appropriate diagnostic tests, providing point-of-service testing during pharmacy visits, adjusting warfarin doses, and referring patients for physician follow-up at appropriate intervals.

Goals

1. Provide appropriate warfarin dosing and monitoring to achieve definite outcomes that improve the patient's quality of life at this facility
2. Provide a systematic outpatient ACC designed to coordinate and optimize the delivery of anticoagulation therapy
3. Optimize therapeutic anticoagulation by minimizing the patient's bleeding risks and thromboembolic events, decreasing the time required for titration to achieve a desired level of anticoagulation, and promoting the efficient use of laboratory tests
4. Determine the appropriateness of anticoagulation therapy in specific patients
5. Maximize the benefits while minimizing the risks (e.g., bleeding) of warfarin therapy
6. Provide inservice programs for medical, nursing, and pharmacy staffs regarding appropriate oral anticoagulation
7. Provide patient education/counseling on anticoagulation. Enhance the patient's involvement in his or her warfarin therapy.
8. Improve patient compliance with warfarin therapy
9. Enhance the identification of potential drug–drug and drug–food interactions involving warfarin
10. Decrease physician workload, expand pharmacy-outpatient services, and obtain appropriate reimbursement for clinical pharmacy services
11. The clinic will provide a peer-reviewed, organized, and standardized protocol for provider credentialing, supervision, patient care management and coordination, communication and documentation, laboratory monitoring, patient selection and assessment, initiation of therapy, maintenance and routine monitoring of therapy, patient education, and patient outcomes.

Eligibility

Patients must be referred to the anticoagulation clinic by their provider. Informed consent must be received from the patient before a pharmacist assumes responsibility for the patient's warfarin therapy.

The referring physician will be responsible for providing the following data on the referral form when requesting pharmacy management of his or her patient:
- Indication for anticoagulation (if prosthetic valve, then type of valve is required)
- Current daily dose
- Expected duration of anticoagulant therapy
- Target INR
- Patients may be accepted into the ACC if they meet the following criteria:
  - Are reliable and willing to follow instructions
  - Are able to keep appointments
  - Have reliable transportation to the hospital
  - Have access to and are accessible by telephone
- Patients may be dismissed from the ACC for the following reasons:
  - If the information listed above is not made available by the primary provider
  - If there are medical contraindications, such as, but not limited to, uncontrolled or severe HTN, bleeding diathesis, pregnancy, alcoholism, active peptic ulcer disease, history of recent major bleeding episode (gastrointestinal [GI], genitourinary [GU], central nervous system [CNS])
  - Unexplained anemia, uncontrolled psychiatric disturbances, or high risk of falling (occupational, history of falling)
  - Lack of appropriate medical follow-up
  - An inability of the pharmacy program to manage more patients because of time and/or space limitations

Referrals

Patients may be enrolled in the ACC through a written referral in the patient's medical record.

Inpatients

- Referral to the ACC may be made by the provider and should be made as early as possible before discharge (preferably two or three days before) or at the time of initial warfarin dosing.
- A pharmacist will visit the patient, review the medical record, confer with the referring physician regarding acceptance into the ACC if necessary.
- After acceptance, the pharmacist will review indications for and the plan of treatment together with the appropriate precautions and adverse effects.
- The patient will be given an anticoagulation information booklet containing a treatment identification card, an appointment date for a follow-up on his/her INR, appropriate patient education literature, and emergency telephone numbers for reaching the pharmacy or the emergency department if pharmacy is unavailable. The need for adherence to pharmacological therapy and appointment instructions will be stressed.
- The patient may be shown the Coumadin® video by the inpatient nursing staff if available and appropriate.

Outpatients

- Referral to the ACC will be made by the provider.
- Patients are entered in the ACC through documentation in the patient's medical record.
- After review of the referral and medical record and, if necessary, conferral with the referring physician, a decision to reject or accept the patient into ACC or schedule for further evaluation will be made.

ACC Appointment Schedule

Patient appointments and continuity of care will be maintained by the Resource Patient Management System (RPMS) scheduling package in addition to the patient's chart. Patient follow-up visits will be scheduled on the basis of the dose adjustment protocol and clinical judgment of the pharmacist and provider. Patients will be required to make an appointment with a provider at least quarterly for routine medical follow-up. ACC visits will be made between provider visits as appropriate.

If a patient does not attend a scheduled ACC visit and has not called to reschedule, adequate follow-up will be ensured by taking the following steps:

- The patient will receive an appointment reminder letter to have his/her INR checked immediately or to reschedule for a follow-up ACC appointment.
- If a patient misses three consecutive appointments or more than four per year, the patient
  - May be dismissed from the ACC service, and the patient's primary provider will need to follow up through the outpatient clinic system. A dismissal from the ACC service will be made available in the patient's medical record.

ACC Visits

Patients will be seen at scheduled appointments by a pharmacist in a timely manner. Providers will provide a written prescription for patients to have pertinent laboratory values monitored by protocol for up to six months. These orders will be maintained in the patient's medical record. Patients will be required to check in with Patient Registration before going to the laboratory for the necessary laboratory values ordered (e.g., INR, PT, complete blood count [CBC], liver function tests [LFT]).

The patient's chart will be requested from the Medical Records Department by the Laboratory Department when the patient presents to have his or her appropriate laboratory monitoring performed for anticoagulation therapy.

After the chart and laboratory results are collected in the pharmacy, the pharmacist will discuss subjective and objective findings in an available counseling room. All information will be reported in the patient's medical record, including

- Current drugs
- Date of last INR order
- Date of referral to the ACC
- Signs and symptoms of overanticoagulation as described in the Pharmacy and Therapeutics Warfarin Protocol
- Recent alterations in diet (include drugs and ethyl alcohol [EtOH] intake)
- Changes in lifestyle, social well-being, or health status
- Adherence with drug regimen
- Status of other problem(s) not related to anticoagulation
- Reason for anticoagulant therapy
- Target INR range
- Today's PT and INR results
- Other laboratory results
- BP and pulse rate
- An assessment of subjective and objective findings as they pertain to the patient's oral anticoagulation therapy
- Drug name, strength, quantity, and directions for use
- Follow-up appointment for INR
  - Recommended follow-up appointment in clinic
  - Referrals to other services as appropriate
  - Patient education documentation

Therapeutic Dose Adjustments

The assigned pharmacist will determine initial dosage and expected duration of therapy schedules with the concurrence of the patient's provider. Subsequent adjustments in the dosing schedule will be made with the intent of maintaining the patient's INR within the goal ranges described by the most recent recommendations of the American College of Chest Physicians and the patient's primary provider.

Patients presenting with INR values outside the therapeutic range, previously maintained in good control, will be interviewed to identify precipitating factors (i.e., diet changes, food interactions, drug interactions, use of OTCs, lifestyle changes, social changes, missed dosages, other disease states, and alcohol use). The warfarin dose will be adjusted on the basis of the clinical interpretation of these factors and the patient's INR value. The dose adjustment protocol will serve as a guideline for therapeutic dose adjustments; however, emphasis will be placed on ease of the treatment regimen and individualization of therapy based on the patient's individual characteristics. A return visit will be scheduled as appropriate.

Referral to Physician

A provider will be notified immediately if the patient requires an evaluation for a significant adverse event or if the INR is considered a critical value by the Laboratory Department. The pharmacist will review with the patient's primary provider any unexpected questions or complications that arise as well as the need for further anticoagulation therapy when the original estimated duration of therapy has been reached. All assessments, SOAP notes, and dosage adjustments will be reviewed and co-signed by a provider through standing order protocol within 48 hours of an anticoagulation visit. Patients will be referred to a provider-only visit every 3 months.

Patient Education

A continuing program of patient education forms the basis for clear patient understanding of anticoagulation therapy. Patients and their relatives/caregivers must be fully informed of the indication for therapy, the nature of the program, and the possible complications. Education begins at the initial clinic visit and is reinforced during subsequent visits. The educational process will be verbal and written (handouts) as well as individualized to account for the patient's ability to comprehend the subject. Patients are to be questioned at each visit for problems in the areas of control, complications, adverse effects, and compliance. Patient education will be documented in the patient's medical record using the national Indian Health Service (IHS) Patient and Family Education protocols and locally developed and approved lesson plans.

Laboratory Monitoring

Laboratory tests will be ordered by protocol or clinical judgment of the pharmacist or the patient's provider. The medical provider will provide the initial laboratory order by writing "INR per protocol for six months (or other appropriate length of time not to exceed six months)" on the patient's medical record. A copy of the INR order will be given to the Laboratory Department, where it will be kept on file. It is recommended that the INR value be checked at least once monthly in a patient on a stable dose of warfarin and within his or her goal INR. The patient's provider will provide the Laboratory Department a valid prescription for PT and INR laboratory orders through this policy, procedure, and protocol by writing "INR per anticoagulation protocol from date A to date B (not to exceed six months)" in the patient's medical record. A copy of the prescription will be kept on file in the Laboratory Department, and this order will be referred to for PT and INR laboratory values tested within these periods. If an INR and PT are requested but a valid prescription is not on file in the Laboratory Department, the Laboratory Department will contact the Pharmacy Department, which will discuss the need for a laboratory prescription with a provider.

References for INR testing

1. American Heart Association recommends a maximum duration between testing for safe monitoring at four-week intervals (Hirsh J, et al. Oral anticoagulants: mechanism of action, clinical effectiveness, and optimal therapeutic range. Chest 1995;108(suppl):231S–46S).
2. CMS (NCDs) recommendations are: "In a patient on stable warfarin therapy, it is ordinarily not necessary to repeat testing more than every two to three weeks" (National Coverage Determinations (NCDs) 11/25/02, www.cms.hhs.gov/ncd/searchdisplay.asp?NCD_ID=80&NCD_vrsn_num=1).
3. "Performing PT tests at intervals of four weeks is recommended for a patient who achieves a stable dose and response. Clinical experience, however, shows that the mean interval for PT testing in many anticoagulation management services is between two and three weeks" Ansell JE, Oertel LB, Wittkowsky AK, eds. Managing Oral Anticoagulation Therapy. New York: Aspen Publishers, 1997:4B-3:3).

Personnel Orientation/Criteria to Participate

Staff pharmacists will be oriented, trained, and supervised in the management of oral anticoagulant therapy for compliance with the latest recommendations of the ACCP and the current hospital Managing Oral Anticoagulation Therapy Policy and Procedure for anticoagulation therapy. Certification will be obtained from the IHS National Clinical Pharmacy Specialist (NCPS) program, and limited medical privileges from the hospital's governing board will be awarded to pharmacists before following in the ACC (with the exception of pharmacists in training to achieve these certifications [see Pharmacist Credentialing]). A copy of the certification and standing orders will be placed in the departmental personnel folder. Pharmacists will be recertified yearly to ensure that appropriate techniques and procedures are maintained.

Pharmacist Credentialing

Pharmacists will be credentialed through a national and local mechanism before receiving limited medical staff privileges. The NCPS program is a credentialing body developed by the IHS to ensure uniformity among IHS pharmacists providing disease state management services. The criteria for recognition as an NCPS in ACCs consider the pharmacist's time with the IHS; credentials; experience; ability to demonstrate with a physician that at least thirty charts can be appropriately and safely managed by the patient following a local policy, procedure, and protocol; a letter of attestation from a physician; and a completed liability claims form. The pharmacist will apply for an NCPS certification through the policy and procedure defined by the NCPS credentialing committee. The pharmacist must then pass the ACC examination with a score of 75% or greater, which tests the pharmacist's knowledge of pathophysiology, pharmacotherapy, monitoring, and adherence to the ACC policy and procedure. A certification of completion will be awarded to the pharmacist by the Chief Pharmacist and Clinical Director. An application will be obtained from the Personnel Department for acceptance into the medical staff. This document will be completed in its entirety and will be submitted for review by the medical staff and hospital governing board. The medical staff will review the pharmacist's application together with at least thirty of the pharmacist's ACC encounters. If approved by the medical staff, the pharmacist's application will be presented to the governing board, and if approved, the pharmacist will receive the privileges to provide anticoagulation therapy as outlined in the Privilege Request form. The pharmacist will receive the privileges outlined in this form; however, the pharmacist will not be a full member of the medical dental staff committee.

Continuous Performance Improvement

Because of the nature of warfarin and its narrow benefit-to-risk ratio, little tolerance can be allowed to ensure the highest level of care possible. Quality indicators for the ACC shall include information such as INR values in goal range, below goal range, and above goal range; serious adverse events; number of patient visits; number of laboratory values evaluated; and patient and provider satisfaction. This information shall be reviewed on a continual basis and recorded in the hospital's performance improvement records.

ANTICOAGULATION SERVICE PROCEDURE

1. The patient's provider enrolls him or her into the ACC by placing a referral for acceptance into the ACC in the patient's medical record. An order is included in the referral enabling the pharmacist to order laboratory tests pertaining to the patient's anticoagulation therapy for one (1) year.
2. The pharmacy accepts the patient into the ACC and schedules a follow-up appointment.
3. The patient reports to patient registration and verifies demographic information.
4. The patient goes to the laboratory to have PT and INR drawn or has the test performed in the pharmacy using an approved point-of-care testing device.
5. The pharmacist evaluates the patient's laboratory results and reviews the patient's medical record.
6. The pharmacist calls the patient and/or caregiver into a private counseling room to assess the anticoagulation therapy.
7. The pharmacist develops an assessment and recommendation.
8. The pharmacist determines an appropriate follow-up appointment.
9. The pharmacist will provide recommendations, patient education, and an appointment slip for the patient's next visit if it is at the pharmacy.

Nomogram for Adjusting Warfarin Therapy Based on Total Weekly Dose

INR Goal 2.0–3.0	INR Goal 2.5–3.5	Recommendation
< 1.4	< 2.0	May add 10–20% of total weekly dose today Increase total weekly dose by 10–20% Return in 1 week
1.5–0.9	2.1–2.4	May add 5–10% of total weekly dose today Increase total weekly dose by 5–10% Return in 2 weeks
2.0–3.0	2.5–3.5	No change Return in 1 month
3.1–3.9	3.6–4.6	May subtract 5–10% of total weekly dose today Or hold today's dose Decrease total weekly dose by 5–10% Return in 2 weeks
4.0–5.0	4.7–5.2	Verify INR with laboratory results May subtract 10–20% of total weekly dose today Or hold 1–2 doses Decrease total weekly dose by 10–20% Return in 1 week
> 5.0	> 5.2	Verify INR with laboratory results Visit with primary care provider Monitor INR until 3 or less Restart with total weekly dose decreased by 20–50% Return daily until controlled

Vitamin K for reversal of anticoagulation

INR above therapeutic but less than 5 No signs of significant bleeding	Hold next dose of warfarin, or lower dose of warfarin, or if INR is only minimally above therapeutic, no intervention may be necessary	Follow-up INR in 1–4 weeks depending on circumstances
INR above 5 but less than 9 No signs of significant bleeding	Hold 1 or 2 doses of warfarin and restart warfarin at a lower dose	Follow-up INR in 3–7 days
INR above 5 but less than 9 No signs of significant bleeding At increased risk of bleeding	Hold next dose of warfarin May give oral (PO) vitamin K (1–2.5 mg)[a]	Follow-up INR in 12–24 hours
For urgent surgery or dental extraction[b] Goal INR to perform surgery is ~1.5	If time permits, hold warfarin; INR will drop below 1.5 in 3–4 days If time is of the essence, PO vitamin K (2–4 mg) may be given	INR will drop over 24 hours If still elevated at 24 hours, an additional 1 or 2 mg may be given Follow-up INR in 12–24 hours
INR greater than 9 No signs of significant bleeding	Hold warfarin Give PO vitamin K (3–5 mg)	INR will drop over 24 hours If still elevated at 24 hours, an additional 1 or 2 mg may be given Follow-up INR in 12–24 hours
Serious bleeding or INR greater than 20	Hold warfarin Give slow intravenous (IV) infusion of vitamin K (10 mg) May consider fresh plasma transfusion or prothrombin complex concentrate	Follow-up INR in 12 hours
Life-threatening bleeding or serious warfarin overdose	Hold warfarin Give slow IV infusion of vitamin K (10 mg) Give prothrombin complex concentrate	Follow-up INR in 12 hours May repeat vitamin K in 6–7 hours if INR not declining
If anticoagulation is necessary after high doses of vitamin K	Administer heparin based on the standard care nomogram **and** Restart warfarin	Continue for 3–7 days until INR is in therapeutic range Vitamin K may cause warfarin resistance after about 1 week

[a]For patients with acute venous thrombosis or arterial embolism, start heparin before surgery and continue after surgery until INR in goal range; for patients with recurrent VTE, mechanical heart valves, or atrial fibrillation, start subcutaneous (SC) heparin or low-molecular-weight heparin (LMWH) after surgery until INR in goal.
[b]Injectable vitamin K may be administered orally if tablet form is not available.
PO vitamin K is more reliable than SC vitamin K (SC vitamin K can have unpredictable and delayed effects); IV vitamin K can cause severe allergic reactions; vitamin K = phytonadione (Mephyton®).

PRIVILEGE REQUEST—PHARMACY
Anticoagulation Service

Requested Privilege	Requested		Approved	
	Limited	Full	Limited	Full
Assessment of patients with regard to anticoagulation therapy (e.g., checking BP and pulse rate; ordering appropriate laboratory tests; questioning patients with regard to general health, adverse effects, and anticoagulation therapy; assessing needs of warfarin therapy using the most recent CHEST Summary Guidelines)				
Adjusting the dose of warfarin by nomogram and clinical assessment using the most recent CHEST Summary Guidelines				
Scheduling patients for follow-up appointments with regard to their anticoagulation therapy to ensure that appropriate steps are taken for patients to follow up in clinic				
To educate patients on warfarin therapy using the anticoagulation lesson plans outlined in the anticoagulation policy and procedure				

_____
Requesting Pharmacist

_____
Chief of Pharmacy

_____
Clinical Director

CHEROKEE INDIAN HOSPITAL
Cherokee, North Carolina

Oral Anticoagulant (Warfarin) Therapy Management Certification

_____ has read and expressed an understanding of the Pharmacy Policy and Procedure Manual Item 11.40 (Oral Anticoagulation Clinic Program) and the most recent recommendations from the American College of Chest Physicians. He/She has been observed in the management of warfarin therapy and is found to possess an acceptable level of competency to independently provide this Warfarin Protocol by:

    1. Educating patients
    2. Ordering appropriate laboratory tests
    3. Adjusting warfarin doses to maintain appropriate therapy
    4. Reappointing patients for follow-up

_____   _____
Pharmacist   Date

_____   _____
Chief of Pharmacy Services   Date

Concurrence:

_____   _____
Clinical Director   Date

ANTICOAGULATION DRUG THERAPY MANAGEMENT PROTOCOL

Submitted by: Debra Lopez

Created: August 2005

This DTM protocol is to comply with the pharmacy and medical practice acts regarding DTM by a pharmacist under the written protocol of a physician. The procedures, protocols, practices, and other items contained within these documents are intended to be helpful reminders for the pharmacists and physicians of this institution. In no instance should the contents of these documents be considered standards of professional practice or rules of conduct or for the benefit of any third party. The documents herein are guidelines only and allow professional discretion and deviation where the individual health care provider deems variation appropriate as allowed by law.

The individual physicians authorized to prescribe drugs and responsible for the delegation of DTM in the Anticoagulation Clinic are _____.

The clinical pharmacists who are authorized to prescribe drugs under the physician initiated protocol and who will carry out the DTM as delegated are _____, and his/her current resident.

In accordance with the incorporated treatment guidelines, the clinical pharmacist may provide care for patients in the ACC under the physician-initiated protocol to include:

1. Assesses patients' therapeutic needs as specified by physician consult regarding anticoagulation therapy. Disease states/ailments treated with anticoagulation therapy include, but are not limited to, DVT, PE, stroke, TIA, bioprosthetic and mechanical heart valves, hypercoagulable states, peripheral vascular disease (PVD), and acute MI.
2. Evaluates pharmacological and non-pharmacological treatment regimens.
3. Orders, interprets, and conducts all pertinent laboratory studies.
4. Initiates and adjusts drugs in accordance with attached pharmacological privileges.
5. Provides patient education regarding disease(s) and pharmacological and non-pharmacological therapy.
6. Documents patient visits, patient care, and treatment decisions in the medical record. The referring physician and primary care physician (PCP) will have access to such medical records. Initial and subsequent follow-up documentation will be placed in the patient's medical record on a regular basis.
7. Consults with referring physician, the PCP, and other members of the health care team, as appropriate.
8. Obtains authorization from the physician for deviations from the protocol.
9. The schedule for physician review and status reports to the physician is based on each individual patient. The services provided to the patient by the pharmacist will be available to or provided to the physician after each clinic visit and on an as-needed basis. A supervising physician will also meet regularly with the clinical pharmacists to review the DTM protocol and patient care.
10. This protocol does not delegate diagnosis to the clinical pharmacists.
11. The clinical pharmacists will use treatment guidelines for DTM of anticoagulation therapy from the CHEST guidelines (CHEST 2001;119:January 2001 supplement).

This Drug Therapy Management protocol was formulated and approved by:

_____   _____
M.D./Date   Medical Director   M.D./Date

_____   _____
M.D./Date   M.D./Date

Requesting Practitioners:

_____   _____
Pharm.D., CDE/Date   Pharm.D./Date

Anticoagulation Clinic Protocol: Clinical Pharmacists

Clinical pharmacists are the responsible providers for the anticoagulation clinic. The following procedure is authorized:
- Review the clinical record including indications for the anticoagulant, PT/INR, and drugs.
- Renew or alter current prescriptions for warfarin under the supervision of the designated physician.
- Initiate the stool guaiac test if patient experiences hematochezia.
- Provide patient instruction regarding the safe and appropriate use of anticoagulation therapy.
- Use anticoagulation guidelines when prescribing anticoagulants.
- Clinical concerns will be addressed to the primary care provider.

General Dosing Instructions
- Use 5-mg tablets whenever possible.
- When alternate dosage is needed twice weekly, use on Monday and Friday.
- When alternate dosage is needed once weekly, use on Friday.
- Start warfarin using the following guidelines:
  - If the patient is younger than 70 years and/or weighs more than 60 kg, give 5 mg daily and check the PT/INR in four to six days.
  - If the patient is older than 70 years and/or weighs less than 60 kg; has liver disease, CHF, or inadequate nutrition; or is at high risk of bleeding, start with 2.5 mg daily and check the PT/INR in four to six days.
- Refer to the protocol flow charts for the dosage protocol.
- Management of excessive prolongation of INR: If the INR is more than 6, send the patient to the laboratory for venipuncture PT/INR.

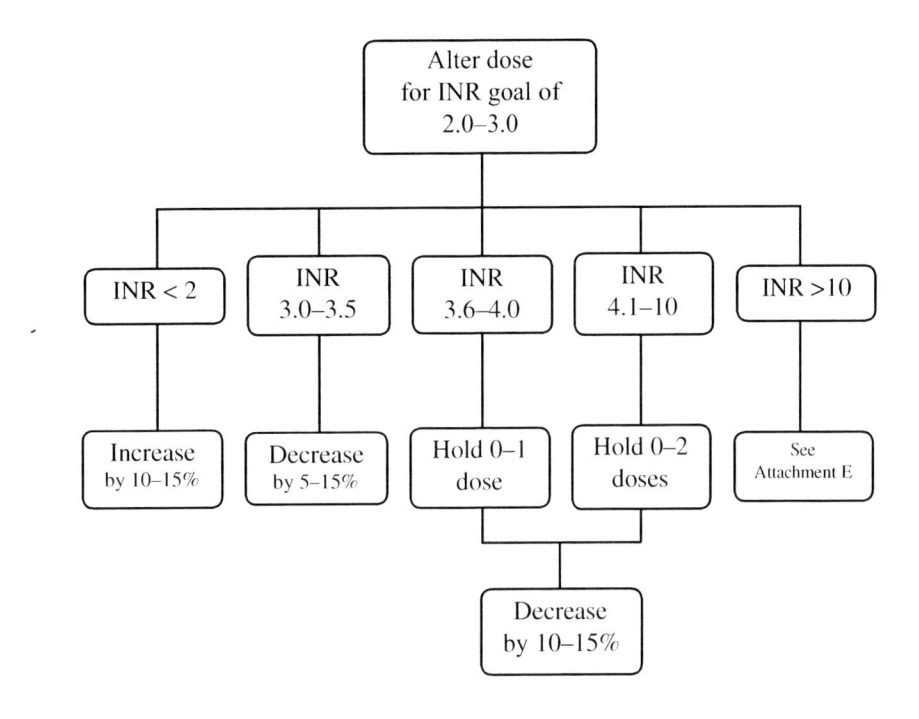

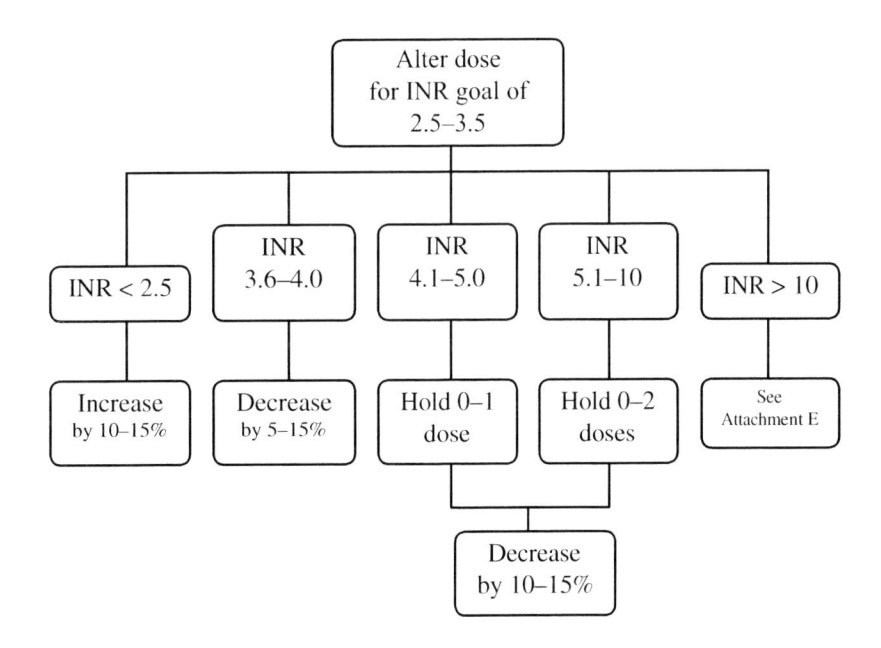

```
                    Alter dose
                   for INR goal of
                      2.0–3.0
    ┌──────┬──────────┬──────────┬──────────┬──────────┐
  INR < 2   INR       INR        INR         INR >10
            3.0–3.5   3.6–4.0    4.1–10
    │        │         │          │           │
 Increase  Decrease  Hold 0–1   Hold 0–2     See
 by 10–15% by 5–15%  dose       doses        Attachment E
                       │          │
                       └────┬─────┘
                         Decrease
                         by 10–15%
```

```
                    Alter dose
                   for INR goal of
                      2.5–3.5
    ┌──────┬──────────┬──────────┬──────────┬──────────┐
  INR < 2.5  INR       INR        INR         INR > 10
             3.6–4.0   4.1–5.0    5.1–10
     │        │         │          │           │
  Increase  Decrease  Hold 0–1   Hold 0–2     See
  by 10–15% by 5–15%  dose       doses        Attachment E
                       │          │
                       └────┬─────┘
                         Decrease
                         by 10–15%
```

NOTE: Because of tablet size, adjustment for an increase or decrease falling beyond recommended dose by up to 3% percent is deemed acceptable. Unless other concerns are present, an adjustment by up to 3% does not need prior verification by a physician.

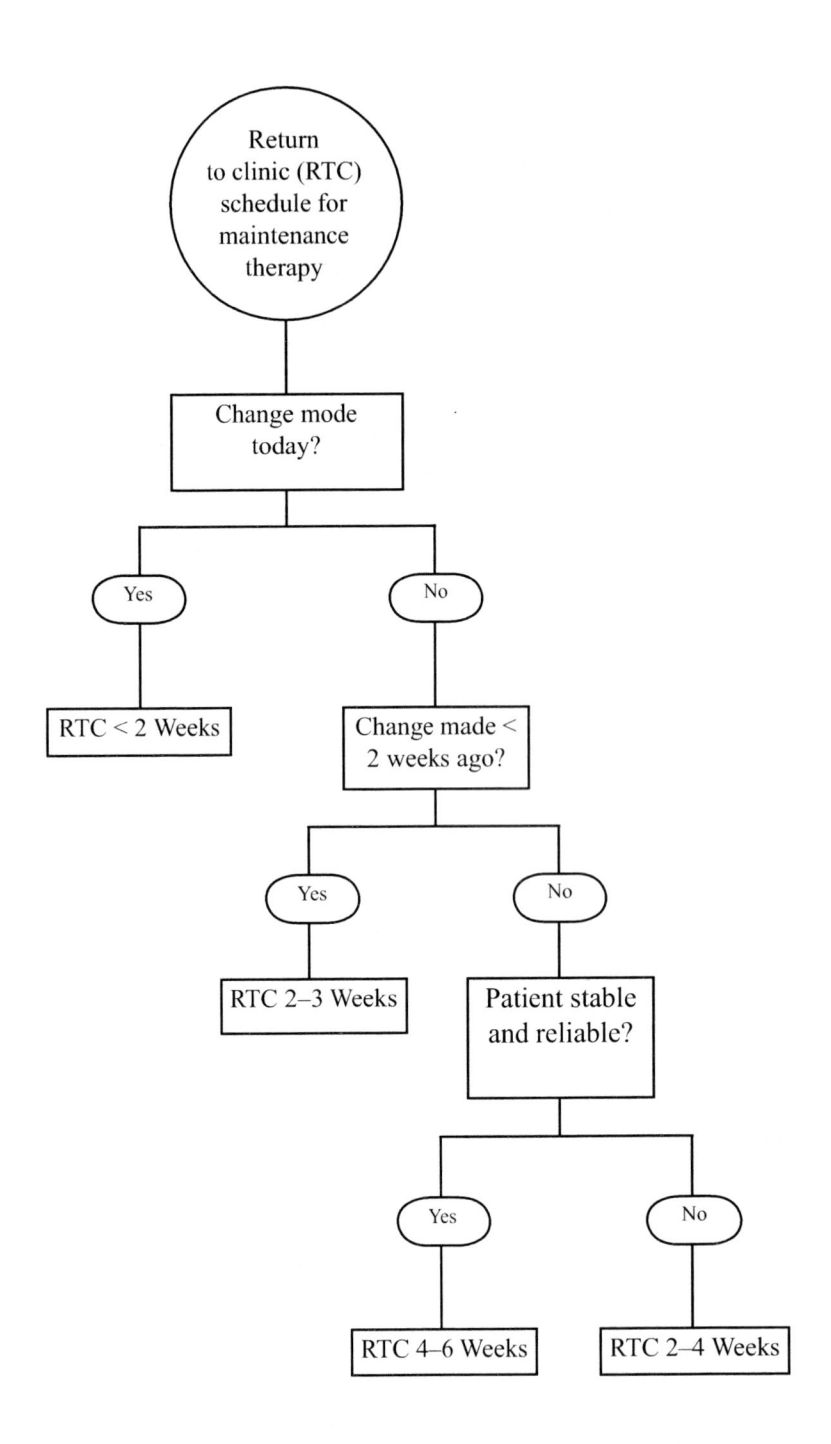

```
                    ┌─────────────┐
                   (   Return     )
                   ( to clinic(RTC))
                   ( schedule for  )
                   (  maintenance  )
                   (    therapy    )
                    └──────┬──────┘
                           │
                   ┌───────┴───────┐
                   │  Change mode  │
                   │    today?     │
                   └───────┬───────┘
                     ┌─────┴─────┐
                   (Yes)        (No)
                     │           │
              ┌──────┴─────┐  ┌──┴──────────────┐
              │ RTC < 2 Weeks│ │ Change made <   │
              └──────────────┘ │ 2 weeks ago?    │
                               └────────┬────────┘
                                  ┌─────┴─────┐
                                (Yes)        (No)
                                  │           │
                         ┌────────┴──┐  ┌─────┴────────┐
                         │RTC 2–3 Weeks│ │Patient stable│
                         └─────────────┘ │ and reliable?│
                                         └──────┬───────┘
                                           ┌────┴────┐
                                         (Yes)     (No)
                                           │         │
                                   ┌───────┴──┐  ┌───┴──────┐
                                   │RTC 4–6 Wk│  │RTC 2–4 Wk│
                                   └──────────┘  └──────────┘
```

ADULT ANTICOAGULATION PROTOCOL—CDTM

Submitted by: Kelly Ragucci

Revised: November 2005

Purpose

To establish guidelines for the monitoring of anticoagulation therapy in adult patients and to clearly define the roles/responsibilities of the physicians and collaborating pharmacists. The purpose of the service is to provide continuity of care to patients who require anticoagulation; enhance patient care through education, monitoring, and close follow-up; and reduce adverse events associated with anticoagulation therapy.

Provider Qualifications

A pharmacist providing anticoagulation DFM must be credentialed by the department of pharmacy services and meet minimal competencies required for their practice area. Until credentialing is obtained, a pharmacist may work under the direct supervision of the credentialed pharmacist. These physicians must be MUSC-credentialed physicians and have a signed CDTM agreement for anticoagulation management with the credentialed pharmacist.

Procedure

Referral

The referring physician will provide the pharmacist with the following: date of anticoagulation initiation, present anticoagulation dose, inr goal/range, reason for therapy, length of therapy, and other pertinent information. It is also the responsibility of the referring physician, or his/her designee, to be available for consultation. The pharmacist has the right to decline the management of a patient based on perceived inappropriateness of therapy.

Clinic Visits

The patient will follow the general policies and procedures concerning registration and will report to the laboratory to have blood work drawn if necessary. Afterward, the patient will meet with the pharmacist to discuss laboratory results and other pertinent information. Other forms of communication may be used and will be determined by the pharmacist and the patient.

- Physical assessment
  - Visual inspection
- Initiate drug therapy
  - The pharmacist is not authorized to initiate drug therapy under this protocol without first contacting a physician.
- Modify or discontinue drug therapy
  - Therapeutic and nontherapeutic values
    - After evaluation and consideration of all contributing factors, including missed/extra doses, drug changes, dietary changes, and potential bleeding problems, dosage adjustments will be made according to the flow sheets in figure 1. Patients will then schedule a PT/INR blood draw and follow-up appointment with the clinic. Regardless of the INR value, if a patient has signs or symptoms of serious bleeding or clotting, the referring physician will be contacted by the clinic, or the patient will be sent to the emergency department. When the estimated duration of anticoagulation therapy is complete, the referring physician will be notified, and a consensus will be reached between the clinic and the physician before therapy discontinuation.
    - All orders will be written according to CDTM anticoagulation protocol and signed by the credentialed pharmacist. Prescriptions may be written or called into the patient's pharmacy by the credentialed pharmacist, as an agent of the physician, by telephone order.
  - Planned surgeries and procedures
    - Patients will be instructed to inform all health care providers about warfarin therapy. On notification of planned procedures, the pharmacist will contact the referring physician. Plans for interruption of therapy will be made and forwarded to the appropriate surgeon/physician. The patient will follow up for PT/INR laboratory values within seven to ten days of restarting warfarin therapy.
- Order appropriate tests
  - The pharmacist is authorized to order the following laboratory tests to monitor the efficacy and toxicity of anticoagulation therapy (see figure 1).
    - PT/INR
    - CBC

Prepared by Medical University of South Carolina, Charleston, South Carolina

- Perform point-of-care testing
  - The pharmacist is authorized to perform INR point-of-care testing, with an MUSC-approved device.
- Administer drugs
  - The pharmacist is not authorized to administer drugs under this protocol without first contacting a physician.
- Refer patients
  - The pharmacist is authorized to refer patients to their physician or to the emergency department.
- Participation in/coordination of clinical research
  - Not applicable in this protocol
- Patient education
  - An extensive longitudinal program of patient education will be provided. Patients and family members/caretakers will be provided the following information:
    - Purpose of the anticoagulation service and follow-up procedures
    - Indication for warfarin therapy
    - Goal INR
    - Signs and symptoms of bleeding and what to do if it occurs
    - Signs and symptoms of thrombus or emboli and what to do if it occurs
    - Instructions on how to take warfarin and the importance of adherence
    - What to do if a dose is missed
    - Identification of warfarin dose by color
    - Drug–diet interactions (e.g., Vitamin K–containing foods)
    - Drug–drug interactions (prescription, OTC, and herbal products)
- Documentation
  - All patient encounters will be documented in the progress notes of the EMR using the clinical pharmacy anticoagulation note template (figure 2). All notes will be sent to the referring provider by the EMR system.
- Billing for services
  - Patients will be billed for services in accordance with the MUSC Department of Pharmacy
  - Services ambulatory care billing policy (B06)

All other procedures will be performed according to the general policies and procedures of the clinic.

Quality Assurance/Outcomes

Data will be continuously monitored to ensure patients are receiving optimal care. Outcomes of the anticoagulation protocol will include, but not be limited to, the percentage of patients at goal INR, response to therapy, and serious adverse events. Process tracking will also occur to confirm adherence to the protocol. These results will be presented quarterly to the appropriate pharmacy coordinator and manager.

References

1. Dalen JE, Hirsh J, Guyatt GH, eds. Seventh American College of Chest Physicians consensus conference on antithrombotic and thrombolytic therapy. Chest 2004;126(3 suppl):163S–696S.
2. Kearon C, Hirsh J. Management of anticoagulation before and after elective surgery. N Engl J Med 1997;336:1506–11.
3. Ansell JE, ed. Managing Oral Anticoagulation Therapy: Clinical and Operational Guidelines. Gaithersburg, MD: Aspen Publishing, 1997.

Figure 1. Dosage adjustment protocols

Low Intensity INR (Goal 2-3)

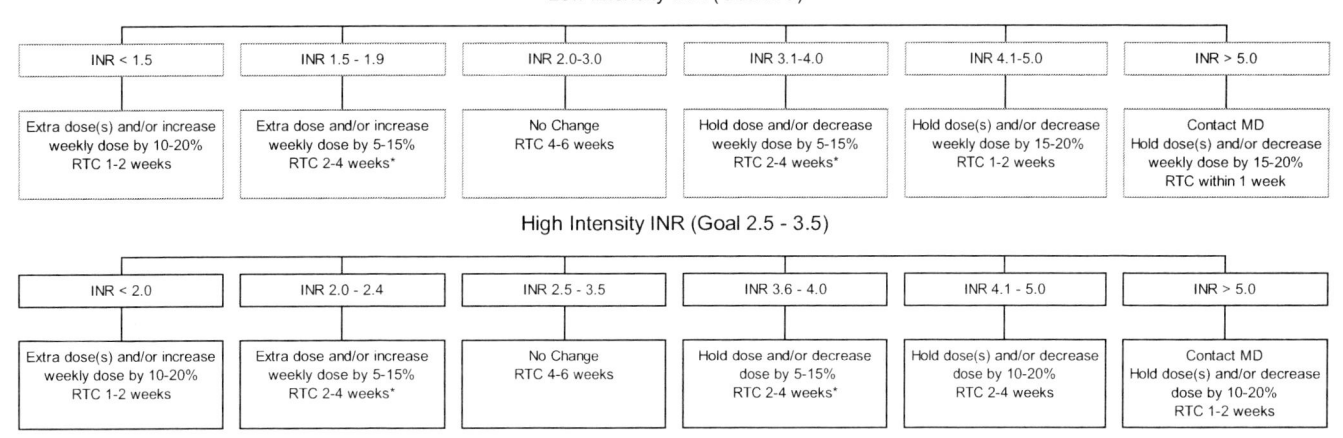

INR < 1.5	INR 1.5 - 1.9	INR 2.0-3.0	INR 3.1-4.0	INR 4.1-5.0	INR > 5.0
Extra dose(s) and/or increase weekly dose by 10-20% RTC 1-2 weeks	Extra dose and/or increase weekly dose by 5-15% RTC 2-4 weeks*	No Change RTC 4-6 weeks	Hold dose and/or decrease weekly dose by 5-15% RTC 2-4 weeks*	Hold dose(s) and/or decrease weekly dose by 15-20% RTC 1-2 weeks	Contact MD Hold dose(s) and/or decrease weekly dose by 15-20% RTC within 1 week

High Intensity INR (Goal 2.5 - 3.5)

INR < 2.0	INR 2.0 - 2.4	INR 2.5 - 3.5	INR 3.6 - 4.0	INR 4.1 - 5.0	INR > 5.0
Extra dose(s) and/or increase weekly dose by 10-20% RTC 1-2 weeks	Extra dose and/or increase weekly dose by 5-15% RTC 2-4 weeks*	No Change RTC 4-6 weeks	Hold dose and/or decrease dose by 5-15% RTC 2-4 weeks*	Hold dose(s) and/or decrease dose by 10-20% RTC 2-4 weeks	Contact MD Hold dose(s) and/or decrease dose by 10-20% RTC 1-2 weeks

*Dosage adjustment may not be necessary.
**Dose should be increased or decreased after two consecutive super- or subtherapeutic INR values.

Warfarin Drug Interactions[a]

Drug–Food Interactions That Have Been Reported to Increase the Effects of Warfarin
Acetaminophen, alcohol, amiodarone, anabolic steroids, chloral hydrate, cimetidine, ciprofloxacin, clofibrate, disulfiram, erythromycin, fluconazole, isoniazid, itraconazole, metronidazole, miconazole, omeprazole, phenylbutazone, piroxicam, propafenone, propranolol, quinidine, phenytoin, sulfamethoxazole/trimethoprim, sulfinpyrazone, tamoxifen, tetracycline, flu vaccine

Drug–Food Interactions That Have Been Reported to Decrease the Effects of Warfarin
Barbiturates, carbamazepine, chlordiazepoxide, cholestyramine, dicloxacillin, griseofulvin, nafcillin, rifampin, sucralfate, foods with high vitamin K content/enteral feeding

[a]This is not a comprehensive list of warfarin interactions. Any changes in drugs will be appropriately addressed.

FIGURE 2—Anticoagulation Note Template

Date: ___/___/___
Title: CLIN PHARM ANTICOAG—APCC UDC
Providers: _____
Contact type: In-clinic visit, Telephone follow-up (f/u)
Duration of visit: 15 minutes
Laboratory: Indication: DVT, PE, CVA. AFIB, MVR, AVR, Thrombophilia, Other
Note entered by: JOE SCHMO

A 50-year-old man who presents to the Clinical Pharmacist for anticoagulation management and education. Patient is without complaints regarding warfarin therapy.

Warfarin therapy: Date of initiation: 1/1/1
Lab: Date of initiation: 1/1/01
Lab: CURRENT DOSE: 5 mg qod
Lab: Tablet Strength: 5 mg
Lab: Therapy Duration: 6 MONTHS
Lab: Total Weekly Dose: 35 mg
Lab: RF for Bleeding: CONCOMITANT ASA
Lab: RF for Thrombo: INTERNATIONAL FLIGHT ATTENDANT
Missed doses? NO
Bleeding or bruising? NO
Change in urine or stool color? NO
EtOH use? NO
Dietary changes? NO
New prescriptions or OTC/herbal products? NO
Any upcoming surgical or dental procedures? NO
Any increased edema, leg pain, or other thromboembolic symptoms? NO
Other concerns: NONE

PT from OACIS
INR from OACIS

Desired Range: 2.0—3.0
Laboratory: Goal INR: 2.5

Assessment: INR is above the desired range. Dosage adjustment is warranted. INR is below the desired range. Dosage adjustment is warranted. INR is within the desired range. Dosage adjustment is warranted.

Plan: NO CHANGES
Laboratory: Plan (new dose): Continue current dose.
Laboratory: Total Weekly Dose: Same
Laboratory: % increase/decrease: 0%
Laboratory: Date of follow-up: 4 WEEKS

Instructed patients to monitor themselves for signs or symptoms of bleeding and thromboembolism and to report to the ER if symptoms arise. Patients verbalized understanding of all instructions and have been instructed to call the clinic with comments or questions New patient education—Educated patient on the indication for anticoagulation; interpretation of the INR; importance of adherence with drugs and visits; avoidance of ASA, nonsteroidal anti-inflammatory drugs (NSAIDs), and alcohol; and instructions to report any drug initiation or discontinuation. Discussed importance of consistency with intake of vitamin K–containing foods, informing health care providers of Coumadin therapy. Reviewed signs and symptoms of bleeding. Patient supplied with Coumadin alert card and encouraged to get a medic alert bracelet.

COUMADIN CLINIC DISMISSAL LETTER

Submitted by: Pamela L. Stamm

Revised: June 2003

(Sent by certified mail receipt requested on letterhead.)

Date:

Dear_____,

    We have identified a problem regarding your attendance at scheduled clinic and laboratory appointments. You missed Coumadin clinic on _____ [day and date] and failed to have your blood tested as scheduled on _____ [day and date]. We have tried to contact you multiple times and have used the police department to manage your medical issues.

    Your medical condition requires continuous follow-up to ensure appropriate management. Also, you are taking Coumadin®. This drug may cause serious problems if not monitored regularly. You must take your Coumadin® each day as we have discussed to keep your blood thin and to best prevent more clotting. Without visits to us or your doctor and appropriate blood thinning, you are at risk of life-threatening problems such as clotting or bleeding.

    These important issues have been previously discussed with you. You have not attended your Coumadin Clinic appointments as you had agreed. As a result, we are unable to monitor your condition appropriately. Due to your pattern of missed appointments and our inability to reach you, we feel you are not a candidate for Coumadin® therapy at this time. You are dismissed from Coumadin Clinic effective immediately. This means we will no longer be contacting you or attempting to manage your Coumadin®. You need to stop taking your Coumadin® today. You also need to follow up with your primary medical care provider for continued evaluation and management of your medical conditions. We recommend that you contact your medical provider at _____ to schedule an appointment as soon as possible.

    Failure to contact your primary medical care provider immediately and to return for follow-up will prevent needed monitoring of your medical conditions.

    You may contact either _____ [Business Manager] at _____ or _____ [Medical Director] at _____ Monday through Friday 8:00 A.M.–5:00 P.M. with any questions or concerns about this letter. If there is no answer, please leave your name and number where you can be reached. If you believe you may be having a problem with your Coumadin®, seek immediate medical assistance.

Sincerely,

_____

[Name], Clinical Pharmacist

REMINDER OF MISSED APPOINTMENTS

Submitted by: Pamela L. Stamm

Revised: June 2003

(Sent by certified letter receipt requested on letterhead.)

[Pt. Address]

Date:

Dear_____,

    We have been trying to reach you by telephone regarding a missed _____ [laboratory or clinic] appointment on _____ [day and date] regarding your Coumadin® therapy. Coumadin® requires frequent visits and laboratory work to ensure appropriate management. We need to see you to ensure that your blood is "thin enough" but not "too thin." If your blood is too "thin," you may bleed. If your blood is too "thick," you could experience leg or lung clots or worse. These situations could be life threatening.

    We have discussed with you the need for laboratory work and the need to be available by telephone after laboratory work if your dose needs to be changed. You have agreed to this requirement, but we have consistently been unable to reach you by telephone. We recommend that you call the clinic today at _____ to reserve our next available Coumadin Clinic appointment. We will draw blood from your finger at that clinic appointment. Your attention toward this matter is greatly appreciated. Continue taking your Coumadin® at the same time each day to keep your blood thin. We will change your dose at your appointment if it is needed. If you have any concerns regarding this matter, please contact us at _____.

Sincerely,

_____
[Name], Clinical Pharmacist

CC: Primary Care Physician, Office Manager

ACUTE DEEP VEIN THROMBOSIS TREATMENT WITH LOW-MOLECULAR-WEIGHT HEPARIN PROTOCOL

Submitted by: Betsy Blake

Created: 2000

Background

Each year, more than six hundred thousand people in the United States are hospitalized for DVT. The traditional initial treatment of these patients has required hospital admission for the administration of a continuous infusion of intravenous unfractionated heparin for 5–7 days accompanied by frequent monitoring of the activated partial thromboplastin time (APTT). However, recent studies demonstrate that in selected patients, outpatient treatment using LMWH is as safe and effective as adjusted doses of unfractionated intravenous heparin administered in the hospital. The favorable pharmacokinetic profile of LMWHs allow them to be administered subcutaneously without laboratory monitoring in a dose determined by the patient's weight. Enoxaparin (Lovenox®) is the only LMWH approved by the FDA for the outpatient treatment of acute DVT.

Rationale

In 1999, 292 patients were discharged from the MUSC with a diagnosis of acute DVT without PE. The average length of hospital stay was 12 days. Of these 292 patients, 61 had an admission diagnosis of DVT without PE. The average length of stay for these patients was about 5 days.

Several analyses have been published demonstrating the economic benefit of LMWHs compared with unfractionated heparin for the outpatient treatment of acute DVT. In 1998, Groce reported patient outcomes and cost analysis associated with a multidisciplinary outpatient DVT protocol established in a 532-bed nonprofit teaching hospital. During a 26-month period, 125 patients were treated for acute DVT on an outpatient basis. All patients successfully completed an average of 5.23 days of enoxaparin, with 4.26 days of treatment as outpatients, leading to a drop in average length of hospitalization from 5.4 days to 0.97 days. About 98% of patients required no rehospitalization for any reason, including recurrence of DVT or bleeding complications. The preliminary results of these 125 patients demonstrated a cost avoidance of $2,470.68 per patient with a total cost avoidance of $308,835.17 for the hospital.

Objective

To develop a multidisciplinary outpatient DVT Treatment Protocol for use by the MUSC to provide patients with a safe and effective alternative to the traditional management of acute DVT while avoiding the costs associated with a prolonged hospital stay.

PHYSICIAN'S PROTOCOL

Treatment of Acute Deep Vein Thrombosis with Low-Molecular-Weight Heparin in Adults

This protocol is intended to facilitate early hospital discharge and appropriately prepare the patient for outpatient treatment of DVT with enoxaparin (Lovenox®).

Patients must meet the following **inclusion criteria:**

- ❑ Proximal DVT or symptomatic calf DVT
- ❑ Age older than 18 years
- ❑ Medically and hemodynamically stable
- ❑ Continuum of Care Manager has determined that patient/caregiver is able to obtain enoxaparin (Lovenox®) for outpatient use and is willing and able to self-administer drug or that patient meets criteria for home health to administer drug at home.

This protocol **should not** be used for patients who meet **any of the following exclusion criteria:**

- ❑ Pregnancy, breastfeeding, or childbearing potential without adequate contraception
- ❑ Presence of current active bleeding process, active peptic ulcer disease, or familial bleeding diathesis
- ❑ Previous history of two or more episodes of DVT or PE
- ❑ Concurrent symptomatic PE
- ❑ Inability to receive enoxaparin (Lovenox®) because of unstable coexisting condition
- ❑ History of heparin-induced thrombocytopenia
- ❑ Hypersensitivity to enoxaparin sodium, heparin, or pork products
- ❑ Potential for drug non-adherence
- ❑ Lack of language or learning skills conducive to self-management and/or unsuitable home environment to support therapy
- ❑ Inability to attend follow-up visits because of geographic inaccessibility
- ❑ Disorders contraindicating anticoagulation therapy
- ❑ Presence of known deficiency of antithrombin III, protein C, protein S, resistance to activated protein C, or other known hypercoagulable states
- ❑ Creatinine clearance (CrCl) < 30 mL/minute
- ❑ Weight > 150 kg

If patient meets inclusion criteria and does not meet any of the exclusion criteria, proceed with the preprinted orders, "Admission Orders for Patients with Deep Vein Thrombosis Being Discharged on Enoxaparin."

Prepared by Medical University of South Carolina, Charleston, South Carolina

Admission Orders for Patients with Deep Vein Thrombosis to be Discharged on Enoxaparin

- ☐ Initiate nursing clinical protocol for "Admission of Patients with Deep Vein Thrombosis Discharged on Enoxaparin." **Patient has met inclusion/exclusion criteria for protocol.**
- ☐ Notify Continuum of Care Manager of admission and need for home enoxaparin.
- ☐ Vital signs routine. Obtain patient's height and weight NOW.
- ☐ Baseline laboratory values STAT if not previously done, **before starting** enoxaparin (Lovenox®) or warfarin (Coumadin®): partial thromboplastin time (PTT), PT/INR, CBC, BMP.
- ☐ Daily PT/INR starting on Day 3 of warfarin (Coumadin®). Draw next PT/INR on _____.
- ☐ CBC every three days while receiving enoxaparin (Lovenox®).
- ☐ Stool for occult blood with next bowel movement; then before discharge if possible.
- ☐ Diet:_____
- ☐ Activity: bed rest with bathroom privileges Day 1. Day 2, up as desired in room. While in bed, keep affected leg elevated.
- ☐ Antiembolic stockings/sequential compression device if appropriate.
- ☐ Notify pharmacist on service to provide drug instruction.
  If no pharmacist is present on service, page adult pharmacist on call at pager ID #17284.
- ☐ Notify physician when INR is 2–3 for two consecutive days.

Drugs:
- ☐ Allergies:_____
- ☐ Precautions: Avoid intramuscular injections, aspirin or aspirin-containing compounds, and nonsteroidal anti-inflammatory drugs unless prescribed by a physician.
- ☐ If on IV heparin therapy, discontinue now.
- ☐ Enoxaparin (Lovenox®) 1 mg/kg every twelve hours subcutaneously NOW if not on heparin or 30–60 minutes after discontinuation of IV heparin.
  Actual patient weight in kg:_____ × 1 mg/kg = _____ mg
  Rounded up or down to the nearest 10 mg = enoxaparin_____ mg subcutaneously every twelve hours.
- ☐ Warfarin (Coumadin®) _____ mg × 1 NOW.

For pain:
- ☐ Acetaminophen 650 mg PO every 6 hours p.r.n. pain (TOTAL acetaminophen dose/day from ALL sources should NOT exceed 4 grams/day).
- ☐ Hydrocodone 5 mg/Acetaminophen 500 mg PO, 1 tablet for mild or 2 tablets for moderate pain every 6 hours p.r.n. (TOTAL acetaminophen dose/day from ALL sources should NOT exceed 4 grams/day).
- ☐ Oxycodone 5 mg/Acetaminophen 325 mg (Percocet®), 1 tablet for mild or 2 tablets for moderate pain every 6 hours p.r.n. (TOTAL acetaminophen dose/day from ALL sources should NOT exceed 4 grams/day).
- ☐ Oxycodone 5 mg PO, 1–2 tablets every 3–4 hours p.r.n. for moderate to severe pain.
- ☐ Other

For constipation:
- ☐ Milk of Magnesia (MOM®) 30 mL orally every day as needed.
- ☐ Docusate 100 mg orally twice daily as needed.

Additional orders:

- ☐ Notify M.D. for BP <_____,>_____, Heart rate (HR) <_____,>_____, Temperature <_____,>_____ and:

Physician signature_____ Date_____ Time_____
Physician pager ID# _____

Discharge Orders for Early Discharge of Patient with Deep Vein Thrombosis to be Discharged on Enoxaparin

- ❏ Initiate nursing clinical protocol for "Early Discharge of Patients with Deep Vein Thrombosis."
  Date of Discharge _____
  Activity:_____
  Diet:_____

Discharge Disposition
- ❏ Home or self-care (DIS)
- ❏ Home with durable medical equipment (DME)
- ❏ Home with home health services including nursing, occupational therapy, physical therapy, ST (HHS)
- ❏ Continuum of Care Manager has determined method for obtaining outpatient enoxaparin, home health and laboratory specimens.
- ❏ Notify pharmacist on service or adult pharmacist on call to provide final drug counseling and documentation.
- ❏ Discharge after patient care complete and discharge instructions have been provided.
- ❏ Provide patient with a copy of discharge orders.

Discharge Instructions:
- ❏ Patient to call 911 for any signs of chest pain, shortness of breath, or uncontrolled bleeding.
- ❏ Call physician for increased warmth, tenderness, or redness to affected limb or for any signs of bleeding.

Discharge Drugs (list even if not providing a prescription):
- ❏ Enoxaparin (Lovenox®):_____mg subcutaneously (SC) every twelve hours (rounded up or down to the nearest 10 mg) until INR of 2–3 for two consecutive days.
  (Prefilled syringes include 30, 40, 60, 80, and 100 mg.)
- ❏ Warfarin (Coumadin®):_____mg orally every day. First dose given on date:_____.
- ❏ Notify ambulatory clinical pharmacist if appropriate.

Appointments:

A. Outpatient laboratory tests: Should be drawn **EARLY MORNING**.
  ◦ CBC on the following date: _____(consider drawing every three days while on enoxaparin)
  ◦ PT/INR on the following date:_____
  ◦ Results to be forwarded to: Dr._____ at (telephone)_____.
  ◦ Laboratory tests to be drawn by (please circle or fill in) home health or _____ outpatient laboratory.
  ◦ Fax laboratory orders to laboratory at: (fax number):_____.

B. Physician Appointments (within five days of discharge): _____.
  ◦ Fax discharge orders to primary care physician at (fax number): _____.

I have discussed the risks and benefits of administration of low-molecular-weight heparin for the treatment of deep vein thrombosis with the patient/caregiver, and he/she agrees to the use of this therapy as an outpatient.

PHYSICIAN _____ Date_____
Time _____Pager #_____

PRIMARY CARE AND CHOLESTEROL MANAGEMENT GROUP SERVICE AGREEMENT, NOTE TEMPLATES, LETTERS, EVALUATION, AND CONSULT

Submitted by: Francine Farnsworth

Created: March 2006

Date:_____

Nomenclature: Cholesterol Management Group
Clinic meets: Weekly on most Thursday mornings
Clinic hours:
Interdisciplinary representation: Primary Care Clinical Pharmacist, Nutrition Service Representative, Social Work Representative

Mission

To perform pharmacotherapeutic management and provide patient education by an interdisciplinary format regarding lipid disorders. The cumulative goal is the reduction in cardiovascular disease (CAD) through risk factor modification, lipid-lowering, reduction in adverse events, and improved clinical outcomes.

Objectives

- To identify and assist in managing patients with hyperlipidemia who are at risk of CAD
- To reduce the risk of CAD and improve clinical outcomes by means of lipid lowering
- To identify and manage adverse events of lipid-lowering agents
- To initiate, modify, and monitor drug therapy incorporating laboratory results
- To provide patient and provider education regarding lipid management including non-pharmacological lifestyle modification

Criteria for enrollment

Patients selected are those with elevated cholesterol (low-density lipoprotein [LDL] and/or triglycerides) concentrations in the past four months. Additional criteria may be determined by the Cholesterol Management Group Coordinator and/or Primary Care Chief.

Primary care shall

- Review enrollment criteria and establish appropriateness for enrollment in Pharmacotherapy Lipid Clinic.
- Complete Pharmacotherapy Lipid Clinic consult, indicating patient history and indications
  - Establish LDL goal
  - Current lipid-lowering **drug**(s), or lipid-lowering drug previously taken, including reason for discontinuance and ADRs
  - Other prescription, OTC, herbal product, and home remedies
  - Exercise regimen or enrolled in VA exercise program
  - Consulted to dietitian
- Order fasting laboratory results if not done within three months of consult to include (these laboratory results will be ordered by clinical pharmacist before the appointment):
  - Lipid profile
  - LFT
  - Optional, per provider's preference
    - Thyroid-stimulating hormone (TSH), glycosylated hemoglobin (HgA1c), basic metabolic panel (BMP), or creatine phosphokinase (CPK)

Cholesterol Management Group Shall

- Evaluate patients with hyperlipidemia diagnosis
- Assist in determining personal LDL goal and risk (if not provided)
- Document visit-in-progress note using template provided and assigning co-signatories when appropriate
- Titrate and/or initiate lipid-lowering drugs as indicated
- Review and facilitate approval of nonformulary drug requests for lipid-lowering therapies as indicated

Algorithm:

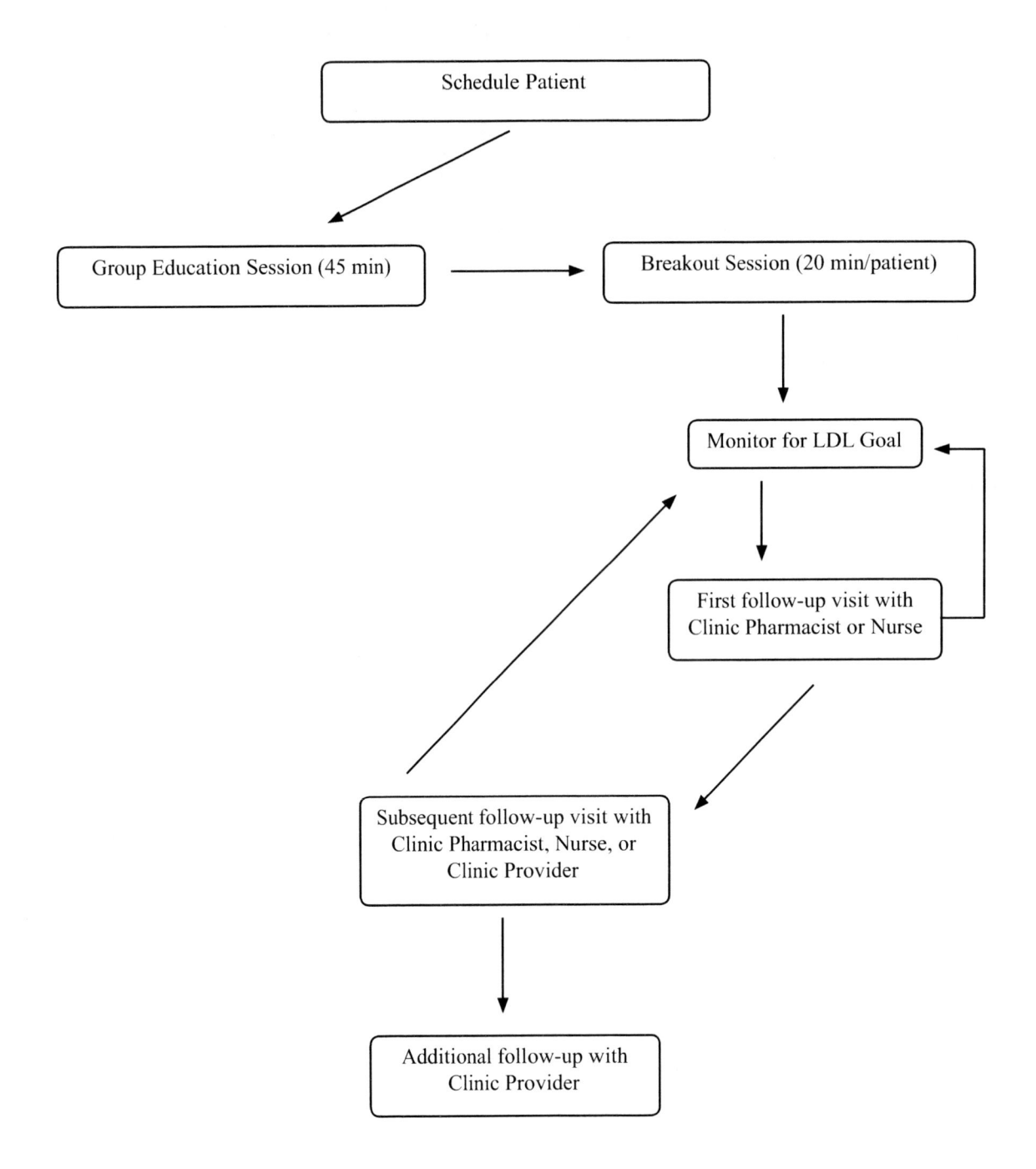

```
                    Schedule Patient
                           │
                           ▼
   Group Education Session (45 min) ──▶ Breakout Session (20 min/patient)
                                                    │
                                                    ▼
                                          Monitor for LDL Goal ◀─┐
                                                    │            │
                                                    ▼            │
                                       First follow-up visit with│
                                       Clinic Pharmacist or Nurse┘
                                                    │
                                                    ▼
             Subsequent follow-up visit with
             Clinic Pharmacist, Nurse, or
             Clinic Provider
                        │
                        ▼
             Additional follow-up with
             Clinic Provider
```
(arrow also returns from Subsequent follow-up visit back to Monitor for LDL Goal)

Pharm.D. Cholesterol Note Template

Name:_____SSN: _____DOB:_____

Primary Care Provider: [TIU TPBN PCP]_____
Allergies/ADRs:_____

Purpose of Visit: Patient is a_____year-old [PATIENT RACE] [PATIENT SEX] who presents to Cholesterol Management Group (CMG) for evaluation of elevated cholesterol values.

Patient's medical history is significant for the following:_____
Reviewed previous clinic note(s) and laboratory values:_____

S: Patient presents to CMG today in <u>no acute distress</u>.

Social History (SH):   Tobacco use:_____
                              EtOH consumption: _____
                              Diet: _____
                              Exercise:_____

Objective:
        Vitals: _____
            Weight: _____
            Height: _____
        Active drugs:_____
        OTC/Herbal/Non-VA drug(s):_____
        Laboratory tests: (lipid profile; LFT)_____

A/P:

1. Hyperlipidemia—(Controlled/Uncontrolled). Goals LDL <____mg/dL; high-density lipoprotein (HDL) more than 40 mg/dL; triglycerides: less than 150 mg/dL; total cholesterol: less than 200 mg/dL.
   - Tolerating/Not tolerating ____ cholesterol drug(s) well.
   - Per patient agreement, will initiate (cholesterol-lowering drug[s]). Counseled patient on possible adverse effects, dose, and frequency. Will reevaluate FLP in about eight to twelve weeks; appointment letter to be mailed to patient.
   - Reviewed and discussed cholesterol laboratory values and rationale for goals in addition to signs/symptoms of heart disease and stroke.
   - Encouraged continued therapeutic lifestyle changes (dietary modifications, increasing physical activity/exercise as tolerated, smoking cessation, decreasing EtOH consumption).
   - Laboratory results pending/will contact patient when laboratory results received to discuss therapeutic plan and follow-up (if needed).
   - Asked patient to contact clinic if any questions/concerns arise before next clinic visit. Patient agreed with plan and verbalized understanding of above.

New Drugs/Refills:_____
Consults:_____
Future Appointments: _____

Group Education Cholesterol Note Template

Name:_____SSN: _____DOB:_____

Cholesterol Management Group Education Note

During a 45- to 50-minute session on |TODAY'S DATE|, discussed the following in a multidisciplinary format:

(1) cholesterol and types of cholesterol;
(2) importance of cholesterol lowering;
(3) goal values;
(4) drugs used to treat elevated cholesterol and rationale for use (including, but not limited to, possible adverse effects, applicable laboratory monitoring parameters, and dosing frequencies);
(5) importance of clinic follow-up;
(6) healthy eating/types of fats and dietary modifications;
(7) weight loss;
(8) additional lifestyle modifications (e.g., physical activity, smoking cessation, alcohol consumption); and
(9) other social issues.

Presented in PowerPoint format with accompanying handout of entire presentation.

CHOLESTEROL GROUP PATIENT INTRODUCTION LETTER

March 2006

Dear Veteran:

We are excited to tell you about a new service available at the Veteran's Administration Medical Center-Salem (VAMC–Salem) called the "Cholesterol Management Group." This is an exciting educational program for patients with high cholesterol values or patients who were recently prescribed a cholesterol-lowering drug(s) by their primary care provider.

Why is cholesterol lowering important? Even though a little cholesterol is needed for our bodies to function, too much cholesterol can be bad. High cholesterol values can cause blockage in our arteries, which may lead to a heart attack or stroke.

Your primary care provider has identified you to be scheduled in our Cholesterol Management Group. Enclosed, you will find a letter with two appointments at the VAMC–Salem.

The first appointment (9:00–9:45 A.M.) is the educational presentation. This 45-minute session will provide you with a basic understanding of cholesterol and why cholesterol lowering is important. In addition, you will learn about the different drugs your provider may prescribe, as well as other diet and lifestyle changes that are used to help lower cholesterol.

The second appointment will be an individual meeting with a Clinical Pharmacist to discuss your cholesterol results, drugs, diet and activity values, and other questions you may have.

Because fasting laboratory work is necessary to accurately evaluate your cholesterol, *we ask that you please check in at least 1 hour before the appointment and report to the laboratory.* We ask you to *not eat or drink anything for 10–12 hours before having your blood drawn.* (However, it is okay to drink water and take necessary drugs.)

If you have any questions or concerns, please contact your Primary Care Clinic: Clinic 1—(540) 982-2463, ext. 3252; Clinic 2—(540) 982-2463, ext. 3250; or Clinic 3—(540) 982-2463, ext. 3258.

Sincerely,

Cholesterol Management Group

Cholesterol Management Group—Post Evaluation

To allow us to have a better understanding of your needs, please take a few minutes to answer the following questions. Please circle one choice for each question. Thank you!

Before attending this class today:		
1. Were you provided any information about this appointment?	Yes	No
2. Is this class scheduled at a convenient time?	Yes	No
After listening to today's presentation:		
3. Did you learn about		
a. Cholesterol and the different types of cholesterol (LDL, HDL)	Yes	No
b. Goals for the different types of cholesterol and triglycerides	Yes	No
c. Drugs used to help lower cholesterol and triglycerides	Yes	No
d. Possible adverse effects of cholesterol-lowering drugs	Yes	No
e. Value of laboratory work and follow-up appointments	Yes	No
4. Did you learn about		
a. Healthy eating/healthier food choices	Yes	No
b. Types of dietary fats in foods	Yes	No
c. How to follow a low-fat/low-cholesterol diet	Yes	No
5. Did you learn about		
a. Physical activity/exercise	Yes	No
b. Smoking cessation	Yes	No
c. Limiting alcohol use	Yes	No
6. Do you feel that you now have a better understanding of how to help lower your cholesterol?	Yes	No
7. I would recommend this class to others who want to know more about their cholesterol	Yes	No
8. In the future, I would prefer to receive my cholesterol follow-up by: Clinic appointment Telephone		

Additional Comments:

CHOLESTEROL MANAGEMENT GROUP—PROVIDER CONSULT

Introduction

This clinic is intended for treating patients whose primary problem is hyperlipidemia.

If this patient has DM with his/her last HgA1c > 8.0, refer to Metabolic Clinic (Primary Care consult section).

Please note that patients will be asked to fast for 10 to 12 hours and present to the laboratory for fasting blood work before the appointment.

In addition, patients will be scheduled for an appointment with the Clinical Pharmacist assigned to their respective clinic to review their individual cholesterol goals and laboratory results, to review incorporation of lifestyle modifications and current drugs, etc.

Consult Information

Describe history of dyslipidemia (text box): _____
_____
_____
_____

Problem list (medical history) (extracted from patient's EMR): _____
_____
_____
_____

History of ADRs and/or drug interactions (extracted from patient's EMR): _____
_____
_____
_____

Active outpatient drugs (extracted from patient's EMR): _____
_____
_____
_____

Selected laboratory results (most recent—extracted from patient's EMR):

        BMP_____
        Hepatic function panel_____
        Lipid profile_____

Has patient been seen by dietitian?   ❏ Yes   ❏ No
If not, has a consult been placed?   ❏ Yes   ❏ No

Patient's target LDL (check appropriate box):
        ❏ Less than 70 mg/dL
        ❏ Less than 100 mg/dL
        ❏ Less than 130 mg/dL
        ❏ Less than 160 mg/dL

CARDIOVASCULAR RISK EDUCATION AND MANAGEMENT PROGRAM PROTOCOL

Submitted by: Kathy Fit

Created: April 2006

Background

About 34% of all Americans have some form of CAD. CAD was identified as a cause of about one-third of all deaths in 2002. A number of risk factors have been identified for CAD, including, but not limited to, HTN, dyslipidemia, DM, metabolic syndrome, obesity, inactivity, and nicotine dependence. At least 27% of adults have at least two major risk factors for CAD. The most common combination includes HTN and dyslipidemia.

It is estimated that fifty million Americans have HTN. About 30% of these patients are unaware that they have HTN. Even when patients are aware of their current condition and are being treated for it, only about one-third reach their BP goals. The documented benefits of medical treatment aimed toward achieving BP goals are significant. However, as seen from the above national data, our current health care system struggles to achieve these BP goals. Statistics also show that about 41–49% of all American adults have elevated LDL cholesterol (higher than 130 mg/dL), and an additional 15–40% have low HDL values (less than 40 mg/dL). Both of these abnormalities have been linked to an increase in CAD, and several studies have shown that appropriate treatment can lower the patient's risk.

Many initiatives in the health care community have been implemented to educate and encourage health care providers to identify and aggressively treat all patients with HTN and dyslipidemia to their appropriate goals. The purpose of this program is to enhance the physician's treatment and further lower the patient's cardiovascular risk by patient education and recommendations for medical management, which would be implemented only with the physician's approval.

Qualifications of the Pharmacist

She is a clinical pharmacist who has completed her Pharm.D. degree and is a registered pharmacist in this state. She also holds an appointment as assistant professor in the Department of Pharmacy Practice. Pharmacy residents who may be participating in this protocol have their Pharm.D. degrees and are registered pharmacists in this state. She is also currently managing the smoking cessation program here at High Point/Winston-Salem (WGHP).

Policy

The clinical pharmacist, pharmacy residents, and pharmacy students completing rotations under the supervision of the clinical pharmacist will follow this written protocol.

Organization

- The program will be managed by a clinical pharmacist.
- All patients must be referred by a WGHP physician to the program and, to be accepted, be willing to participate.
- Patients may be denied acceptance into the program if
  - The program is no longer able to manage additional patients because of time, space, or personnel constraints.
  - Patients are on dialysis or have had kidney transplants—requiring specialist care.
- All appointments will last about thirty minutes (initial and follow-up).
- All recommendations for lifestyle modifications and drug therapy will be based on the JNC-VII and ATP-III guidelines, as well as the NCEP Report detailing the implications of recent trials on the ATP-III guidelines. Summary charts of goal BP, lifestyle modifications, and use of particular antihypertensive agents for compelling indications are included in Appendix B.

Monitoring Data Program

A cardiovascular risk reduction computer program, developed by Pfizer, will be used. This computer database helps track patients' outcomes and assists in the development of reminder letters to patients. The system helps clinicians track patients who have missed their appointments and are due for follow-up. This program also helps create standard documentation notes and allows tracking of additional cardiovascular risk factors such as blood glucose and fasting lipid panel parameters. Management of these risk factors is essential to the control of CAD, and appropriate recommendations will be made to the physician if the clinical pharmacist deems it necessary.

Procedures

Guidelines for Referrals

Each patient should be referred to the physician-directed/pharmacist-managed cardiovascular risk education and management program on a case-by-case basis. Once a physician determines the patient needs more education and additional follow-up on HTN, hyperlipidemia, or both, which is provided through this program, a referral should be filled out and given to the receptionist staff (referral box in the receptionist area in family practice). On the referral form, the physician can indicate which services he or she would like the clinical pharmacist to focus on. Please see Appendix D for an example of the referral form. Any health care practitioner (nurse, medical assistant, physician's assistant, etc.) can complete the form, but the physician must sign the referral form. It is requested that the physician document his or her referral to the cardiovascular risk education and management program in the patient's medical chart.

Patient Confidentiality

Pharmacy residents and pharmacy students may be present and participate in the program because of the teaching agreement between WellGroup HealthPartners and Midwestern University Chicago College of Pharmacy. All patients will be verbally informed that, as part of their treatment, these individuals will have access to their medical information. All of their information will remain confidential according to the Health Insurance Portability and Accountability Act (HIPAA) regulations and policies in place at this institution. All individuals participating in this program have undergone the appropriate HIPAA training.

Responsibilities of the Clinical Pharmacist

Under this protocol, the pharmacist will be able to participate in the following activities:
- Educate the patient regarding HTN, dyslipidemia, complications of HTN and/or dyslipidemia, appropriate lifestyle modifications, and drugs.
- Recommend and implement appropriate lifestyle modifications.
- Measure the patient's weight, height, BP, and pulse.
- Recommend appropriate drugs and/or dose modifications to treat the patient's BP to goal.
  - These recommendations will only be implemented after physician approval.
- Recommend appropriate drugs and/or dose modifications to treat patient's lipids to goal.
  - These recommendations will only be implemented after physician approval.
- Recommend appropriate laboratory work to monitor safety and efficacy of drugs used in the treatment of HTN and/or dyslipidemia.
  - These recommendations will only be implemented after physician approval.
- Identify other cardiovascular risk factors (e.g., DM, nicotine dependence) and make appropriate recommendations to the physician.
- Write or call in prescriptions for the recommended drugs as a verbal order, after physician approval.
- Order appropriate laboratory work, after physician approval.
- Document all activities and recommendations in the patient's chart.

Documentation

- All interaction with patients will be documented in the patient's medical chart.
- Notes will be sent to the referring physician for co-signature.

Billing

- A level 1 visit will be billed incident to the referring physician. A 99211 billing code will be used for all of these patients.

Quality Management

This protocol will be reviewed annually by the clinical pharmacist and faculty physicians and updated as needed. It will also be updated more often if necessary, based on any new treatment guidelines for HTN.

The first appointment will include (thirty minutes):
- Measurements and assessments
  - Height
  - Weight
  - BP (average of two measurements)
  - Pulse rate
- Any indication of lower extremity edema
- A detailed patient interview to obtain pertinent medical history, drug history, family history, and social history
- An assessment of cardiovascular risk factors according to JNC-VII and ATP-III guidelines
- A determination of BP goals
  - Goal BP is less than 140/90 mm Hg for most patients.
  - Goal BP is less than 130/80 mm Hg for patients with DM or chronic kidney disease (CKD).
- Determination of goal LDL values will be based on the presence of major risk factors as identified in ATP-III and a patient's Framingham Score, if applicable.
- Assessment of patient compliance and motivation
- Recommendations for lifestyle modifications (exercise and diet changes)

- Recommendations for drug initiation and/or dose modifications. These recommendations would only be implemented when approved by the referring physician, the covering physician, or, if neither is available, the supervising physician. Recommendations will be based on each individual case using the JNC-VII and ATP-III guidelines. **(Summary is available in Appendix B.)**
- Recommendations for laboratory work needed. Will only be ordered with physician's approval. **(See General Laboratory Work Recommendations in Appendix C.)**

Patient education
- Significance of BP measurements and goals of treatment
- Significance of lipid parameters and goals of treatment
- Potential complications of HTN and dyslipidemia including CAD, HF, cerebrovascular accidents, and renal failure
- Lifestyle modifications
- Drugs
- Other cardiovascular risk factors such as DM and smoking cessation will also be evaluated.
- Even though management of DM is outside the scope of this protocol, the pharmacist will recommend therapy choices to the physician for managing these risk factors, if appropriate.
- If the physician approves these recommendations and requests implementation, the pharmacist will provide instructions to the patient and document them in the patient's chart.
- Smoking cessation education will be provided to the patient based on the smoking cessation protocol if the patient is motivated and ready to attempt smoking cessation.
- Subsequent follow-up visits will be scheduled as needed for management. If the patient needs BP monitoring, then subsequent visits may be scheduled every one to four weeks. If the patient needs only lipid management, then subsequent visits may be scheduled in one to three months.
- All notes will be forwarded to the referring physician for co-signature.
- All patients will be encouraged to contact the Pharm.D. with any questions or problems. Patients will be instructed to contact their PCP if they need immediate attention and are not able to reach the Pharm.D.

Subsequent follow-up visits (thirty minutes)
- Measurements and assessments
  - Weight
  - BP (average of two measurements)
  - Pulse rate
  - Any indication of lower extremity edema
- Assessment of patient compliance and motivation
- Recommendations for lifestyle modifications (exercise and diet changes)
- Recommendations for drug initiation and/or dose modifications. These recommendations would only be implemented after approval by the referring physician, the covering physician, or, if neither is available, the supervising physician.
- Recommendations for laboratory work if needed. Will only be ordered with physician's approval.
- Reinforcement of educational elements from the initial visit, if necessary.
- All patients will be encouraged to contact the Pharm.D. with any questions or problems. Patients will be instructed to contact their primary care physician if they are not able to reach the Pharm.D. and need immediate attention.
- All notes will be forwarded to the referring physician for co-signature.
- Subsequent visits will be scheduled as appropriate.

Clinic hours *(may not be available every week, depending on the other responsibilities of the pharmacist)*
- Monday: 9:00 A.M.–2:00 P.M.
- Tuesday: 1:00–5:00 P.M.
- Thursday: 9:00 A.M.–5:00 P.M.

Discharge criteria from program:
- At least two consecutive BP measurements at goal on the same drug regimen at least three months apart
- At least two consecutive lipid measurements at goal on the same drug regimen for at least six months
- Referring physician will be notified of patient discharge.
- Patients can also be discharged from the program if they refuse to participate or have multiple (three or more documented) no-shows for appointments. All of these cases will be discussed with the referring physician before discharge.

Appendix A—Recommendations for Treatment of HTN

Table 1: Classification and management of BP in adults—JNC-VII
Figure 1: Algorithm for treatment of HTN—JNC-VII
Table 2: Suggested lifestyle modifications together with potential effects on systolic BP—Table 5 JNC-VII
Table 3: Recommended drugs for compelling indications—Table 8 JNC-VII

Special Management Considerations
- Hypertensive Urgencies and Emergencies
  - If a patient presents with significantly elevated BP (more than 180/120 mm Hg), repeat measures will be performed, and the following actions will be taken
    - Contact referring physician immediately
    - Contact supervising physician
    - Refer patient to emergency department or extended hours if neither of the above is available.
  - Patients will be managed on the basis of the advice of the previously discussed physicians.

Appendix B—Recommendations for Treatment of Dyslipidemia

ATP-III at a Glance

Appendix C— Recommended Laboratory Monitoring

- Recommended laboratory work
- All patients with HTN will need a recent BMP and a spot albumin–creatinine ratio test on admission to the program.
  - "Recent" is defined as within the past six months or as clinically indicated.
  - This information is needed to determine the appropriate goal BPs for the patient and the appropriate drug therapy.
- If a patient is initiated on <u>diuretics</u>
  - Serum K+ and creatinine
    - Baseline
    - Within two to four weeks of initiation
    - Then, every six to twelve months
  - Uric acid concentrations—if patient has a history of gout and/or develops symptoms
- If a patient is initiated on an angiotensin-converting enzyme inhibitor (ACEI) or an angiotensin receptor blocker (ARB)
  - Patients who would be considered at high risk of developing hyperkalemia
    - Patients with DM
    - Creatinine clearance (CrCl) less than 30 mL/minute
    - Elderly
    - Decompensated HF
    - Volume-depleted or sodium-depleted patients
    - Patients taking potassium-sparing diuretics, potassium supplements, nonsteroidal anti-inflammatory drugs (NSAIDs), or celecoxib
  - Serum potassium and creatinine concentrations should be followed closely in the above patients.
    - Potassium and creatinine
      - Baseline
      - One to two weeks after initiation or dose change
      - Then, every three months
    - An increase of less than 35% above baseline in the serum creatinine can be tolerated as long as hyperkalemia does NOT develop.
  - In patients who are NOT at risk of renal artery stenosis or hyperkalemia
    - Potassium and creatinine
      - Baseline
      - Three to four weeks after initiation or dose change
      - Every six to twelve months
    - An increase of less than 35% above baseline in the serum creatinine can be tolerated as long as hyperkalemia does NOT develop.
- **All other drugs**
  - No specific laboratory parameters are required.

Appendix D—Referral Form

Clinical Pharmacy Referral Form

This is the form for all the services that are available from the clinical pharmacy program at WellGroup HealthPartners.

Referring Physician: _____ Office Ext.: _____
Patient Name: _____ Chart #: _____
Patient's Telephone # _____ Gender: Female   Male
DOB: ___ / _____ / _____

<u>Please select the service(s) of interest</u>

- ❏ Hypertension (modifications implemented only after physician review)
- ❏ Hyperlipidemia (modifications implemented only after physician review)
- ❏ Drug profile review/herbal product review (modifications implemented only after physician review)
- ❏ Smoking cessation—Please answer the two questions below if requesting smoking cessation services.

Additional Smoking Cessation Information

1. Additional Diagnosis Code: _____
   (Some providers will only reimburse smoking cessation if the patient has a medical condition that is negatively affected by smoking.)
2. **Please indicate how you would like for the clinical pharmacist to initiate drug therapy for smoking cessation.**
- ❏ **Initiate drug therapy based on the protocol. No need to consult physician.**
- ❏ Recommend drug therapy and consult physician before initiating drug therapy.

I consider this referral to the Clinical Pharmacy Program a necessary part of this patient's medical care:

Physician Signature: _____ Date: _____

References

1. American Heart Association. Heart Disease and Stroke Statistics—2005 Update. Dallas, TX: AHA, 2004.
2. National High Blood Pressure Education Program Coordinating Committee. The Seventh Report of the Joint National Committee on Detection, Evaluation, and Treatment of High Blood Pressure. NIH Publication No. 03-5233. Washington, DC: U.S. Department of Health and Human Services, 2003.
3. Burt VL, Cutler JA, Higgins M, Horan MJ, Labarthe D, Whelton P, et al. Trends in the prevalence, treatment, and control of hypertension in the adult US population: Data from the health examination surveys, 1960 to 1991. Hypertension 1995;26:60–9.
4. Palmer BF. Managing hyperkalemia caused by inhibitors of the renin-angiotensin-aldosterone system. N Engl J Med 2004;351:585–92.

CLINICAL PHARMACY CARDIAC RISK SERVICE

Submitted by: Brian Sandhoff and Sheila Kasten

Revised: October 2006

Policy Statement

Since 1998, the Clinical Pharmacy Cardiac Risk Service (CPCRS) has aggressively sought to improve, maintain, or limit the degradation in functional status of members with CAD. The focus of CPCRS is long-term drug management for patients to ensure that appropriate cholesterol-lowering and HTN drugs are initiated, doses are adjusted as necessary, and follow-up laboratory tests are completed to achieve cholesterol and BP goals.

The clinical pharmacy specialist or clinical pharmacist, working in collaboration with the PCP or cardiologist, is authorized to adjust drug doses as needed to achieve defined therapeutic goals. Drug- or disease-related laboratory tests may also be ordered by the clinical pharmacy staff member.

Protocols

- Patients with CAD may be referred to CPCRS by
  - PCP
  - Cardiologist
  - CAD Registry *(CPCRS will contact patient's PCP or cardiologist to see if physician desires patient to be enrolled in service)*
  - Cardiac Rehabilitation Nurses *(CPCRS will contact patient's PCP or cardiologist to see if physician desires patient to be enrolled in service)*
- CPCRS enrollment criteria
  - History of MI
  - History of percutaneous transluminal angioplasty
  - History of coronary artery stent placement
  - History of coronary artery bypass graft
  - History of unstable angina
  - History of blockage (50% or more, or moderate occlusion) in one or more coronary vessels
  - History of positive thallium test with evidence of infarction
- Patients not meeting one of the above criteria for enrollment into the CPCRS will be referred back to their PCP for care.

A clinical pharmacy specialist or clinical pharmacist will contact a patient by telephone if drug adjustments or other patient-specific information is likely necessary to improve clinical outcomes. Patients contacted by telephone will also be sent a letter or e-mail informing them of their results and reinforcing the information discussed on the telephone. Patients who are stable clinically (cholesterol/BP controlled and on appropriate drugs as defined below) may be contacted by letter or e-mail only informing the patient of their laboratory test results and next scheduled follow-up. Patients will be contacted as directed in the attached protocols.

- Please see the following appendices for additional information
  - Cholesterol management protocol (Appendix A)
  - HTN management protocol (Appendix B)
  - Myalgia/CPK management protocol (Appendix C)
  - Alanine aminotransferase (ALT) management protocol (Appendix D)
  - Laboratory monitoring protocol (Appendix E)
  - Diabetes/Prediabetes screening protocol (Appendix F)
  - Drug interaction protocol (Appendix G)
  - Renal dosing of cholesterol drugs for patients with CKD (Appendix H)
  - Cholesterol-lowering drug dosing ranges (Appendix I)
- Lipid-lowering therapy
  - Threshold for evaluation/intervention LDL more than 100 mg/dL
    - Goal LDL less than 100 mg/dL or less than 70 mg/dL (for patients at very high risk of recurrent cardiac events—defined as patients with CAD and one or more of the following: DM, current tobacco users, diffuse atherosclerotic vascular disease, per cardiology, metabolic syndrome, or initial and recurrent acute coronary syndrome events)
  - Encourage appropriate lifestyle modification/encourage participation in applicable Kaiser Permanente resources.
  - Initiate and monitor lipid-lowering therapy after the prescription of such therapy by a licensed Kaiser Permanente physician.
    - When patients on cholesterol-lowering drugs have no clear indication, minimal or no response, or OTC alternatives, the drug may be discontinued unless there is another reason for its use (e.g., pleiotropic effects, heart protection with statins).
    - Drugs will be initiated or titrated on the basis of the cholesterol management protocol (Appendix A). Patient specifics (e.g., history of patient intolerances to drugs or decreased re-

nal function) may necessitate initiating cholesterol-lowering drugs at lower doses than those specified in Appendix A. For these patients, drugs may be adjusted more slowly within the dose range as described in Appendices H and I.
- Aspirin
  - All patients should be screened for ASA use.
    - If a patient is not on ASA and does not have a contraindication for use, ASA therapy should be initiated.
    - If a patient is not on ASA because of a contraindication, the reason for the patient not being on ASA should be documented in the EMR called KP HealthConnect and patient tracking system (HealthTrac).
  - β-Blockers post-MI
    - All patients should be screened for β-blocker initiation post-MI.
    - If a patient is not on a β-blocker and does not have a contraindication for use, β-blocker therapy should be initiated pending physician approval.
    - If a patient is not on a β-blocker because of a contraindication, the reason patient is not on β-blocker should be documented in EMR (HealthConnect) and patient tracking system (HealthTrac).
  - ACEI initiation in patients with DM
    - All patients with DM should be screened for ACEI initiation.
    - If a patient is not on an ACEI and does not have a contraindication for use, ACEI should be initiated and titrated, as tolerated, to a target dose of lisinopril 20 mg daily.
    - If a patient is not on an ACEI or at target dose because of a contraindication or adverse effect, the reason for patient not being on an ACEI or at target dose should be documented in EMR (HealthConnect) and patient tracking system (HealthTrac).

The clinical pharmacy specialist or clinical pharmacist should document information obtained from the patient in the EMR (HealthConnect).

The clinical pharmacy specialist or clinical pharmacist should communicate with the physician within 24 hours by electronic encounters in the EMR (HealthConnect) after initiation of a new drug or to notify the physician of a titration of a drug per the attached protocols.

When encountering possible ADRs, the CPCRS clinical pharmacy specialist or clinical pharmacist should ensure that proper documentation is made in both the EMR (HealthConnect) and HealthTrac. When a patient's safety may be jeopardized by continued use of the offending drug, the CPCRS clinical pharmacy specialist or clinical pharmacist may ask the patient to temporarily stop the drug until the ADR information can be communicated to the PCP or other physician for a final determination on whether the drug should be permanently discontinued.

When encountering patients with drug–drug interactions that require intervention, the CPCRS clinical pharmacy specialist or clinical pharmacist should make an adjustment to medical therapy using the information in Appendix G.

Patients enrolled in CPCRS should be tracked using a comprehensive computerized database, HealthTrac. HealthTrac acts as a tracking system to prevent patients from being lost to follow-up. CPCRS should send reminders to patients encouraging them to have their laboratory work drawn. Patients should be telephoned if they fail to show up for a laboratory appointment. All related activities and outcomes should be documented in HealthTrac as well as in the EMR (HealthConnect).

The CPCRS conducts quarterly quality assurance peer reviews to ensure that the CPCRS clinical pharmacy specialists and clinical pharmacists are following the protocols of the CPCRS and documenting required information as described above in both the EMR (HealthConnect) and HealthTrac.

References

1. Scandinavian Simvastatin Survival Study Group. Randomized trial of cholesterol lowering in 4444 patients with coronary artery disease: The Scandinavian Simvastatin Survival Study. Lancet 1994;344:1383–89.
2. Heart Protection Collaborative Group. MRC/BHF Heart Protection Study of cholesterol lowering with simvastatin in 20,536 high-risk individuals: A randomized placebo controlled trial. Lancet 2002;360:7–22.
3. The Long Term Intervention with Pravastatin in Ischaemic Disease (LIPID) Study Group. Prevention of cardiovascular events and death with pravastatin in patients with coronary artery disease and a broad range of initial cholesterol values. N Engl J Med 1998;339:1349–57.
4. Sacks FM, Pfeffer MA, Moye LA, et al. The effect of pravastatin on coronary events after myocardial infarction in patients with average cholesterol levels. N Engl J Med 1996;335:1001–9.
5. Expert Panel on Detection, Evaluation, and Treatment of High Blood Cholesterol in Adults. Executive summary of the third report of the National Cholesterol Education Program (NCEP) expert panel on detection, evaluation, and treatment of high blood cholesterol in adults (Adult Treatment Panel III). JAMA 2001;285:2486–97.
6. Chobanian AV, Bakris GL, Black HR, et al.; for the National High Blood Pressure Education Pro-

gram Coordinating Committee. Seventh Report of the Joint National Committee on prevention, detection, evaluation, and treatment of high blood pressure. Hypertension 2003;42:1206–52.
7. American Diabetes Association. Treatment of hypertension in adults with diabetes. Diabetes Care 2003;26(suppl 1):S80–2.
8. Kris-Ehterton PM, Harris WS, Appel LF; for the Nutrition Committee. AHA Scientific Statement: Fish consumption, fish oil, omega-3 fatty acids, and cardiovascular disease. Circulation 2002;106:2747–57.
9. Khan NA, McAlister FA, Campbell NC, et al. The 2004 Canadian recommendations for the management of hypertension. Part II. Therapy. Can J Cardiol 2004;20:41–59.
10. National Kidney Foundation Guideline. K/DOQI clinical practice guidelines for chronic kidney disease: evaluation, classification, and stratification. Kidney Disease Outcome Quality Initiative. Am J Kidney Dis 2002;39(suppl 1):S1–S246.
11. American Diabetes Association. Standards of care for patients with diabetes mellitus. Diabetes Care 2003;26(suppl 1):S33–50.
12. Cannon CP, Braunwald E, McCabe CH, et al.; for the Pravastatin or Atorvastatin Evaluation and Infection Therapy—Thrombolysis in Myocardial Infarction 22 Investigators. Intensive versus moderate lipid lowering with statins after acute coronary syndromes. N Engl J Med 2004;350:1495–504.
13. Nissen SE, Tuzcu EM, Schoenhagen P, et al.; for the Reversal Investigators. Effect of intensive compared with moderate lipid lowering therapy on progression of coronary atherosclerosis: a randomized controlled trial. JAMA 2004;291:1071–80.
14. Sandhoff BG, Nies LK, Olson KL, et al.; for the Clinical Pharmacy Cardiac Risk Service Study Group. Clinical pharmacy cardiac risk service for managing patients with coronary artery disease in a health maintenance organization. AJHP 2007;64:77–84.

Approval

Chief, Clinical Pharmacy [Date]
Cardiovascular Services

Supervisor, Clinical Pharmacy [Date]
Cardiac Risk Service

Medical Director, Clinical [Date]
Pharmacy Cardiac Risk Service

Manager, Clinical Pharmacy [Date]

RDC, Internal Medicine [Date]

RDC, Family Medicine [Date]

Medical Director, Pharmacy [Date]
Use and Therapeutics

Executive Director, Pharmacy [Date]
Operations and Therapeutics

Appendix A: Cholesterol Management Protocol

Patients with CAD and the following risk factors should be targeted for LDL <70 mg/dL:

- ☐ Diabetes Mellitus
- ☐ Current tobacco users
- ☐ Diffuse atherosclerotic vascular disease
- ☐ As instructed by cardiologist
- ☐ Metabolic syndrome
- ☐ Recurrent events
- ☐ Initial ACS events

FLP

All new patients with TC>135mg/d should be started on Lovastatin 80mg/d or Simvastatin 40mg/d (pending generic availability

If previous LDL >155 mg/dL-initiate Simvastatin 80mg/d

All patients LDL goal is <100mg/dL unless patients are at very high risk*
Non-HDL goal is 30 mg/dL higher than LDL goal (e.g. Goal LDL <70mg/dL, then non-HDL goal <100mg/dL)

LDL and Non-HDL at goal; TG <400 mg/dL:

Continue Lovastatin 80mg/d or Simvastatin 40mg/d

NOTE: If pt already on Lovastatin 80mg/d and LDL and Non-HDL controlled consider changing to Simvastatin 40mg/d.

If LDL above goal:

- ☐ Change to Simvastatin 80mg/d

Isolated TG elevation:

TG > 200 mg/dL AND Non-Hdl<160
- ☐ Initiate Super-DHA 500mg BID and titrate to dietitian
- ☐ Refer to dietitian

If TG remain >400 mg/dl
- ☐ Add gemfibrozil 600mg BID OR
- ☐ Add fenofibrate 54- 160mg QD in the following patients:
  ➤ Previous myalgias or CPK elevation >250 mg/dL
  ➤ Patient on any statin
  ➤ Patients on Ezetimibe

If LDL remains above but near goal (≤15 mg/dL above goal) OR HDL is below 50mg/dL:
- ☐ Continue Simvastatin 80mg/d and ADD Slo-niacin 250mg BID and titrate to 1500mg/d in divided doses

If LDL remains above goal (>15mg/dL): See options below:

NOTE: Use clinical judgement/patient preference for more aggressive therapy to achieve LDL<70 mg/dL. Mitigating circumstances may preclude more aggressive treatment**

- ☐ Change to Vytorin(simvastatin/ezetimibe) 40/10/d or 80/10/d per prior authorization criteria
- ☐ Change to Atorvastatin 80mg/d
- ☐ Change to Rosuvastatin 40mg/d
- ☐ Addition of plant stanols/sterols to current lipid lowering therapy
- ☐ Add ezetimibe (Zetia) 10mg/d per prior authorization criteria
- ☐ Add niacin or Slo-niacin to statin therapy
- ☐ Add bile acid sequestrant therapy to statin therapy
- ☐ **When determining response to non-formulary medications, there must be at least 15% reduction in LDL after initiation to continue therapy**

**Mitigating circumstances that may alter LDL goals and/or strategies

- ☐ Patient financial consideration
- ☐ Creatinine Clearance < 30 ml/min
- ☐ Age (>85)
- ☐ Life expectancy < 2 years
- ☐ Recent co-morbid history/instability
- ☐ Critical Drug interactions
- ☐ Close proximity of LDL to 70 mg/dL (defined as LDL between 70-80) and achievement of at least 40% reduction from baseline LDL cholesterol

Prepared by Kaiser Permanente, Aurora, Colorado

Appendix B—HTN Management Protocol

CPCRS Guideline for the Treatment of HTN

This guideline summarizes the CPCRS approach to treating HTN in Colorado Kaiser Permanente enrollees with established CAD. Authoritative guidelines exist for the treatment of HTN (JNC-VII). Although there is consensus in many areas regarding the treatment of HTN, other areas remain contentious and debated. This guideline emphasizes efforts that are supported by currently available randomized controlled trial evidence of benefit and demonstrated cost-effectiveness. It is likely that the specific approach to treating HTN will evolve as new evidence is published.

A. Non-pharmacological Treatment

Lifestyle changes recommended in all patients with pre-HTN and HTN

Dietary Approaches to Stop Hypertension (DASH) diet (low in fat and high in fruit and vegetables, with low-fat dairy products)
Sodium restriction 2 g or less of sodium daily
Weight reduction if body mass index (BMI) is 25 kg/m^2 or higher
Exercise (moderate intensity) on most days of the week.
Limit alcohol to one drink (women) or two drinks (men)

B. Pharmacological Treatment

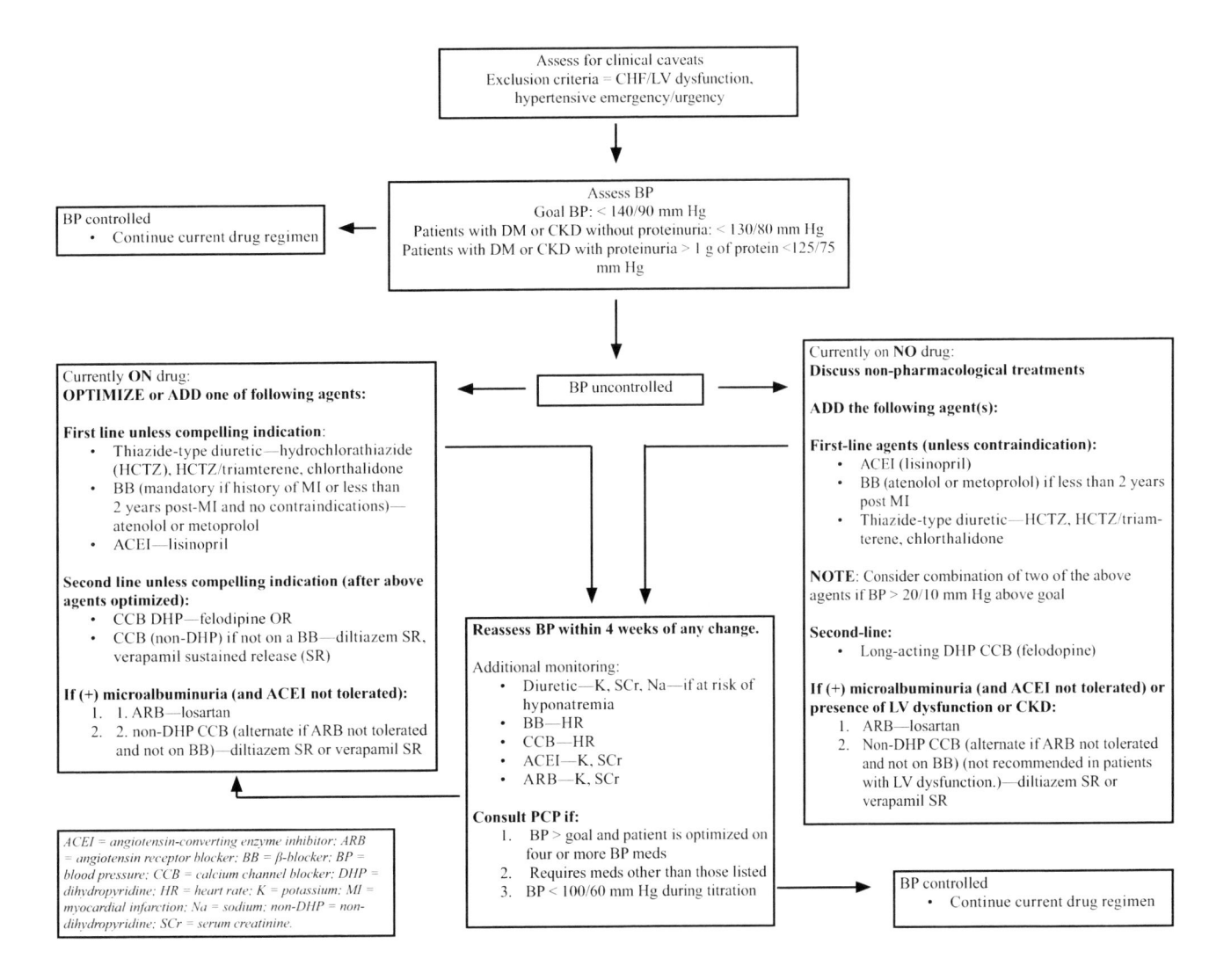

Assess for clinical caveats
Exclusion criteria = CHF/LV dysfunction, hypertensive emergency/urgency

↓

Assess BP
Goal BP: < 140/90 mm Hg
Patients with DM or CKD without proteinuria: < 130/80 mm Hg
Patients with DM or CKD with proteinuria > 1 g of protein <125/75 mm Hg

→ **BP controlled**
- Continue current drug regimen

↓

BP uncontrolled

Currently ON drug:
OPTIMIZE or ADD one of following agents:

First line unless compelling indication:
- Thiazide-type diuretic—hydrochlorathiazide (HCTZ), HCTZ/triamterene, chlorthalidone
- BB (mandatory if history of MI or less than 2 years post-MI and no contraindications)—atenolol or metoprolol
- ACEI—lisinopril

Second line unless compelling indication (after above agents optimized):
- CCB DHP—felodipine OR
- CCB (non-DHP) if not on a BB—diltiazem SR, verapamil sustained release (SR)

If (+) microalbuminuria (and ACEI not tolerated):
1. 1. ARB—losartan
2. 2. non-DHP CCB (alternate if ARB not tolerated and not on BB)—diltiazem SR or verapamil SR

Currently on NO drug:
Discuss non-pharmacological treatments

ADD the following agent(s):

First-line agents (unless contraindication):
- ACEI (lisinopril)
- BB (atenolol or metoprolol) if less than 2 years post MI
- Thiazide-type diuretic—HCTZ, HCTZ/triamterene, chlorthalidone

NOTE: Consider combination of two of the above agents if BP > 20/10 mm Hg above goal

Second-line:
- Long-acting DHP CCB (felodopine)

If (+) microalbuminuria (and ACEI not tolerated) or presence of LV dysfunction or CKD:
1. ARB—losartan
2. Non-DHP CCB (alternate if ARB not tolerated and not on BB) (not recommended in patients with LV dysfunction.)—diltiazem SR or verapamil SR

Reassess BP within 4 weeks of any change.

Additional monitoring:
- Diuretic—K, SCr, Na—if at risk of hyponatremia
- BB—HR
- CCB—HR
- ACEI—K, SCr
- ARB—K, SCr

Consult PCP if:
1. BP > goal and patient is optimized on four or more BP meds
2. Requires meds other than those listed
3. BP < 100/60 mm Hg during titration

→ **BP controlled**
- Continue current drug regimen

ACEI = angiotensin-converting enzyme inhibitor; ARB = angiotensin receptor blocker; BB = β-blocker; BP = blood pressure; CCB = calcium channel blocker; DHP = dihydropyridine; HR = heart rate; K = potassium; MI = myocardial infarction; Na = sodium; non-DHP = non-dihydropyridine; SCr = serum creatinine.

Prepared by Kaiser Permanente, Aurora, Colorado

Laboratory Follow-up

If mild electrolyte changes occur (i.e., noncritical values) in patients on diuretics, ACEIs, or ARBs, potassium supplementation (KCl 10–80 mEq orally daily) may be prescribed, dosage adjustments to antihypertensive drugs made, or dietary changes (i.e., change in potassium or fluid intake) advised, and the physician will be notified within twenty-four hours if drug changes are made. In general, 10 mEq of KCl will raise serum K+ by 0.1 mEq/L, and dosing of KCl supplements will be based on this dosage guideline. If diuretics are discontinued, potassium supplementation may be adjusted or stopped, and the physician will be notified within 24 hours.

Clinical Caveats

Clinical exclusions from the CPCRS HTN Treatment Guidelines

CHF, EF 40% or less
- Optimization of hypertensive regimen will be deferred to the CHF clinic
- If not already enrolled in the CHF clinic, will be referred for enrollment
- HealthConnect note will be forwarded to Heart Failure Clinic pooled in basket: Heart Failure/Franklin

Systolic BP more than 180 mm Hg and/or diastolic BP more than 110 mm Hg
- PCP or designee will be contacted.

Clinical Caveats Care Pathways

Nephropathy (more than 1 g of proteinuria)
- If followed by outside Nephrology, HTN management will be deferred to outside Nephrology.
- If not followed by outside Nephrology, can refer to RMDM clinic
  - Patients with stage 3 CKD (estimated GFR 30–60 mL/minute) plus comorbidities (CAD and/or DM) are eligible to be enrolled in RMDM.
  - SCr more than 2.5, or if large increase in SCr (i.e., 0.5 mg/dL or more), notify PCP or RMDM clinic

Four or more HTN drugs and BP above goal
- An assessment of the current hypertensive regimen will be completed.
- If the current hypertensive regimen is not optimized, regimen will be optimized.
- If the current hypertensive regimen is optimized, the PCP will be consulted regarding treatment options.

Noncompliance with laboratory/BP monitoring
- Patient will be contacted by telephone or letter.
- If laboratory results/BP monitoring is not completed within one month of missed laboratory letter, the PCP will be notified and BP will be reassessed at the next scheduled encounter.

Patient refusal
- The PCP will be notified (HealthConnect note will be forwarded to the PCP's basket).

Hypotensive (systolic BP less than 100 mm Hg, diastolic BP less than 60 mm Hg)
- If systolic BP is less than 100 mm Hg or diastolic BP is less than 60 mm Hg, the patient will be assessed for symptoms of hypotension (dizziness, lightheadedness, and fatigue).
- If symptomatic, hypertensive drugs will be downtitrated or discontinued as appropriate.
- If asymptomatic, the PCP will be consulted to determine if any action is necessary.

Appendix C: CPK Management Protocol

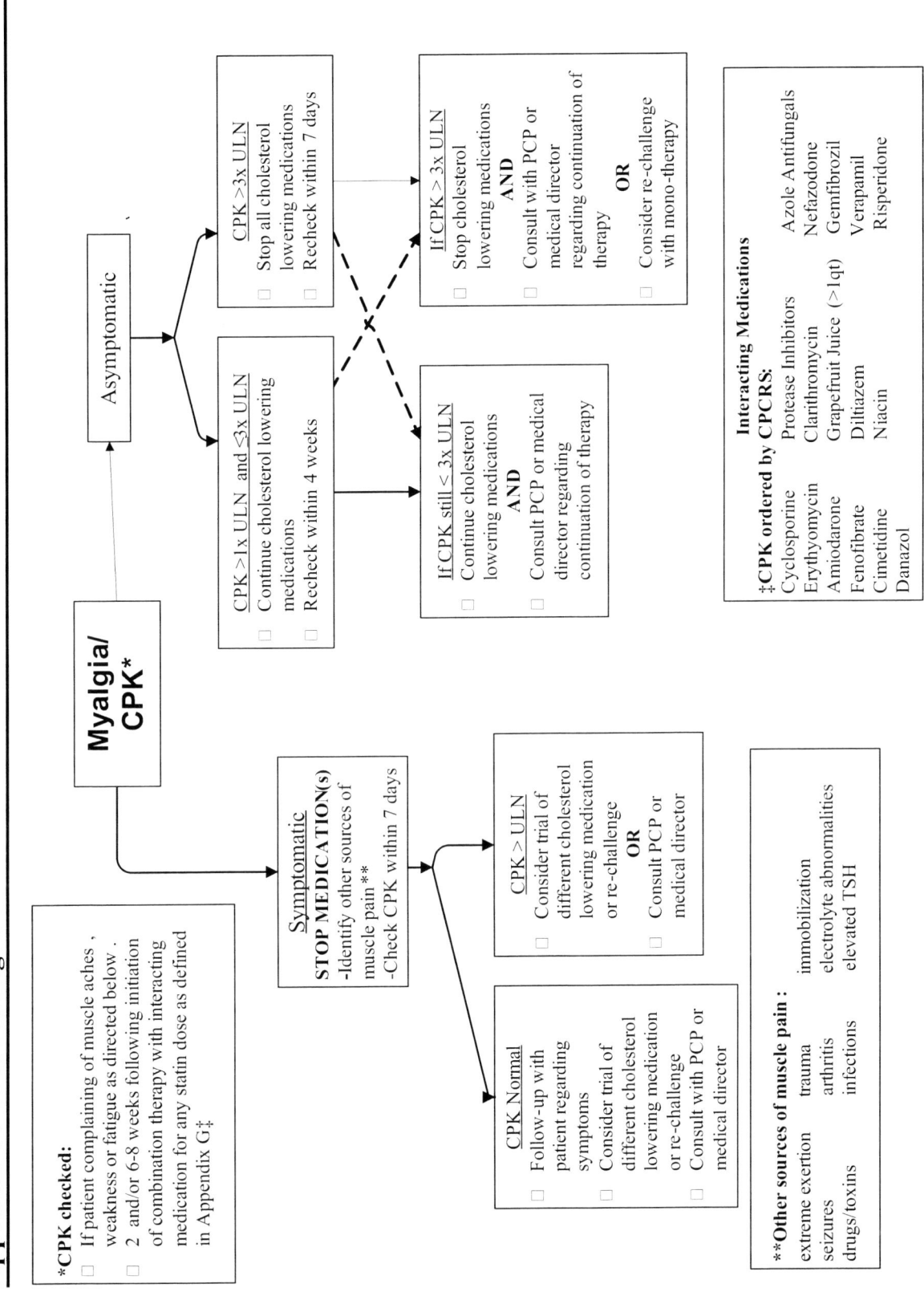

*CPK checked:
- ☐ If patient complaining of muscle aches, weakness or fatigue as directed below.
- ☐ 2 and/or 6-8 weeks following initiation of combination therapy with interacting medication for any statin dose as defined in Appendix G‡

Myalgia/ CPK*

Asymptomatic

CPK >1x ULN and <3x ULN
- ☐ Continue cholesterol lowering medications
- ☐ Recheck within 4 weeks

CPK >3x ULN
- ☐ Stop all cholesterol lowering medications
- ☐ Recheck within 7 days

If CPK still < 3x ULN
- ☐ Continue cholesterol lowering medications
  AND
- ☐ Consult PCP or medical director regarding continuation of therapy

If CPK > 3x ULN
- ☐ Stop cholesterol lowering medications
  AND
- ☐ Consult with PCP or medical director regarding continuation of therapy
  OR
- ☐ Consider re-challenge with mono-therapy

Symptomatic
STOP MEDICATION(s)
- Identify other sources of muscle pain**
- Check CPK within 7 days

CPK Normal
- ☐ Follow-up with patient regarding symptoms
- ☐ Consider trial of different cholesterol lowering medication or re-challenge
- ☐ Consult with PCP or medical director

CPK > ULN
- ☐ Consider trial of different cholesterol lowering medication or re-challenge
  OR
- ☐ Consult PCP or medical director

**Other sources of muscle pain:

extreme exertion	trauma	immobilization
seizures	arthritis	electrolyte abnormalities
drugs/toxins	infections	elevated TSH

Interacting Medications

‡CPK ordered by CPCRS:

Cyclosporine	Protease Inhibitors	Azole Antifungals
Erythyomycin	Clarithromycin	Nefazodone
Amiodarone	Grapefruit Juice (>1qt)	Gemfibrozil
Fenofibrate	Diltiazem	Verapamil
Cimetidine	Niacin	Risperidone
Danazol		

ULN = upper limits of normal.

Prepared by Kaiser Permanente, Aurora, Colorado

Appendix D: ALT Management Protocol

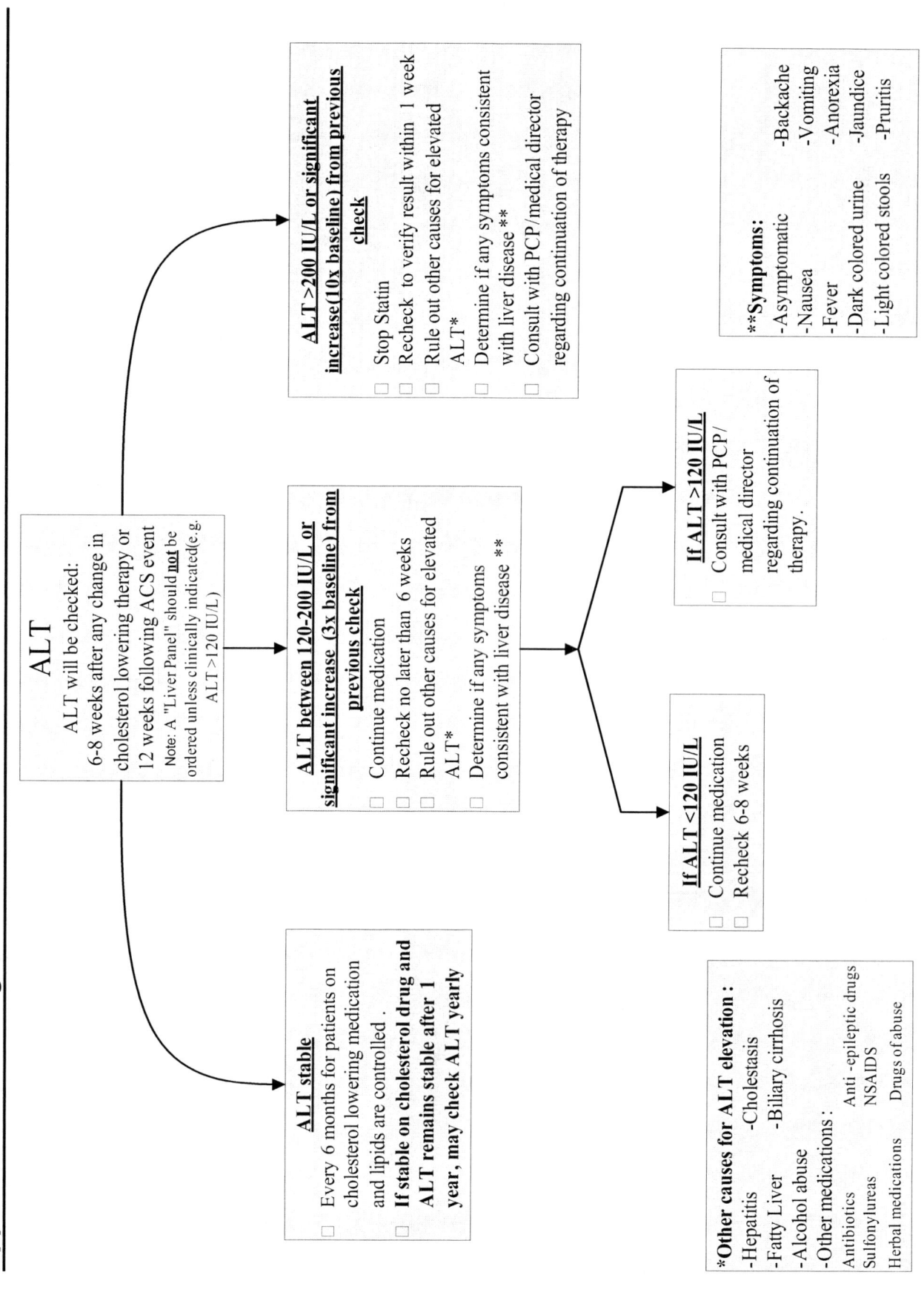

ALT

ALT will be checked:
6-8 weeks after any change in cholesterol lowering therapy or 12 weeks following ACS event
Note: A "Liver Panel" should **not** be ordered unless clinically indicated (e.g. ALT >120 IU/L)

ALT stable
- Every 6 months for patients on cholesterol lowering medication and lipids are controlled.
- **If stable on cholesterol drug and ALT remains stable after 1 year, may check ALT yearly**

ALT between 120-200 IU/L or significant increase (3x baseline) from previous check
- ☐ Continue medication
- ☐ Recheck no later than 6 weeks
- ☐ Rule out other causes for elevated ALT*
- ☐ Determine if any symptoms consistent with liver disease **

If ALT <120 IU/L
- ☐ Continue medication
- ☐ Recheck 6-8 weeks

If ALT >120 IU/L
- ☐ Consult with PCP/medical director regarding continuation of therapy.

ALT >200 IU/L or significant increase (10x baseline) from previous check
- ☐ Stop Statin
- ☐ Recheck to verify result within 1 week
- ☐ Rule out other causes for elevated ALT*
- ☐ Determine if any symptoms consistent with liver disease **
- ☐ Consult with PCP/medical director regarding continuation of therapy

---

*Other causes for ALT elevation:
- Hepatitis
- Cholestasis
- Fatty Liver
- Biliary cirrhosis
- Alcohol abuse
- Other medications:
  Antibiotics   Anti-epileptic drugs
  Sulfonylureas   NSAIDS
  Herbal medications   Drugs of abuse

**Symptoms:
- Asymptomatic   - Backache
- Nausea   - Vomiting
- Fever   - Anorexia
- Dark colored urine - Jaundice
- Light colored stools - Pruritis

Prepared by Kaiser Permanente, Aurora, Colorado

Appendix E— Laboratory Monitoring Protocol

Laboratory Monitoring Procedures for CPCRS

The following information is intended to serve as a guide for providers caring for patients enrolled in the Clinical Pharmacy Cardiac Risk Service.

The following tests will be obtained at **BASELINE** at enrollment into CPCRS:

Fasting lipid profile (FLP)	10–12 weeks after an acute coronary event 6 months after enrollment if previous FLP controlled/stable 2 months after enrollment if previous FLP uncontrolled or more than 6 months from last FLP
ALT	ALT will be ordered with first FLP as described above unless patient is not taking a cholesterol drug AND previous FLP is controlled/stable. A "Liver Panel" should not be ordered unless clinically indicated (e.g., abnormal ALT > 120 U/L).
Fasting plasma glucose (FPG)	For patients without DM: If most recent is more than 3 years before enrollment or 10–12 weeks after an acute coronary event No FPG will be obtained for patients with DM.
HgA1c	If most recent is more than 1 year before enrollment and patient has received a diagnosis of DM
Thyroid profile	If most recent is more than 1 year before enrollment for patients with uncontrolled FLP (on or off drugs)
Creatinine	If most recent is more than 1 year before enrollment for all patients enrolled in CPCRS

The following tests will be obtained routinely by CPCRS:

FLP	6–8 weeks after any change in cholesterol drug 2–6 months after non-pharmacological interventions Every 6 months for patient on cholesterol drug and controlled. If stable on cholesterol drug and FLP remains controlled after 1 year, may check FLP yearly. Annually if patient not on cholesterol drug and controlled	All results will be reviewed and signed by CPCRS providers and addressed per the FLP algorithm. Exceptions: Providers will be notified of all patients with triglycerides > 1,000 mg/dL and HDL < 15 mg/dL.
ALT	6–8 weeks after any change in cholesterol drug 2 months after non-pharmacological interventions Every 6 months for patient on cholesterol drug and controlled. If stable on cholesterol drug and ALT remains normal after 1 year, may check ALT yearly. Should not be ordered if FLP controlled/stable and NOT on a cholesterol drug. A "Liver Panel" should not be ordered unless clinically indicated (e.g., abnormal ALT > 120 U/L).	Normal results will be reviewed and signed by CPCRS providers. Abnormal results per ALT monitoring guidelines
FPG	Routine screening every 3 years for patients without DM (if not done by the PCP). Screen at 1- to 2-year intervals if two or more of the following: history of gestational DM, first-degree relative with DM, polycystic ovarian syndrome (PCOS), age older than 40, nonwhite, BMI more than 25, new-onset hypertriglyceridemia Yearly for patients with impaired FPG (between 100 and 125) if not done by the PCP 6–8 weeks after initiation/adjustment of niacin Repeat fasting glucose if clinically indicated	FPG ≤ 99 will be reviewed and signed by CPCRS providers New fasting blood glucose (FBG) ≥ 100 mg/dL, refer to the prediabetes algorithm Stable FBG > 100 mg/dL will be reviewed and signed by CPCRS providers.
HgA1c	Ensure that at least one HgA1c is completed yearly if not ordered by the PCP.	HgA1c < 8% and stable will be reviewed and signed by CPCRS providers. HgA1c ≥ 8% or unstable will be sent to the PCP for evaluation.

Prepared by Kaiser Permanente, Aurora, Colorado

Thyroid profile	Treatment-resistant lipids (on cholesterol drugs) and no previous TSH (more than 1 year) Routine screening (every year) for patients on thyroid supplementation with controlled cholesterol (if not already done by PCP) If patient is symptomatic with myalgia	Normal results will be reviewed and signed by CPCRS providers. Abnormal TSH results will be sent to the PCP for review and signoff.
Creatinine	Every year if not done by the PCP Within 1–4 weeks after initiation/dosage increase of a diuretic, ACEI, or ARB If patient is symptomatic with myalgia	Normal or stable results (defined as no increases during previous 6 months) will be reviewed and signed by CPCRS providers. Abnormal or unstable results will be sent to the PCP for review and signoff.
Uric acid	If patient is starting niacin therapy and has no prior uric level 6–8 weeks after initiation/dosage increase of niacin Annually for patients on stable doses of niacin	Normal results will be reviewed and signed by CPCRS providers. Abnormal results will be sent to the PCP for review and signoff.
CPK	2 weeks and/or 6–8 weeks after initiation/change of combination therapy (obtain baseline CPK if combination therapy expected in the future) as defined in Appendix G If patient is symptomatic with myalgia If significant change in pharmacotherapy (i.e., potential drug interaction and dose titration)	Normal results will be reviewed and signed by CPCRS providers. Abnormal results per CPK monitoring guidelines
Microalbumin	Routine screening every year for patients with DM if not done by PCP	Normal or stable results will be reviewed and signed by CPCRS providers. Abnormal results will be sent to PCP for review and signoff.
Potassium	Within 1–4 weeks after initiation/dosage increase of ACEI/ARB/diuretic May recheck within 7 days of abnormal reading to confirm	Normal results will be reviewed and signed by CPCRS providers. Abnormal results per HTN guidelines Critical: < 3.0 mEq/L and > 6.0 mEq/L sent to PCP
Sodium	Within 1–4 weeks if starting or titrating diuretic **AND** patient at risk of hyponatremia (elderly or history of hyponatremia) May recheck within 7 days of abnormal reading to confirm	Normal results will be reviewed and signed off by CPCRS providers. Abnormal results per HTN guideline Critical < 120 mEq/L and > 160 mEq/L sent to PCP
High-sensitivity C-reactive protein (HsCRP)	If patient resistant to starting/changing CAD drugs (statins/ACE/HTN drugs)	All results will be signed off by CPCRS.

Appendix F—CPCRS Guideline for Screening for Diabetes/Prediabetes

Adapted from the Kaiser Permanente Colorado Region guidelines for Screening of Diabetes/Prediabetes
This is an informational guideline not intended to replace clinical judgment. Independent clinical judgment should be exercised by providers using this algorithm.

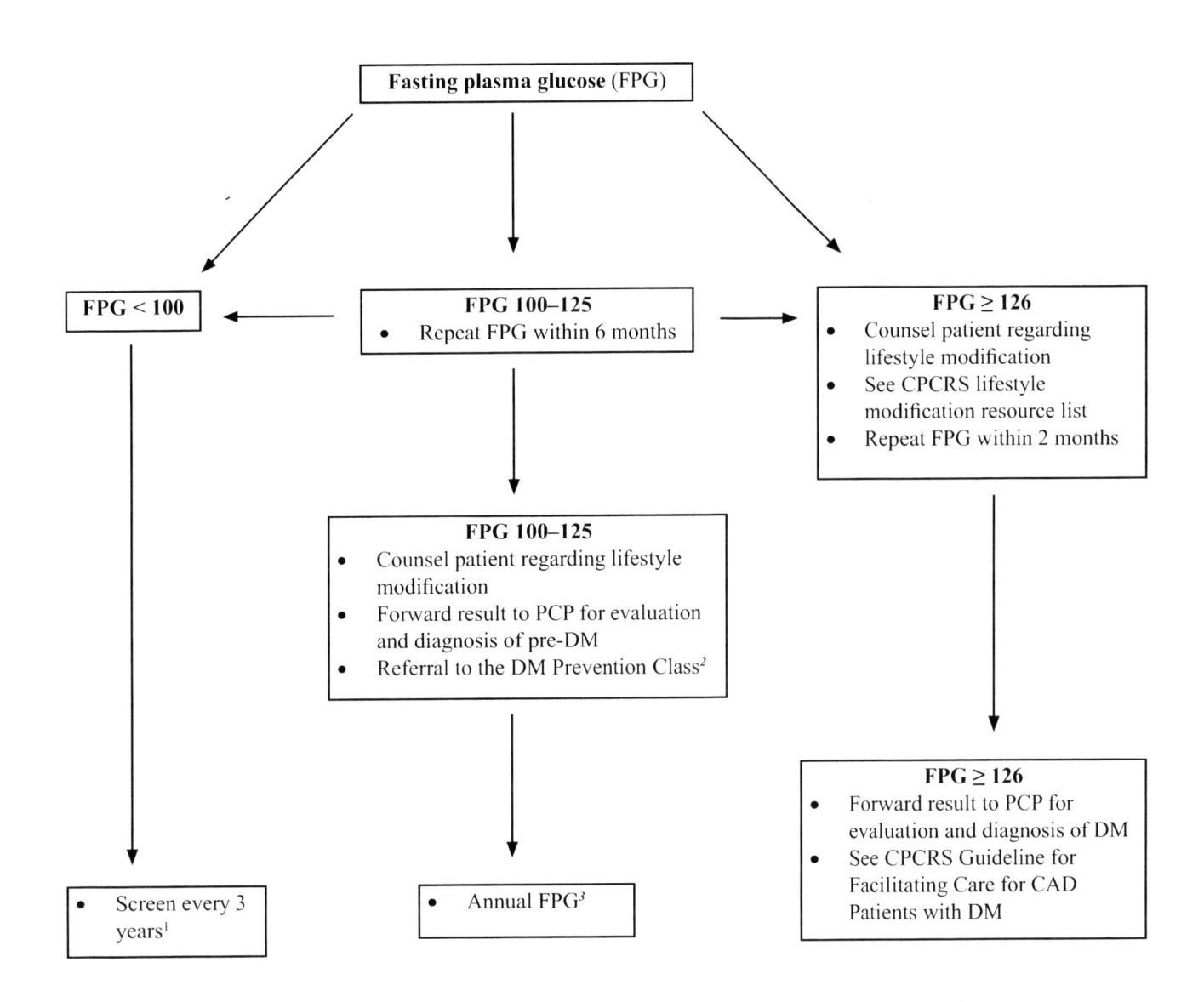

```
                          ┌─────────────────────────────┐
                          │ Fasting plasma glucose (FPG)│
                          └─────────────────────────────┘
                    ↙                ↓                    ↘
        ┌─────────┐      ┌──────────────────────┐      ┌──────────────────────────────┐
        │ FPG<100 │ ←─── │     FPG 100–125      │ ───→ │          FPG ≥ 126           │
        └─────────┘      │ • Repeat FPG within  │      │ • Counsel patient regarding  │
                        │   6 months            │      │   lifestyle modification     │
                        └──────────────────────┘      │ • See CPCRS lifestyle        │
              │                   ↓                    │   modification resource list │
              │       ┌──────────────────────────┐    │ • Repeat FPG within 2 months │
              │       │      FPG 100–125         │    └──────────────────────────────┘
              │       │ • Counsel patient        │
              │       │   regarding lifestyle    │
              │       │   modification           │
              │       │ • Forward result to PCP  │
              │       │   for evaluation and     │
              │       │   diagnosis of pre-DM    │
              │       │ • Referral to the DM     │
              │       │   Prevention Class²      │
              │       └──────────────────────────┘
              │                   ↓                              ↓
              ↓                                   ┌──────────────────────────────┐
      ┌──────────────┐        ┌──────────────┐    │          FPG ≥ 126           │
      │ • Screen     │        │ • Annual FPG³│    │ • Forward result to PCP for  │
      │   every 3    │        └──────────────┘    │   evaluation and diagnosis   │
      │   years¹     │                            │   of DM                      │
      └──────────────┘                            │ • See CPCRS Guideline for    │
                                                  │   Facilitating Care for CAD  │
                                                  │   Patients with DM           │
                                                  └──────────────────────────────┘
```

1.	If two or more of the following, consider screening at 1- to 2-year intervals: history of gestational diabetes,* first-degree relative with diabetes, PCOS, age > 40, nonwhite, BMI > 25, new-onset hypertriglyceridemia.
2.	Refer to the Diabetes Prevention Class if patient is able to make lifestyle modification; consider age, prognosis, and current functional status.
3.	Consider screening more often if helpful in tracking success of lifestyle modification.

Prepared by Kaiser Permanente, Aurora, Colorado

Appendix G—Statin Drug Interaction Protocol

Interacting Drug	Therapeutic Option	CPK
Cyclosporine	Convert to/initiate pravastatin or rosuvastatin	6–8 weeks
Protease inhibitors Indinavir, nelfinavir Ritonavir, saquinavir, lopinavir Fosamprenavir, atazanavir, darunavir Tipranavir	Convert to/initiate pravastatin or rosuvastatin	6–8 weeks
Azole anti-fungals: Fluconazole, ketoconazole Itraconazole, voriconazole	Completely stop statin therapy for duration of anti-fungal therapy **OR** convert/initiate pravastatin or rosuvastatin for duration of anti-fungal therapy	6–8 weeks
Macrolide antibiotics (except for azithromycin): Erythromycin, clarithromycin	Completely stop statin therapy for duration of macrolide therapy **OR** convert/initiate pravastatin or rosuvastatin for duration of macrolide therapy	6–8 weeks
Nefazodone	Convert to/initiate pravastatin or rosuvastatin	6–8 weeks
Amiodarone	Limit/reduce dose to: Lovastatin 40 mg daily Simvastatin 20 mg daily Atorvastatin 10 mg daily Vytorin 20/10 mg daily If LDL not controlled on above doses, consider conversion to pravastatin or rosuvastatin therapy	6–8 weeks
Nondihydropyridine CCBs: Verapamil, diltiazem	Limit/reduce dose to: Lovastatin 40 mg daily Simvastatin 40 mg daily Atorvastatin 40 mg daily Vytorin 40/10 mg daily If LDL not controlled on above doses, consider conversion to pravastatin or rosuvastatin therapy	6–8 weeks
Fibrate Gemfibrozil	Convert patient to fenofibrate 54–160 mg daily	6–8 weeks
Fenofibrate	Preferred	2/6–8 weeks
Cimetidine	No statin preference or dose limit	2/6–8 weeks
Risperidone	No statin preference or dose limit	2/6–8 weeks
Danazol	No statin preference or dose limit	2/6–8 weeks
Niacin	No statin preference or dose limit	6–8 weeks
Grapefruit juice (> 1 qt daily)	No statin preference or dose limit	2/6–8 weeks

Prepared by Kaiser Permanente, Aurora, Colorado

Appendix H—Dosing Recommendations of Cholesterol-Lowering Drugs for Patients with CKD

Estimated CrCl ≥ 30 mL/minute
Lovastatin 20–80 mg/day
Simvastatin 20–80 mg/day
Vytorin 10/10–80/10 mg/day
Atorvastatin 10–80 mg/day
Rosuvastatin 5–40 mg/day
Pravastatin 10–80 mg/day

Estimated CrCl < 30 mL/minute
Lovastatin 10–40 mg/day
Simvastatin 10–40 mg/day
Vytorin 10/10–40/10 mg/day
Atorvastatin 10–80 mg/day
Rosuvastatin 5–10 mg/day
Pravastatin 10–80 mg/day
No change in statin dosing is needed for people on dialysis.

Estimated CrCl < 50 mL/minute
Fenofibrate 54 mg/day
Gemfibrozil 300 mg twice daily

Appendix I—Dosing Ranges for Cholesterol-Lowering Drugs

Drug	Usual Daily Dose Range	Precautions/Contraindications
HMG CoA reductase inhibitors (statins) *listed in order of potency*		
Lovastatin	10–80 mg	Active liver disease, pregnancy, lactation, or myalgias already present; adjust dose in renal disease (Appendix H)
Pravastatin	10–80 mg	
Simvastatin	10–80 mg	
Atorvastatin	10–80 mg	
Rosuvastatin	5–40 mg	
Cholesterol absorption inhibitor		
Ezetimibe	10 mg	Hypersensitivity to ezetimibe, active liver disease
Ezetimibe/simvastatin	10/10–10/80 mg	See ezetimibe and simvastatin
Bile acid sequestrant		
Cholestyramine	4–24 g	Biliary or bowel obstruction
Colestipol	5–30 g (granules) or 2–16 g (tablets)	
Fibrates		
Gemfibrozil	600–1,200 mg	Active liver disease, primary biliary cirrhosis; preexisting gallbladder disease; adjusted doses needed in renal disease (Appendix H)
Fenofibrate	54–160 mg	
Nicotinic acid		
Slo-Niacin	500–2,000 mg	Active liver disease, renal disease, DM, peptic ulcer, gout, gallbladder disease

HMG CoA = 3-hydroxy-3-methylglutaryl coenzyme A.

Prepared by Kaiser Permanente, Aurora, Colorado

CORONARY ARTERY DISEASE SERVICE POLICY AND PROCEDURE

Submitted by: Christopher Lamer

Revised: May 2004

Purpose

A need exists among the Eastern Band of Cherokee Indians to aggressively target and treat CAD. The Cherokee Indian Hospital Pharmacy and Therapeutics Committee has approved the implementation of a Coronary Artery Disease Secondary Prevention Service (CADPS) to ensure close monitoring of patients with a diagnosis of CAD (ICD-9 code of 410.0–414.9). The purpose of the CADPS is to allow pharmacists to clinically manage selected patients who have received the diagnosis of CAD through a collaborative system. The CADPS is designed to augment provider efforts to diminish and/or delay the complications of CAD. This service will contribute to patient management in the primary care model through physician extension and preventive medicine.

Goals

Goals of the CADPS are to enable certified pharmacists to work collaboratively with the medical staff to (a) optimize the health care of Eastern Band of Cherokee Indians who have a diagnosis of CAD and (b) augment provider efforts to delay or diminish the complications of CAD.

Objectives

Objectives of the CADPS are to

- Increase the awareness of CAD and associated risks
- Provide Patient Education related to CAD and related topics using the national IHS Patient and Family Education Protocols
- Optimize pharmacological and non-pharmacological therapies
- Monitor for and reduce ADEs
- Achieve CAD treatment goals as defined by national guidelines

Target Population

The targeted population for the CADPS will be American Indian patients who have established CAD.

Needs Assessment

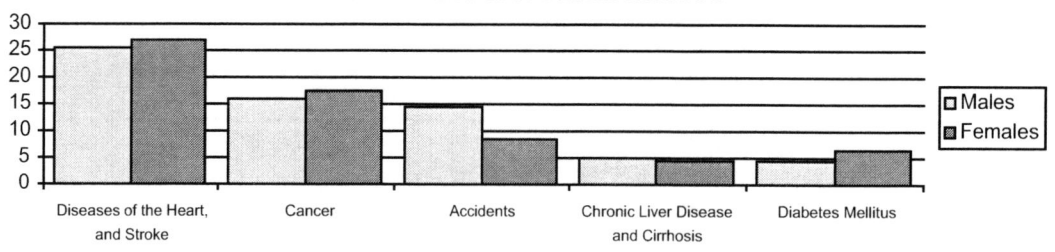

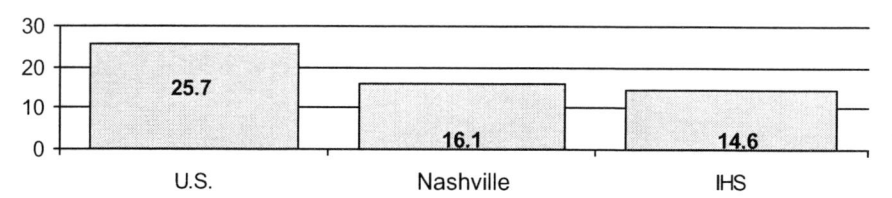

CAD is the leading cause of death among American Indians and Alaska Natives. The "Diseases of the Heart Death Rate" is higher in the Nashville area compared with the rates reported among other American Indians/Alaska Indians. The rise in the incidence of CAD in American Indians is evident in the members of the Eastern Band of Cherokee Indians. One-third (33.4%) of the people who have used CIH for their health care have some type of disease of the heart and/or circulatory system. Of the living patients with a visit to CIH since January 1, 1999, 4.1% have received a diagnosis of CAD (defined by ICD-9 codes 410.0–414.9), and 12.1% have received a diagnosis of DM. The Strong Heart Study found that DM increased the risk of CAD in men by 2.1-fold and in women by 3.5-fold. The risk of CAD among American Indians is very high, and preexisting CAD is the strongest risk factor for subsequent cardiovascular events.

A number of interventions reduce the incidence of CAD and/or subsequent complications. Data published in the *Journal of Clinical Outcomes Management* that defined interventions that reduce the risk of developing CAD were compared to data collected from the CIH database and reported in Table 1.

Pharmacy-based CAD programs (including lipid clinics, CHF clinics, and HTN clinics) demonstrate multiple benefits, including (a) improved patient-outcomes, (b) increased adherence to prescribed therapies, and (c) improved patient and provider satisfaction. Interventions targeting dyslipidemia and HTN through collaborative disease state management, regular patient interaction, and close patient monitoring by a pharmacist will improve clinical quality indicators. Pharmacists contribute to collaborative practices by adding their expertise of drug therapy management, drug safety and monitoring, and patient education. Pharmacists can improve persistence and adherence to prescribed therapies and improve the flow of clinical information between pharmacists and other health care providers. Economic benefits are observed through collaborative programs involving the pharmacist. A number of studies have demonstrated cost-saving benefits through appropriate dosing, monitoring, and evaluation of therapies by the pharmacist.

Clinic Information

CADPS Appointments and Schedule

The CADPS will be conducted in the outpatient pharmacy of CIH and is designed to allow certified pharmacists to collaboratively manage patients who have a diagnosis of CAD through protocol in conjunction with treatment plans outlined by the patient's provider(s). Patient appointments and continuity of care will be maintained by the RPMS scheduling package in addition to the patient's medical record. Patient follow-up visits will be scheduled on the basis of the clinical judgment of the pharmacist and provider. Patients will be required to make an appointment with a provider at least quarterly for routine medical follow-up. CADPS service visits will be made between provider visits as appropriate.

Hours of Operation

The CADPS will operate during the normal working hours of the pharmacy.

Referrals

A medical staff provider may refer patients with a diagnosis of CAD to the CADPS, and referrals will be maintained in the patient's medical record. Providers may refer patients by completing a CADPS referral Patient Care Component (PCC+) form or by contacting the referred certified pharmacist. Once referred, patients will consult a certified pharmacist for follow-up instructions.

Clinic Eligibility

- All patients with a diagnosis of CAD are eligible to participate in the CADPS if they meet the following criteria
    ○ They are reliable and willing to follow instructions.
    ○ Are able to keep appointments

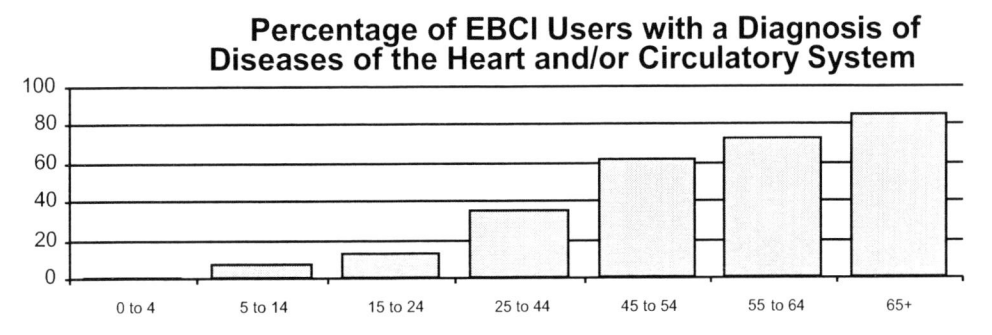

Percentage of EBCI Users with a Diagnosis of Diseases of the Heart and/or Circulatory System

Age Group	Percentage
0 to 4	0
5 to 14	~8
15 to 24	~15
25 to 44	~37
45 to 54	~63
55 to 64	~73
65+	~87

EBCI = Eastern Band of Cherokee Indians

- Have reliable transportation to the hospital
- Have access to and are accessible by telephone
- Patients may be dismissed from the CADPS for the following reasons
  - Required information is not made available by the provider.
  - Lack of appropriate medical follow-up
  - Inability of the pharmacy program to manage more patients because of time and/or space limitations
- Certified pharmacists may participate in the CADPS.
- Noncertified pharmacists will provide services, including (a) increase the awareness of CAD and the associated risks; (b) provide patient education related to CAD and related topics using the national IHS Patient and Family Education Protocols; and (c) monitor for and reduce ADEs.

Referral to Clinic/PCP

Pharmacists may refer patients to other health care providers including a PCP, emergency department provider, physical therapy, behavioral health, nutritionist, DM program, smoking cessation program, or general clinic; all patients must have a provider visit every three months at a minimum or as determined appropriate by the patient's provider. A provider will be notified immediately if the patient requires an evaluation for a significant adverse event or if the laboratory value is considered critical by the Laboratory Department. The pharmacist will review with the patient's primary provider any unexpected questions or complications that arise as well as the need for further therapy. All assessments, SOAP notes, and dosage adjustments will be reviewed and cosigned by a provider through standing order protocol within 24 hours of a CADPS visit. Patients will be referred to a provider-only visit every 3 months.

Appointments

Patients will be seen at scheduled appointments by a pharmacist in a timely manner. The patient's chart will be requested from the Medical Records Department by the pharmacist when the patient presents to the pharmacy for his or her appointment. Once the chart and laboratory results are collected, the pharmacist will discuss subjective and objective findings in an available counseling room. All information will be reported in the patient's medical record, including
- Typical food intake
- Physical activity
- Stress and stressors
- Stress management strategies
- Willingness to make behavioral changes
- Goals of behavioral change
- Laboratory values
  - CARE panels
  - LFTs
  - HgA1c when appropriate
  - Albumin when appropriate
- Vital signs
  - BP
  - Pulse rate
  - Respiratory rate
- Active problems
- Inactive problems
- Major risk factors for CHD
- Risk factors for the metabolic syndrome
- Allergies
- Current drug history
- Date of referral to the CADPS
- Assessment of subjective and objective findings
- Follow-up recommendations
- Recommended follow-up appointment in clinic
- Referrals to other services as appropriate
- Patient education documentation
- Treatment plans
- Goals of therapy

Patients will be assessed in one of three private counseling rooms, which are separate from the pharmacy filling area and the pharmacy waiting room. A PCC+ form will be generated for each patient by a dedicated PCC+ laser printer. Each counseling room is equipped with a sphygmomanometer, a computer with access to an RPMS, a patient chart (graphic interface user), and the Internet. These counseling rooms are conducive to conducting a patient history and limited physical examination. Pharmacists will be allotted a maximum of 10–15 minutes to assess each patient.

Pharmacists will target interventions that have been documented to reduce the risks of developing CAD, including (a) treating dyslipidemia; (b) maximizing BP control; (c) achieving goal HgA1c; (d) optimizing non-pharmacological therapy; and (e) instituting appropriate pharmacological therapy when appropriate, including ASA, β-blockers, and ACEI/ARB. The CIH pharmacy will address this need by use of the available technology and clinical guidelines to manage a CADPS. All information will be documented on the CADPS PCC+ form. The pharmacist will review the visit with a provider within 24 hours of the CADPS visit. If a major intervention is made, the provider will be asked to come to the pharmacy for a face-to-face encounter with the patient. Once an optimal care plan is agreed on, the provider will co-sign the patient's medical record and determine and document the appropriate E&M code.

Collaborative Pharmacist-Provider Face-to-Face Visit

After the pharmacist has collected subjective and objective information, assessed current therapy, and recommended a new treatment plan, a primary care provider may be requested. A provider face-to-face visit will be required at least once monthly for each patient. The pharmacist will call the outpatient nursing staff to request a provider face-to-face visit. If the "Hospitalist System" is in effect, the Hospitalist will be the contact provider for the review of patient visits. Providers who will be involved in the face-to-face visit will go to the outpatient pharmacy department and discuss the service encounter with the pharmacist involved. After the care plan has been discussed and agreed on by all parties involved, the provider will discuss issues regarding therapy, safety, and follow-up services with the patient. Recommendations will be made collaboratively with the provider and the pharmacist, and the provider will indicate the appropriate E/M code on the patient's medical record. For visits that occur between monthly visits, the provider who reviews the standing order protocol is requested to perform an evaluation of the documentation and actions presented by the pharmacist and sign the patient's medical record once an agreed-on treatment plan has been reached. For these incidences, the patient's medical record will indicate that a standing order was carried out and that no provider face-to-face contact occurred.

Role of the Pharmacist

Patient Education
A continuing program of patient education forms the basis for a clear patient understanding of his or her therapy. Patients and their relatives/caregivers must be fully informed of the indication for therapy, the nature of the program, and the possible complications. Education begins at the initial clinic visit and is reinforced at subsequent visits. The educational process will be verbal and written (handouts) as well as individual to account for the patient's ability to comprehend the subject. Patients are to be questioned at each visit for problems in the areas of control, complications, adverse effects, and compliance. Patient education will be documented in the patient's medical record using the national IHS Patient and Family Education protocols and locally developed and approved lesson plans. Certified pharmacists will provide patient education related to CAD and related topics (such as HTN, dyslipidemia, diet, and tobacco cessation) using the national IHS Patient and Family Education Protocols.

Ordering and Monitoring of Laboratory Tests
Certified pharmacists may evaluate the patient's cardiac risk factors per national guidelines and IHS recommendations to determine CHD risk reduction goals.

Certified pharmacists may order laboratory tests pertaining to the monitoring, evaluation, or assessment of CAD or pharmacological therapy as appropriate.

Certified pharmacists may interpret and evaluate laboratory results pertaining to the monitoring, evaluation, or assessment of CAD or pharmacological therapy as appropriate. Laboratory results will be reviewed with a provider within 24 hours. Critical laboratory values or abnormal laboratory results of concern will be reviewed with a provider immediately, as appropriate.

Physical Assessment
Certified pharmacists may provide limited physical assessment including, but not limited to, BP, HR, and respiratory rate.

Pharmacological and Non-pharmacological Optimization
Certified pharmacists may optimize, alter, remove, or add pharmacological therapy pertaining to CAD as appropriate to the individual patient case and the patient's provider. A provider will review all pharmacological interventions made by the certified pharmacist before co-signing the assessment and plan on the patient's medical record. If a major intervention (e.g., dosage adjustment, addition of a new drug) is made, a provider will be contacted and asked to visit with the patient for a brief face-to-face encounter. The provider will be asked to review the patient's medical record and the recommendations made by the certified pharmacist pursuant to a plan of action.

Outcomes Evaluations
Six indicators of adequate secondary prevention of CAD will be measured at baseline and evaluated. These shall include (1) LDL goal of less than 100 mg/dL; (2) BP goal of less than 140/90 mm Hg or less than 130/80 mm Hg; (3) ASA use; (4) β-blocker use; (5) ACEI/ARB use; and (6) HgA1c when appropriate. These six indicators will be documented on the PCC+ form and measured through a search of the RPMS database 6 and 12 months after implementation of the service. Secondary outcomes will be collected and documented on the PCC+ form and will include (a) risk factors associated with CAD and the metabolic syndrome (will also appear on the health summary); (b) appropriate therapeutic monitoring laboratory values; (c) lifestyle habits and activities including nutrition and exercise; (d) willingness to change selected lifestyle habits; (e) perceived stresses; (f) medical histories; and (g) patient education.

Training and Certification
Pharmacists will receive local and national credentialing through the following credentialing bodies: (a) National Institute for Standards in Pharmacy Credentialing (NISPC) Disease State Management in Dyslipidemia; (b) BCPS in pharmacotherapy; or (c) North Carolina Clinical Pharmacy Practitioner certification (NC CPP). Pharmacists who wish to be credentialed must also demonstrate proficiency in the cardiovascular service by following the policies and

procedures outlined herein. To verify correct policies and procedures, each pharmacist will be required to present 30 charts for review to an approved preceptor (a provider or credentialed pharmacist) for review. Once 30 charts have been reviewed, the pharmacist will receive a certificate credentialing him/her as a pharmacist at CIH who is granted the ability to follow the policies and procedures outlined herein. The Cherokee Indian Hospital Policy for pharmacist credentialing will be finalized by submitting an application through the medical/dental staff credentialing process. Once approved, the pharmacist will receive the privileges outlined in this policy. The pharmacist will not be a full member of the medical/dental staff committee.

In addition to the local credentialing process, pharmacists will be required to apply for an NCPS certificate to participate in the service.

Personnel Orientation/Criteria to Participate

Staff pharmacists will receive orientation, training, and supervision in the management of the CADPS in compliance with the latest recommendations and the current hospital P and T Committee's Policy and Procedures. Certification will be obtained locally, nationally, and from the IHS NCPS program. Limited medical privileges from the hospital's governing board will be awarded to pharmacists before they participate in the CADPS (with the exception of pharmacists in training to achieve these certifications). A copy of the certification/standing orders will be placed in the departmental personnel folder. Pharmacists will be recertified yearly to ensure that appropriate techniques/procedures are maintained.

Competency Evaluation

Pharmacists will be required to complete 10 continuing education hours on CAD or a related topic. A CAD examination will be developed to assess the pharmacist's knowledge of diagnosis, assessment, treatment, and monitoring of CAD and the therapies used in the treatment. Competency will be recorded in the pharmacist's personnel file.

Continuous Performance Improvement

Given the nature and consequences of CAD, little tolerance can be allowed to ensure the highest level of care possible. Quality indicators for the CADPS shall include information such as BP, LDL, HDL, triglycerides, total cholesterol, HgA1c, ASA use, β-blocker use, ACEI/ARB use, serious adverse events, risk, number of patient visits, number of laboratory values evaluated, and patient and provider satisfaction. This information shall be reviewed on a continual basis and recorded in the hospital's Quality Assessment and Improvement Manual.

Procedure

The Provider

- The patient's provider enrolls him or her in the CADPS by placing a written request for acceptance into the ACC in the patient's medical record.
- The patient agrees to follow up with a provider every 3 months and to follow up with a credentialed member of the pharmacy staff as requested for the period between provider visits.
- The pharmacy accepts the patient into the CADPS and schedules a follow-up appointment.
- The patient reports to patient registration and verifies demographic information.
- The patient goes to the laboratory when applicable.
- The pharmacist contacts medical records to request that the patient's chart be sent to the pharmacy.
- The pharmacy collects the patient's laboratory results and medical record and calls the patient and/or caregiver into a private counseling room to assess the therapeutic treatment plan.
- The pharmacist develops an assessment and recommendation.

The Pharmacist

- When a major intervention takes place, the pharmacist calls the outpatient department requesting a face-to-face visit with a provider.
  ○ A provider comes to the outpatient pharmacy to review with the pharmacist the patient's current anticoagulation therapy and findings and provides face-to-face care for the patient.
  ○ The provider and the pharmacist collaboratively determine the best possible plan of action for the patient's anticoagulation therapy.
  ○ The provider documents the appropriate E&M code on the patient's medical record.
- Has a provider review the patient's medical record. The provider signs the medical record, and the pharmacist will indicate that the visit was done per standing order.
- The pharmacist determines an appropriate follow-up appointment:
  ○ If within three months of last provider visit, the pharmacist will recommend that the patient make an appointment with an outpatient clinic.
  ○ If within less than one month, the patient will make an appointment in the pharmacy.
- The pharmacist will provide recommendations, patient education, and an appointment slip for the patient's next visit held within the pharmacy.
- The pharmacist will return the medical record to the Medical Records Department.

References

1. American Heart Association. AI/AN and CV Diseases. Statistical Fact Sheet—Populations, 2003:1–4.
2. Schnipper JL, Stafford RS. Secondary prevention of coronary artery disease: Lipid management as a priority for improvement. JCOM 2002;9:371–80.
3. DiTusa L., Luzier AB, Brady G, Reinhart RM, Snyder BD. A pharmacy-based approach to cholesterol management. Am J Manage Care 2001;7:973–9.
4. Bogden PE, Abbott RD, Williamson P, Onopa JK, Koonz LM. Comparing standard care with a physician and pharmacist team approach for uncontrolled hypertension. J Gen Intern Med 1998;13:740–5.
5. Pharmaceutical care services and results in project ImPACT: hyperlipidemia. J Am Pharm Assoc 2000;40:157–65.
6. Garrett DG, Martin LA. The Asheville Project: Participants' perceptions of factors contributing to the success of a patient self-management diabetes program. J Am Pharm Assoc 2003;43:185–90.
7. Simpson SH, Johnson JA, Tsuyuki RT. Economic impact of community pharmacist intervention in cholesterol risk management: An evaluation of the study of cardiovascular risk intervention by pharmacists. Pharmacotherapy 2001;21:627–35.
8. Ellis SL, Carter BL, Malone DC, Billups SJ. Clinical and economic impact of ambulatory care clinical pharmacists in management of dyslipidemia in older adults: The IMPROVE study. Impact of managed pharmaceutical care on resource utilization and outcomes in Veterans Affairs medical centers. Pharmacotherapy 2000;20:1508–16.
9. Crealey GE, McElnay JC, Maguire TA, O'Neill C. Costs and effects associated with a community pharmacy-based smoking-cessation programme. Pharmacoeconomics 1998;14:323–33.

Table 1. Occurrence of Interventions to Reduce CAD[a,b]

Intervention Strategy	Total patients	Population utilizing CIH for health care (%)	Total visits	Data collected from study published in JCOM 2002 (%)
Number of living patients with a visit to CIH since 1/1/99	13,154	100	333,037	NA
Number of living patients with a diagnosis of CAD (ICD-9 codes 410.0–414.9) since 1/1/99	535	4.1	3,415	302
On ASA	275	76.8	1,365	~85
On β-blockers[c]	184	34.3	922	~75
On ACEI/ARBs[d]	440	82.2		
Last BP < 140/90 mm Hg	409	76.4		~62
Last BP < 130/80 mm Hg	258	48.2		~42
Last TC < 200 mg/dL	233	43.6		
Last LDL < 100 mg/dL	255	47.7		~38
Last HDL > 40 mg/dL	246	46.0		
Last TG < 150 mg/dL	65	12.1		
DM	1,591	12.1	32,218	NA

[a]Data collected on August 12, 2002.
[b]ASA is defined as aspirin dispensed through CIH (does not include combination products or OTC products purchased elsewhere).
[c]β-Blockers are defined by atenolol, metoprolol, propranolol, or carvedilol.
[d]ACEI/ARBs are defined by lisinopril, fosinopril, ramipril, benazepril, and losartan.
NA = not applicable; TG = triglycerides.

Protocol Approval

_____
Clinical Director

_____
Chairperson of Pharmacy and Therapeutics Committee

_____
Chief of Pharmacy Services

Privilege Request—Pharmacy
CAD Prevention Service

Requested Privilege	Requested Limited	Requested Full	Approved Limited	Approved Full
Assessing patients (e.g., checking BP and pulse rate; ordering appropriate laboratory tests; questioning patients with regard to general health, adverse effects, and therapy; assessing needs of therapy using the most recent guidelines and recommendations)				
Optimizing therapy by collaborative protocol and clinical assessment using the most recent guidelines				
Scheduling patients for follow-up appointments with regard to their therapy and ensuring that appropriate steps are taken for patients to follow up in clinic				
Patient education using the IHS PFE protocols and lesson plans				

CORONARY ARTERY THERAPY MANAGEMENT CERTIFACTION

_____ has read and expressed an understanding of the Pharmacy Policy and Procedure. He/She has been observed in the management of coronary artery disease and is found to possess an acceptable level of competency to independently provide Coronary Artery Disease Services by:

1. Educating patients
2. Ordering appropriate laboratory tests
3. Adjusting drug doses
4. Scheduling patients for follow-up
5. Referring patients as appropriate

_____   _____
Pharmacist   Date

_____   _____
Chief of Pharmacy Services   Date

Concurrence:

_____   _____
Clinical Director   Date

Continuous Quality Indicators—Outcomes Data Collection Form

Name	Chart #	Date	TC	LDL	HDL	TG	Non-HDL	SBP	DBP	Pulse	Dx DM	Hb A1c	ASA	ACE/ARB	BABA
											☐ Yes ☐ No		☐ Prescrib ☐ Contra ☐ Not Rx'd	☐ Prescrib ☐ Contra ☐ Not Rx'd	☐ Prescrib ☐ Contra ☐ Not Rx'd
											☐ Yes ☐ No		☐ Prescrib ☐ Contra ☐ Not Rx'd	☐ Prescrib ☐ Contra ☐ Not Rx'd	☐ Prescrib ☐ Contra ☐ Not Rx'd
											☐ Yes ☐ No		☐ Prescrib ☐ Contra ☐ Not Rx'd	☐ Prescrib ☐ Contra ☐ Not Rx'd	☐ Prescrib ☐ Contra ☐ Not Rx'd
											☐ Yes ☐ No		☐ Prescrib ☐ Contra ☐ Not Rx'd	☐ Prescrib ☐ Contra ☐ Not Rx'd	☐ Prescrib ☐ Contra ☐ Not Rx'd
											☐ Yes ☐ No		☐ Prescrib ☐ Contra ☐ Not Rx'd	☐ Prescrib ☐ Contra ☐ Not Rx'd	☐ Prescrib ☐ Contra ☐ Not Rx'd
											☐ Yes ☐ No		☐ Prescrib ☐ Contra ☐ Not Rx'd	☐ Prescrib ☐ Contra ☐ Not Rx'd	☐ Prescrib ☐ Contra ☐ Not Rx'd
											☐ Yes ☐ No		☐ Prescrib ☐ Contra ☐ Not Rx'd	☐ Prescrib ☐ Contra ☐ Not Rx'd	☐ Prescrib ☐ Contra ☐ Not Rx'd
											☐ Yes ☐ No		☐ Prescrib ☐ Contra ☐ Not Rx'd	☐ Prescrib ☐ Contra ☐ Not Rx'd	☐ Prescrib ☐ Contra ☐ Not Rx'd
											☐ Yes ☐ No		☐ Prescrib ☐ Contra ☐ Not Rx'd	☐ Prescrib ☐ Contra ☐ Not Rx'd	☐ Prescrib ☐ Contra ☐ Not Rx'd
											☐ Yes ☐ No		☐ Prescrib ☐ Contra ☐ Not Rx'd	☐ Prescrib ☐ Contra ☐ Not Rx'd	☐ Prescrib ☐ Contra ☐ Not Rx'd
											☐ Yes ☐ No		☐ Prescrib ☐ Contra ☐ Not Rx'd	☐ Prescrib ☐ Contra ☐ Not Rx'd	☐ Prescrib ☐ Contra ☐ Not Rx'd
											☐ Yes ☐ No		☐ Prescrib ☐ Contra ☐ Not Rx'd	☐ Prescrib ☐ Contra ☐ Not Rx'd	☐ Prescrib ☐ Contra ☐ NotRx'd
											☐ Yes ☐ No		☐ Prescrib ☐ Contra ☐ Not Rx'd	☐ Prescrib ☐ Contra ☐ Not Rx'd	☐ Prescrib ☐ Contra ☐ NotRx'd
													☐ Prescrib ☐ Contra ☐ Not Rx'd	☐ Prescrib ☐ Contra ☐ Not Rx'd	☐ Prescrib ☐ Contra ☐ NotRx'd

SBP = systolic blood pressure; DBP = diastolic blood pressure; prescrib = prescribed; contra = contraindicated; not rx'd = not prescribed

Sample Dyslipidemia Algorithm

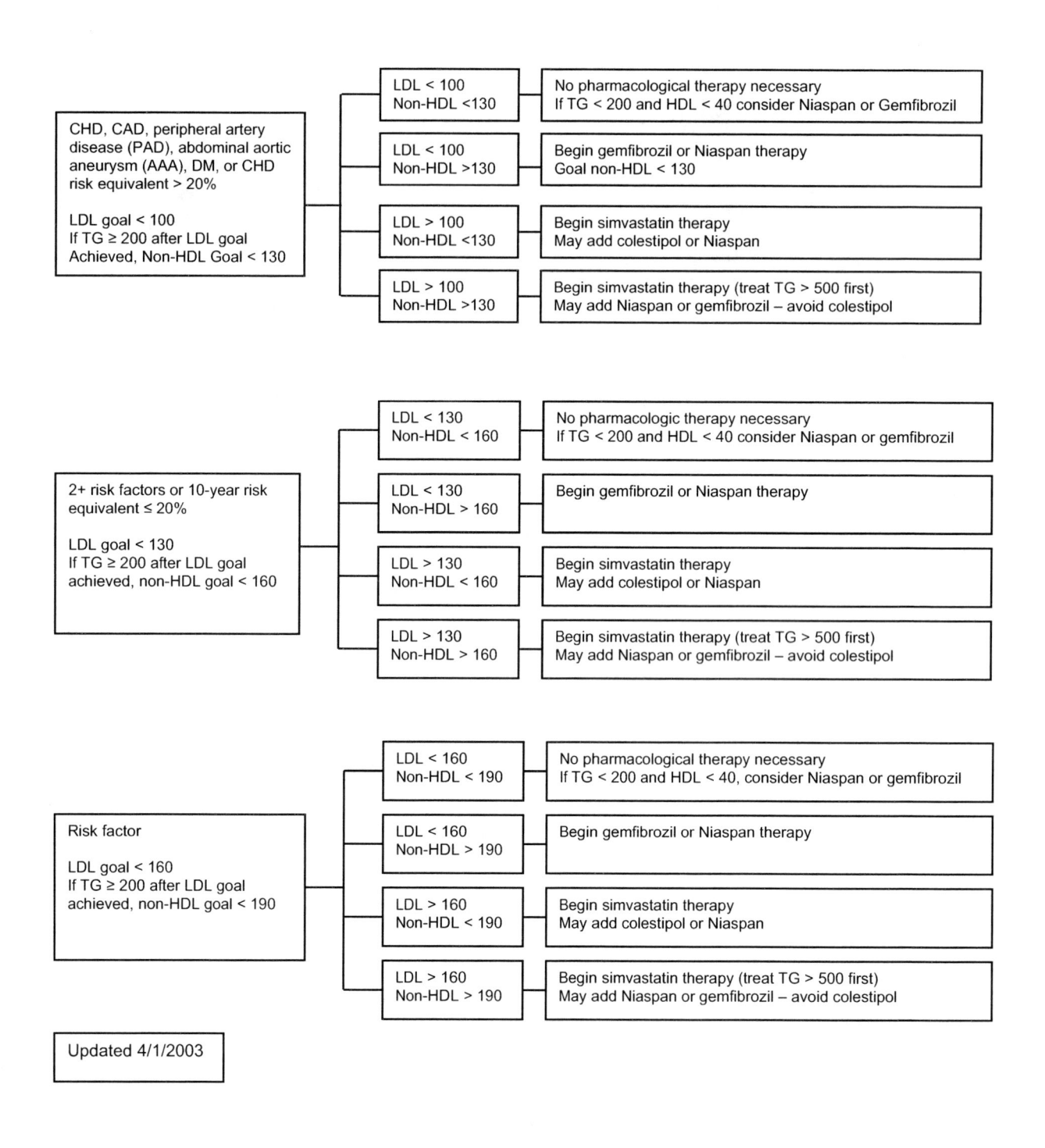

CHD, CAD, peripheral artery disease (PAD), abdominal aortic aneurysm (AAA), DM, or CHD risk equivalent > 20%

LDL goal < 100
If TG ≥ 200 after LDL goal Achieved, Non-HDL Goal < 130

- **LDL < 100 / Non-HDL <130** → No pharmacological therapy necessary. If TG < 200 and HDL < 40 consider Niaspan or Gemfibrozil
- **LDL < 100 / Non-HDL >130** → Begin gemfibrozil or Niaspan therapy. Goal non-HDL < 130
- **LDL > 100 / Non-HDL <130** → Begin simvastatin therapy. May add colestipol or Niaspan
- **LDL > 100 / Non-HDL >130** → Begin simvastatin therapy (treat TG > 500 first). May add Niaspan or gemfibrozil – avoid colestipol

2+ risk factors or 10-year risk equivalent ≤ 20%

LDL goal < 130
If TG ≥ 200 after LDL goal achieved, non-HDL goal < 160

- **LDL < 130 / Non-HDL < 160** → No pharmacologic therapy necessary. If TG < 200 and HDL < 40 consider Niaspan or gemfibrozil
- **LDL < 130 / Non-HDL > 160** → Begin gemfibrozil or Niaspan therapy
- **LDL > 130 / Non-HDL < 160** → Begin simvastatin therapy. May add colestipol or Niaspan
- **LDL > 130 / Non-HDL > 160** → Begin simvastatin therapy (treat TG > 500 first). May add Niaspan or gemfibrozil – avoid colestipol

Risk factor

LDL goal < 160
If TG ≥ 200 after LDL goal achieved, non-HDL goal < 190

- **LDL < 160 / Non-HDL < 190** → No pharmacological therapy necessary. If TG < 200 and HDL < 40, consider Niaspan or gemfibrozil
- **LDL < 160 / Non-HDL > 190** → Begin gemfibrozil or Niaspan therapy
- **LDL > 160 / Non-HDL < 190** → Begin simvastatin therapy. May add colestipol or Niaspan
- **LDL > 160 / Non-HDL > 190** → Begin simvastatin therapy (treat TG > 500 first). May add Niaspan or gemfibrozil – avoid colestipol

Updated 4/1/2003

TG = triglycerides.

Sample HTN Algorithm for Comorbid Conditions

Please consult Drug information, contraindications and specific JNC V guideline criteria prior to initiating HTN therapy. Also be sure to allow a trial of lifestyle modification prior to initiating antihypertensive therapy when appropriate

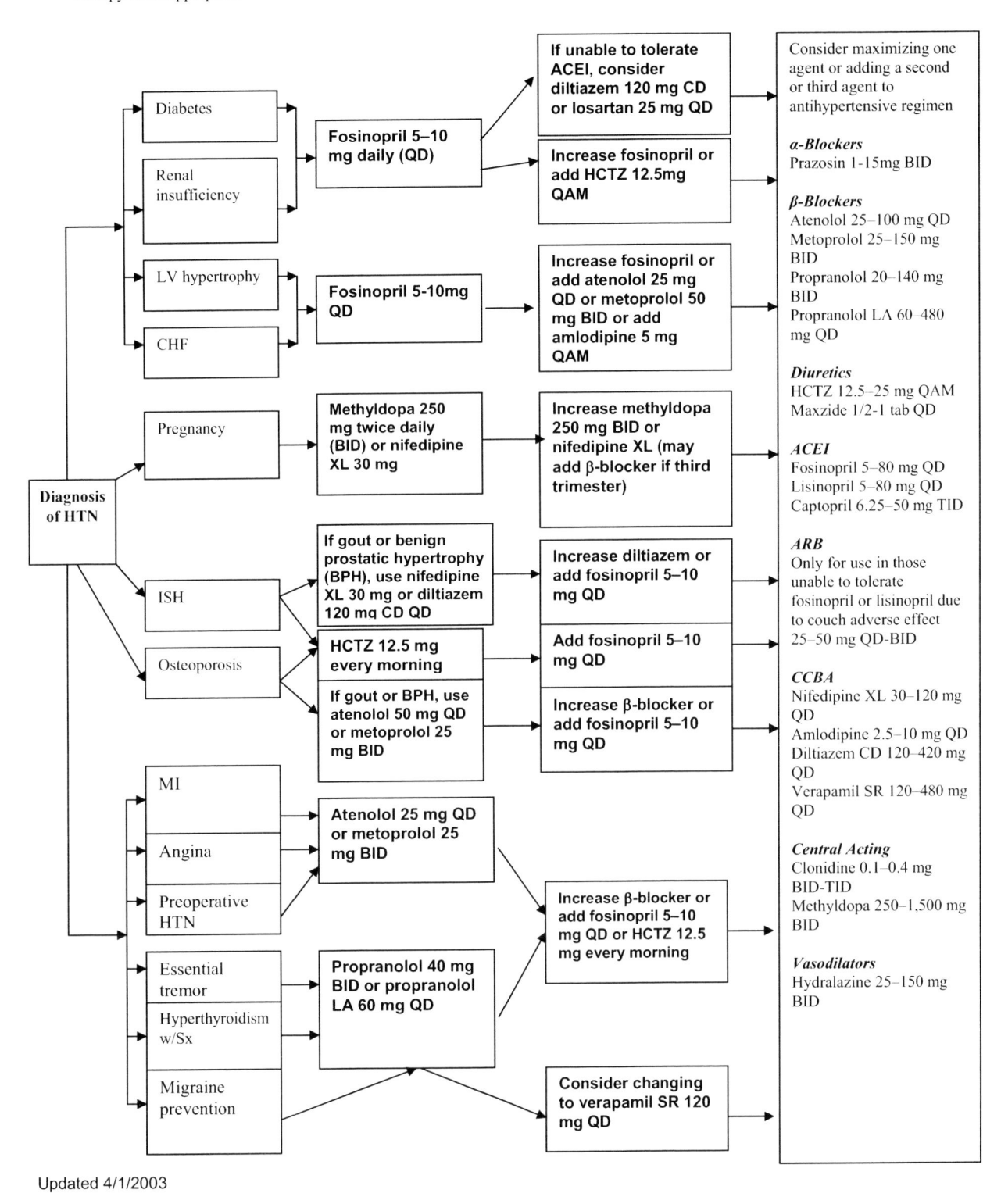

Diagnosis of HTN

- **Diabetes / Renal insufficiency** → Fosinopril 5–10 mg daily (QD)
  - → If unable to tolerate ACEI, consider diltiazem 120 mg CD or losartan 25 mg QD
  - → Increase fosinopril or add HCTZ 12.5mg QAM

- **LV hypertrophy / CHF** → Fosinopril 5-10mg QD
  - → Increase fosinopril or add atenolol 25 mg QD or metoprolol 50 mg BID or add amlodipine 5 mg QAM

- **Pregnancy** → Methyldopa 250 mg twice daily (BID) or nifedipine XL 30 mg
  - → Increase methyldopa 250 mg BID or nifedipine XL (may add β-blocker if third trimester)

- **ISH** → If gout or benign prostatic hypertrophy (BPH), use nifedipine XL 30 mg or diltiazem 120 mg CD QD
  - → Increase diltiazem or add fosinopril 5–10 mg QD

- **Osteoporosis** → HCTZ 12.5 mg every morning
  - → Add fosinopril 5–10 mg QD
  - If gout or BPH, use atenolol 50 mg QD or metoprolol 25 mg BID
  - → Increase β-blocker or add fosinopril 5–10 mg QD

- **MI / Angina / Preoperative HTN** → Atenolol 25 mg QD or metoprolol 25 mg BID
  - → Increase β-blocker or add fosinopril 5–10 mg QD or HCTZ 12.5 mg every morning

- **Essential tremor / Hyperthyroidism w/Sx** → Propranolol 40 mg BID or propranolol LA 60 mg QD

- **Migraine prevention** → Consider changing to verapamil SR 120 mg QD

Consider maximizing one agent or adding a second or third agent to antihypertensive regimen

α-Blockers
Prazosin 1-15mg BID

β-Blockers
Atenolol 25–100 mg QD
Metoprolol 25–150 mg BID
Propranolol 20–140 mg BID
Propranolol LA 60–480 mg QD

Diuretics
HCTZ 12.5–25 mg QAM
Maxzide 1/2-1 tab QD

ACEI
Fosinopril 5–80 mg QD
Lisinopril 5–80 mg QD
Captopril 6.25–50 mg TID

ARB
Only for use in those unable to tolerate fosinopril or lisinopril due to couch adverse effect
25–50 mg QD-BID

CCBA
Nifedipine XL 30–120 mg QD
Amlodipine 2.5–10 mg QD
Diltiazem CD 120–420 mg QD
Verapamil SR 120–480 mg QD

Central Acting
Clonidine 0.1–0.4 mg BID-TID
Methyldopa 250–1,500 mg BID

Vasodilators
Hydralazine 25–150 mg BID

Updated 4/1/2003

HEART FAILURE CLINIC

Submitted by: Allen Shek

Updated: November 2002

Background

CHF is the most common diagnosis-related group for admission both nationally and at SJGH. In a small retrospective admission census analysis (n=1,260) from January 1, 1999, to March 31, 1999, CHF comprised 12% of all inpatient medical admissions at SJGH.

Goals of Heart Failure Clinic (HFC)

1. To retard the progression of HF and improve the quality of care and quality of life for patients with CHF
2. To reduce readmission rates and use of unscheduled clinic and emergency department visits because of CHF exacerbation
3. To facilitate an effective transition of CHF patients from the Cardiology Clinic back to their PCP by providing an interim period of close monitoring, follow-up, and patient education

Scope of HFC

The main purpose of the HFC is to optimize the management of CHF and maintain enrolled patients at their optimal functional status. The HFC is meant to complement rather than replace the care provided by the patient's PCP and to ease the patient load on the SJGH Cardiology Clinic. However, management of several risk factors is an integral part of CHF management and thus cannot be overlooked; they include HTN, hyperlipidemia, smoking cessation, and weight management. The HFC is also designed to optimize the management of the above risk factors as much as possible. For any other primary care issues, patients will be referred back to their PCP.

Circumstances under which the nurse practitioner or clinical pharmacist, hereafter referred to as the "clinician," may perform these functions:

Setting

HFC

Staffing

The clinic will be staffed by a licensed nurse practitioner and a clinical pharmacist. Care may also be provided by Pharm.D. students under the direct supervision of the clinician.

Clinical Privileges

The clinicians may authorize refills for routine drugs in conjunction with the next physician visit. Drug doses for CHF, HTN, and hyperlipidemia will be adjusted and optimized according to guidelines in the Management Protocol section. Specific laboratory tests, including BMP, HgA1c, thyroid function tests, lipid profile, LFTs, and albumin, may be ordered as part of the monitoring.

The clinical pharmacist may not work in the HFC until such privileges have been approved in writing by the Director of Pharmacies.

Supervision

Dr. Ramesh Dharawat, Medical Director of the HFC, will be available for consultation. Dr. Kapre or Dr. Ali will be consulted if Dr. Dharawat is not available.

Patient Inclusion

Before patients are enrolled in the HFC, the following criteria must be met:

1. Patient must have a PCP.
2. Patient must have a diagnosis of nonreversible CHF or dilated cardiomyopathy (DCM) clearly documented in his or her medical record.
3. Patient must have had an echocardiogram performed with an estimated EF within the past twelve months.

The HFC case manager will work closely with the staff in both the inpatient and ambulatory clinic areas to coordinate referral of high-risk patients and ensure continuity of care. Other CHF patients already seen by the Cardiology Clinic, Family Practice, or Internal Medicine Clinic may be referred by their PCP to the HFC for closer follow-up and intense patient education.

Patient Exclusion

Any patient who fails to show up for three or more visits will be referred back to the PCP for follow-up. This will be documented in the patient's medical record.

Development and Approval

Procedures are to be reviewed annually by the nurse practitioner and clinical pharmacist in the HFC team at SJGH and consulting physicians, with direction from the chiefs of Medicine and Cardiology Sections at SJGH. Written changes are to be submitted for approval to the Pharmacy and Therapeutics Committee.

Clinic Flow

At the initial visit, the clinician shall interview the patient and review the medical record to determine:
1. Medical history, cardiovascular risk factors, family history, SH, and allergies
2. History of CHF, etiology of CHF, and last hospitalization secondary to CHF exacerbation
3. Results of last echocardiogram and EKG performed
4. Immunization record for pneumococcal and influenza vaccines

At each visit, the clinician:
1. Assesses the vital signs, pulse oximetry, and blood glucose reading
2. Assesses patient's current weight to establish target weight and evaluate changes. Target weight is defined as the weight at which the patient is at his/her best clinical status.
3. Performs physical examination to assess signs of fluid overload
4. Interviews the patient to assess the presence and severity of fluid retention as well as the S/Sx of CHF exacerbation. Dr. Dharawat or the PCP will be consulted if the patient shows signs of clinical deterioration or is in acute respiratory distress.
5. Determines functional capacity by the distance the patient can walk within two minutes
6. Determine NYHA functional classification (Appendix A)
7. Records the last EKG and/or treadmill test results, if available
8. Reviews and evaluates the most recent laboratory tests for Na, K, BUN, Cr, HgA1c, TSH, T4 free, T3 free, lipid profile, LFT, albumin, and other tests when appropriate
9. Reviews complete drug list, including prescription, OTC, and herbal supplements
10. Assesses drug and diet compliance and adherence
11. Assesses the occurrence of any adverse reactions
12. Assesses the need for dosage or drug adjustment or modification according to the guidelines in the management protocol section
13. Provides patient counseling on diet and lifestyle modification, if necessary, and assesses the need for referral to another specialty clinic or program for optimal management of DM, smoking cessation, and weight management. Every patient will be encouraged to engage in moderate degrees of exercise, as tolerated, to prevent or reverse physical deconditioning. Every patient will be encouraged to attend a two-session weight reduction class offered by the Dietary Department. Patients will be encouraged to measure and record body weight daily at home.
14. Sets up follow-up appointment in three months or sooner depending on patient's stability
15. Completes documentation in the HFC demographic form (Appendix B) and visit note (Appendix C). Original copy of the visit note will be filed in the patient's medical record, and a copy of the visit note and the demographic form will be maintained in the patient's shadow chart, which will be kept confidential in the HFC.

Telemanagement

After the initial visit, patients will be followed up by telephone by the clinician in two days to assess understanding and compliance; then every two weeks for the first month; then every four to six weeks based on patient's clinical status.

During each telemanagement session, the clinician:
1. Obtains daily weight from the patient and adjusts target weight if necessary
2. Interviews the patient to assess compliance
3. Assesses the presence and severity of fluid retention as well as the signs and symptoms of decompensation
4. Adjusts diuretic therapy at the earliest sign of decompensation (e.g., weight increase of 2–3 pounds from target weight). Urgent situations will be reported to Dr. Dharawat or the attending physician on call.
5. Sets up next telemanagement session or early clinic visit with patient
6. Documents action taken in progress notes and HFC Follow-up Log (Appendix D). The progress note will be forwarded to the patient's medical record, and a copy will be kept in the patient's shadow chart.

Triage

Patients will be given telephone numbers of the HFC and case manager for questions or concerns. Patient will be instructed to contact the HFC if he/she gains more than 3 pounds from the target weight. The case manager will then, in turn, triage the questions to either the nurse practitioner or the clinical pharmacist on duty or on call when appropriate. Urgent cases will be referred to the house staff on call.

Discharge

Patients who have been stable with their weight and clinical status for twelve months without an emergency department visit or the need for hospitalization will be considered for discharge from the HFC and monitored by their PCP.

Management Protocol

Primary Focus: CHF

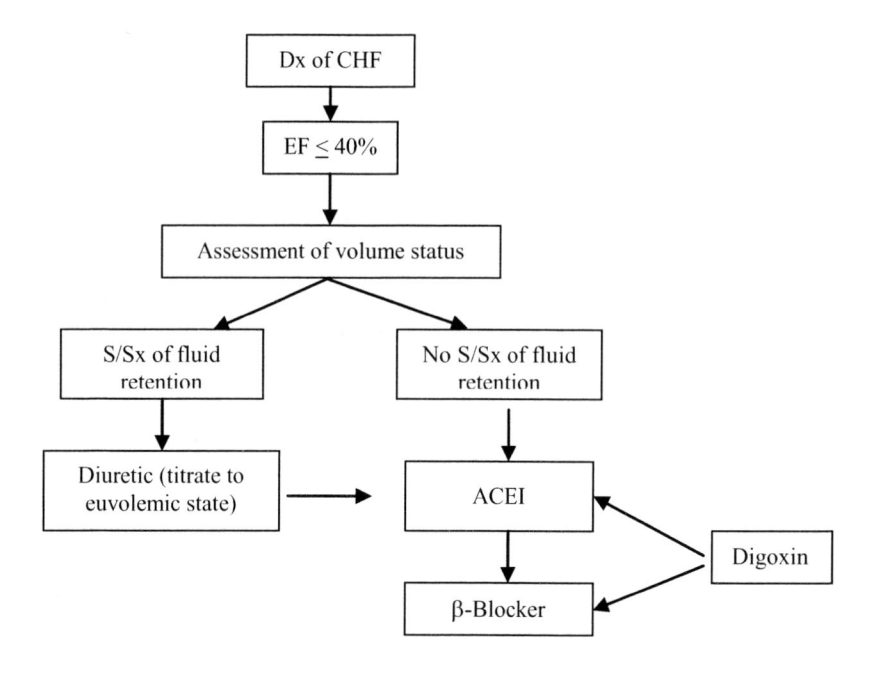

```
Dx of CHF
   ↓
EF ≤ 40%
   ↓
Assessment of volume status
   ↙            ↘
S/Sx of fluid    No S/Sx of fluid
retention        retention
   ↓                ↓
Diuretic (titrate → ACEI ← Digoxin
to euvolemic         ↓      ↗
state)            β-Blocker
```

Dx = diagnosis; S/Sx = signs and symptoms

Diuretics

Every effort should be made to optimize diuretic therapy to eliminate symptoms as well as physical signs of fluid retention, as assessed by jugular venous distension or peripheral edema, or both. Diuretics should not be used alone even if the symptoms of HF are well controlled, but they should generally be combined with an ACEI and a β-blocker. Moderate sodium restriction (3 g/day or less) should also be instituted. Low doses of potassium-sparing diuretics (e.g., spironolactone) may be more effective and better tolerated than potassium and/or magnesium supplements. *NSAIDs should be avoided in patients with HF.*

Diuretics	Initial Dosage	Incremental Dosage	Maximum Dosage	Comment
HCTZ	25 mg once daily	25 mg	200 mg/day	Usual maintenance dose = 25–100 mg/day. Ineffective when CrCl < 30 mL/minute
Metolazone	2.5 mg once daily	2.5 mg	20 mg/day	Effectiveness is maintained even when CrCl < 30 mL/minute.
Furosemide	20 mg once daily	20–40 mg	2–2.5 g/day (in divided doses)	
Spironolactone	25 mg once daily	25 mg	200 mg/day	Spironolactone 25 mg/day added to conventional therapy in patient with severe HF (Class IV) decreased mortality and hospitalization.

Laboratory monitoring for Na, K, Mg, BUN, and Cr should be performed two weeks after initiation or dosage adjustment and every six months thereafter to assess need for K or Mg supplements.

Contraindications
Anuria, hypersensitivity to these compounds

Precautions
Dehydration, hypotension, electrolyte imbalance (e.g., hypokalemia, hypomagnesemia, hypocalcemia), hyperuricemia, photosensitivity

ACEI

ACEIs are recommended to improve symptoms and clinical status and to decrease the risk of death and hospitalization in all patients with mild, moderate, and severe HF who have a left ventricular EF of less than 40%.

Contraindications

Patients who developed angioedema or anuric renal failure from prior exposure, with bilateral renal artery stenosis, and pregnant patients

Precautions

Hypotension (systolic BP < 80 mm Hg), marked increased SCr concentration (more than 3 mg/dL), elevated serum potassium concentration (more than 5.5 mmol/L). Treatment with ACEI should be initiated at very low doses, followed by gradual increments in dose based on patient's tolerance. In controlled clinical trials, the dose of the ACEI was not determined by a patient's therapeutic response but was increased until a large target dose was reached

Table 1: ACEIs Available at SJGH

ACEI	Initial Dosage	Target Dosage	Maximum Dosage
Lisinopril	5 mg QD	40 mg QD	80 mg QD
Benazepril[a]	5 mg daily	40 mg 2 times/day[b]	40 mg 2 times/day
Captopril	6.25–12.5 mg 3 times/day	50 mg 3 times/day	50 mg 3 times/day

[a]Benazepril has not been studied and does not have an FDA indication for use in CHF.
[b]Maximum dosage is set as target dosage because maximum dosage has not been studied.
BID = twice daily; QD = once daily; TID = three times daily

According to the most recent consensus recommendation, there are no differences among available ACEIs in their effects on symptoms, clinical status, mortality, or disease progression. Every effort should be made to increase dose of ACEIs to the target doses shown in clinical trials or to the highest tolerated level, to decrease morbidity and mortality. Laboratory monitoring for K, BUN, and Cr should be performed one to two weeks after initiation or adjustment and periodically thereafter.

β-Blockers

All patients with stable New York Hospital Association Class II and III HF caused by LV systolic dysfunction should receive β-blocker therapy to improve symptoms and clinical status and to decrease risk of death and hospitalization.

Contraindications

Bronchospastic disease, symptomatic bradycardia, or advanced heart block (unless treated with a permanent pacemaker) or patients who have acutely decompensated HF

Precautions

Asymptomatic bradycardia (pulse rate less than 60 beats/minute). As with ACEIs, the dose of β-blockers in controlled clinical trials was not determined by a patient's therapeutic response but was increased until the patient received a prespecified target dose. Most trials did not evaluate whether lower doses would be effective. Nevertheless, β-blockers should be initiated in very low doses, followed by gradual increments in dose (every two to four weeks) if lower doses have been well tolerated

β-Blockers	Initial Dosage	Incremental Dosage	Target Dosage
Atenolol	25 mg/day	Double every 2–4 weeks	100 mg twice daily
Carvedilol[a]	3.125 mg twice daily	Double every 2–4 weeks	25 mg twice daily for < 85 kg 50 mg twice daily for > 85 kg
Metoprolol XL	12.5–25 mg/day	Double every 2–4 weeks	200 mg/day

[a]If atenolol cannot be tolerated even at the lowest dose, carvedilol should be used as an alternate β-blocker.

Digoxin

Digoxin is recommended to improve the clinical status of patients with HF caused by LV systolic dysfunction and should be used in conjunction with diuretics, an ACEI, and a β-blocker. The drug appears to have no or little effect on survival.

Contraindications

Patients with significant sinus or atrioventricular block, unless patient has a permanent pacemaker

Precautions

Patients receiving other drugs that can depress sinus or atrioventricular nodal function (e.g., amiodarone or a β-blocker). Therapy with digoxin is commonly initiated and maintained at a dose of 0.25 mg every day. A lower dose of 0.125 mg daily or every other day may be appropriate, particularly in patients older than seventy years or in those with impaired renal function.

Laboratory monitoring for digoxin value, serum K, Mg, BUN, and Cr should be performed two weeks after initiation or adjustment and periodically thereafter unless digoxin toxicity is suspected. Vital signs should be monitored for bradycardia.

Hydralazine and Isosorbide Dinitrate

The combination of hydralazine and isosorbide dinitrate should not be substituted for ACEIs in patients who are tolerating ACEIs without difficulty. Despite the lack of data with vasodilator combinations in patients who are intolerant of ACEIs, the combined use of hydralazine and isosorbide dinitrate should be considered a therapeutic option in such patients, particularly in those who cannot take an ACEI because of angioedema or severe renal insufficiency.

Angiotensin II Receptor Blockers (ARBs)

According to the most recent consensus recommendation, there is no persuasive evidence that ARBs are equivalent or superior to ACEIs in the treatment of CHF. Therefore, ARBs should not be substituted for ACEIs in patients who are tolerating ACEIs without difficulty. However, despite the lack of conclusive evidence supporting the efficacy of these drugs in HF, it is reasonable to substitute an ACEI with an ARB in patients who are intolerant to ACEIs because of angioedema or intractable cough.

Secondary Focus

HTN

Target BP is 120/80 mm Hg or lower, if tolerated, because it is considered optimal for cardiovascular risk. When adjusting diuretics, ACEI, and β-blocker, optimal BP control will be targeted in addition to aiming for symptom control and target dosage. If BP control cannot be optimized with the above agents, the patient's PCP will be consulted for further management.

Hyperlipidemia

Management of hyperlipidemia will be according to the Clinical Protocol for the Ambulatory Care Dyslipidemia Management Clinic.

Reference

1. Consensus Recommendations for the management of chronic heart failure. On behalf of the membership of the Advisory Council to Improve Outcomes Nationwide in Heart Failure. Am J Cardiol 1999;83:1A–38A.

Appendix A—New York Heart Association (NYHA) CHF Classification

Class I	Patients with cardiac disease but without resulting limitation of physical activity. Ordinary physical activity does not cause undue fatigue, palpitation, dyspnea, or anginal pain.
Class II	Patients with cardiac disease resulting in slight limitation of physical activity. They are comfortable at rest. Ordinary physical activity results in fatigue, palpitation, dyspnea, or anginal pain.
Class III	Patients with cardiac disease resulting in marked limitation of physical activity. They are comfortable at rest. Less than ordinary activity causes fatigue, palpitation, dyspnea, or anginal pain.
Class IV	Patients with cardiac disease resulting in inability to carry on any physical activity without discomfort. Symptoms of heart failure or the anginal syndrome may be present even at rest. If any physical activity is undertaken, discomfort is increased.

Reprinted with Permission. www.americanheart.org. ©2007, American Heart Association, Inc.

Reference

1. Konstam M, Dracup K, Baker D, et al. Clinical Practice Guideline 11: Heart failure: Evaluation and care of patients with left-ventricular systolic dysfunction. Rockville, MD: U.S. Department of Health and Human Services, Agency for Health Care Policy and Research, 1994. AHCPR Publication 94-0612.

Appendix B

San Joaquin General Hospital

Heart Failure Clinic (HFC)

Name:_____ DOB:_____ PCP:_____

Street Address:_____ Phone:_____ Date:_____

City/State:_____

PMH:_____
_____

Family History: _____
_____

Social History: Tobacco:_____ EtOH: _____ Illicit Drug:_____

Allergies:_____

CHF <u>diagnosed</u> since:_____

Pneumonvax® given on: _____
_____

Flu Shot last given on: _____
_____ Last Hospitalization on:
_____
_____ _____
_____ _____

	Etiology
☐	Idiopathic
☐	Alcoholic
☐	S/P MI
☐	HTN
☐	Valvular heart disease
☐	Others:

Echo last done on: _____ LVEF: _____%	EKG last done on:_____
Echo last done on: _____ LVEF: _____%	EKG last done on:_____
Echo last done on: _____ LVEF: _____%	EKG last done on:_____
Echo last done on: _____ LVEF: _____%	EKG last done on:_____
Echo last done on: _____ LVEF: _____%	EKG last done on:_____
Echo last done on: _____ LVEF: _____%	EKG last done on:_____
Echo last done on: _____ LVEF: _____%	EKG last done on:_____
Echo last done on: _____ LVEF: _____%	EKG last done on:_____
Echo last done on: _____ LVEF: _____%	EKG last done on:_____

Last Updated On	Initial

Appendix C

San Joaquin General Hospital

Heart Failure Clinic (HFC) Visit Note

Date of visit:_____ Phone:_____

Patient's Medical History:_____
_____
_____

Allergies:_____

Patient's overall assessment: Better   Same   Worse

Tobacco:_____ EtOH:_____

Complaints:_____
_____
_____

BP: _____/_____   HR: _____ Wt: _____ lb

O_2 Sat: _____ % BS: _____ mg/dL

Pulmonary Exam		
Pulmonary edema (PE)	Yes	No
JVD	Yes	No
S3	Yes	No

Symptoms		
Dyspnea on exertion	Yes	No
Orthopnea	Yes	No
Paroxysmal nocturnal dyspnea	Yes	No
Number of pillows:		

Functional Status:
Walked _____ ft in 2 min
NYHA Class: I II III IV

EKG:
Treadmill:

Date	Labs	Value
	Na+	
	K+	
	BUN	
	Cr	
	HgA1c	
	TSH	
	T4 free	
	T3 free	
	T-CHL	
	TG	
	HDL	
	LDL	
	AST	
	ALT	
	Albumin	

Drugs:

Diuretics:_____
_____

ACEI: _____

β-Blocker: _____

Antiplatelet: _____

Others: _____
_____
_____
_____
_____
_____

Appendix D

San Joaquin General Hospital

Heart Failure Clinic Follow-up Log

Phone:_____

Date	Phone F/U	Clinic Visit	Wt (lb)	Target Wt (lb)	Symptoms Stable		Compliance with Meds		Action/Comment	Next F/U
	☐	☐			Y	N	Y	N		
	☐	☐			Y	N	Y	N		
	☐	☐			Y	N	Y	N		
	☐	☐			Y	N	Y	N		
	☐	☐			Y	N	Y	N		
	☐	☐			Y	N	Y	N		
	☐	☐			Y	N	Y	N		
	☐	☐			Y	N	Y	N		
	☐	☐			Y	N	Y	N		
	☐	☐			Y	N	Y	N		
	☐	☐			Y	N	Y	N		
	☐	☐			Y	N	Y	N		
	☐	☐			Y	N	Y	N		
	☐	☐			Y	N	Y	N		

F/U = follow up

AMBULATORY BLOOD PRESSURE MONITORING REFERRAL SERVICE

Submitted by: Michael Ernst

Created: January 2001

Background

The Ambulatory Blood Pressure Monitoring (ABPM) referral service of the Family Care Center at the University of Iowa Hospitals and Clinics processes about one hundred referrals annually from both the Family Medicine and Internal Medicine outpatient clinics. The service was initiated in January 2000 and is codirected by a clinical pharmacist and a physician. The service is designed to both help optimize the evaluation and care of hypertensive (or suspected hypertensive) patients and provide a teaching opportunity for the medical residents of the Family Medicine and Internal Medicine clinics.

Equipment

- SpaceLabs 90217—An ultralite ambulatory BP monitor (SpaceLabs Medical, Inc.; Redmond, WA) (*www.spacelabsmedical.com*)
- Extra-large, large, regular, small BP cuffs
- Spacelabs ABP Report Management System software, version 2.00
- Sphygmomanometer
- Stethoscope

Typical Indications For Referral[a]

1. Suspected white-coat HTN
2. Evaluation of response to antihypertensive therapy/treatment resistance
3. Discrepant office/home BP readings
4. BP lability
5. Suspected hypotension

[a]*Home BPs or other out-of-office BPs are encouraged before proceeding to ABPM.*

Procedures

1. Physician fills out a consult to the service. Consult is evaluated by clinical pharmacist for appropriateness (home BP monitoring or other out-of-office BPs is encouraged first).
2. Pharmacist contacts patient to schedule visit.
3. Current drugs, including antihypertensive regimen (if applicable) are reviewed at the patient visit.
4. Monitor is programmed to record BP every 20 minutes during daytime hours (0600–1800) and every 30 minutes for nighttime hours (1800–0600).
5. Patient is instructed regarding the ABPM session and fitted with a monitor. Patient is sent with an information sheet and activity log.
6. Patient returns monitor and activity log the next day.
7. Monitor is downloaded and processed by the clinical pharmacist.
8. Clinical pharmacist documents results of ABPM session in clinical note (see sample below) with M.D. codirector as cosigner.
9. Clinical pharmacist discusses results of the session directly with the ordering physician, and makes verbal recommendations for adjustment of therapy (if applicable).

Information Obtained from ABPM

1. 24-hour mean, maximum/minimum BP, HR
2. Daytime, nighttime mean, maximum/minimum BP, HR
3. BP load
4. Dipping status
5. Individual BP readings

Billing

1. CPT 93790 (Ambulatory BP Monitor 24hr Interpretation and Report)
2. CPT 93786 (Ambulatory BP Monitor 24 hr)

References

1. Ernst ME, Bergus GR. Patient satisfaction with ambulatory blood pressure monitoring in a primary care setting in the United States: a cross-sectional survey. BMC Fam Pract 2003;4:15.
2. Ernst ME, Bergus GR. Non-invasive, 24-hour ambulatory blood pressure monitoring: Overview of technology and clinical applications. Pharmacotherapy 2002;22:597–612.
3. Ernst ME, Bergus GR. Ambulatory blood pressure monitoring. South Med J 2003;96:563–8.
4. Ernst ME, Bergus GR. Ambulatory blood pressure monitoring: technology with a purpose. Am Fam Physician 2003;67:2262–70.

B-lb 24 Hour Ambulatory Blood Pressure Monitoring (Copy - Discard Confidentially) - Final

Outpatient Visit	Date of Service 02/17/2006 Visit #608
FCC - Im Faculty	Hospital #
Page 1 of I	Name
File most recent, confidentiaHy discard previous versions of the same visit	Birth Date/Age/Sex 60 YRs F
(print date/ume 3/2/063 10PM)	IDX# OCLIN

HISTORY OF PRESENT ILLNESS
Ms. _____ is a 60-year-old female with hypertension under uncertain control. She is currently treated with ramipril 10 mg/d. She was referred for further evaluation of her BP profile via 24hr ambulatory BP monitoring, which she underwent 2/27/06-2/28/06. - MEE

TECHNICAL COMMENTS Total scan time = 23 hrs, 20 mm. 52 successful readings obtained (90% of total attempted). - MEE

SUMMARY OF RESULTS
24hr mean BP = 127/71 mmHg
Daytime hrs (0600–2200) mean BP = 137/77 mmHg
Nighttime hrs (2200–0600) mean BP = 107/59 mmiHg
24hr mean heart rate (range) = 86 bpm (65–118)

During the daytime hrs (0600–2200), 56.8% of SBP readings were above period limits (>135 mmHg) and 10.8% of DBP readings were above period limits (>85 mmHg).

During the nighttime hrs (2200–0600), 20.0% of SBP readings were above period limits (>120 mmHg) and 0% of DBP readings were above period limits (>80 mmHg).

Further breakdown of 24hr SBP profile is as follows:

Time (hrs)	%SBP>120	%SBP>135	%SBP>140	%SBP>160
0800–1600	84.2	47.4	42.1	5.3
1600–2400	93.8	50.0	31.3	0
2400–0800	23.5	23.5	23.5	11.8

Further breakdown of 24hr DI3P profile is as follows:

Time (hrs)	%DBP>80	%DBP>85	%DBP>90	%DBP>100
0800–1600	15.8	0	0	0
1600–2400	37.5	18.8	6.3	0
2400–0800	23.5	5.9	5.9	0

Overall, during the entire testing period, 46.2% of SBP readings were above period limits (>135 mmllg daytime; >120 mmI-Ig nighttime). 7.7% of DBP readings were above period limits (>85 mmflg daytime; >80 mmHg nighttime). - MEE

UNSTRUCTURED DOCUMENTATION
Results relayed to patient by phone 3/2/06 at 1237pm. - SJW

REVIEWERS/CONTRIBUTORS
Final Reviewer: _____ MD /Electronically Signed 03/02/2006
Initial Reviewer: MEE/Michael Ernst, Pharm D, Staff/Electronically Signed 03/02/2006

Document #0005-94-0244 Dictated/Initiated 03102/2006 11:37

UNIVERSITY OF IOWA HOSPITALS AND CLINICS

HYPERTENSION CLINIC

Submitted by: Sara Klockars and Melissa Rice

Created: 2004

Purpose

To offer a convenient, less expensive, multidisciplinary, high-flow group clinic for the management of patients with HTN according to national guidelines (Kaiser Permanente Colorado [KPCO] and JNC-VII.

Target Population

Inclusion

- Age 18 or older
- HTN diagnosis
- BP more than 130/80 mm Hg with chronic kidney disease or DM
- BP more than 140/90 mm Hg all others
- Patient prefers group clinic (with other patients)

Exclusion

- Clinically unstable patients
- Patient prefers to see PCP
- Patient requires work-up for secondary causes of HTN

Referral Procedure/Scheduling

Who can refer?

- Physicians
- Midlevel providers (Nurse Practitioners and Physician Assistants)
- Nursing staff by refill protocol
- Clinical Pharmacy Specialists
- Other health care providers

How do you refer?

- Book directly into HTN clinic schedule
- Send referral in EMR to "HTN clinic booking," and staff will outreach to schedule an appointment

Schedule

- Maximum of 25 patients per 2-hour period

Location

Information Shared When Appointment Scheduled

- Group co-pay (usually less expensive than regular office visit)
- Visits take about 15 to 20 minutes; need to arrive on time
- Bring list of all drugs (including OTC and natural products) for review.
- Bring list of home BP readings.
- Bring home BP machine.
- HTN clinic is for evaluation and treatment of HTN only. If patient desires a complete examination or has other concerns that need to be evaluated, a separate appointment must be scheduled with the PCP.
- Seen individually by clinical pharmacy specialist, midlevel, or physician
- Registered nurse (RN) available to provide education on nutrition, home BP monitoring, smoking cessation, etc.

HTN Clinic Procedures

Staffing

- Physician
- Midlevel
- Clinical Pharmacy Specialist
- Registered Nurse
- Medical Assistant (MA) or Licensed Practical Nurse (LPN)

Clinic operation

- Patients will register at front desk, obtain check-in slip, and follow signs to Hidden Falls Group Clinic Room.
- Patient takes a seat in reception area and rests for at least five minutes.

MA/LPN duties

- Setup
  - Begin setup for clinic thirty minutes before first scheduled patient (put out signs, etc.)
  - Print a copy of the HTN clinic schedule for each station
- Check-in
  - Start checking in patients at least 15 to 20 minutes before the start of the HTN clinic to avoid a backup of patients at the beginning of clinic.

- Bring patients to MA/LPN station (after they have rested for at least 5 minutes).
    - BP in right and left arm of each patient, heart rate
    - Height, weight, and BMI calculation (only if patient has <u>never</u> visited the HTN clinic before)
    - Ask about tobacco history and document.
    - Please record BP at time of measurement to ensure BP is in chart when patient is seen by provider.
- Pull up patient's chart in EMR from HTN clinic schedule, open group visit note, and start documentation in nursing notes.
- Direct patient to the nurse education station in the middle of the room. The check-in sheets will be called by physician, midlevel, or clinical pharmacy specialist (providers).
- Patient flow
    - Watch the waiting area and nurse education station areas to ensure that patients aren't being overlooked or skipped.
        - Everyone in the nurse education area should already have been checked in, with the exception of family members that may have come with the patients.
- Cleanup
    - Place all signs and materials in their appropriate storage areas.
        - Keep the schedule to mail "missed appointment" letters to the no-show patients.

RN education duties

- Equipment setup
    - Literature/supplies
    - BP cuffs and portable mercury sphygmomanometer from Primary Care Procedure room A (small, medium, and large cuffs)
- Duties
    - Initial 15 to 30 minutes assist MA or LPN with check-in of the first three to six patients
    - Instruct members either before or after seeing physician, Nurse Practitioner, or Clinical Pharmacy Specialist for visit, on proper use of home BP monitor. Also, check home BP monitors for accuracy as needed.
    - Discuss and answer questions from members regarding contents of regional handout titled "High Blood Pressure: Your Steps Toward Control."
    - Discuss diet and exercise with the patient (handouts and visual aids on diet, exercise, the DASH diet available).
    - Discuss smoking cessation and tools available to assist.
    - Regional class information on diet, cholesterol, and tobacco cessation can also be shared with the patient through the Rocky Mountain Health Quarterly.
    - Document education in Nursing Notes portion of EMR.

Physician, Midlevel Practitioner, and Clinical Pharmacy Specialist Duties

- Providers will obtain patients from the nurse education station.
- Open Encounter note in medical record already started by MA/LPN and/or RN and insert documentation tool "Hypertension Clinic Colorado"
- Providers will review
    - Clinic BP
    - Home BP readings
    - Current drugs and compliance
    - Past drugs, adverse reactions, and allergies
    - Risk factors (family history, tobacco use, etc.) and other disease states
    - Clinical Pharmacy Specialists can enroll patients in Collaborative Drug Therapy Management HTN protocol and/or can consult with prescriber in clinic.
    - Drugs will be adjusted, and laboratory tests will be ordered (for Clinical Pharmacy Specialists, according to CDTM protocol or verbal order).
    - KPCO and JNC-VII guidelines will be followed.
    - Follow-up plan will be communicated to patient verbally and written on an after visit summary (to be printed and given to patient) and will include:
        - BP in clinic today
        - BP goal (and if it has or has not been reached)
        - Drug changes
        - Lifestyle recommendations (e.g., exercise plan, smoking cessation information)
        - Laboratory follow-up
        - Follow-up appointment information
    - If follow-up HTN clinic appointment is needed, patient can be scheduled directly into HTN clinic schedule or provider can send referral in EMR to "HTN clinic booking," and staff will outreach to schedule an appointment.
    - Physician and/or midlevel will review, cosign, ensure all encounters are coded accurately, and close all EMR encounters.

ADULT HYPERTENSION PROTOCOL

Submitted by: Andrea Wessell

Created: May 2005

Purpose

To establish guidelines for the monitoring of antihypertensive therapy in adult patients and to clearly define the roles/responsibilities of the physicians and collaborating pharmacists. The purpose of the service is to provide continuity of care to patients who require antihypertensive therapy, enhance patient care through education, monitoring, and close follow-up, and reduce adverse events associated with antihypertensive therapy.

Provider Qualifications

A pharmacist providing antihypertensive drug therapy management must be credentialed by the Department of Pharmacy Services and meet minimal competencies required for their practice area. In addition, until credentialing is obtained, the pharmacist or pharmacy student will work under the direct supervision of the credentialed pharmacist. The physicians must be MUSC-credentialed physicians and have a signed CDTM agreement for anticoagulation management with the credentialed pharmacist.

Procedure

Referral

The referring physician will provide the clinic with the following: goals for patient referral, present antihypertensive drugs, a list of other comorbid disease states, and other pertinent information including prior diagnostic studies and laboratory parameters listed in Appendix A, Table 4.

Clinic Visits

Procedure

The patient will follow the general policies and procedures regarding registration. If laboratory work is necessary, the patient will report to the laboratory. The patient will meet with the pharmacist after the laboratory work has been drawn. (See Appendix A, Table 4 for recommended laboratory monitoring).

- During the first visit, the following topics will be addressed
  - Medical history, surgical history, social history, and family history
  - Current drugs (prescription and nonprescription)
  - HTN education
  - Pathophysiology of disease state
  - Complications of HTN
  - Goals of therapy (see Appendix A, Tables 1 and 2)
  - Lifestyle modifications (see Appendix A, Table 3)
  - Antihypertensive drugs (see Appendix B)
- During follow-up visits, the following topics will be addressed
  - Compliance with therapy (drugs, diet, exercise)
  - Efficacy of therapy and need for adjustment
  - HTN education reinforcement
- Follow-up visits will be scheduled at 2 weeks to 6 months depending on patients' responses to and adherence with treatment.

Physical Assessment

- The pharmacist may perform or review the following physical assessments on each visit
  - Visual inspection (i.e., peripheral edema)
  - Weight
  - Vital signs (BP and pulse rate)

Drug Management

- The pharmacist is authorized to initiate, modify, or discontinue the following drugs (Appendix A, Tables 5 and 6, Appendix B)
  - Diuretics
  - β-Blockers
  - ACEIs
  - ARBs
  - Calcium channel blockers
  - $α_1$-blockers
  - Vasodilators
  - Central $α_2$-agonists
  - ASA
- The pharmacist will contact the referring physician on the initiation of the above drugs or if a drug requires discontinuation. *All orders will be written according to CDTM HTN Protocol and signed by the credentialed pharmacist.*
- The pharmacist will provide drug education when a new drug is initiated and at follow-up visits.
- The pharmacist will refer the patient to their physician for drug refills, unless prior arrangements have been made and are documented on the referral form.

Drug Administration

- This protocol does not authorize the pharmacist to administer any drug.
- Laboratory monitoring

- According to patient-specific factors and other recent laboratory values, the pharmacist is authorized to order the following laboratory tests when clinically warranted
  - Comprehensive metabolic panel
  - Urinalysis
  - Microalbumin-creatinine ratio
  - Uric acid
- Perform Point-of-Care testing
  - Not applicable for this protocol
- Participation in/coordination of clinical research
  - Not applicable for this protocol

Patient Referral

The pharmacist may refer patients to a registered dietician for more in-depth medical nutrition therapy. The pharmacist will refer patients to the emergency department or referring physician, as clinically indicated, or for BP less than 90/60 mm Hg or more than 160/100 mm Hg or for pulse rate less than 55 beats/minute or more than 120 beats/minute.

- Documentation
  - All patient encounters will be documented in the EMR using the clinical pharmacy note templates. All notes will be sent to the referring provider by the EMR or Oacis system.
- Billing for services
  - Patients will be billed for services in accordance with the MUSC Department of Pharmacy Services Ambulatory Care Billing Policy (B06)
  - All other procedures will be performed according to the general policies and procedures of the clinic.
- Clinic Discharge
  - Patients will be discharged from the clinic when they have achieved the goals set by the referring physician or when they decide no longer to receive care. Also, the pharmacist, in conjunction with the referring physician, may decide to discharge the patient from the services of the clinic.

Quality Assurance/Outcomes

Data will be continuously monitored to ensure that patients are receiving optimal care. Outcomes of HTN management will include, but not be limited to, the percentage of patients at goal BP and the change in BP from initial referral. These results will be presented as requested to the appropriate pharmacy coordinator and manager.

References

1. Chobanian AV, Bakris GL, Black HR, et al. The Seventh Report of the Joint National Committee on the Prevention, Detection, Evaluation, and Treatment of Hypertension (JNC VII). Hypertension 2003;42:1206–52.
2. National Heart, Lung and Blood Institute, JNC VII Express. Available at http://www.nhlbi.nih.gov/guidelines/hypertension/express.pdf. Accessed May 20, 2008.
3. Klasco RK, ed. DRUGDEX® system. Greenwood Village, CO: Thomson MICROMEDEX. (Edition expires 9/2008.)

Appendix A

The Seventh Report of the Joint National Committee on the Prevention, Detection, Evaluation, and Treatment of Hypertension (JNC-VII)

Table 1: Classification of HTN

BP Classification	SBP (mm Hg)		DBP (mm Hg)
Normal	< 120	And	< 80
Pre-HTN	120–139	Or	80–89
Stage 1	140–159	Or	90–99
Stage 2	≥ 160	Or	≥ 100

Table 2: Goal Blood Pressures by Population

Population	Goal BP (mm Hg)
General	< 140/90
DM Renal disease (GFR < 60 mL/minute or albuminuria)	< 130/80

Table 3: Recommended Lifestyle Modifications

Weight reduction
Aerobic physical activity
At least thirty minutes most days of the week
Dietary Approaches to Stop Hypertension (DASH) diet
Rich in fruits and vegetables, low in saturated fat
Dietary sodium reduction
< 2.4 g Na or < 6 g NaCl
Moderation of alcohol consumption
Less than two drinks per day for men, one for women

Table 4: Recommended Diagnostic and Laboratory Tests before Therapy Initiation

12-lead ECG
Urinalysis
Blood glucose
Hematocrit
Potassium
Creatinine
Calcium
Lipid profile

Table 5: Compelling Indications

Compelling Indication	Diuretic	β-Blocker	ACEI	ARB	CCB	Aldosterone Antagonist
HF						
Post-MI						
Increased CAD risk						
DM						
Renal disease						
History of stroke						

Table 6: HTN Management for Patients without Compelling Indications

BP Classification	Lifestyle Modifications	Initial Drug Therapy
Normal	Encourage	No drugs indicated
Pre-HTN	Yes	No drugs indicated
Stage 1 HTN	Yes	Thiazide diuretics for most—may consider ACEI, BB, CCB, ARB, or combination
Stage 2 HTN	Yes	Two-drug combination for most—thiazide diuretics and ACEI or ARB or CCB or BB

Appendix B— Drug Classes Used to Treat HTN

ACEIs

Mechanism of Action
- Inhibits the conversion of angiotensin I to angiotensin II

Contraindications
- Hypersensitivity to active component of any ACEI
- Bilateral renal artery stenosis
- Pregnancy
- Angioedema
- Hyperkalemia

Precautions
- Severe hypotension may occur in patients who are sodium and/or volume depleted
- Use with caution in patients with collagen vascular diseases, valvular stenosis, recent anesthesia
- Hepatic disease

Adverse Drug Effects
- 1–10%: headache, dizziness, fatigue, cough
- Less than 1%: hypotension, tachycardia, hyperkalemia, rash, photosensitivity, angioedema, increased SCr

Drug Interactions
- NSAIDs: reduced hypotensive effects of ACEIs
- Lithium: increased serum lithium concentrations, may result in symptoms of toxicity
- Potassium supplements
- Potassium-sparing diuretics

Monitoring
- BMP

Table 1: Available ACEIs and Doses

Drug (trade name)	Usual Dose Range (mg/day)[a]	Usual Starting Dose (mg)	Daily Frequency
Benazepril (Lotensin)[b]	10–40	10	1–2
Captopril (Capoten)[b]	25–100	6.25	2–3
Enalapril (Vasotec)[b]	2.5–40	2.5	1–2
Fosinopril (Monopril)[b]	10–40	10	1
Lisinopril (Prinivil, Zestril)[b]	10–40	5	1
Moexipril (Univasc)[b]	7.5–30	7.5	1
Perindopril (Aceon)	4–8	4	1–2
Quinapril (Accupril)	10–40	10	1
Ramipril (Altace)	2.5–20	2.5	1
Trandolapril (Mavik)	1–4	1–2	1

[a]Titrate slowly for four to six weeks.
[b]Generic available.

β-Blockers

Mechanism of Action
- Inhibition of adrenergic stimulation by a blockade of the β-adrenergic receptor

Contraindications
- Cardiogenic shock
- Hypersensitivity to any ingredient in β-blockers
- Decompensated HF
- Second- or third-degree atrioventricular block
- Severe sinus bradycardia

Precautions
- Anesthesia/surgery (myocardial depression)
- Abrupt withdrawal should be avoided—taper for one to two weeks.
- Bronchospastic disease (use cardioselective β-blockers)
- CHF
- DM
- Hyperthyroid/thyrotoxicosis
- Peripheral vascular disease

Adverse Drug Effects
- More than 10%: bradycardia, depression, fatigue, dizziness
- 1–10%: reduced peripheral circulation, hypotension, diarrhea, nausea, rash, wheezing, impotence
- Less than 1%: nightmares, Raynaud's phenomenon, decreased exercise tolerance

Drug Interactions
- Ergot alkaloids: peripheral ischemia
- Amiodarone, clonidine, hydralazine, non-DHP CCBs: increased effect/toxicity of β-blocker

Table 2: Available β-Blockers and Doses

Drug (trade name)	Usual Dose Range (mg/day)	Usual Starting Dose (mg)	Daily Frequency
Atenolol (Tenormin)[a]	25–100	50	1
Bisoprolol (Zebeta)[a]	2.5–10	5	1
Carvedilol (Coreg)[b]	12.5–50	6.25	2
Labetolol (Normodyne, Trandate)[a,b]	200–800	100	2
Metoprolol (Lopressor)[a]	50–450	50	2
Metoprolol XL (Toprol XL)	50–450	50	1
Propranolol (Inderal)[a]	40–240	40	2
Propranolol long acting (Inderal LA)	60–180	60	1

[a]Generic available.
[b]α- and β-blocking activity.
XL = extended release.

Thiazide Diuretics
    Mechanism of Action
        ◦ Inhibit the reabsorption of sodium and chloride in the ascending Loop of Henle and early distal tubule and increase the urinary excretion of sodium and chloride
    Contraindications
        ◦ Anuria
        ◦ Hypersensitivity
        ◦ Potassium more than 5.5 mEq/L (potassium-sparing diuretics)
    Precautions
        ◦ Electrolyte imbalance (hypokalemia, hyponatremia)
            ▪ Hyperuricemia
            ▪ Hepatic disease
            ▪ Lupus erythematosus
            ▪ Kidney disease (most agents will be ineffective with CrCl less than 30 mL/minute; indapamide and metolazone may be beneficial in these patients)
    Adverse Drug Effects
        ◦ Electrolyte imbalance (K, Mg, and Na)
        ◦ Possible dehydration, dizziness
        ◦ Photosensitivity, Stevens-Johnson syndrome, rash
        ◦ Impotence
    Drug Interactions
        ◦ NSAIDs—Decrease diuretic, natriuretic, and antihypertensive effects of thiazides
        ◦ Lithium—May induce lithium toxicity by decreased lithium excretion
    Monitoring
        ◦ BMP
        ◦ Uric acid
        ◦ Volume status

Table 3: Selected Thiazide Diuretics and Doses

Drug (trade name)	Usual Dose Range (mg/day)	Usual Starting Dose (mg)	Daily Frequency
HCTZ (Microzide/Oretic)[a]	12.5–25	12.5	1
Chlorothiazide (Diuril)[a]	125–500	125	1

[a]Generic available.

CCBs
    ◦ Non-DHPs
    ◦ DHPs

    Mechanism of Action
        ◦ Inhibit calcium ions from entering the "slow channels" or select voltage-sensitive areas of vascular smooth muscle or myocardium during depolarization.
        ◦ Non-DHPs predominantly work on the myocardium.
        ◦ DHPs predominantly work on peripheral circulation in the vascular smooth muscle.
    Contraindications
        ◦ Non-DHPs
            ▪ Acute MI with pulmonary congestion
            ▪ Cardiogenic shock
            ▪ Hypersensitivity to any component of non-DHPs
            ▪ Hypotension (less than 90 mm Hg systolic)
            ▪ Second- or third-degree atrioventricular block (except with functioning pacemaker)
            ▪ Severe CHF
            ▪ Sick sinus syndrome (except with functioning pacemaker)
        ◦ DHPs
            ▪ Hypersensitivity to any component of DHP
    Precautions
        ◦ Non-DHPs
            ▪ Concurrent β-blocker use
            ▪ Digital ischemia, ulceration, or gangrene
            ▪ First-degree atrioventricular block
            ▪ GI hypermotility or obstruction (extended-release dosage forms)
            ▪ Liver dysfunction
            ▪ Renal dysfunction
        ◦ DHPs
            ▪ Concurrent β-blocker use
            ▪ CHF
            ▪ Edema
            ▪ Hypertrophic cardiomyopathy
            ▪ Hypotension
            ▪ Liver dysfunction
            ▪ Renal dysfunction
            ▪ Sick sinus syndrome
    Adverse Drug Effects
        ◦ All CCBs
            ▪ Dizziness
            ▪ Flushing
            ▪ Headache
            ▪ Hypotension
            ▪ Nausea
        ◦ Non-DHPs
            ▪ Bradycardia
            ▪ Constipation
            ▪ Gingival hyperplasia
        ◦ DHPs
            ▪ Peripheral edema
            ▪ Reflex tachycardia

Drug Interactions
- Non-DHPs
  - Amiodarone—increased effect/toxicity of amiodarone
  - β-blockers—increased effect/toxicity of β-blockers
  - Cyclosporine, sirolimus, tacrolimus—increased immunosupressant values
  - Digoxin—increased effect/toxicity of digoxin
  - Dofetilide—increased effect/toxicity of dofetilide
  - Fentanyl—severe hypotension or increased fluid volume
  - Lovastatin, simvastatin—increased effect/toxicity of statin
- DHPs
  - Amiodarone—increased effect/toxicity of amiodarone
  - Cyclosporine, sirolimus, tacrolimus—increased immunosuppressant values
  - Fentanyl—severe hypotension or increased fluid volume

Monitoring
- Peripheral edema (DHPs)

Table 4: Selected CCBs and Doses

Drug (Trade Name)	Usual Dose Range (mg/day)	Usual Starting Dose (mg)	Daily Frequency
Diltiazem ER[a] (Cardizem CD, Dilacor XR, Tiazac)[b]	180–480	180	1
Diltiazem SR[a] (Cardizem SR)[b]	120–360	120	2
Verapamil IR[a] (Calan, Isoptin)[b]	80–360	80	2 or 3
Verapamil LA[a] (Calan SR, Isoptin SR, Covera HS, Verelan PM)[b]	120–360	120	1 or 2
Amlodipine (Norvasc)	2.5–10	5	1
Nifedipine LA[a] (Adalat CC, Procardia XL)	30–60	30	1
Felodipine (Plendil)	2.5–10	5	1

[a]Generic available.
[b]Non-DHPs.
ER = extended release; SR = sustained release; IR = instant release; LA = long acting

ARBs

Mechanism of Action
- Block the angiotensin II receptor thereby inhibiting the vasoconstrictive and aldosterone-secreting effects of angiotensin II

Contraindications
- Hypersensitivity to any component of ARB
- Pregnancy
- Bilateral renal artery stenosis
- History of angioedema with an ACEI
- Hyperkalemia

Precautions
- Use with caution in patients receiving potassium-sparing diuretics or potassium-supplements
- Use with caution in volume-depleted patients
- Hepatic disease

Adverse Drug Effects
- Hyperkalemia

Drug Interactions
- Potassium-sparing diuretics
- Potassium supplements

Monitoring
- BMP

Table 5: Available ARBs and Doses

Drug (trade name)	Usual Dose Range[a] (mg/day)	Usual Starting Dose (mg)	Daily Frequency
Candesartan (Atacand)	8–32	16	1
Eprosartan (Tevetan)	400–800	600	1 or 2
Irbesartan (Avapro)	150–300	150	1
Losartan (Cozaar)	25–100	50	1 or 2
Olmesartan (Benicar)	20–40	20	1
Telmisartan (Micardis)	20–80	40	1
Valsartan (Diovan)	80–320	80	1

[a]Slow titration; increase dose every two weeks as necessary.

α_1-Blockers

Mechanism of action
- Blocks postsynaptic α-adrenergic receptor, resulting in vasodilation of veins and arterioles

Contraindications
- Hypersensitivity

Precautions
- Concomitant use of other antihypertensives
- Carcinoma of the prostate
- Dizziness, lightheadedness
- Hepatic disease
- Orthostatic hypotension
- Recent cerebrovascular event
- Syncope

Adverse Drug Effects
- More than 10%: syncope, dizziness/orthostatic changes
- 1–10%: somnolence, nervousness, anxiety, abnormal vision
- Less than 10%: hypotension, tachycardia, depression

Drug Interactions
- Additive effects with other antihypertensives
- Phosphodiesterase type 5 (PDE5) inhibitors

Monitoring
- Mental status changes

Table 6. Available α_1-Blockers

Drug (trade name)	Usual Dose Range (mg/day)[a]	Usual Starting Dose (mg)	Daily Frequency
Doxazosin (Cardura)[b]	1–16	1	1
Prazosin (Minipress)[b]	2–20	1	2–3
Terazosin (Hytrin)[b]	1–20	1	1–2

[a]Slow titration for several weeks.
[b]Generic available.

Central α_2-agonist (Clonidine)

Mechanism of action
- Stimulates α_2-adrenoreceptors in the brain stem, reducing sympathetic outflow and producing a decrease in vasomotor tone and heart rate

Contraindications
- Hypersensitivity to any component of clonidine

Precautions
- Use with caution in patients with impaired renal function, cerebrovascular disease, sinus node dysfunction, or coronary disease.
- Do not abruptly discontinue. If discontinuation is necessary, gradually taper for one week.
- Avoid use in patients who are hemodynamically unstable.

Adverse Drug Effects
- More than 10%: orthostatic hypotension, rebound HTN, bradycardia, drowsiness
- 1–10%: mental depression, fatigue, constipation
- Less than 1%: palpitations, tachycardia, insomnia, vivid dreams

Drug Interactions
- TCAs, antagonize antihypertensive effects of clonidine
- β-Blockers may potentiate bradycardia and rebound HTN.

Monitoring
- Mental status changes

Table 7: Selected α_2-agonists

Drug (trade name)	Usual Dose Range (mg/day)[a]	Usual Starting Dose (mg)	Daily Frequency
Clonidine (Catapres)[b]	0.2–1.2	0.1	2–4
Clonidine transdermal patch (Catapres-TTS)	0.1–0.3	0.1	Transdermal patch to be worn for 7 days

[a]Titrate by 0.1 mg every one to two weeks if needed.
[b]Generic available.

Vasodilators

Mechanism of Action
- Increase intracellular concentrations of cyclic guanosine monophosphatec (GMP) resulting in direct arteriolar smooth muscle relaxation therefore decreasing the amount of systemic pressure in the arterial system.

Contraindications
- Dissecting aortic aneurysm
- Pheochromocytoma (minoxidil)
- Hypersensitivity

Precautions
- Angina
- CAD
- Cerebrovascular disease/cerebrovascular accident
- CHF (without adequate diuretic therapy)
- Dialysis/impaired renal function
- Fluid retention
- MI (within prior thirty days)
- Pericardial effusion
- Pericarditis
- Tachycardia

Adverse Drug Effects
- More than 10%: CHF, edema, tachycardia, hypertrichosis (minoxidil), drug-induced lupus (hydralazine)
- 1–10%: fluid/electrolyte imbalance, GI upset

- Less than 1%: angina, leukopenia, anemia, thrombocytopenia, Stevens-Johnson syndrome, pericardial effusion

Drug Interactions
- Additive effects with other antihypertensives

Monitoring
- BMP
- Body weight (minoxidil)
- Volume status

Table 6: Available α_1-Blockers

Drug (trade name)	Usual Dose Range (mg/day)[a]	Usual Starting Dose (mg)	Daily Frequency
Hydralazine (Apresoline)**	25–100	10	2–4
Minoxidil (Loniten)[b]	2.5–80	1	1–2

[a]Titrate weekly as needed.
[b]Generic available.

SMOKING CESSATION PROGRAM PROTOCOL

Submitted by: Kathy Fit

Created: October 2005

Purpose/Background

Tobacco addiction is the number one preventable cause of premature death. It has been estimated that 435,000 people die annually in this country as a result of tobacco-related illness. Patients have a difficult time with smoking cessation, and as a health care organization committed to quality health care, we need to make every effort to assist patients in this task. Several studies have proven that assistance with smoking cessation, including counseling and pharmacological therapy, is effective in aiding patients to quit. This new clinical pharmacy program can provide such a service, and this formal protocol would standardize the service and enable the clinical pharmacist, if the referring physician agrees on the referral form, to prescribe under the protocol.

Qualifications of the Pharmacist

She is a clinical pharmacist who has completed her Pharm.D. degree. She completed a one-year specialty residency in primary care with an emphasis on education and is a registered pharmacist in this state. She is also an assistant professor in the Department of Pharmacy Practice. Pharmacy residents who participate in this protocol also have their Pharm.D. degrees and are registered pharmacists in this state.

Policy

The clinical pharmacist, pharmacy residents, and pharmacy students completing rotations under the supervision of the clinical pharmacist will follow this written protocol.

Organization

- The program will be managed by a clinical pharmacist.
- At times, a pharmacy resident and/or pharmacy students may also be at the site and will participate in the following activities under the supervision of the clinical pharmacist.
- All patients must be referred by their PCP to the program to participate.
- All patients must participate in the group education class before the individual follow-up appointments with the pharmacist.
- Once the group education class is complete, the patient will make a 15-minute individual appointment with the pharmacist to discuss and decide on the best therapy (nicotine replacement, bupropion, or no drug therapy) for the patient.
- The clinical pharmacist will then conduct a telephone follow-up with the patient on a scheduled basis.
- About 4 to 6 weeks after the patient's quit date, the patient will make another individual 15-minute follow-up appointment to assess the status of smoking cessation, the adverse effects, and the plan for tapering the drug therapy.
- The BP, pulse rate, and weight will be measured at each individual patient visit.
- Clinic hours (may not be available every week, depending on the other responsibilities of the pharmacist)
  - Group education class (90 minutes)
  - Individual appointments (15 minutes) for two visits
    - The first appointment will be made for as soon as possible after the group class.
    - The second appointment will be made four to six weeks after the patient's quit date.

Procedures

Guidelines for Referrals

Each patient should be referred to the physician-directed/pharmacist-managed smoking cessation program on a case-by-case basis. Once the physician has a patient who is **seriously interested** in smoking cessation a referral should be filled out and given to the receptionist staff (referral box in the receptionist area in Family Practice). Any health care practitioner (nurse, medical assistant, and physician's assistant, etc.) can complete the form but the physician must sign the referral form. It is requested that the physician document his or her referral to the smoking cessation program in the patient's medical chart, as well. The patient will then be able to make an appointment.

On the referral form the physician must indicate one of the following management options:

- Initiate drug therapy based on the protocol. No need to consult physician before prescribing.
- Recommend drug therapy and consult physician before prescribing.

Prepared by WellGroup HealthPartners, Chicago Heights, Illinois

Patient Confidentiality

Pharmacy residents and pharmacy students may be present and participating in the program as a result of the teaching agreement between WellGroup HealthPartners and Midwestern University Chicago College of Pharmacy. All patients will be verbally informed that as part of their treatment these individuals will have access to their medical information. All of their information will remain confidential according to the HIPAA regulations and policies in place at this institution. All individuals participating in this program have undergone the appropriate HIPAA training.

Clinic Visits

Initial Group Class

The clinical pharmacist, pharmacy resident, or pharmacy student (under supervision of the clinical pharmacist or pharmacy resident) will see all referred patients for an initial group smoking cessation class. The following topics will be addressed in the class (90 minutes)—see Appendix A for details of group visit:
- Fagerström Nicotine Dependency Test
- Health consequences of smoking and of quitting
- Individual motivating factors
- Assessing smoking triggers
- Coping with cravings
- Dealing with withdrawal symptoms
- Preparing and setting a quit date
- Rewards
- Review of nicotine replacement and/or bupropion SR
- Proper education regarding drug, including dose and potential adverse effects
- Other Web-based and telephone resources to aid in the process
- Patients will also receive a number of written patient education materials that reinforce the above topics to take home.

Clinic Visits

First Individual Follow-up Visit (15 minutes)—to be scheduled after the group education class
- Brief medical history including
  - Medical conditions
  - Current prescription, OTC, and herbal drug use
  - Assess whether any drugs need to be adjusted once smoking has stopped
  - Drug allergies
  - Alcohol and drug use
- Patient's smoking history
- Reinforce quit date
- BP, pulse rate, and weight will be measured and documented.
- Choose nicotine replacement therapy and/or bupropion SR, and provide detailed education regarding the product chosen, if appropriate.
- **Based on the physician's referral, the pharmacist will either**
  - **Initiate drug therapy independently as described in Appendix B or**
  - **Recommend appropriate drug therapy but consult with the PCP before initiating therapy**

Second Individual Follow-up Visit (15 minutes)—To be scheduled 4 to 6 weeks after quit date.
- Success of smoking cessation
- Congratulations and encouragement
- Efficacy of nicotine replacement or bupropion SR
- Adverse effects of nicotine replacement products or bupropion SR
- How much of the nicotine replacement product is being used?
- Changes in mood, appetite, breathing (overall well-being)
- Discuss coping strategies for cravings.
- Remind patients of the rewards.
- Number of cigarettes (if any) since the quit date. What was the source of the slip?
- If the patient did relapse or never quit, set a new quit date.
- Assess the need for continued drugs and whether a decrease in dose is appropriate if using nicotine replacement therapy.

Telephone Follow-up

Patients will be asked if the pharmacy staff could conduct telephone follow-ups between individual appointments and after, as deemed appropriate. If the patient refuses, then this portion of the protocol will not be implemented. Once the patient is seen in the smoking cessation program, his or her name and contact information will be added to the Smoking Cessation Follow-Up List. This list will contain the patient's name, medical record number, telephone number, address, quit date, what smoking cessation drugs are being used, and scheduled contact times for the next three months. The clinical pharmacist, pharmacy resident, or pharmacy student (under the supervision of the clinical pharmacist or pharmacy resident) will make these telephone calls.
- The patient will be contacted at the following dates:
  - One week after the scheduled quit date
  - Three weeks after the scheduled quit date
  - Two months after the scheduled quit date
  - Three months after the scheduled quit date
- During the telephone follow-up calls, the following topic areas will be discussed with the patient:
  - Success of smoking cessation
  - Congratulations and encouragement
  - Efficacy of nicotine replacement or bupropion

- Adverse effects of nicotine replacement products or bupropion
- How much of the nicotine replacement product is being used
- Changes in mood, appetite, breathing (overall well-being)
- Discuss coping strategies for cravings
- Remind patients of the rewards
- Number of cigarettes (if any) since the quit date. What was the source of the slip?
- If the patient did relapse or never quit, set a new quit date.
- Assess the need for continued drugs.

All telephone calls will be documented. Two attempts will be made for each patient at each scheduled follow-up date. If, after these two attempts, the patient cannot be reached, the patient will be called at the next scheduled follow-up time. All attempts will be documented in the patient's chart, noting time, date, who placed the call, and the result of the call.
- Responsibilities of the Clinical Pharmacist
  - Under this protocol, the pharmacist will be able to perform the following activities:
    - Decide whether nicotine replacement therapy and/or bupropion will be used for the specific patient on the basis of medical history, concurrent drugs, and the patient's desires. It is possible that no drug therapy will be initiated if it is not appropriate. The clinical pharmacist will also decide the dose, route, and duration of therapy. (Appendix B contains information regarding drug therapy.)
    - If the physician indicates so on the referral, the pharmacist will consult the physician before initiating any of the drug therapy.
    - Write or call in prescriptions for the smoking cessation drugs described in this protocol (prescribing under protocol)
    - If the physician indicates so on the referral, the pharmacist will consult the physician before doing so.
    - Discontinue any smoking cessation products as necessary.
    - No smoking cessation products will be ordered for any pregnant or nursing patients if not specifically prescribed by the referring physicians. However, behavioral counseling and techniques will be provided.

Documentation

Attendance at group education classes will be documented in the patient's medical chart. All individual clinic visits will be documented in a SOAP method and will be entered in the progress notes section of the medical chart. All telephone calls will be documented with the date, time, who placed the call, and a brief note describing the patient's success, current status of drug use, and future plans. All prescriptions written by the pharmacist or called into the pharmacy will be documented in the progress notes. All prescriptions will be written with the pharmacist's signature and the referring physician's name. The smoking cessation program will also keep a shadow file on all of the referred patients, including a copy of the referral form and all progress notes and telephone call documentation.

Program Discharge

Patients will be discharged from the program when they have successfully stopped smoking and when 3 months from their quit date has passed. Patients may be discharged sooner from the program if they never quit smoking or relapse and they have no desire to quit again at the moment. Some patients may stay in the program longer if they need more assistance; this decision will be made on a case-by-case basis. After discharge, the patient will still have contact information for the program if they have questions or problems.

Billing

When the clinical pharmacist or pharmacy resident sees a patient, a level 1 visit will be billed incident to the referring physician.

Quality Improvement

This protocol will be reviewed annually by the clinical pharmacist and faculty physicians and updated as needed. It will also be updated more frequently if necessary based on any new smoking cessation product availabilities or new guidelines.

References:

1. American Cancer Society. Tobacco and cancer. Available at http://www.cancer.org/docroot/PED/ped_10.asp. Accessed June 19, 2008.
2. Zhu S, Melcer T, Sun J, Rosbrook B, Pierce JP. Smoking cessation with and without assistance: A population-based analysis. Am J Prev Med 2000;18:305–11.

Appendix A— Description of Material at Group Visits

Assessing Nicotine Dependence: Fagerström Test Points

1. How soon after you wake up do you smoke your first cigarette?
   - ❏ Within 5 minutes
   - ❏ 6 to 30 minutes
   - ❏ 31 to 60 minutes
   - ❏ After 60 minutes
2. Do you find it difficult to refrain from smoking in places where it is forbidden (for example, movie theater and church)?
   - ❏ Yes
   - ❏ No
3. Which cigarette would you most hate to give up?
   - ❏ The first one in the morning
   - ❏ Any other
4. How many cigarettes per day do you smoke?
   - ❏ 10 or fewer
   - ❏ 11–20
   - ❏ 21–30
   - ❏ 31 or more
5. Do you smoke more often during the first hours after waking than during the rest of the day?
   - ❏ Yes
   - ❏ No
6. Do you smoke if you are so ill that you are in bed most of the day?
   - ❏ Yes
   - ❏ No

Total score of 0–5: low to moderate nicotine dependence
Total score of 6–10: high nicotine dependence

Health Consequences of Smoking

Did you know:
- Four hundred thirty-five thousand people die each year in this country because of tobacco-related illness.
- Cigarettes kill more people than alcohol, car accidents, AIDS, suicide, homicide, and illegal drugs combined.
- The Centers for Disease Control and Prevention estimates that smokers typically live about 14 years shorter than nonsmokers.
- Three thousand nonsmokers also die of lung cancer each year from inhaling secondhand smoke.
- Four thousand substances are in cigarette smoke, and 63 are known to be linked with cancer.

Smoking increases your risk of these diseases/problems:
- Heart Disease
- Cancer
  - Lung (87% of all cases)
  - Oral, larynx, esophagus, bladder, kidney, pancreas, stomach, and cervix
- COPD
- Stroke
- Cataract formation
- Osteoporosis
- Pregnancy complications
- Increased risk of middle ear infections, respiratory infections, and asthma in children exposed to secondhand smoke

Health Consequences of Quitting

What happens after I quit smoking?
- <u>Twenty minutes after quitting</u>: BP returns to a level close to before your last cigarette. Temperature of your hands and feet increases to normal.
- <u>Eight hours after:</u> The carbon monoxide level in your blood returns to normal.
- <u>Twenty-four hours after:</u> Your risk of a heart attack decreases.
- <u>Two weeks to three months after:</u> Your circulation improves and your lung function increases up to 30%.
- <u>One to nine months after quitting:</u> Coughing, sinus congestion, fatigue, and shortness of breath decrease; cilia (tiny hairlike structures that move mucus out of the lungs) regain normal function, increasing the ability to handle mucus, clean the lungs, and reduce infection.
- <u>One year after quitting:</u> The excess risk of CHD is half that of a smoker.
- <u>Five years after quitting:</u> Your stroke risk is reduced to that of a nonsmoker 5 to 15 years after quitting.
- <u>Ten years after quitting:</u> The lung cancer death rate is about half that of a continuing smoker. The risk of cancer of the mouth, throat, esophagus, bladder, kidney, and pancreas decreases.
- <u>Fifteen years after quitting:</u> The risk of CHD is that of a nonsmoker.

Individual Motivating Factors
- Why do you want to quit? (group discussion)
- Develop "Reasons to Quit" cards.

Assessing Smoking Triggers
- Use a tobacco log to help determine individual triggers.
- Common triggers
  - Coffee breaks
  - Friends who smoke
  - Driving in the car
- Develop ways to avoid these triggers or how to cope.

Cravings—How to Cope?
- Drink plenty of fluid.
- Suck on sugarless candy, lollipops, chew sugarless gum, toothpicks, and straws.
- Munch on carrot or celery sticks.
- Play with a stress ball or a rubber band.
- Take a walk.
- Call someone or visit with someone.
- Read your reasons to quit card.
- Take a bath or shower.
- Play with children or pets.
- Deep breathing
- Visualization
- Delay—will subside in a few minutes
- Brush teeth or rinse with mouthwash.

Dealing with Slips
- Just because you smoke one cigarette does not mean you need to smoke a whole pack.
- A slip does not mean it is over. Just reset a quit date and start again.

Nicotine Withdrawal Symptoms—What Do I Do?

Withdrawal Symptom	Activity
Dry mouth or sore throat	Sip cold water. Chew sugarless gum or suck on sugarless candy.
Headaches	Try a warm bath or shower. Try relaxation or meditation techniques.
Insomnia	Avoid caffeine after 6:00 p.m. Try relaxation techniques.
Constipation	Drink plenty of fluids and increase the amount of vegetables, fruit, and other fiber in your diet.
Difficulty concentrating	Plan workload appropriately. Avoid extra stress during the first few weeks.
Fatigue	Take naps if possible. Slow down and let the body heal.
Hunger	Drink water and low calorie drinks. Eat low-fat and low-calorie snacks.
Irritability	Take walks; try relaxing hot baths; try relaxation techniques
Coughing	Drink fluids; suck on cough drops or sugarless hard candy

Preparing and Setting a Quit Date
Setting a quit date
- Should be within the next 30 days
- Maybe consider a date of some significance
  - Birthday or anniversary, etc.

Preparing for Your Quit Date: "Break the Habit"
- One to two weeks before the quit date
  - Make smoking inconvenient.
  - Make smoking unpleasant.
  - Do not smoke automatically.
  - Limit tobacco use.
- Day before quit date
  - Throw away all remaining cigarettes, and put away lighters and ashtrays.
  - Make a dental appointment for a cleaning.
- Right after quitting
  - Tell everyone so you will have support.
  - Clean home and work.
  - Give yourself a reward.
  - Avoid triggers.

Rewards
Reward yourself for not smoking on significant anniversary dates
- On your quit date, one week, two weeks, three weeks, one month, two months, three months, six months, one year, and then every year
  - Examples: Buy yourself something special; go out to a nice restaurant.
- Open a new account or start a piggy bank.
  - Deposit all the money you would have normally spent on cigarettes; then, on your one-year anniversary, do something very special.
- Go on vacation.

Treatment Options
- Will review each drug with class—see Appendix B for drug details
  - Nicotine patch
  - Nicotine gum
  - Nicotine lozenge
  - Nicotine nasal spray
  - Nicotine inhaler
  - Bupropion SR (Zyban®)

Other Resources for Support
- **Illinois Tobacco Helpline**
  (800) 548-8252
- **Nicotine Anonymous**
  (877) 879-6422
  www.nicotine-anonymous.org (accessed June 2008)
- **Office on Smoking & Health**
  Centers for Disease Control and Prevention
  (770) 448-5705
  www.cdc.gov/tobacco (accessed June 2008)
- **American Cancer Society**
  (800) ACS-2345
  www.cancer.org (accessed June 2008)
- **National Cancer Institute**
  (800) 422-6237
- www.nicorette.com (accessed June 2008)
- www.nicoderm.com (accessed June 2008)
- www.commitlozenge.com (accessed June 2008)
- www.nicotrol.com (accessed June 2008)
- www.tobaccofree.org (accessed June 2008)

Appendix B—Drug Therapy Protocol

Pharmacological agents have been proven to help many patients quit smoking. The following document discusses all of the possible first-line drug therapies that may be chosen by the pharmacist to assist the patient with smoking cessation. Specific products for the patient will be chosen on the basis of the patient's medical history and preference. In this document, the doses, administration, contraindications, precautions, adverse effects, and patient education points will be described.

Nicotine Patch—OTC

Product Availabilities and Dosing

Nicoderm CQ ❏ 21 mg, 14 mg, 7 mg ❏ 24-hour patch	Nicotrol ❏ 15 mg, 10 mg, 5 mg ❏ 16-hour patch
More than 10 cigarettes/day ❏ 21 mg for 4–6 weeks ❏ 14 mg for 2 weeks ❏ 7 mg for 2 weeks 10 or fewer cigarettes/day ❏ 14 mg for 6 weeks ❏ 7 mg for 2 weeks	More than 10 cigarettes/day ❏ 15 mg for 6 weeks ❏ 10 mg for 2 weeks ❏ 5 mg for 2 weeks 10 or fewer cigarettes/day ❏ NOT recommended
Generic patch ❏ 22 mg, 11 mg ❏ 24-hour patch	More than 15 cigarettes/day ❏ 22 mg for 6 weeks 15 or fewer cigarettes/day ❏ 11 mg for 6 weeks

Adapted from Rx for Change: Clinician-assisted tobacco cessation. The Regents of the University of California, University of Southern California, and Western University of Health Sciences. Copyright © 1999–2007, with permission.

Administration
- Apply to a hairless area on the body between the neck and the waist.
- Sites must be rotated.
- A new patch will be applied daily.

Contraindications
- Concurrent cigarette smoking
- Recent MI (2 weeks or less)
- Serious underlying arrhythmias
- Serious or worsening angina

Precautions
(Will discuss with physician before starting therapy for these patients.)
- Pregnancy
- Severe uncontrolled HTN (160/100 mm Hg or more)

Adverse Effects
- Local skin irritation
- Vivid dreams
- Insomnia

Patient Education
- Rotation of application sites
- Techniques to avoid vivid dreams
- Proper disposal of patch

Nicotine Gum—OTC

Product Availabilities: Nicorette 2 mg and 4 mg
  Generic versions
Dose: 25 or more cigarettes/day—4 mg
Less than 25 cigarettes/day—2 mg

Taper for 12 Weeks
- Weeks 1–6: Chew 1 piece every 1–2 hours.
- Weeks 7–9: Chew 1 piece every 2–4 hours.
- Weeks 10–12: Chew 1 piece every 4–8 hours.
- Maximum is 24 pieces per day.

Administration
- Chew until "peppery" sensation is felt.
- Park between cheek and gum until sensation is gone.
- Chew gum again until sensation is felt again and place between cheek and gum.
- Repeat for 30 minutes.
- Do not eat or drink for 15 minutes before using gum and during gum use.

Contraindications
- Dentures
- Temporomandibular joint disorder
- Recent MI (two weeks or less)
- Serious underlying arrhythmias
- Serious or worsening angina

Precautions
(Will discuss with physician before starting therapy for these patients.)
- Pregnancy
- Severe uncontrolled HTN (160/100 mm Hg or higher)

Adverse Effects
- Mouth and/or jaw soreness
- Hiccups
- Dyspepsia
- Hypersalivation

Patient Education
- Proper chew and park technique
- Avoidance of food and drink when using the gum
- Rotation of areas for parking the gum

Nicotine Lozenge—OTC

Product Availabilities: Commit® 2 mg and 4 mg
Dose: First cigarette 30 minutes or less from awakening—4 mg
First cigarette more than 30 minutes from awakening—2 mg

Taper for Twelve Weeks
- Weeks 1–6: 1 lozenge every 1–2 hours
- Weeks 7–9: 1 lozenge every 2–4 hours
- Weeks 10–12: 1 lozenge every 4–8 hours
- Maximum is 20 lozenges/day.

Administration
- Allow the lozenge to dissolve slowly in your mouth.
- Move the lozenge back and forth while dissolving.
- Avoid chewing or swallowing the lozenge.
- Do not eat or drink for 15 minutes before the lozenge and while using the lozenge.

Contraindications
- Recent MI (2 weeks or less)
- Serious underlying arrhythmias
- Serious or worsening angina

Precautions
(Will discuss with physician before starting therapy for these patients.)
- Pregnancy
- Severe uncontrolled HTN (160/100 mm Hg or higher)

Adverse Effects
- Nausea
- Hiccups
- Cough
- Heartburn
- Headache

Patient Education
- Proper technique—to move around mouth and NOT to chew or swallow
- Avoidance of food or drink while using the lozenge
- Nicotine release may result in a warm and tingling feeling

Nicotine Inhaler—Prescription Only

Product Availabilities: Nicotrol inhaler—10-mg cartridge, which delivers 4 mg
Dose: 6–16 cartridges/day for 3 months and then reduce gradually for 3 months

Administration
- Insert 1 cartridge in mouthpiece and inhale deeply on the mouthpiece.
- Take about 3 or 4 puffs per minute.
- There is enough nicotine in one cartridge for 20 minutes of active puffing.
- Use at least 3 cartridges per day but no more than 16 cartridges.
- Do not eat or drink anything for 15 minutes before and during inhaler use.

Contraindications
- Recent MI (2 weeks or less)
- Serious underlying arrhythmias
- Serious or worsening angina
- Severe reactive airway disease

Precautions
(Will discuss with physician before starting therapy for these patients.)
- Pregnancy
- Severe uncontrolled HTN (160/100 mm Hg or more)

Adverse Effects
- Mouth or throat irritation
- Unpleasant taste
- Cough
- Runny nose
- Hiccups
- Headache

Patient Education
- Proper inhalation technique
- Proper storage

Nicotine Nasal Spray—Rx Only

Product Availabilities: Nicotrol NS (0.5 mg of nicotine in each spray.)

Dose
- 1 or 2 doses per hour (8–10 doses/day) for first 6 to 8 weeks
- 1 dose = 2 sprays (1 spray in each nostril)
- Taper dose during weeks 6–12 (no optimal schedule available)
- DO NOT exceed 5 doses/hour or 40 doses/day.

Administration
- Unit must be primed before first use and if not used for 24 hours.
- Blow nose before using nasal spray.

- ❏ Tilt head back slightly and breathe through mouth.
- ❏ Insert unit into nostril and spray 1 dose into each nostril.
- ❏ Do not sniff or breathe in during the spray.
- ❏ Avoid blowing nose for 2 to 3 minutes after spraying.
- ❏ Wait 5 minutes after administering medicine to drive or operate heavy machinery.

Contraindications
- ❏ Chronic nasal disorders
- ❏ Severe reactive airway disease
- ❏ Recent MI (2 weeks or less)
- ❏ Serious underlying arrhythmias
- ❏ Serious or worsening angina

Precautions
(Will discuss with physician before starting therapy for these patients.)
- ❏ Pregnancy
- ❏ Severe uncontrolled HTN (160/100 mm Hg or higher)

Adverse Effects
- ❏ Nasal or throat burning
- ❏ Runny nose
- ❏ Tearing
- ❏ Sneezing
- ❏ Cough
- ❏ Headache

Patient Education
- ❏ Proper technique for inhalation
- ❏ Avoid driving or operating heavy machinery for five minutes after using product.
- ❏ Dependence is possible.

Miscellaneous: Risk of dependence is highest with this formulation.

Bupropion SR—Rx Only
Product availabilities: Zyban and generic formulations—150 mg

Dose
- ❏ 150 mg every morning for 3 days; then increase to 150 mg twice daily
- ❏ Use for 7 to 12 weeks; may be used for up to 6 months
- ❏ Doses need to be reduced in kidney impairment.
  - ❏ Specific guidelines are not available, so clinical judgment must be used.
- ❏ Doses must be reduced in liver impairment.
  - ❏ Severe hepatic cirrhosis—150 mg every other day

Administration
- ❏ Bupropion sustained release should be taken 12 hours apart.
- ❏ If patients have trouble with insomnia, second dose of bupropion can be taken 8 hours after the first morning dose.
- ❏ If patient is unsuccessful by the end of 6 weeks, therapy should be discontinued because it is unlikely to be effective.

Contraindications
- ❏ History of a seizure disorder
- ❏ History of anorexia or bulimia
- ❏ Use of a monoamine oxidase (MAO) inhibitor within the past 14 days
- ❏ Concomitant bupropion therapy
- ❏ Simultaneous discontinuation of alcohol or sedatives

Precautions
(Will discuss with physician before starting therapy for these patients.)
- ❏ Pregnancy

Drug Interactions
- ❏ The following agents should be used with caution with bupropion.

May lower the seizure threshold	May lower the efficacy of bupropion	May increase toxicity of bupropion	Bupropion may increase toxicity of these agents by CYP2D6 inhibition
Antidepressants Antipsychotics Systemic steroids Tramadol Theophylline	Carbamazepine Phenobarbital Phenytoin	Cimetidine Ritonavir	Aripiprazole Carvedilol Desipramine Dextromethorphan Flecainide Fluoxetine Haloperidol Imipramine Metoprolol Mirtazapine Nortriptyline Paroxetine Propafenone Propranolol Risperidone Sertraline Thioridazine

Adverse Effects
- ❏ Insomnia
- ❏ Dry mouth
- ❏ Dizziness
- ❏ Rash
- ❏ Constipation
- ❏ Seizure risk (0.1%)

Patient Education
- Risk of seizures
- Avoidance of alcohol

Additional Information

It has been documented that the polycyclic aromatic hydrocarbons in tobacco smoke are responsible for several drug interactions. The polycyclic aromatic hydrocarbons are known to increase the metabolism of certain CYP enzymes, specifically CYP1A1 and CYP1A2. The following table contains drugs/substances that may need to be adjusted as the patient stops smoking because the enzyme induction will no longer be a problem.

Drug/Substance Name	Description of Interaction
Caffeine	Smoking increases clearance; caffeine levels may increase after cessation; reduce caffeine intake as needed.
Insulin	Smoking may decrease insulin absorption due to vasoconstriction; monitor blood glucose concentrations and adjust accordingly after cessation.
Chlorpromazine, clozapine, fluvoxamine, haloperidol, mirtazapine, and olanzapine	Smoking increases clearance of these substances; monitor patient and decrease doses if necessary after cessation.
Flecainide and mexiletine	Same as above
Theophylline	Clearance is increased 58–100% by smoking; monitor drugs closely whenever smoking is started, stopped, or changed and adjust accordingly.

Adapted from Rx for Change: Clinician-assisted tobacco cessation. The Regents of the University of California, University of Southern California, and Western University of Health Sciences. Copyright © 1999–2007, with permission.

The pharmacist will review the patient's chart to see whether he or she is currently on any of these drugs and will inform the physician of the need to adjust dosages.

References

1. Corelli RL, Hudmon KS. Tobacco use and dependence. In: Koda-Kimble MA, Young L, Kradjan WA, Guglielmo BJ, Alldredge BK, eds. Applied Therapeutics: The Clinical Use of Drugs, 8th ed. Baltimore: Lippincott, Williams & Wilkins, 2005:85-1 to 85-29.
2. Nicotine (drug evaluation). Klasco RK: DRUGDEX® system (electronic version). Greenwood Village, CO: Thomson Micromedex. Available at www.thomsonhc.com. Accessed June 2008.
3. Nicotine Polacrilex (drug evaluation). Klasco RK: DRUGDEX® system (electronic version). Greenwood Village, CO: Thomson Micromedex. Available at www.thomsonhc.com. Accessed June 2008.
4. Commit® Lozenge Product Information. Available at www.commitlozenge.com. Accessed June 2008.
5. Nicotrol® Inhaler package insert. Pfizer, February 2005.
6. Nicotrol® NS package insert. Pfizer, February 2005.
7. Bupropion (drug evaluation). Klassco RK: DRUGDEX® system (electronic version). Greenwood Village, CO: Thomson Micromedex. Available at www.thomsonhc.com. Accessed June 2008.
8. Zyban® package insert. GlaxoSmithKline, August 2005.

Appendix C—Smoking Cessation Program Referral Form

A clinical pharmacist manages the smoking cessation program. The patients, once referred, will be scheduled for three separate visits:
- A 90-minute group visit
- A 15-minute individual visit once the group class is completed
- A 15-minute individual follow-up visit 4–6 weeks after their quit date

Details regarding the clinical pharmacist's responsibilities and the program are outlined in the smoking cessation program protocol. Please review before referring patients to the program.

Referring Physician:_____Office Ext:_____
Patient Name: _____Record #:_____
Patient's Telephone #:_____Gender: ☐ female ☐ male
DOB: _____/_____/_____

Diagnosis Code:_____
To get reimbursement, a diagnosis is needed in addition to nicotine dependence. Certain providers will pay for smoking cessation if the patient has another medical condition negatively affected by smoking or if they are on drugs that are affected by smoking.

Please indicate how you would like the clinical pharmacist to initiate drug therapy for smoking cessation:

- Initiate drug therapy based on the protocol. No need to consult physician before prescribing.
- Recommend drug therapy and consult physician before initiating drug therapy.

I consider this referral to the Smoking Cessation Program to be a necessary part of this patient's medical care:

Physician Signature:_____ Date:_____

Prepared by WellGroup HealthPartners, Chicago Heights, Illinois

SMOKING CESSATION CLINIC POLICY AND PROCEDURE

Submitted by: Lori Wilken

Created: March 2006

Purpose

- Describe the roles of the Smoking Cessation Clinic (SCC) with regard to the process of helping patients stop smoking, as well as within the College of Pharmacy and university structure
- Increase the likelihood of a smoker becoming abstinent by using clinically proven pharmacological and behavioral techniques
- Provide consultative services to health care providers on tobacco dependence and related issues
- Serve as an information resource for patients enrolled in the SCC
- Provide educational programs and inservices to medical, nursing, and pharmacy staff regarding various aspects of tobacco dependence
- Conduct research regarding tobacco dependence and related areas
- Serve as an educational site for pharmacy students, pharmacy practice residents, medical students, medical residents, and nursing students

Definitions

For the purpose of this guideline, the following definitions apply:

Abstinence—Not to smoke any cigarettes or cigars or use any form of tobacco for a period
Behavioral modification—Using various behavioral techniques to effect a change in an unwanted behavior
Carbon monoxide measurement—Measurement of exhaled carbon monoxide using a handheld device
Fagerström score—Measurement of nicotine dependence based on a 10-point questionnaire
First-line smoking cessation drugs—First-line drugs include nicotine gum, patches, inhaler, lozenges and nasal spray, and bupropion suspended release.
Gemini—Computerized documentation system at UICMC
Lapse or slip—An episode of reverting back to the unwanted behavior that is not permanent
Relapse—Reverting back to the unwanted behavior permanently
Smoker—Any person who smokes tobacco
Spirometry—Breathing test used to screen for airway obstruction
Stage of change—Estimation of readiness to change an unwanted behavior (i.e., smoking) based on a continuum of change model
Tobacco user—any person who smokes cigarettes or cigars or uses spit tobacco

Policy

Cigarette smoking is the chief preventable cause of morbidity and mortality in the United States.

We at the University of Illinois at Chicago Medical Center believe that promoting and assisting with the process of smoking cessation in each of our patients is integral to the mission of the Medical Center.

Procedure

Consultation and referral

- Any health care provider may refer their patient to the SCC. A prior authorization may be necessary for some insurance carriers to cover the service provided. Patients may also refer themselves to the clinic.

Appointments

- Appointments are made by calling patient registration.

Hours of operation

- Individual appointments:
  - Tuesdays and Fridays 1:00–4:30 P.M.
  - Thursdays 8:00–11:30 A.M.

Location

- Internal Medicine Center
- Pulmonary Clinic

Patient Reception/Check-In

- Patients will sign in at the front desk and will wait to be called by the SCC pharmacotherapist.

Physician Contact

- The physician covering Pulmonary Clinic may elect to examine and interview the patient. Clinical notes requiring a physician's signature will be reviewed and signed by the designated physician of the Pulmonary Clinic.

Clinical Privileges
- The SCC pharmacotherapist is authorized to perform the following functions:
  ○ Initiate smoking cessation drug(s) for patients seen in the SCC as an agent of the designated physician overseeing the SCC
  ○ Authorize refills for smoking cessation drugs for patients monitored in the SCC as an agent of the designated physician overseeing the SCC

Clinic Procedures
Individual Visit 1—Baseline
- Referral information
- Pack-year history
- Reasons why the smoker wants to quit smoking
- Motivation and confidence to quit smoking
- Previous quit attempts including length of success, time of last attempt, method used, and efficacy of method
- Barriers to stopping smoking
- Medical problem list
- Drug list and allergies
- SH identifying other current or past addictions, alcohol use, smoking history, occupation, diet, and exercise
- Insurance
- BP, pulse rate, weight, Fagerström score, carbon monoxide reading, and spirometry
- Stage of change (precontemplation, contemplation, preparation, action, and maintenance) based on patient's identified quit date
- Behavioral and drug recommendations and education
- Follow-up scheduled
- Documentation of the above information in Gemini and forwarded to the billing physician and the referring health care provider

Individual Visit 2–8—Follow-up Visits
- Triggers, plans, barriers
- Relapse prevention
- Motivation to continue abstinence
- Drug efficacy, proper use and adverse effects, refills
- Behavioral modification recommendations and education
- Problem list or drug changes
- Stage of change (precontemplation, contemplation, preparation, action, and maintenance) based on patient's identified quit date and success to date
- Follow-up scheduled

- Documentation of the above information in Gemini and forwarded to the referring health care provider.
- Documentation will be forwarded to the designated physician overseeing the SCC for written prescription authorization, if necessary

Telephone Calls or Mailings
- Telephone calls may be made by smoking cessation personnel or designated assistants (e.g., students, residents) for the following reasons:
  ○ Improve motivation of patient
  ○ Determination of abstinence
  ○ Missed appointment/rescheduling
  ○ Hospital consultation follow-up
- Drug follow-up
- Personnel will identify themselves and state that they are calling on behalf of the UIC Smoking Cessation Clinic.
- Mailing of abstinence certificates, reminder letters, and surveys will be sent on clinic stationery.
- Documentation of telephone calls and mailings will be completed in Gemini.

Patient Education
Behavioral Modification
- Tally sheet to identify triggers
- Written Trigger Plan
- Stress and time management
- Healthy diet and exercise recommendations
- Educational smoking cessation book

Drug
- Advantages and disadvantages of each drug
- Proper use, adverse effects, expectations, and cost of each drug
- Demonstration of each drug
- Drug education sheet(s)
- Prescription

Follow-up Procedures
- Follow-up appointments are based on the smoker's desire to quit smoking, the smoker's ability to return for clinic appointments, and the clinician's judgment.
- Guidelines for follow-up based on stage of change:
  ○ Precontemplation: Three months or patient schedules an appointment when he/she is ready to quit smoking.
  ○ Contemplation: One to three months or patient schedules an appointment when he/she is ready to quit smoking.
  ○ Preparation: One to two weeks based on the chosen quit date

- Action: One week to one month depending on necessary support and drug use. Patient should be followed in person for at least one month of abstinence
- Maintenance: Three to twelve months after quit date with in-person visits or telephone counseling

Billing

- Level 1 visit, coded for Tobacco Abuse (305.1) and other patient-specific disease states related to smoking
- Level 2 and higher may be billed if the patient is seen and examined by the covering pulmonologist.

Training/Teaching

- Pharmacy students, residents, nursing students, and medical students and residents may receive training in smoking cessation at the UIC SCC.
- Pharmacy students may receive experience through the Ambulatory Care Clerkship rotation or an independent elective course PMPR 380/390. Pharmacy residents may choose the SCC as one of their ambulatory care clinics for one month or as their longitudinal clinic for six months or longer.
- Other health care students and residents may contact the SCC personnel to observe and participate in the smoking cessation clinic.

Before seeing patients independently, the following criteria must be completed:

1. Discussion of required readings with the preceptor
2. Observation of the smoking cessation counselor/preceptor for one to two weeks
3. Seeing patients in the presence of the preceptor for at least one week
4. Presenting the patient to the preceptor before discharging the patient

---

Director, Pharmacy Services   Date

Pharmacist   Date

References

1. Fiore MC, Bailey WC, Cohen SJ, et al. Treating tobacco use and dependence. Clinical practice guideline. Rockville, MD: U.S. Department of Health and Human Services. Public Health Service, June 2000. Available at www.surgeongeneral.gov (Accessed June 2008).
2. Kennedy DT, Paulson DM, Eddy TD, et al. A smoking-cessation program consisting of extensive counseling, pharmacotherapy, and office spirometry: Results of a pilot project in a veteran's administration medical center. Pharmacotherapy 2004;24:1400–7.
3. McGhan WF, Smith MD. Pharmacoeconomic analysis of smoking-cessation interventions. Am J Health Syst Pharm 1996;53:45–52.
4. Vogt TM, Selvin S, Widdowson G, Hulley SB. Expired air carbon monoxide and serum thiocyanate as objective measures of cigarette exposure. Am J Public Health 1977;67:545–9.
5. Wilken LA, Winkler SR, Weathermon RA. The pharmacist's role in substance use disorders. In: The University of the Sciences in Philadelphia. Remington: The Science and Practice of Pharmacy, 21st ed. Philadelphia: Lippincott, Williams & Wilkins, 2005:2303–17.

SMOKING CESSATION PROGRAM COLLABORATIVE PRACTICE AGREEMENT

Submitted by: Ila Harris

Revised: 2006

Under Minnesota law, the Pharmacy Practice Act allows pharmacists to practice under a Collaborative Practice Agreement with individual physicians. Pharmacists may participate in the practice of managing and modifying drug therapy on a case-by-case basis according to a written protocol between the specific pharmacist and the individual physician(s) who is/are responsible for the patient's care and authorized to prescribe drugs.

By signing this document, the named physicians agree that the named pharmacist may enter into a Collaborative Practice with them for the management of smoking cessation in patients according to the attached protocol for the Smoking Cessation Program. By signing this document, the physician agrees with the smoking cessation management outlined in the attached protocol. Resident physicians are supervised by the faculty physicians listed; therefore, the signatures approve the referral of the resident physician's patients to the Smoking Cessation Program.

SMOKING CESSATION PROGRAM AND COLLABORATIVE AGREEMENT APPROVED BY

PHARMACIST CLINICIAN

_____
Name   Date
License #:_____

FACULTY PHYSICIANS

_____   _____
Name   Date   Name   Date
License #:_____   License #:_____

DATE OF IMPLEMENTATION:
DATES ANNUAL REVIEW COMPLETED:

Under Minnesota law, the Pharmacy Practice Act allows pharmacists to practice under a Collaborative Practice Agreement with individual physicians. Pharmacists may participate in the practice of managing and modifying drug therapy on a case-by-case basis according to a written protocol between the specific pharmacist and the individual physician(s) who is/are responsible for the patient's care and authorized to prescribe drugs.

The named pharmacy residents below may enter into a Collaborative Practice with the physicians named on the previous page for the management of smoking cessation in patients according to the attached protocol for the Smoking Cessation Program.

SMOKING CESSATION PROGRAM AND COLLABORATIVE AGREEMENT

PHARMACY RESIDENTS

Prepared by Bethesda Family Medicine, St. Paul, Minnesota

Purpose/Background

A formal protocol at Bethesda Clinic for smoking cessation was felt to be necessary. The clinical pharmacist frequently sees patients for smoking cessation. It is necessary to contact the physician before a prescription is given, and the primary physician is often unavailable. Multiple studies have shown the advantages of effective counseling and behavioral therapies for a patient to successfully quit smoking. The clinical pharmacist, pharmacy resident, and pharmacy student are able to provide this type of counseling and support to patients who are ready to quit. A formal protocol would standardize the counseling and allow the pharmacist to prescribe under protocol.

Qualifications of Pharmacists

Ila M. Harris is a clinical pharmacist who has both her B.S. Pharm. and Pharm.D. degrees. She completed a one-year specialty pharmacy residency in Family Medicine. She has been in practice after completing her residency since 1994, and she is a registered pharmacist. She is also a BCPS. Pharmacy residents involved in this protocol have their Pharm.D. degrees and are registered pharmacists.

Policy

The clinical pharmacist, any pharmacy residents, and students doing rotations under the supervision of the clinical pharmacist will follow this written protocol.

Organization

The clinical pharmacist will coordinate the smoking cessation program. Pharmacy residents will also see patients. Pharmacy students who may see patients will do so under the supervision of the clinical pharmacist or pharmacy resident. Patients who are interested in quitting smoking and desire assistance will be seen.

After the initial appointment, follow-up telephone calls will be made to assess the patient's progress. These telephone calls will be documented in the patient's chart and can be made by the clinical pharmacist, pharmacy resident, or pharmacy student under the supervision of the clinical pharmacist.

Procedures

Guidelines for Referral

Under Minnesota law for Collaborative Practice Agreements, all patients must be referred to the pharmacist on a case-by-case basis. When a physician has a patient who is interested in smoking cessation, the physician will refer the patient to the clinical pharmacist for smoking cessation. The physician will document the referral in their progress note in the medical chart. The patient will make an appointment to meet with the clinical pharmacist at a later date. Depending on the schedule of the pharmacist and the patient, the clinical pharmacist may see the patient immediately on the same day.

Clinic Visits

Patients will be seen by the clinical pharmacist, pharmacy resident, or pharmacy student (under the supervision of the clinical pharmacist or pharmacy resident) for a smoking cessation visit. There are several key points that will be discussed in this conversation (See Appendix A, which will be used during the visit):
- Patient's smoking history
- Patient's stage of smoking cessation and willingness to quit
- Fagerström Nicotine Dependency Test
- Health consequences of smoking and of quitting
- Assessment of smoking triggers
- Coping with cravings
- Preparing for the quit date
- Rewards for self on anniversary dates
- Choice of nicotine replacement and/or bupropion (Zyban®) or varenicline (Chantix®), followed by proper education on the drug, including proper administration and potential adverse effects.
- Patient will also be given a list of other smoking cessation programs/resources to contact for further assistance and support.

Telephone Follow-up

Patients will be asked if they would like to receive follow-up telephone calls. If they prefer not to, or if they do not have a telephone, then this portion of the protocol will not be followed. The patient will be telephoned within one to two weeks of the quit date and then whenever necessary. These telephone calls can be made by the clinical pharmacist, pharmacy resident, or pharmacy student under the supervision of the clinical pharmacist.
- During this initial telephone call, the following items will be addressed
  - Success of smoking cessation
  - Congratulations and encouragement
  - Efficacy of nicotine replacement and/or bupropion (Zyban®) or varenicline (Chantix®)
  - If using as-needed nicotine replacement, how often is it being used?
  - Adverse effects from drugs
  - Changes in mood, appetite, breathing, etc.
  - Discuss coping with cravings.
  - Remind patient of rewards.
  - Number of cigarettes (if any) since quit date. If patient has smoked again, what triggered it?
  - If patient relapsed or did not quit, discuss setting a new quit date.
  - Assess need for continued smoking cessation drugs

All telephone calls will be documented on telephone call shingles. One attempt will be made to contact the patient. If the patient is unable to be reached, then a message will be left. If the patient does not have an answering machine, then another call may be attempted.

Clinical Activities Provided by the Clinical Pharmacist

Under this protocol, the clinical pharmacist/pharmacy resident is authorized to decide if nicotine replacement and/or bupropion (Zyban®) or varenicline (Chantix®) will be used in a specific patient based on the patient's desires and other medical conditions. The duration of treatment will also be decided. The specific form of nicotine replacement (e.g., patch, gum, lozenge, inhaler, nasal spray) will be selected by the clinical pharmacist. It may be decided that no drugs will be used.

This protocol will also authorize the clinical pharmacist/pharmacy resident to write or call in a new prescription for smoking cessation drugs (prescribing under protocol). For written prescriptions, the names of both the referring physician and the clinical pharmacist will be used, as authorized by the protocol.

This protocol also authorizes the clinical pharmacist/pharmacy resident to discontinue any smoking cessation drugs, when deemed appropriate.

If patient is pregnant or nursing, no drugs will be used unless authorized by the physician, but counseling for behavioral modification will be provided.

Documentation

Each initial smoking cessation visit will be documented in a SOAP note format in the progress notes of the patient's medical chart. The note will document the referral by stating, "This patient referred to the smoking cessation program by Dr. _____." Further documentation of telephone follow-up will occur on the telephone call shingles placed in the progress notes of the patient's medical chart. If a prescription is written or phoned in by the clinical pharmacist, the drug, dose, quantity, and number of refills will be documented in the SOAP note.

Billing

When the clinical pharmacist or pharmacy resident sees the patient, a level 1 visit will be billed.

Termination of care

A patient will be discontinued from the smoking cessation program when he or she has successfully stopped smoking or sooner if the patient does not quit or relapses and does not wish to set a new quit date. Patients will be monitored for a longer period if they express desire or if it is believed necessary. It will be made clear to patients that they can call at any time if they have any problems or questions or if they desire another attempt at quitting.

Quality Improvement

The protocol will be reviewed yearly by the clinical pharmacist and faculty physicians and revised as needed.

Appendix A

Quitting Smoking
YOU CAN DO IT!

Getting a better understanding of your smoking

How much do you smoke? _____

How long have you smoked? _____

Have you tried to quit before? How many times? _____

What methods did you use? Which helped? _____

Have you been successful? For how long? _____

Why did you relapse in the past? _____

What is different this time? _____

Why do you smoke? _____

What scares you about quitting? _____

Why do you want to quit? (Motivators for quitting)

1) _____

2) _____

3) _____

4) _____

How badly do you want to stop smoking? _____

Do you think you can successfully stop smoking with our help? _____

Triggers for Smoking

_____
_____

QUIT DATE: _____

    Fagerström score: _____

    Pharmacological treatment used: _____

_____
_____

Office Use Only:

Date Called				
Quit? New quit date set? Any other information? Additional follow-up needed?				

Assessing Nicotine Dependence: Fagerström Score

	1	2	3	4
How soon after you wake do you smoke your first cigarette?	> 1 hour	½–1 hour	6–30 minutes	< 5 minutes
Do you find it difficult to refrain from smoking in places where it is forbidden?	No	Yes		
Which cigarette would you hate to give up the most?	Any other	First of the morning		
How many cigarettes/day do you smoke?	< 10	11–20	21–30	> 31
Do you smoke the most in the morning?	No	Yes		
If you are so ill that you are in bed most of the day, do you still smoke?	No	Yes		

Total score of 0–5: LOW to MODERATE nicotine dependence SCORE:_____
Total score of 6–10: HIGH nicotine dependence

More than four hundred thirty thousand smokers die each year from smoking-related illnesses in the United States.
Four thousand substances are in cigarette smoke; sixty-three are known carcinogens.
Most quitters need multiple attempts at quitting before they are successful.

Smoking increases your risk of these conditions/problems:
• Heart disease
• Cancer
◦ Lung, mouth, throat, stomach, cervical, bladder, pancreatic, esophageal, others
• Stroke
• Emphysema
• Chronic bronchitis
• Pneumonia
• Adverse pregnancy outcomes
• Death from smoking
◦ More than 430,000 smoking-related deaths in the United States each year
◦ Almost one in five deaths is attributable to smoking.
◦ Secondhand smoke is responsible for 3,000 lung cancer deaths each year and 37,000 heart disease deaths.
Is it too late to prevent these problems?
What happens after I quit smoking?
• One year after quitting, your risk of heart disease is cut in half.
• Three to five years after quitting, your risk of bladder, mouth, and esophagus cancer is cut in half.
• Ten years after quitting, your risk of lung cancer is cut in half.
• Fifteen years after quitting, the risk of heart disease is the same as if you never smoked.
• Five to fifteen years after quitting, the risk of stroke is the same as if you never smoked.
• Eleven to fifteen years after quitting, the risk of dying is almost the same as if you never smoked.

Coping with cravings
- ❏ Avoid places where people are smoking (bars, casinos)
- ❏ Ask friends not to smoke in front of you
- ❏ Note card with reasons for quitting (where cigarettes usually are)
- ❏ Chew sugarless gum; suck on candy
- ❏ Lollipops, toothpicks, straws
- ❏ Keep a rubber band around wrist; play with it if you need something to do with your hands
- ❏ Munch on carrot and celery sticks
- ❏ Brush your teeth
- ❏ Take a walk, exercise
- ❏ Call a friend; visit a friend
- ❏ Play with children or pets
- ❏ Deep breathing
- ❏ Mini-mental vacation
- ❏ Take a bubble bath; shower
- ❏ Take up a new hobby

Quit Date: _____

Getting ready for the quit date!
- Tell friends about quitting and quit date
- Identify support system
- Mark calendar
- Post signs of why you want to quit around your house/apartment
- Start to cut down on cigarettes (very slowly)
- Change brands
- Different hand/side of mouth
- Rate how much you really need each cigarette (1–10; if 5 or fewer, put it away)
- Different room; smoke outside only or in garage
- Change routine

Day before quit date
- Clean and "freshen" house and car
- Do laundry; take coats to dry cleaner
- Throw away cigarettes, ashtrays, lighters, matches (outside home)
- Make sure you have plenty of gum, candy, mints, toothpicks, straws, etc.

On quit date
- Keep busy; plan activities
- Stay away from favorite chair, room
- Eat meals in different room
- Stay in nonsmoking areas

Rewards
Reward yourself for not smoking
- On quit date, each month, one year, then every year
- Buy something special, take time for yourself
- Open up new account; deposit money normally spent on smoking
- At the end of one year of not smoking, do something really nice!

Enforce Total Abstinence
1. This is a lifetime commitment.
2. Do not even have "just one puff"!!
3. If you slip just once, renew your commitment; remember, this time you CAN stay off cigarettes.

Treatments
Bupropion (Zyban®, Wellbutrin®)
- Non-nicotine treatment; increases amount of dopamine
- Helps physical and psychological addiction; helps withdrawal symptoms
- Most people say it makes cigarettes taste bad.
- Dosage: 150 mg (1 tablet) once daily in the morning for 3 days and then twice daily for 2 to 3 months
  ○ Start on: _____
  ○ Set quit date 1 to 2 weeks after starting.
- Take 12 hours apart. If insomnia occurs, take 8 hours apart (second dose earlier).
- <u>Adverse effects</u>: dry mouth, insomnia

Varenicline (Chantix®)
- Non-nicotine treatment; partially blocks the effects of nicotine and partially has the same effect
- Dose: Days 1–3: 0.5 mg once daily
  ○ Days 4–7: 0.5 mg twice daily
  ○ Day 8—end of treatment: 1 mg twice daily
- Quit date should be set 1 week after starting Chantix.
  ○ Start on: _____
- Treatment duration is 12 weeks. If smoking successfully stopped at 12 weeks, continue for additional 12 weeks.
- In general, use with other nicotine replacement products is not recommended.
  ○ Causes four times more nausea, headache, vomiting, dizziness, stomach problems, and fatigue
  ○ This may also happen if you smoke while taking Chantix at a higher dose.
- <u>Adverse effects</u>: nausea, insomnia, constipation, flatulence, vomiting

Nicotine Patch
Nicoderm CQ® (24 hours)—OTC: 21 mg (4 weeks), 14 mg (2 weeks), 7 mg (2 weeks)
Nicotrol® (16 hours)—OTC: 15 mg (8 weeks)
Habitrol® (24 hours)—Rx: 21 mg (4 weeks), 14 mg (2 weeks), 7 mg (2 weeks)
ProStep® (24 hours)—Rx: 22 mg (4 weeks), 11 mg (4 weeks)
  **Start with lower strength if you smoke fewer than 15 cigarettes/day.*
- Apply patch to hairless area between neck and waist; rotate sites.

- Don't smoke when using patches!!
- <u>Adverse effects</u>: skin irritation, vivid dreams, insomnia, GI tract complaints

Nicotine gum (Nicorette®—OTC)
- Nicotine replacement
- Start on quit date; use gum ONLY after stopping smoking.
- Directions
  - Chew until peppery taste or "tingling" is felt and then "park" the gum between gum and cheek until sensation is gone (usually one to three minutes).
  - Rechew every few minutes and "park" again.
  - Chew each piece for 30 minutes, one every 1 to 2 hours; don't eat or drink anything but water when chewing.
- Maximum: Thirty *2-mg* pieces or twenty *4-mg* pieces
- Decrease dose slowly; use for 6 months only.
- <u>Adverse effects</u>: Mouth and jaw soreness, hiccups, stomach discomfort, indigestion

Nicotine Lozenge (Commit® Lozenge—OTC)
- Nicotine replacement (sugar free)
- Start on quit date; use ONLY after stopping smoking.
  - Directions: Suck on lozenge until you feel a tingle; then, shift it from one side of the mouth to the other periodically; let it dissolve; don't chew or swallow; it will take 20 to 30 minutes to dissolve.
  - Do not eat or drink for 15 minutes before lozenge or while the lozenge is in the mouth.
  - Use one every 1 to 2 hours during the day for 6 weeks; then every 2 to 4 hours for 3 weeks; then every 4 to 8 hours for 3 weeks; then D/C
  - For 2- or 4-mg lozenges: Use 2 mg if first cigarette is more than 30 minutes after wakening and 4 mg if within 30 minutes.

Nicotine Inhaler
(Nicotrol Inhaler®—Prescription)
- Plastic device that looks like a cigarette
- 80 puffs = 4 mg of nicotine (about 20 minutes of active puffing)
- Directions: 3–4 puffs/minute for 20 to 30 minutes
- Four inhalers used per day (minimum)
- Decrease use after 3 months, maximum duration: 6 months
- <u>Adverse effects</u>: cough, mouth/throat irritation

Nicotine Nasal Spray
(Nicotrol NS®—Prescription)
- Two sprays = 1 mg of nicotine
  - Directions for use: One or two sprays per hour (one in each nostril); don't exceed 10 sprays/hour or 40 sprays/24 hours
  - <u>Adverse effects</u>: nasal and throat irritation, runny nose, sneezing

Other resources to help you quit:
Freedom from Smoking
Online program (free)
www.lungusa.org
Click on "Quit Smoking"

Clean Break of Minnesota
Online program ($149)
www.cleanbreak.com

Nicotine Anonymous
Meetings are open to those who have quit or those who want to quit.
Local live, telephone, and Internet meetings are available.
www.nicotine-anonymous.com (Accessed June 2008)

Other Web sites:
www.quitplan.com (Accessed June 2008)
www.cancer.org (Accessed June 2008)
www.lungusa.org (Accessed June 2008)
www.quitnet.org (Accessed June 2008)
www.tobaccofree.org (Accessed June 2008)
www.quit4life.com (geared toward adolescents) (Accessed June 2008)
www.quitsmokingchat.com (Accessed June 2008)

Sources
- Clinical Practice Guideline. Treating Tobacco Use and Dependence. Washington, DC: U.S. Department of Health and Human Services, Public Health Service, June 2000.
- Dale LC, Hurt RD, Offord KP, et al. High dose nicotine patch therapy: percentage of replacement and smoking cessation. JAMA 1995;274:1353–8.
- Jorenby DE, Smith SS, Fiore MC, et al. Varying nicotine patch dose and type of smoking cessation counseling. JAMA 1995;274:1347–52.
- Nicotrol Inhaler prescribing information. St. Louis, MO: Pharmacia Corporation, 2001.
- Nicotrol Nasal Spray prescribing information. St. Louis, MO: Pharmacia Corporation, 2001.
- Zyban Prescribing information. Research Triangle Park, NC: GlaxoSmithKline, August 2001.

ADULT TOBACCO CESSATION PROTOCOL

Submitted by: Kelly Ragucci

Revised: December 2006

Purpose

To establish guidelines for the management and education of tobacco cessation in adult patients and to clearly define the roles/responsibilities of the physicians and collaborating pharmacists. The purpose of the service is to provide continuity of care to patients who require tobacco cessation; enhance patient care through education, monitoring, and close follow-up; and reduce adverse events associated with tobacco cessation therapy.

PROVIDER QUALIFICATIONS

A pharmacist providing tobacco cessation drug therapy management (DTM) must be credentialed by the Department of Pharmacy Services and meet minimal competencies required for their practice area. Until credentialing is obtained, a pharmacist may work under direct supervision of the credentialed pharmacist. The physicians must be MUSC credentialed and have a signed CDTM agreement for tobacco cessation management with the credentialed pharmacist.

PROCEDURE

Referral

The referring physician will provide the clinic with comorbid diseases to include, but not be limited to, any history of MI, arrhythmias, seizures, eating disorders, and vascular disease. If preferred by provider, specific pharmacotherapy recommendations for tobacco cessation may be made.

Clinic Visits

Procedure
- The patient will follow the general policies and procedures concerning registration and will then meet with the pharmacist.
- First visit—The following points will be addressed
  - Tobacco use history
  - Pregnancy test and/or birth control assessment
  - Transtheoretical model of behavioral change and willingness to quit (Figure 1)
  - Fagerström nicotine dependence test (Appendix I)
  - Availability of self-help material and behavioral therapy
  - Additional education and management based on assessed stage of change (Figure 1)
- Stages of change include
  - Precontemplation—Patient is not thinking about quitting in the next 6 months.
  - Contemplation—Patient is thinking about quitting in the next 6 months.
  - Preparation—Patient plans to quit within the next 30 days.
  - Action—Patient is actively engaged in the behavioral change.
  - Maintenance—Patient has sustained the behavioral change for 6 months or more.

Follow-up visits

(To be determined by the patient and pharmacist)
- Precontemplation phase
  - Follow-up is not required by the pharmacist, because the patient does not want to quit.
- Education and management will occur for all patients in the contemplation, preparation, or action phase.
- Contemplation phase
  - Patients will be seen quarterly.
- Preparation and Action phase
  - Once the patient has set a quit date
    - The patient will be provided a prescription, if necessary, during the preparation phase.
    - The patient will be educated on drugs selected and adverse effects.
    - The patient will schedule an appointment within one week after the quit date and then at least monthly.
  - In addition to clinic visits, the pharmacist will telephone the patient weekly for the first month as necessary, based on goal achievement. After the first month, a telephone follow-up schedule will be determined in concert with the patient.

Physical assessment

The pharmacist may perform or will review the following physical assessments at each visit
- Visual inspection for signs of smoking, chest pain, or angina
- Vital signs: to include BP and pulse rate (regular or irregular)
- Drug management

Prepared by Medical University of South Carolina, Charleston, South Carolina

- The pharmacist is authorized to initiate, modify, discontinue, and determine duration of treatment of the following drugs
  - Nicotine replacement therapy
  - Nicotine patch
  - Nicotine gum
  - Nicotine nasal spray
  - Nicotine inhaler
  - Nicotine lozenge
  - Bupropion SR
  - May consider combination therapy or an alternative nicotine replacement therapy
  - Choice of drug will be determined by the pharmacist and patient according to specific characteristics of the patient and their preference. Choice of drug may also be dictated by referring physician preference.
- The pharmacist will contact the referring physician when the above drugs are initiated or if a drug requires discontinuation. All orders will be written according to CDTM Tobacco Protocol and signed by the credentialed pharmacist. Prescriptions may be written or called into the patient's pharmacy by the credentialed pharmacist, as an agent of the physician, by telephone order.
- The pharmacist will provide drug education when a drug is initiated and at follow-up visits.
- Laboratory monitoring
  - The pharmacist is not authorized to order laboratory tests under this protocol. If tests need to be ordered to determine appropriate therapy, the pharmacist will contact the referring physician.
- Drug refills
  - The pharmacist will refer the patient to his or her physician for drug refills unless prior arrangements have been made.
- Perform point-of-care testing
  - The pharmacist is not authorized to perform point-of-care testing under this protocol.
- Drug administration
  - The pharmacist is not authorized to administer drugs under this protocol.
- Patient referral
  - The pharmacist may refer patients to behavioral therapy, the emergency department, or the referring physician as clinically indicated.
- Participation in/coordination of clinical research
  - Not applicable for this protocol
- Documentation
  - All patient encounters will be documented in the Progress Notes section of the EMR.
  - All notes will be sent to the referring provider by the EMR.
- Billing for services
  - Patients will be billed for services in accordance with the MUSC Department of Pharmacy Services Ambulatory Care Billing Policy.
- Clinic discharge
  - The patient will be discharged when the maintenance phase has been achieved or when the patient decides he or she no longer wishes to receive care. In addition, the pharmacist, in consultation with the referring physician, may decide to discharge the patient from the clinic.
- All other procedures will be performed according to the general policies and procedures of the clinic.

Quality Assurance/Outcomes

Data will be continuously followed to ensure that patients are receiving optimal care. The primary outcomes followed will include, but not be limited to, tobacco cessation rates and serious adverse events. Process tracking will also occur to confirm adherence to the protocol. These results will be presented biannually to the appropriate pharmacy coordinator and manager.

References

1. Fiore MC, Bailey WC, Cohen SJ, et al. Treating tobacco use and dependence: Clinical practice guideline. Rockville, MD: U.S. Department of Health and Human Services, Public Health Service, 2000. Available at www.surgeongeneral.gov/tobacco/. Accessed June 1, 2008.
2. The Regents of the University of California. Rx for Change clinical practice guideline. Available at http://rxforchange.ucsf.edu/. Accessed June 1, 2008.

Figure 1. Transtheoretical model of behavior change and willingness to quit.

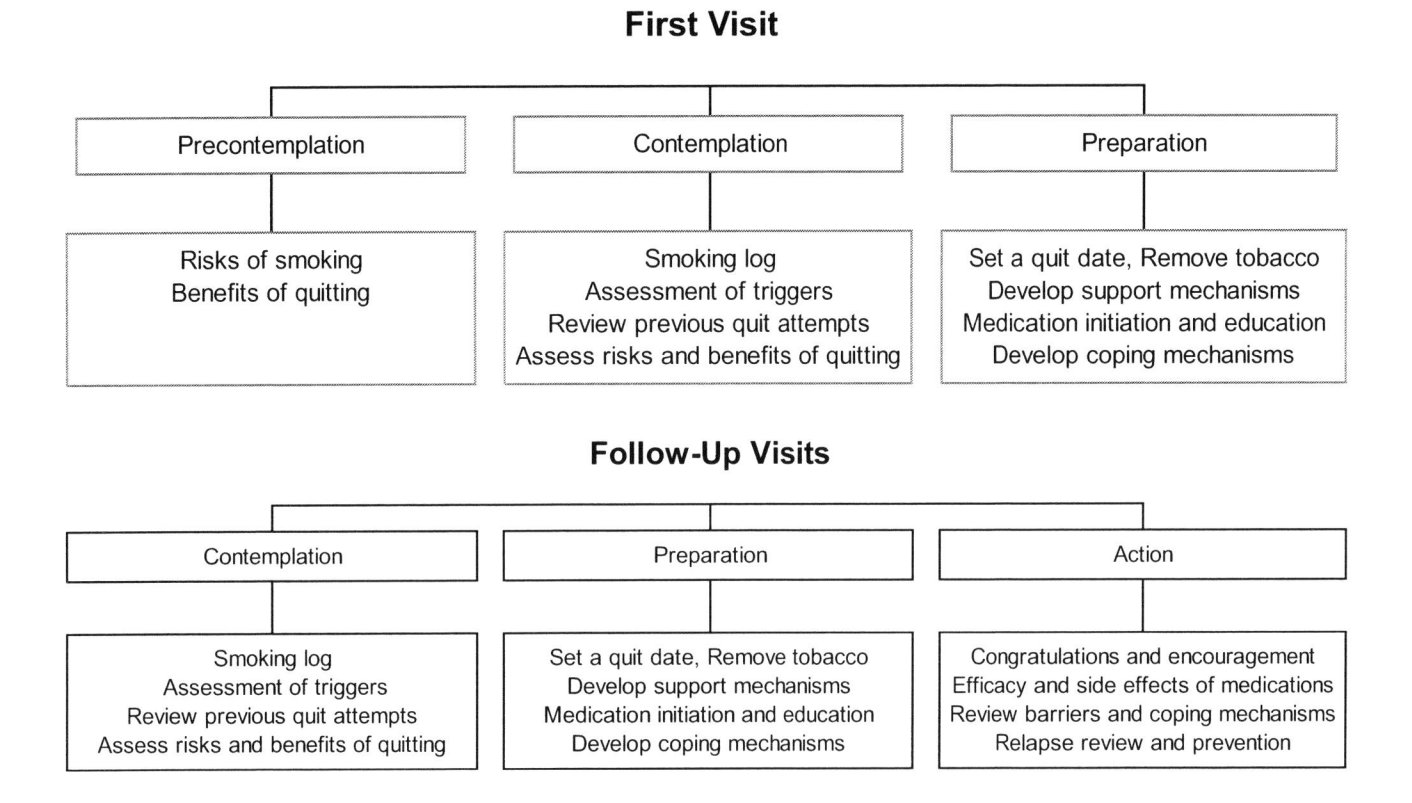

First Visit

Precontemplation	Contemplation	Preparation
Risks of smoking Benefits of quitting	Smoking log Assessment of triggers Review previous quit attempts Assess risks and benefits of quitting	Set a quit date, Remove tobacco Develop support mechanisms Medication initiation and education Develop coping mechanisms

Follow-Up Visits

Contemplation	Preparation	Action
Smoking log Assessment of triggers Review previous quit attempts Assess risks and benefits of quitting	Set a quit date, Remove tobacco Develop support mechanisms Medication initiation and education Develop coping mechanisms	Congratulations and encouragement Efficacy and side effects of medications Review barriers and coping mechanisms Relapse review and prevention

Copyright © 1982 by Division of Psychotherapy (29). American Psychological Association. Adapted with permission. The official citation that should be used in referencing this material is Psychotheor Res Pract Train 1982;19:276–88

Appendix I

Fagerström Tolerance Scale

Participant ID:_____
Date:___/___/___

Write the number of the answer that is most applicable on the line to the left of the question.

_____1. How soon after you awake do you smoke your first cigarette?

0. After 30 minutes
1. Within 30 minutes

_____2. Do you find it difficult to refrain from smoking in places where it is forbidden, such as the library, theater, or doctors' office?

0. No
1. Yes

_____3. Which of all the cigarettes you smoke in a day is the most satisfying?

0. Any other than the first one in the morning
1. The first one in the morning

_____4. How many cigarettes a day do you smoke?

0. 1–15
1. 16–25
2. More than 26

_____5. Do you smoke more during the morning than during the rest of the day?

0. No
1. Yes

_____6. Do you smoke when you are so ill that you are in bed most of the day?

0. No
1. Yes

_____7. Does the brand you smoke have a low, medium, or high nicotine content?

0. Low
1. Medium
2. High

_____8. How often do you inhale the smoke from your cigarette?

0. Never
1. Sometimes
2. Always

SCORING INSTRUCTIONS: *Add up your responses to all the items. Total scores should range from 0 to 11, where 7 or greater suggests physical dependence on nicotine.*

TOTAL SCORE:_____

Reference

1. Heatherton TF, Kozlowski LT, Frecker RC, Fagerstrom KO. The Fagerstrom Test for Nicotine Dependence: A revision of the Fagerstrom Tolerance Questionnaire. Br J Addict 1991;86:1119–27.

Appendix II: Tobacco Cessation Drugs

Bupropion SR (Zyban)

- Dose: 150 mg every day for 3 days; then 2 times per day for 2 to 3 months. Some patients may require longer maintenance therapy for up to 6 months. The quit date is set for about 10 days after initiation of bupropion.
    - Dose should not exceed 300 mg daily because of a dose-dependent increased risk of seizure.
    - Dosing frequency must be reduced in hepatic impairment and renal impairment. There are no specific recommendations for this dosing reduction; clinical judgment will be used. In severe cirrhosis, the dose should be 150 mg every other day.
    - Administration
        - Agent may be used safely with nicotine replacement therapy.
        - If insomnia occurs, the doses may be taken 8 hours apart.
        - Dose may be decreased to 150 mg every day if adverse effects occur.
        - If patient has made no progress after 7 weeks, may consider discontinuing therapy.
- Contraindications: Bupropion will not be used in patients with seizure disorders, with a history

or a current diagnosis of anorexia or bulimia, or with concomitant MAO inhibitors.
- ❑ Additional concerns: If patient is pregnant, treatment will be discussed with the referring physician before beginning therapy.
- ❑ Drug interactions: Bupropion inhibits CYP2D6 isoenzyme; therefore, it may be necessary to adjust the doses of drugs that are metabolized through this enzyme. These drugs include amitriptyline, bisoprolol, carvedilol, clozapine, desipramine, dextromethorphan, flecainide, fluoxetine, haloperidol, imipramine, labetolol, metoprolol, nortriptyline, oxycodone, paroxetine, promethazine, propafenone, propranolol, risperidone, sertraline, tamoxifen, thioridazine, timolol, tramadol, trazodone, and venlafaxine. In addition, codeine and hydrocodone may be ineffective if used with bupropion. If a patient is receiving any of these drugs, the situation will be discussed with the referring physician so that any necessary adjustments can be made. Bupropion should be used with caution in conjunction with other drugs that may decrease the seizure threshold (e.g., SSRIs, tramadol, theophylline, antipsychotics, systemic steroids, use/cessation of alcohol use); however, they may still be used together under this protocol if deemed appropriate by the clinical pharmacist. The above drug interactions are not all-inclusive.
- ❑ Adverse effects: Common adverse effects include insomnia (30–40%) and dry mouth (11%). These adverse effects usually lessen with continued use. Adverse effects that are less common but associated with discontinuation of treatment include tremors (3.4%) and rash (2.4%).

Verenicline (Chantix)

- ❑ Dose: 0.5 mg daily on days 1–3; 0.5 mg twice daily on days 4–7; 1 mg twice daily thereafter (weeks 2–12)
- ❑ Contraindications: Hypersensitivity to verenicline tartrate or any component of the formulation
- ❑ Additional patient education: Doses should be taken after eating, with a full glass of water; nausea and insomnia are adverse effects that are usually temporary; if symptoms persist, notify your health care provider. Dose tapering is not necessary when discontinuing treatment.
- ❑ Drug interactions: Successful cessation of smoking may alter the pharmacokinetic properties of other drugs (e.g., theophylline, warfarin, insulin).
- ❑ Adverse effects: Common adverse effects (5% or more and twice the rate observed in placebo-treated patients) include nausea, sleep disturbances (insomnia, abnormal dreams), constipation, flatulence, and vomiting.

Nicotine replacement therapy

(nicotine patch, gum, nasal spray, inhaler, and lozenge)
- ❑ Nicotine patch
  - ❑ Dose: See Table 1.

Table 1: Recommended Nicotine Patch Regimen

Product	Light Smoker	Heavy Smoker
Nicotrol (OTC, 16-hour)	≤ 10 cigarettes/day	> 10 cigarettes/day Step 1 (15 mg for 6 weeks) Step 2 (10 mg for 2 weeks) Step 3 (5 mg for 2 weeks)
Nicoderm CQ (OTC, 24-hour)	≤ 10 cigarettes/day Step 2 (14 mg for 6 weeks) Step 3 (7 mg for 2 weeks)	> 10 cigarettes/day Step 1 (21 mg for 6 weeks) Step 2 (14 mg for 2 weeks) Step 3 (7 mg for 2 weeks)
Generic (prescription, 24-hour) (formerly Habitrol)	≤10 cigarettes/day Step 2 (14 mg for 6 weeks) Step 3 (7 mg for 2 weeks)	> 10 cigarettes/day Step 1 (21 mg for 4 weeks) Step 2 (14 mg for 2 weeks) Step 3 (7 mg for 2 weeks)
Generic (OTC, 24-hour) (formerly ProStep)	≤15 cigarettes/day 11 mg for 6 weeks	> 15 cigarettes/day 22 mg for 6 weeks

- ❑ Altered regimens may be used, depending on patient-specific issues and clinical judgment.
- ❑ Patient's starting patch dose will be correlated to his/her current cigarette intake; one cigarette = 1 mg of nicotine. The maximum dose of patches proven to be safe and effective is 44 mg.
- ❑ If current smoking is less than 15 cigarettes per day, may consider starting with 14-mg patches.
- ❑ Administration: Apply patch to hairless area between neck and waist, rotating sites.
- ❑ Contraindications: Smoking while on the patch; immediately post-MI (within 2 weeks), serious arrhythmias, worsening angina
  - ❑ Additional concerns: If patient is currently pregnant or has severe vascular disease, treatment will be discussed with the referring physician before therapy is begun.
  - ❑ Adverse effects: Skin irritation (50%), vivid dreams (may switch to sixteen-hour patch), insomnia, GI complaints
- ❑ Nicotine gum (Nicorette—OTC)
  - ❑ Dose: 25 or more cigarettes/day: 4 mg; less than 25 cigarettes/day: 2 mg. Weeks 1–6: one piece every 1½ hours. Weeks 7–9: one piece every 2 to 4 hours. Weeks 10–12: one piece every 4 to 8 hours
    - ❑ Maximum, 24 pieces/day
  - ❑ Administration: Slowly chew until peppery,

minty, or citrus taste or "tingling" in mouth; then "park" the gum between gum and cheek until sensation is gone (usually 1 to 3 minutes). Slowly rechew every few minutes and "park" again. Chew each piece for 30 minutes, with one piece every 1 to 2 hours. Do not eat or drink anything except water 15 minutes before or during chewing. Taper dose slowly.
  - Duration: Up to 12 weeks
  - May be useful for as-needed use only, especially in combination with other agents
- Contraindications: Post-MI (within 2 weeks), serious arrhythmias, or serious or worsening angina
- Other concerns: If patient is currently pregnant or has severe vascular disease, treatment will be discussed with the referring physician before beginning therapy.
- Adverse effects: Chewing the gum too rapidly may cause excessive release of nicotine, resulting in lightheadedness, nausea, irritation of throat and mouth, hiccups, and indigestion. Additional adverse effects include mouth soreness, hiccups, dyspepsia, and jaw muscle ache.
- Nicotine nasal spray (Nicotrol NS—Prescription)
  - Dose: 1 or 2 sprays per hour (one in each nostril), not to exceed 5 sprays per hour or 40 sprays in 24 hours. Two sprays (one in each nostril) = 1 mg of nicotine.
  - Administration: Tilt head slightly back and do not inhale, sniff, or swallow while spray is being administered. A minimum of 8 doses (16 sprays) should be used each day.
    - Not to be used for more than 6 months
  - Precautions: Chronic nasal problems (polyps, allergies, etc.) or severe reactive airway disease. There is a higher abuse potential than with other nicotine replacement therapy because of the quick absorption.
  - Contraindications: Immediately post-MI (within 2 weeks), serious arrhythmias, or serious or worsening angina
  - Additional concerns: If patient is currently pregnant or has severe vascular disease, treatment will be discussed with the referring physician before beginning therapy.
  - Adverse effects: Nasal and throat irritation, runny nose, sneezing, watery eyes, coughing
- Nicotine inhaler (Nicotrol Inhaler—Prescription)
  - Dose: About 80 puffs = 4 mg of nicotine = one cartridge
  - Administration: 3 or 4 puffs/minute (continuous puffing) for 20 to 30 minutes; will use a minimum of 4 cartridges/day; recommended to use at least 6 cartridges/day. Eating and drinking should be avoided for the 15 minutes before and during use.
    - Recommended duration of therapy is 6 months, with gradual reduction during the last 12 weeks.
    - Inhaler should be stored at temperatures greater than 4.4°C, because delivery of nicotine will significantly decrease at lower temperatures.
  - Contraindications: Post-MI (within 2 weeks), serious arrhythmias, or serious or worsening angina
  - Additional concerns: If patient is currently pregnant or has severe vascular disease, treatment will be discussed with the referring physician before beginning therapy.
  - Adverse effects: Cough and mouth/throat irritation
- Nicotine lozenge (Commit—OTC)
  - Dose: 20 lozenges/day and/or 5 lozenges in 6 hours (maximum)
  - Patients smoking their first cigarette within 30 minutes of waking should be advised to use the 4-mg lozenge. Those smoking their first cigarette after 30 minutes of waking should use the 2-mg lozenge.
  - Administration: Weeks 1–6: 1 lozenge every 1 to 2 hours. Weeks 7–9: 1 lozenge every 2 to 4 hours. Weeks 10–12: 1 lozenge every 4 to 8 hours. Place lozenge in mouth and allow it to slowly dissolve for 20 to 30 minutes. Minimize swallowing and occasionally move the lozenge from one side of your mouth to the other. Do not chew or swallow lozenge. Do not eat or drink anything 15 minutes before using or while using the lozenge. Use at least 9 lozenges per day for the first 6 weeks.
  - Precautions: Contains phenylalanine 3.4 mg/lozenge
  - Contraindications: Immediately after MI (within 2 weeks), serious arrhythmias, or serious or worsening angina
  - Additional concerns: If patient is currently pregnant or has severe vascular disease, treatment will be discussed with the referring physician before beginning therapy.
  - Adverse effects: Cough, mouth/throat irritation, nausea, hiccups, and heartburn

PHARMACY ASTHMA PROGRAM
Submitted by: Allen Shek

Created: September 2001

Purpose

- To improve care and ensure optimal outcome in the patient population with asthma through thorough patient education, optimal drug management, and close monitoring
- To prevent unnecessary emergency department visits and hospitalizations due to asthma

Policy

- The participating pharmacists are required to first complete the Health Plan of San Joaquin (HPSJ) Certification Program in asthma patient care.
- When optimizing drug therapy, the participating pharmacists shall adhere to the HPSJ treatment protocol, in consultation with the patient's PCP.
- The participating pharmacist must comply with all documentation procedures to maintain provider status and be eligible for reimbursement of cognitive services rendered.

Procedure

Pharmacist Training/Participation

- HPSJ provides an annual asthma certification program for pharmacists. Pharmacists who have completed this program are eligible to participate as providers of the HPSJ pharmacy asthma program.
- Only pharmacists certified through the above program can complete patient assessment forms and forms required for billing of cognitive services.
- Certified pharmacists must have a consultation area to conduct the patient assessment and interview.

Patient Identification

- Any one of the following criteria may indicate the need for patient enrollment in the HPSJ Pharmacist Asthma Program
    - Emergency department visit for asthma exacerbation in past 12 months
    - Hospitalization(s) for asthma in past 12 months
    - Use of more than one canister of albuterol in 30 days
    - Increased use of short-acting β-agonists (e.g., greater than 3 or 4 times per day)
    - Overuse or misuse of long-acting β-agonists
    - Nonadherence to inhaled anti-inflammatory drugs (e.g., refilling the prescription less often than indicated by the directions)
    - Poor tolerance to physical activity (e.g., exercise-induced asthma)
    - Missing schooldays or workdays because of asthma symptoms
- HPSJ is responsible for sending a list of patients at high risk of asthma exacerbation to participating pharmacists. HPSJ will use claims data to develop this list.
- Certified pharmacists are responsible for identifying HPSJ patients who meet the inclusion criteria and pursuing enrollment for these patients.

Patient Enrollment

- HPSJ members who have agreed to participate in the Pharmacy Asthma Program must complete and sign a Patient Consent Form.
- PCPs can also identify patients and refer them to participating pharmacists.
- The pharmacist provider will contact the patient's PCP by fax to request participation with the collaborative practice agreement. The fax will include a brief description of the Pharmacy Asthma Program (from HPSJ) and a Protocol Referral Form (Appendix A). The physician will need to sign this and fax it back to the pharmacist for patient enrollment to occur.
- If the PCP does not respond within one week, a letter from the medical director of this program will be faxed to the PCP to encourage participation.
- If the PCP is still not willing to respond/participate within one week, these data will be collected and provided to HPSJ.

Patient Education

- The certified pharmacists will
    - Conduct an Initial Assessment and classify asthma severity according to the NHLBI guidelines (Appendix B).
    - Be responsible for reviewing the patient's profile to determine what type of clinical intervention is required and provide appropriate asthma education with written material based on patient's understanding. Areas to cover shall include, but not be limited to, the following
        - What is asthma?

- Triggers
- Asthma diary
- Metered-dose inhaler (MDI)/spacer and peak flow meter techniques
- Nebulizer use
- Smoking cessation (if applicable)
- Action plan
- Assess inhaler and spacer techniques and provide remedial training if needed
- Optimize drug therapy according to HPSJ Treatment Protocol (Appendix C) (see below)
- Teach self-monitoring techniques (peak flow meter/rescue inhaler use)
- Develop a home treatment plan for the patient when appropriate data have been collected

Therapy Optimization

- The pharmacist will be responsible for optimizing drug therapy based on patient-specific issues (special needs, compliance issues, etc.) and HPSJ treatment protocols (Appendix C).
- During each visit, the pharmacist will perform basic auscultation to assess the presence of wheezing. In addition, inhaler/spacer technique, drug adherence, and environmental control must be considered.
- Any potential changes in therapy will be discussed with the PCP, and the PCP must provide approval before implementation. Appropriate documentation in a visit note must be made for such communication.
- Documentation
  - Pharmacists must submit a copy of the consent form and visit note to HPSJ, if requested.
  - Each patient interaction will be documented on the appropriate forms and kept in shadow charts in the participating pharmacy.
  - The visit note will be faxed to the PCP after each appointment.
  - The home treatment plan will be faxed to the PCP when developed.

Billing

- Billing for the cognitive services provided will be done electronically (similar to prescriptions) with payment directly to the pharmacist.
- HPSJ recognizes only claims submitted by certified pharmacists with active provider status. If the provider is not certified by HPSJ or is without active provider status, the claim will be denied.
- The pharmacist is responsible for keeping all appropriate documentation of cognitive services in the shadow charts. This documentation may be requested by HPSJ any time after billing.

HPSJ Pharmacy Asthma Program Structure

Patient Identification

- Patients will be identified for enrolment by HPSJ, PCP, or certified pharmacist providers. Patients will meet criteria for enrollment if any one of the following is true: (1) use more than one canister of albuterol in 30 days, (2) emergency department visit in the past 12 months, or (3) hospitalization for asthma in the past 12 months.

Physician Participation

- The PCPs will be informed of the initiation of this program and the pharmacists involved before the identification of patients.
- Once patients are identified, the pharmacist provider will contact the PCP of the targeted patient to request participation with the collaborative practice agreement. This fax contact will include a brief description of the program from HPSJ and a "protocol referral form" (Appendix A) for monitoring and management based on treatment protocol (Appendix C) approved by the medical director of this program. The physician will need to sign this and fax it back to the pharmacist.
- Two levels of services can be requested by the PCP
  - Education only or
  - Education with drug optimization
- If the PCP does not respond within one week, a letter from the medical director of this program will be faxed to the PCP to encourage participation.
- If the PCP is still not willing to respond/participate, these data will be collected and provided to HPSJ.

Pharmacist Duties

1. Complete the certification programs
2. Identify HPSJ patients who meet inclusion criteria and contact the respective PCPs as described above
3. After receiving consent from both the patient and PCP, the pharmacist will
   a. Provide asthma education with written material based on patient's understanding
   b. Assess current symptoms and classify asthma severity according to the NHLBI guidelines (Appendix B)
   c. Assess inhaler and spacer technique and provide remedial training if needed
   d. Perform basic auscultation to assess the presence of wheezing
   e. Optimize drug therapy based on treatment protocols (Appendix C)
   f. Teach self-monitoring (peak flow meter/rescue inhaler use)

  g. Develop a home treatment plan with the pharmacist's contact number
4. All patient interactions will be documented in the visit notes provided and be kept in shadow charts in the participating pharmacy.
5. The visit note will be faxed to the PCP.
6. Billing for the cognitive services provided will be done electronically (similar to prescriptions) with payment directly to the pharmacist.
7. Set up next appointment for monitoring and assess need for remediation per steps 3a–c. Consider discharging patients from service if therapy is optimized and no exacerbations for 6 months or more.

HPSJ Involvement

- The Health Plan will
    - Be responsible for assisting with identification of the target patients through data evaluation for emergency department use, hospitalization, etc.
    - Inform physicians of the pharmacist asthma program and encourage participation
    - Be financially responsible for payment to pharmacists for services rendered
    - Assist with data evaluation for study outcomes

HPSJ PHARMACY ASTHMA PROGRAM SCHEMATIC

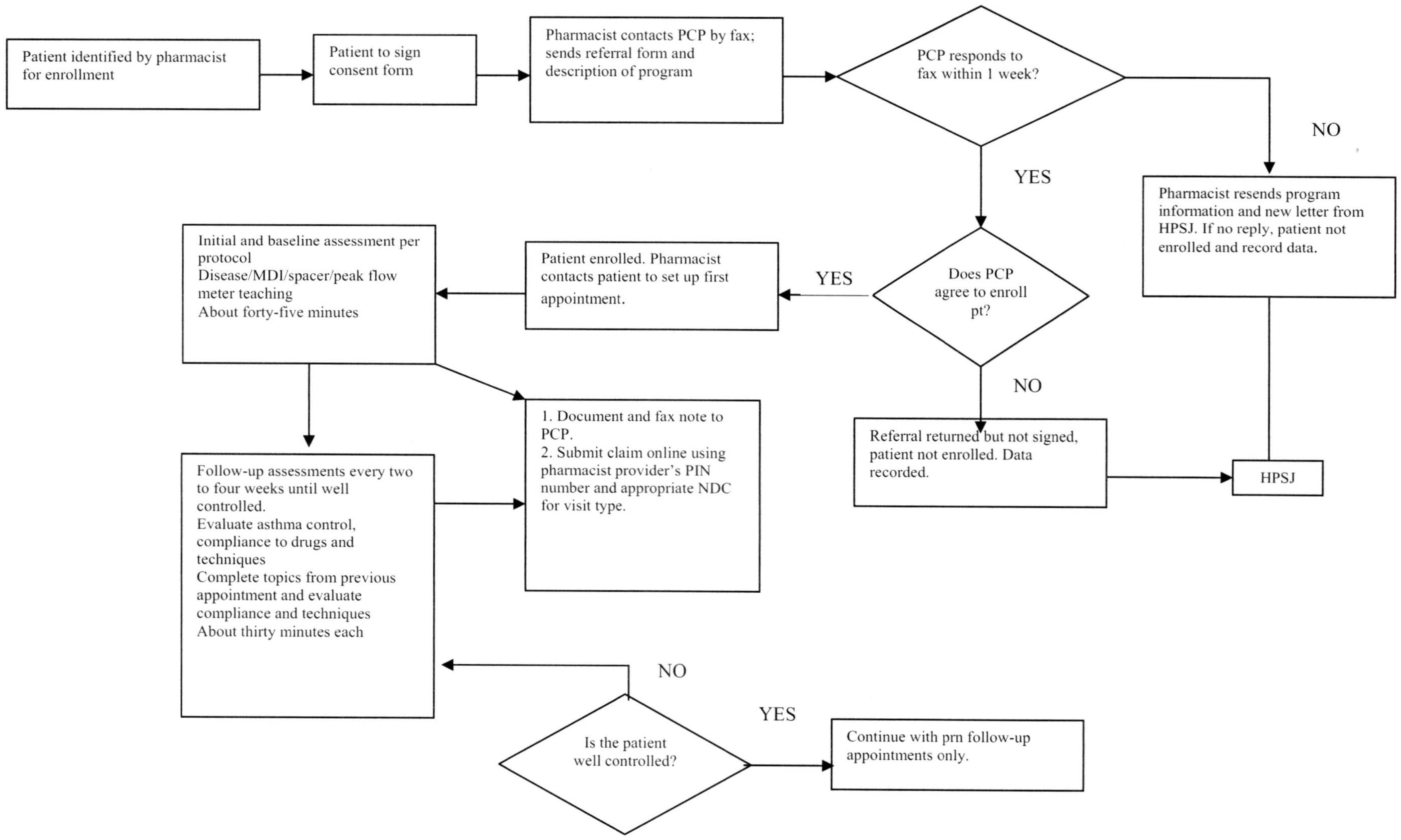

```
Patient identified by pharmacist for enrollment
          │
          ▼
Patient to sign consent form
          │
          ▼
Pharmacist contacts PCP by fax; sends referral form and description of program
          │
          ▼
     ◇ PCP responds to fax within 1 week? ◇
          │
   NO ────┴──── YES
   │            │
   ▼            ▼
Pharmacist    ◇ Does PCP agree to enroll pt? ◇
resends            │
program       YES ─┴─ NO
information        │        │
and new            │        ▼
letter from        │   Referral returned but not signed,
HPSJ. If no        │   patient not enrolled. Data recorded.
reply, patient     │        │
not enrolled       │        ▼
and record         │       HPSJ
data.              │
   │               ▼
   ▼          Patient enrolled. Pharmacist contacts patient to set up first appointment.
  HPSJ             │
                   ▼
         Initial and baseline assessment per protocol
         Disease/MDI/spacer/peak flow meter teaching
         About forty-five minutes
                   │
                   ▼
         1. Document and fax note to PCP.
         2. Submit claim online using pharmacist provider's PIN number and appropriate NDC for visit type.
                   │
                   ▼
         Follow-up assessments every two to four weeks until well controlled.
         Evaluate asthma control, compliance to drugs and techniques
         Complete topics from previous appointment and evaluate compliance and techniques
         About thirty minutes each
                   │
                   ▼
         ◇ Is the patient well controlled? ◇
                   │
            NO ────┴──── YES
            │              │
            ▼              ▼
     (back to claim    Continue with prn
      submission)      follow-up appointments only.
```

Appendix A—HPSJ Pharmacy Asthma Program Referral Form

Health Plan of San Joaquin

Pharmacy Asthma Management Referral Form

Patient Name:_____ Date of Service: _____
Address:_____ City/State/Zip:_____
Telephone #:_____ DOB:_____
Diagnosis (ICD-9):_____

Patient referred to:_____ Phone# _____
　　　　　　　　　　　　　　Pharmacist/Pharmacy

I am requesting that the above Pharmacy/Pharmacist provide this patient with asthma education and therapy optimization per the HPSJ Asthma Pharmacy Program Protocol.
I consider these services a necessary part of this patient's medical care.

_____　　　_____
 Physician's Signature　　　　　　　　　　　　　　　　　Date

Physician's Name (Please Print): _____
Address of practice: _____
Telephone #: _____ Physician's UPIN_____

Appendix B—HPSJ Asthma Severity Classification

Severity[a]	Daytime Symptoms	Nocturnal Symptoms	Lung Function[b]
Step 4 Severe persistent	Symptoms > 3 times/day Frequent exacerbations	> 3 times/week	FEV_1 or PEFR $\leq$ 60% predicted PEF variability > 30%
Step 3 Moderate persistent	Symptoms every day Exacerbations > 1 time/week	> 1 time/week	FEV_1 or PEFR > 60% to < 80% predicted PEF variability > 30%
Step 2 Mild persistent	Symptoms > 2 times/week < 1 time/day	> 2 times/month	FEV_1 or PEFR $\geq$ 80% predicted PEF variability > 20–30%
Step 1 Mild intermittent	Symptoms $\leq$ 2 times/week	$\leq$ 2 times/month	FEV_1 or PEFR $\geq$ 80% predicted PEF variability < 20%

[a] An individual should be assigned the most severe grade in which any feature occurs.
[b] Refer to individual peak flow meter for the predicted PEFR based on patient's sex, age, and height.
Adapted from Figure 3-4a, NHLBI guidelines, Expert Panel Report 2, 1997.
FEV = forced expiratory volume; PEFR = peak expiratory flow (rate).

Appendix C—Treatment Protocol

Recommended Chronic Treatments for Adult Asthmatic Patients[a,b]

Severity	Long-Term Control	Quick Relief
Severe persistent	High-dose anti-inflammatory: Fluticasone 220 µg: ≥ 2 puffs twice daily or Budesonide DPI 4 puffs daily AND <u>Long-acting bronchodilator</u>: Salmeterol 2 puffs every 12 hours AND/OR <u>Leukotriene modifier</u>: Montelukast 10 mg orally every night	Albuterol 2 puffs every 4–6 hours as needed
Moderate persistent	<u>Medium-dose anti-inflammatory</u>: Fluticasone 110 µg: 1–3 puffs twice daily OR Budesonide DPI 2 or 3 puffs daily AND <u>Long-acting bronchodilator if nocturnal symptoms persists</u>: Salmeterol 2 puffs every 12 hours	Albuterol 2 puffs every 4–6 hours as needed
Mild persistent	<u>Low-dose anti-inflammatory</u>: Fluticasone 110 µg: 1 puff twice daily or Triamcinolone 2–5 puffs twice daily	Albuterol 2 puffs every 4–6 hours as needed
Mild intermittent	None needed	Albuterol 2 puffs every 4–6 hours as needed

[a] Adapted from NHLBI Guidelines with drugs covered by HPSJ as of July 18, 2001.
[b] Adequacy of treatment should be reviewed every 1–6 months, depending on the patient's severity and response. If control is not maintained after reviewing patient drug technique, adherence, and environmental control, consider step-up therapy. If control is maintained for more than 6 months, a gradual stepwise reduction in long-term control drugs may be considered.

Recommended Chronic Treatments for Child Asthmatic Patients[a]

Severity	Long-Term Control	Quick Relief
Severe persistent	<u>High-dose anti-inflammatory</u>: Fluticasone 220 µg: ≥ 1 puff twice daily OR Budesonide DPI ≥ 2 puffs once daily AND <u>Long-acting bronchodilator</u>: Salmeterol 2 puffs every 12 hours AND/OR <u>Leukotriene modifier</u>: Montelukast 4 mg orally every night (2–5 years old) ***Montelukast 5 mg orally every night (6–14 years old)***	Albuterol 2 puffs every 4–6 hours as needed
Moderate persistent	<u>Medium-dose anti-inflammatory</u>: Fluticasone 110 µg: 1 or 2 puffs twice daily OR Budesonide DPI 1 or 2 puffs once daily AND <u>Long-acting bronchodilator if nocturnal symptoms persists</u>: Salmeterol 2 puffs every 12 hours[b]	Albuterol 2 puffs every 4–6 hours as needed
Mild persistent	Low-dose anti-inflammatory: Fluticasone 44 µg: 1 or 2 puffs twice daily OR Triamcinolone 2–4 puffs twice daily	Albuterol 2 puffs every 4–6 hours as needed
Mild intermittent	None needed	Albuterol 2 puffs every 4–6 hours as needed

[a] Adequacy of treatment should be reviewed every 1–6 months, depending on the patient's severity and response. If control is not maintained, after reviewing patient drug technique, adherence, and environmental control, consider step-up therapy. If control has been maintained for more than 6 months, a gradual stepwise reduction in long-term control drugs may be considered.
[b] For children older than 4 years; use spacer.

METERED-DOSE INHALER SPACER PROTOCOL— POLICY AND PROCEDURE

Submitted by: Allen Shek

Created: September 2006

Authorizing Prescriber Statement for Initiation of an MDI Spacer Order

California-licensed pharmacists listed in Appendix A1 who are employed by the pharmacy indicated in Appendix A1 and who are acting as delegates for _____, M.D., may initiate an order for an MDI spacer for the patients listed in Appendix A2 according to and in compliance with Article 3 of the Business and Professions code 4052.(a).(5) unless the patient's treating physician makes a specific request to exclude his or her patient from this protocol.

Qualifications of Persons Initiating an MDI Spacer Order
- Current California Pharmacist Licensure
- Completion of Health Plan of San Joaquin (HPSJ)/Premier Pharmacists Networks' (PPN) asthma intervention orientation/training
- Active employment with a pharmacy contracted to participate in the HPSJ/PPN asthma intervention program

Policies
- A standard form will be used to guide the pharmacist's assessment of the patient's asthma severity and appropriateness of therapy (Appendix B) and will be maintained as documentation.
- The pharmacist will notify the protocol physician and the patient's treating provider within 24 hours of the initiation of an order for an MDI spacer (see Appendix C).

Authorizing Prescriber

Physician's Name: _____ Affiliation: _____

Address: _____

Phone: _____ Fax: _____ Pager/Mobile: _____

E-mail: _____

Physician CA license number: _____ Physician DEA number: _____

_____   _____
Date   MD

This authorization will be in effect through February 28, 2007, unless rescinded earlier in writing by either party. Any changes in the protocol must be agreed on by both parties.

Developed by HealthPlan of San Joaquin, Stockton, California, and Premier Pharmacists Network, Sacramento, California

APPENDIX A1—Principal Authorized Pharmacist and Pharmacy

Pharmacy Information

Pharmacy where initiation of MDI spacer orders will occur

Pharmacy Name _____

Street _____ City _____ Zip _____

Pharmacy license # _____ E-mail: _____

Phone _____ Fax _____

Pharmacist in Charge of Program Implementation at This Pharmacy

Printed name _____ CA License # _____

Signature _____ Date _____

Additional Pharmacists Employed by This Pharmacy Authorized to Initiate an MDI Spacer Order

Printed name _____ **License #** _____ **Date** _____

Signature _____ **Date** _____

Printed name _____ **License #** _____ **Date** _____

Signature _____ **Date** _____

Printed name _____ **License #** _____ **Date** _____

Signature _____ **Date** _____

Printed name _____ **License #** _____ **Date** _____

Signature _____ **Date** _____

Printed name _____ **License #** _____ **Date** _____

Signature _____ **Date** _____

Printed name _____ **License #** _____ **Date** _____

Signature _____ **Date** _____

Appendix A2—Eligible Patients

Printed name _____ **HPSJ ID #** _____ **Treating MD** _____

Printed name _____ **HPSJ ID #** _____ **Treating MD** _____

Printed name _____ **HPSJ ID #** _____ **Treating MD** _____

Printed name _____ **HPSJ ID #** _____ **Treating MD** _____

Printed name _____ **HPSJ ID #** _____ **Treating MD** _____

Appendix B—Standardized Assessment/Documentation Form

HPSJ Asthma MTM Program
FAX the Completed Form to: (916) 290-0853

Patient: Name: _IF AVAILABLE,_ DOB: __/__/__
Pharmacy:
Name: _AFFIX PRESCRIPTION_
Address: _LABEL HERE_
Phone Number: _____

Date: _____ Patient's HPSJ ID: _____

1) Ask the patient to tell you about their asthma. How frequently do they have symptoms during the day and at night? Use this information to rate the patient's asthma severity:

Severity:	Mild Intermittent		Mild Persistent		Moderate Persistent		Severe Persistent	
Daytime Sx:	○	<2x/wk	○	>2x/wk	○	QD	○	>3x/day
Nocturnal Sx:	○	<2x/mo	○	>2x/mo	○	>1 x/wk	○	>3x/wk

**If the patient has symptoms > 2 x/wk, be sure to tell them that you can help them gain better control of their asthma, which should improve their health and quality of life. (Complete the rest of this form)

2) Ask the patient to tell you about their asthma drugs. What do they take and how do they take them?

Controller drug(s) Prescribed			Rescue drug(s)		
Drug	Sig (actual use)		Drug	Sig (actual use)	

3) Rate the patient's drug adherence:

a. Controller drug: b. Rescue drug:
○ Overuse ○ Underuse ○ Appropriate   ○ Overuse ○ Underuse ○ Appropriate

Tell the patient you'd like to talk about how they use their inhalers so they can be sure they're getting the best possible benefit from them. Have them demonstrate their technique for using the inhalers.

4) Rate the patient's inhaler technique:

a. MDI: ○ Correct ○ Incorrect   b. DPI: ○ Correct ○ Incorrect

5) Does the patient have a spacer with MDI?   ○ Yes and uses regularly ○ Yes but does not use ○ No

6) Considering the symptom severity and how the patient is taking their drugs, please rate the adequacy/appropriateness of their current regimen:

○ Appropriate ○ Inappropriate

Additional Comments:

7) If the therapy is inappropriate/inadequate, please indicate the action(s) you took to optimize the therapy (select all that apply):

○ Educated the patient on the importance of controller drug(s) (i.e., improving compliance)
○ Trained the patient on appropriate inhaler (MDI or DPI) technique
○ Furnished and educated the patient on the use of a spacer
○ Contacted the patient's prescriber to recommend a change in therapy. If so, what was the result?
  ○ Increased dose of controller drug: _____
  ○ Addition of controller drug: _____
  ○ Change in controller drug _____
  ○ Left a message
  ○ Prescriber refusal
  ○ Other (please describe) _____

8) Does the patient have a significant need for additional, more intensive education/training? ○ Yes ○ No

_____
Signature

Pharmacist's Name (Print): _____

Appendix C—Prescriber Notification Form

RE: Patient Name: _____ DOB: _____

Send to:	From:
Attention:	Pharmacy Name:
Fax Number:	Phone Number:
Date:	Number of Pages, Including Cover: 2
❑ URGENT ☒ REPLY ASAP ❑ PLEASE COMMENT ❑ PLEASE REVIEW ❑ FOR YOUR INFORMATION	

Dear Dr.

Health Plan of San Joaquin has partnered with Premier Pharmacists Network to develop an innovative asthma intervention program designed to improve asthma drug therapy. Through this program, participating pharmacies administer brief consultations provided by licensed pharmacists to targeted HPSJ patients who frequent their pharmacy to obtain refills of rescue inhalers. The purpose of this program is to work together with you to educate and consult with your patients in determining how to get the most out of their prescribed asthma drugs.

During my consultation with the patient named above, it became apparent that the addition of a spacer would very likely improve the efficacy of their metered-dose inhaler. The purpose of this fax is to notify you that I initiated an order for a spacer pursuant to a protocol with _____, MD, who is the Medical Director of HPSJ.

Please do not hesitate to contact me if you would like to discuss any issues regarding this fax. On behalf of Health Plan of San Joaquin and Premier Pharmacists Network, I appreciate your efforts in helping this patient get the most out of their asthma drug therapy.

Sincerely,

_____

cc: _____, MD—Fax: (XXX) XXX-XXXX

ASTHMA SHARED MEDICAL APPOINTMENT

Submitted by: Teresa Klepser

Created: January 2007

Background

The Behavioral Risk Factor Surveillance System (BRFSS) is a state-based, random-digit–dialed survey of the noninstitutionalized civilian U.S. population 18 years and older. The survey collects information about modifiable risk factors for chronic diseases and other leading causes of death each year from the 50 states, the District of Columbia, and three U.S. territories. In 2001, the BRFSS collected and summarized asthma prevalence data for adults from the 8 states that used the adult asthma history module. Findings from the 2001 BRFSS indicated the overall current asthma prevalence for the 8 states that were surveyed was 7.7% (95% CI = 7.3–8.1%). Current asthma prevalence varied from 5.3% (South Dakota) to 9.0% (Michigan). Among respondents with current asthma, 82.7% reported no visits to an emergency department during the preceding 12 months; 71.0% reported no urgent visits to a physician; and 54.4% reported routine checkups for asthma during the preceding 12 months. An estimated 71.6% of respondents with current asthma reported no days of activity limitation, 60.9% reported no days of disturbed sleep, and 21.8% reported having no symptoms during the preceding 30 days. An estimated 47.2% of respondents with current asthma reported no asthma attack or episode during the preceding 12 months. Based on these National Statistics, some asthmatic patients are currently uncontrolled.

National Asthma Guidelines emphasize the importance of the key elements of asthma care—classification, provision of controller drugs, and education about self-management skills. Unfortunately, patients and providers may rely mostly on acute-care needs when it comes to addressing asthma. A planned-care visit is a proactive clinical encounter that focuses on overall patient goals and other aspects of care that are not usually delivered during an acute-care visit. A planned-care visit for asthma is strongly recommended and is reimbursed by insurance carriers. The NHLBI recommends yearly visits for mild intermittent asthma, 6-month visits for mild persistent asthma, 4-month visits for moderate persistent asthma, and 3-month visits for severe persistent asthma.

Studies have shown that relying on acute-care asthma needs may lead to missed opportunities. One study described an innovative approach to asthma management by family physicians that involved scheduling groups of planned-care asthma visits on the same days, referred to as "Asthma Days." Organized asthma clinic days have been shown to increase clinic yearly revenue. The program generated more than $5,600 (excluding allergy testing, which was billed separately by an outside laboratory) during the 3-month period from charges that would have been lost. It was speculated that if 20 patients with persistent asthma received two planned-care visits per patient per year at $65 per visit, $2,600 in additional income would be generated. In many cases, the clinical care and counseling may support a level 4 office visit and pulmonary function testing. According to national guidelines, pulmonary function testing could be reasonably included once or twice per year at $40–$75 per test, which would generate $800–$3,000 in additional revenue. Regarding patient satisfaction, 92% of their patients felt that the visits improved their asthma care. Classification rates for these patients increased from about 20% to more than 90%, the use of inhaled corticosteroids increased from 50% to 87%, and the number of patients with persistent asthma who had action plans increased from 20% to 80%.

Rationale

- Asthma is a key component of the Healthy People 2010 objectives. Eight objectives address asthma:
  - 24-1 Reduce asthma deaths;
  - 24-2 Reduce hospitalizations for asthma;
  - 24-3 Reduce hospital emergency department visits for asthma;
  - 24-4 Reduce activity limitations among individuals with asthma;
  - 24-5 Reduce the number of school or workdays missed by individuals with asthma because of their asthma;
  - 24-6 Increase the proportion of individuals with asthma who receive formal patient education, including information regarding community and self-help resources, as an essential part of the management of their condition;
  - 24-7 Increase the proportion of individuals with asthma who receive appropriate asthma care according to the NAEPP guidelines; and
  - 24-8 Establish in 25 or more states a surveillance system for tracking asthma deaths, illnesses, disabilities, impact of occupational and environmental factors on asthma, access to medical care, and asthma management.
- According to the ProMed Quality Assurance and Utilization Review Committee June meeting, our asthma audits evaluated two indicators: (1) documentation of a written asthma action plan and (2) documentation of anti-inflammatory drugs in persis-

tent asthma. Each indicator is set at a threshold of 90%. During the March 2006 audit, written asthma action plans were documented in 25% of the charts, and anti-inflammatory medicines were documented in 71% of the audited charts. At that meeting, it was suggested to develop a plan to improve these asthma indicators.
- ProMed Family Practice has used the Shared Medical Appointment model since 2003 for male and female physical examinations, bone mineral density scan reviews, and DM examinations. To improve the ProMed asthma indicators, a shared medical appointment model is discussed.

Objectives of the Asthma Shared Medical Appointment

- To increase patient asthma knowledge
- To increase clinic revenue regarding asthma patients
- To increase the percentage of written asthma action plans
- To increase the percentage of anti-inflammatory drugs in patients with persistent asthma
- To decrease the number of emergency department visits in the past 6 months
- To decrease the number of hospital admissions in the past 6 months

Procedure

Identifying Potential Asthma Patients

All asthma claims for the past 12 months may be searched using the code 493.xx in our computerized billing system. With each provider's permission, letters will be mailed to each of these potential patients to explain the asthma shared medical appointment. Follow-up telephone calls will be made to identify patients interested in the asthma shared medical appointment model.

Scheduling Asthma Shared Medical Appointments

Patients who are interested in an asthma shared medical appointment may contact or may be contacted by the ProMed Shared Medical Appointment marketing scheduler at (269) 324-8523. Once an appointment is made, information regarding the shared medical appointment will be mailed to the patient. The patient will receive a reminder call the day before the scheduled appointment from the marketing scheduler.

Components of the Shared Medical Appointment

The basic objective of a shared medical appointment is to provide the patient with clinical management based on both the National Asthma Education and Prevention Program (NAEPP) guidelines and the patient's individual needs. For this reason, each of the shared medical appointments will target the following key processes of care:
- Patient self-assessment;
- Review of symptoms and direct observation of the patient's inhaler technique;
- Objective clinical reassessment by peak flow meter or spirometry;
- Clinical examination and assessment, with revision of treatment plan;
- Classification of asthma;
- Discussion of goal setting and self-management, including development or review of an Asthma Action Plan, which is a written guide for patients that provides a basic outline for self-management according to their symptoms and/or pulmonary function parameters;
- Teaching technique for a patient's specific delivery device, including the use of a spacer;
- Review triggers of asthma and how to control of those triggers;
- If appropriate, providing a prescription of inhaled corticosteroids or appropriate alternative drug for all patients with persistent asthma and thorough discussion of their use, adverse effects, and safety; and
- Scheduling of a follow-up appointment at the time of checkout.

Conducting the Shared Medical Appointment

This will be a 90-minute appointment for five to eight adult patients with the diagnosis of asthma. The providers and staff include a nurse practitioner, pharmacist, nursing staff (RN, LPN, or medical assistant), nurse specialist, and marketing scheduler.

To help identify the important elements of care that are recommended for asthma visits and to ensure proper documentation, a special documentation form for the asthma shared medical appointment was created. Before the shared medical appointment, the nurse specialist completes specific data elements on the documentation form and has the form ready for review by the provider.

When the patient arrives for his or her shared medical appointment, he or she will join the provider in a session room, where he or she will be addressed individually. Each patient will be asked to complete an asthma status questionnaire at check-in. The asthma status questionnaire will be the Asthma Action America's five-item Asthma

Control Test, which is available online at http://www.asthmaactionamerica.org/i_have_asthma/control_test.html. (Accessed June 10, 2008.)

In the session room, the nurse practitioner will complete a head-to-toe assessment as appropriate for the diagnosis of asthma and answer any personal health questions. The nurse practitioner will discuss a written asthma action plan, laboratory results, drugs, diagnostic testing, and any conditions the patient feels comfortable discussing in the session room. The nurse practitioner and pharmacist will also educate the patients on the following topics according to the Michigan Asthma Resource Kit:
- Signs and symptoms of worsening asthma
- Measures to control asthma triggers
- Written asthma action plan
- Monitor use of β_2-agonist inhalers
- Using peak flow meters appropriately
- Proper inhaler technique

Written information regarding the above topics will be given to the patients. The Michigan Asthma Resource Kit will be used to provide copyrightable written information.

Toward the end of the session, each patient will have asthma prescriptions renewed, if necessary; immunizations updated; laboratory and diagnostic testing ordered; and all return visits or special procedure appointments scheduled.

Evaluation

- The following measures of the asthma shared medical appointment will be collected and summarized annually:
  - Patient asthma quiz before and after each asthma shared medical appointment
  - Dollar value of asthma charges/revenue
  - Percentage of written asthma action plans by chart audits
  - Percentage of anti-inflammatory drugs in patients with persistent asthma by chart audits
  - Number of emergency department visits by chart audits
  - Number of hospital admissions by chart audits

References

1. National Institutes of Health National Heart, Lung, and Blood Institute. National Asthma Education and Prevention Program Guidelines (NAEPP). NAEPP Expert Panel Report 2. NIH Publication No. 97–4051. Available at www.nhlbi.nih.gov. Accessed June 10, 2008.
2. National Institutes of Health National Heart, Lung, and Blood Institute. National Asthma Education and Prevention Program Guidelines (NAEPP). NAEPP Expert Panel Report Guidelines for the Diagnosis and Management of Asthma-Update on Selected Topics 2002. NIH Publication No. 02–5075. Available at www.nhlbi.nih.gov. Accessed June 10, 2008.
3. Elward KS. Asthma days: An approach to planned asthma care. Fam Pract Manag 2004;11:43–8.
4. Centers for Disease Control and Prevention. MMWR 2003;52:381–4.
5. Asthma Initiative of Michigan. Michigan Asthma Resource Kit: Tools for quality asthma care. Available at www.michiganasthma.com. Accessed June 10, 2008.

ADULT TYPE 2 DIABETES PROTOCOL

Submitted by: Andrea Wessell

Revised: September 2006

Purpose

To establish guidelines for the monitoring of DM therapy in adult patients and to clearly define the roles/responsibilities of the physicians and collaborating pharmacists. The purpose of the service is to provide continuity of care to patients who require DM therapy; enhance patient care through education, monitoring, and close follow-up; and reduce adverse events associated with DM therapy.

Provider Qualifications

A pharmacist providing DM DTM must be credentialed by the Department of Pharmacy Services and meet minimal competencies required for his/her practice area. Until credentialing is obtained, the pharmacist will work under the direct supervision of a credentialed pharmacist. The physicians must be MUSC credentialed and have a signed CDTM agreement for DM management with the credentialed pharmacist.

Procedure

Referral

- The referring physician will provide the clinic with the following:
  - Patient comorbidities
  - Current drugs
  - Current pertinent laboratory values
  - Goals for patient therapy
  - Other pertinent information

It is the responsibility of the referring physician, or his or her designee, to be available for consultation. The pharmacist has the right to decline the management of a patient based on perceived inappropriateness of therapy, patient-specific risk factors, or barriers to treatment (e.g., nonadherence with drugs, visits). All patients must have blood work drawn at an MUSC laboratory and must report to their prospective clinic for visits. Telephone visits will not be conducted.

Clinic Visits

Procedure

The patient will follow the general policies and procedures concerning registration and will report to the MUSC laboratory to have blood drawn, if necessary. Afterward, the patient must meet with the pharmacist to discuss laboratory results and other pertinent information.

- First Visit—During the initial visit, the following information will be discussed and recorded
  - Patient information
  - Medical, family, and social history
  - Current drugs
  - Past DM therapy
  - Diet
  - Self-monitoring of blood glucose (SMBG)
  - Risk factors
  - Treatment plan and goals
  - Disease state education
  - Drug education
  - Smoking cessation as indicated (Refer to Smoking Cessation Protocol)
- Follow-up Visits—The following will be discussed and recorded (See Appendix A)
  - Effectiveness of therapy
  - Tolerability of therapy
  - Risk factors
  - DM goals
  - Treatment plan including therapy adjustments
  - Disease state education
  - Therapeutic lifestyle changes
  - Drug education
- Follow-up visits will be scheduled at 2 weeks to 6 months depending on the patients' response to and adherence with treatment.

Physical Assessment—The following may be performed or reviewed when indicated
  - Visual inspection for ADEs (e.g., jaundice, rash, flushing)
  - Weight
  - Vital signs (e.g., BP, pulse rate)
  - Foot examination
  - Drug Management (Appendices B–C)

The pharmacist is authorized to initiate, modify, or discontinue the following:
  - Oral antihyperglycemic drugs (Appendices B and C)
  - Sulfonylureas
  - Biguanides
  - TZDs
  - α-Glucosidase inhibitors
  - Meglitinides
  - Combination products of the above
  - Injectable DM drugs (Appendices B and C)
  - Insulins

- Incretin mimetics
- Noninsulin synthetic analogs
- Inhaled DM drugs (Appendix D)
- Insulin
- Aspirin (Appendix E)

The pharmacist will contact the referring physician on initiation of the above drugs or if a drug requires discontinuation. All orders will be written according to CDTM Diabetes Protocol and signed by the credentialed pharmacist. Prescriptions may be written or called into the patient's pharmacy by the credentialed pharmacist, as an agent of the physician, by telephone order.

The pharmacist will provide drugs and proper administration education when a new drug is initiated and at follow-up visits.

The pharmacist will refer the patient to his or her physician for drug refills unless prior arrangements have been made.

Drug Administration
- This protocol does not authorize the pharmacist to administer any drug.

Laboratory Monitoring
According to patient-specific factors and other recent laboratory values, the pharmacist is authorized to order the following laboratory tests when clinically warranted
- BMP
- HgA1c
- Urinalysis
- Microalbumin-creatinine ratio
- Hepatic panel
- FLP: total cholesterol, triglycerides, high-density lipoprotein, and low-density lipoprotein
- Pulmonary function tests

Point-of-Care Testing
The pharmacist is authorized to perform the following test as clinically warranted, if available
- Fingerstick blood glucose

Patient Referrals
- The pharmacist may refer the patient to a dietician, podiatrist, dentist, ophthalmologist, PCP, or referring physician as necessary.
- If a patient requires acute care, an additional physical examination, or diagnostic testing, the pharmacist is authorized to refer patients to their physician or to the emergency department as clinically indicated.

Patient Education
An extensive longitudinal program of patient education will be provided according to goals set by the pharmacist and patient.
- General overview
- Goals of therapy
- Drug education
- SMBG
- Medical Nutrition Therapy
- Acute complications/Contacting referring physician
- Chronic complications associated with hyperglycemia
- Goal setting and problem solving
- Psychosocial aspects

Participation In/Coordination of Clinical Research
- Not applicable for this protocol

Documentation
- All patient encounters will be documented in the progress notes section of the EMR. All notes will be sent to the referring provider by the EMR.

Billing for Services
- Patients will be billed for services in accordance with the MUSC Department of Pharmacy Services Ambulatory Care Billing Policy.
- All other procedures will be performed according to the general policies and procedures of the clinic.

Clinic Discharge
The patient will be discharged from the clinic when he or she has achieved the goals set by the referring physician or when the patient decides he/she no longer wishes to receive care. In addition, the pharmacist, in conjunction with the referring physician, may decide to discharge the patient from the services of the clinic.

Quality Assurance/Outcomes

Data will be continuously monitored to ensure that patients are receiving optimal care. Outcomes of DM management will include, but not be limited to, change in HgA1c from initial referral, percentage of patients at goal HgA1c, and any serious adverse events. Process tracking will also occur to confirm adherence to the protocol. These results will be presented quarterly to the appropriate pharmacy coordinator and manager.

References

1. American Diabetes Association. Standards of medical care in diabetes. Diabetes Care 2006;29:S4–S42. Available at www.care.diabetesjournals.org/content/vol29/suppl_1/. Accessed June 8, 2008.
2. American Heart Association and American Diabetes Association. Thiazolidinedione use, fluid retention, and congestive heart failure: A consensus statement from the American Heart Association and American Diabetes Association. Diabetes Care 2004;27:256. Available at http://care.diabetesjournals.org/cgi/content/full/27/1/256.
3. Klasco RK, ed. DRUGDEX® system. Greenwood Village, CO: Thomson MICROMEDEX. (Edition expires 3/2006.)
4. DeFranzo RA. Pharmacologic therapy for type 2 diabetes. Ann Intern Med 1999;131:281–303.5.
5. Joslin Diabetes Center and Joslin Clinic. Clinical guidelines for adults with diabetes. Available at http://www.joslin.org/Files/Adult_Guideline_Graded.pdf.

[AU6]

Appendix A—ADA Standards of Medical Care in DM

Table 1: Glycemic Goals for Adults with DM

Glycemic Parameter	Goal	Monitoring Frequency
HgA1c	< 7%	Every 3 months until at goal; then twice yearly
Preprandial glucose	90–130 mg/dL	Patient-specific
Peak postprandial glucose	< 180 mg/dL	Patient-specific

Table 2: Treatment Goals for the Prevention of Macrovascular Complications in Adults with DM

Parameter	Goal	Monitoring Frequency
BP	< 130/80 mm Hg	Each visit
LDL cholesterol	< 100 mg/dL or < 70 mg/dL	At least annually, more often until at goal
HDL cholesterol	> 40 mg/dL in men > 50 mg/dL in women	At least annually, more often until at goal
Triglycerides	< 150 mg/dL	At least annually, more often until at goal

Table 3: Standard Monitoring for Microvascular Complications

Microvascular Complication	Screening Tool	Monitoring Frequency
Nephropathy	Urine microalbumin-creatinine ratio	At diagnosis, then yearly
Peripheral neuropathy	Foot examination assessing the following: Sensation Foot structure and gait Skin integrity Vascular status	Yearly by health care provider or at each visit for patients with existing neuropathies Daily quick assessment by patient
Retinopathy	Dilated eye examination performed by an ophthalmologist	Annually

Table 4: Drugs Known to Cause Hyperglycemia

Diuretics	Sympathomimetics
Corticosteroids	CCBs
Isoniazid	Nicotinic acid
Estrogens	Antipsychotics
Phenytoin	

Table 5: Signs and Symptoms of Hyperglycemia

Polyuria	Dry mouth
Polydipsia	Dry, itchy skin
Polyphagia	Poor wound healing
Fatigue	Recurrent infections
Blurred vision	

Table 6: Signs and Symptoms of Hypoglycemia

Dizziness	Mental confusion
Shaking	Unsteadiness
Sweating	Visual disturbances
Hunger	Headache

Table 7: Treatment of Hypoglycemia

- Foods that contain 15 g of carbohydrates
- 3 teaspoons or packets of sugar
- 6 Lifesavers candies
- 6 saltine crackers
- ½ cup of fruit juice
- 1 cup of milk
- ½ cup of regular soft drink
- Glucose tablets

Appendix B—Oral Drugs Used for Glycemic Control in DM

Second-Generation Sulfonylureas

Mechanism of Action
- Stimulate insulin release from pancreas
- Contraindications
- Diabetic ketoacidosis

Precautions
- More likely to cause hypoglycemia when calorie intake is deficient, after prolonged exercise, when alcohol is ingested, or with other hypoglycemic agents
- Allow several days between dose titrations

Adverse Reactions
- 1–10%: hypoglycemia, nausea, dizziness, GI upset, allergic skin reactions, anorexia

Drug Interactions
- Additive effects with other hypoglycemic agents
- H_2-antagonists, β-blockers, TCAs, NSAIDs, and azole antifungals may cause increased effects of sulfonylureas.
- Cholestyramine, rifampin, and thiazide diuretics may decrease effects of sulfonylureas.
- Concomitant administration with drugs known to cause hyperglycemia may lead to loss of glycemic control with sulfonylureas.

Monitoring
- Signs and symptoms of hypoglycemia
- Blood glucose
- HgA1c
- Kidney function

Table 1: Available Second-Generation Sulfonylureas

Drug (trade name)	Usual Dose Range (mg/day)	Usual Starting Dose (mg)	Daily Frequency
Glimepiride (Amaryl)	1–4	1–2	1
Glipizide (Glucotrol)[a,b]	5–10	5	2
Glipizide XR (Glucotrol XL)[a]	5–10	5–10	1
Glyburide (Diabeta, Micronase)[b,c]	1.25–20	1.25–5	1–2
Glyburide micronized (Glynase)[a]	0.75–6	0.75–3	1–2

[a]Generic available.
[b]Available in combination with metformin (Metaglip)
[c]Available in combination with metformin (Glucovance)

Biguanides

Mechanism of Action
- Increase glucose metabolism in skeletal muscle
- Decrease hepatic production of glucose
- Decrease intestinal absorption of glucose

Contraindications
- Renal dysfunction (SCr > 1.5 mg/dL in men, 1.4 mg/dL in women)
- Systolic HF treated with drugs
- Acute or chronic metabolic acidosis
- Concomitant use of iodinated radiocontrast media

Precautions
- Hold agent before any surgical procedure or radiographic studies and for 48 hours after or until renal function is recovered.
- Avoid in patients with impaired liver function.
- Reduce GI adverse effects by initiating at a lower dose and giving just before meals.
- Titrate every 1 to 2 weeks as tolerated.

Adverse Reactions
- More than 10%: anorexia, nausea, abdominal discomfort, diarrhea, flatulence, constipation, metallic taste
- 1–10%: urticaria, photosensitivity, decreased vitamin B_{12} concentrations, hypoglycemia

Drug Interactions
- Cimetidine increases plasma concentrations of metformin

Monitoring
- Signs and symptoms of hypoglycemia
- Blood glucose
- HgA1c
- Kidney function at baseline; then yearly or as needed

Table 2: Selected Biguanides

Drug (trade name)	Usual Dose Range (mg/day)	Usual Starting Dose (mg)	Daily Frequency
Metformin (Glucophage)[a,b]	500–2,000	500	1–3
Metformin XR (Glucophage XR)	500–2,000	500	1

[a]Generic available.
[b]Available in combination with rosiglitazone (Avandamet), glyburide (Glucovance), and glipizide (Metaglip)

TZDs

Mechanism of Action
- Increase PPAR (gamma) target cell response to insulin
- Decrease hepatic production of glucose
- Decrease insulin resistance

Contraindications
- Type 1 DM
- NYHA Class III and IV CHF

- Diabetic ketoacidosis
- Elevated LFTs (> 2.5 times the upper limit of normal)

Precautions
- NYHA Class I and II CHF or patients at risk of developing CHF (monitor S/Sx of fluid retention closely)
- Mildly impaired liver function

Adverse Reactions
- More than 10%: upper respiratory tract infections, headache
- 1–10%: hypoglycemia, edema, myalgia

Drug Interactions
- Insulins

Monitoring
- Signs and symptoms of hypoglycemia
- Blood glucose
- HgA1c
- Signs and symptoms of edema, including weight gain and shortness of breath
- LFTs at baseline and then periodically thereafter

Table 3: Available TZDs

Drug (trade name)	Usual Dose Range (mg/day)	Usual Starting Dose (mg)	Daily Frequency
Pioglitazone (Actos)	15–45	15	1
Rosiglitazone (Avandia)[a,b]	2–8	2	1–2

[a] 4 mg twice daily determined to be more efficacious than 8 mg once daily.
[b] Available in combination with metformin (Avandamet)

Meglitinides

Mechanism of Action
- Stimulates insulin release from pancreas

Contraindications
- Type 1 DM
- Diabetic ketoacidosis

Precautions
- Must be administered with meals because of risk of hypoglycemia

Adverse Reactions
- More than 10%: hypoglycemia, upper respiratory tract infections
- 1–10%: arthralgia, diarrhea, sinusitis, dizziness, flu symptoms

Drug Interactions
- Additive effects with other agents that may cause hypoglycemia

Monitoring
- Signs and symptoms of hypoglycemia
- Blood glucose
- HgA1c

Table 4: Available Meglitinides

Drug (trade name)	Usual Dose Range (mg/day)	Usual Starting Dose (mg)	Daily Frequency
Repaglinide (Prandin)	0.5–4	0.5	2–4 In response to meals
Nateglinide (Starlix)	120–360	60	Twice daily before meals

α-Glucosidase Inhibitors

Mechanism of Action
- Delays digestion of carbohydrates in small intestine

Contraindications
- Irritable bowel syndrome
- Colonic ulceration, partial intestinal obstruction, or predisposition to intestinal obstruction
- Chronic intestinal diseases associated with marked disorders of digestion and absorption
- Cirrhosis
- Diabetic ketoacidosis

Precautions
- Requires patient understanding for proper administration

Adverse Reactions
- More than 10%: abdominal pain, diarrhea, flatulence

Drug Interactions
- Concomitant use of intestinal adsorbents and digestive enzyme preparations with carbohydrate-splitting enzymes may reduce the effect of α-glucosidase inhibitors.
- Miglitol may reduce the bioavailabilty of propranolol and ranitidine.

Monitoring
- Signs and symptoms of hypoglycemia
- Blood glucose
- HgA1c
- LFTs

Table 5: Available α-Glucosidase Inhibitors

Drug (trade name)	Usual Dose Range (mg/day)	Usual Starting Dose (mg)	Daily Frequency
Miglitol (Glyset)	75–300	25	3 times/day with first bite of each meal
Acarbose (Precose)	75–300[a]	25	3 times/day with first bite of each meal

[a] Only patients weighing > 60 kg should be considered for dose titration above 50 mg 3 times/day.

Appendix C—Insulin

Mechanism of Action
- Promotes the cellular uptake of glucose, fatty acids, and amino acids and their conversion to glycogen, triglycerides, and proteins

Dosing
- Initial doses for patients with type 1 DM: ~0.5 U/kg/day
- Initial doses for patients with type 2 DM: ~0.3–0.5 U/kg/day

Precautions
- Requires patient understanding for proper administration and management of adverse effects

Adverse Reactions
- Hypoglycemia
- Local allergic reactions
- Lipohypertrophy at injection site
- Weight gain

Monitoring
- Signs and symptoms of hypoglycemia
- Blood glucose
- HgA1c

Table 7: Pharmacokinetics of Available Rapid-Acting Insulin Preparations

Insulin Type	Onset (hours)	Peak (hours)	Duration of Action (hours)
Aspart (Novolog)	0.25	0.5–1	1–3
Lispro (Humalog)	0.5	0.5–2.5	3–4

Table 8: Pharmacokinetics of Available Short-Acting Insulin Preparations

Insulin Type	Onset (hours)	Peak (hours)	Duration of Action (hours)
Regular	0.5–1	2–3	3–6

Table 9: Pharmacokinetics of Available Intermediate-Acting Insulin Preparations

Insulin Type	Onset (hours)	Peak (hours)	Duration of Action (hours)
NPH (isophane)	2–4	4–10	10–16
Lente (zinc suspension)	2–4	4–12	12–18

Table 10: Pharmacokinetics of Available Long-Acting Insulin Preparations

Insulin Type	Onset (hours)	Peak (hours)	Duration of Action (hours)
Ultralente (extended zinc suspension)	6–10	10–16	18–20

Table 11: Pharmacokinetics of Available Basal Insulin Preparations

Insulin Type	Onset (hours)	Peak (hours)	Duration of Action (hours)
Glargine (Lantus)	2–4	None	24

Table 12: Pharmacokinetics of Available Combination Insulin Preparations

Insulin Type	Onset (hours)	Peak (hours)	Duration of Action (hours)
50% NPH/50% Regular	0.5–1	2–5.5	10–16
70% NPH/30% Regular	0.5–1	2–12	10–16
Novolog mix 70/30	0.25	1–4	15–18
Humalog mix 75/25	0.5	1–6.5	10–16

Appendix D—Clinical Pharmacy Diabetes Education Documentation Template

Title: *CLINICAL PHARMACY- DIABETES
MEDICAL UNIVERSITY OF SOUTH CAROLINA
Providers: *
Referred by: *
SUBJECTIVE: Year old female with type 1 2 diabetes mellitus referred to contact by the clinical pharmacist for diabetes education and management.
Other issues include del del cpdeHPI

MEDICAL HISTORY: *
FAMILY HISTORY: *
SOCIAL HISTORY: *
DIETARY HABITS: del
ACTIVITY: del
PSYCHOSOCIAL ISSUES: del
CURRENT DRUGS: none
Allergies: NKDA
DIABETES REGIMEN:
SSInsulin
OBJECTIVE:
VITALS:
Insert Vitals from today (BP, Pulse):
Insert Vitals from today (Temp, Height, Weight):

LABORATORY RESULTS: none

ASSESSMENT/PLAN:
Patient with newdx controlled uncontrold diabetes and is at a risk for developing complications due to dmcomp. SMBG level within below above desired range. Patient is not monitoring blood sugars appropriately. HgA1C not at goal. Patient would benefit from education regarding dmedu. PatternMgt

TESTING SUPPLIES: del
MONITORING: Instructed to monitor blood glucose del
MEDICAL NUTRITION THERAPY: del
Instructed patient to:
ACTIVITY PLAN: del ActivPlan
PHARMACOTHERAPY: del cpMedPlan
Reviewed proper use of glipizide glyburide metformin metf/glyb rosiglitaz pioglitza insuln use and the associated SE.
Instructed patient to notify clinic if SE develop. RevHYPO
COST OF MEDS: del medassist
delCARDIOVASCULAR: del
delRENAL: del
delEYES: del
delFEET: del
delOTHER EDUCATION: del
delGOALS: del
delEDUCATIONAL MATERIALS: Patient provided with written materials discussing del
delREQUIRED MONITORING: del
FOLLOW-UP: for diabetes management in 1 2 3 4 6 weeks months
Patient encouraged to contact the clinic with signs and symptoms of hyperglycemia or hypoglycemia and any questions or concerns. Patient caregiver verbalized understanding of educational points. Reinforcement required at subsequent visits. Plan discussed with and agreed on by *.

ENDOCRINOLOGY DIABETES CARE CLINIC

Submitted by: Candis Morello and Ryan Suemoto

Revised: February 2007

Pt/ID# _____ DOB: _____ PCP _____

	Dates →→ Laboratory date/visit date							
Diabetes Care	HgA1c ≥ 4 times/year, goal < 7.0%							
	FPG ≥ 4 times year							
	BUN/SCr or CrCl At least every 6 months							
	Microalbumin-UrCr At least every year							
	Urine protein-UrCr ratio							
	LFTs: ALT/AST At least every 3–6 months CK: as needed							
	Weight (lb) Every visit							
	BMI Every visit Ht:							
Cholesterol	Lipids At least yearly, more if abnormal LDL < 100 or < 70 (see algorithm)	TC TG HDL LDL	TC TG HDL LDL	TC TG HDL LDL	TC TG HDL LDL	TC TG HDL LDL	TC TG HDL LDL	TC TG HDL LDL
HTN	BP Goal ≤ 130/80 mm Hg (see algorithm)							
	K+ (if on ACE, ARB, or diuretic)							
Misc.	TSH At least every year							
	Other laboratory results							
Drugs	DM drugs Refer to key							
	Drug changes							
Education	Nutritional Assistant As needed at least every 2 years (NMCSD classes—outpatient)							
	Educational Assistant As needed (NMCSD classes: Phase)							
	Exercise (exercise tolerance test) Once							
	SMBG review Every visit							
	Blood glucose monitor tr/rev Initial; then as needed							
Health Maintenance	Hypoglycemia frequency Every visit							
	Foot check Every visit							
	Eye examination At least every year							
	Patient care management visit At least every 3–6 months							
	Other: medical history							
	PAP/mammogram Influenza vaccine Every year Pneumonia vaccine							

Call me on:

To discuss:
_____
_____
_____

Next visit:
_____
_____
_____
_____
_____

DIABETES CARE CLINIC IN ENDOCRINOLOGY

Diabetes Treatment Plan for: _____ Date: _____

Seen by (circle): Candis M. Morello, Pharm.D., CDE Pager #: _____
Ryan T. Suemoto, Pharm.D. Pager #: _____

Clinic Telephone: _____
If I am unavailable, please ask to leave me a **"telephone consult."**

Physician today: _____, MD or _____, MD

→ Diabetes: _____

→ Blood pressure: _____

→ Cholesterol: _____

→ Health maintenance: _____

Other: _____
_____
_____

→ Call if you have any questions or concerns and ask to leave a **"telephone consult"** if I am unavailable.

	General Goals		Today's Values
Diabetes	Blood glucose	Fasting: 70–125 Premeal: 90–130 At bedtime: 80–140	
	HgA1c	< 7.0%	
Blood pressure	If no protein in urine	< 130/80 mm Hg	
	If protein in urine	≤ 125/75 mm Hg	
Cholesterol	Total cholesterol	< 200	
	Triglycerides	< 150	
	HDL (good cholesterol)	> 40 if man > 50 if woman	
	LDL (bad cholesterol)	< 100 or > 70	

→ **Have fasting laboratory work drawn at least 3–7 days before your next visit.

→ **Bring logbook, glucose meter, and folder to EVERY clinic VISIT!

Endocrinology Diabetes Care Clinic Follow-Up Visit

Date:_____ PCM:_____ Diabetes Type: 1 or 2 ____ Year of diagnosis:_____
Age:_____ BP:_____ Pulse:_____ Temp:_____ HT:_____ WT:_____ BMI:_____

Drugs:	Drug allergy?	Current Diabetes Regimen:	PMH: ❏ Type __ Diabetes
			❏ Hyperlipidemia
			❏ HTN ❏ Thyroid d/o
			Social Hx:
			Smoking Y N
			ETOH Y N
			Pain (rank 1–10):

Subjective

Yes No
❏ ❏ Complaints currently
❏ ❏ Foot lesions noted by patient
❏ ❏ Paresthesias
❏ ❏ Vision changes
❏ ❏ Polyuria/Polyphagia/Polydipsia
❏ ❏ Chest pain
❏ ❏ Hypoglycemic events

                   AM   Lunch   PM   HS
SMBG (range/avg):_____

Nutrition:_____

Activity:_____

Objective

Injection sites: ❏ Normal
Feet: ❏ Normal Monofilament Test ❏ 2+ Pulses in Lower Extremities ❏ No Lesions ❏ No Fungus

Health Maintenance/Laboratory Results: Date_____

HgA1c   BP   Microalbumin   Urine-creatinine *ratio: (μg/mg)*   UA

TC   TG   HDL   LDL   ALT/AS   TTSH   CK

Eye examination (date and results)

Over →

Assessment/Plan

1. DM Control: ❏ *Excellent*   ❏ *Fair*   ❏ *Poor*

2. BP:

3. Lipids:

4. Other: Patient to call if questions or concerns

5. Health Maintenance (nutrition, activity, referrals)
❏ Nutrition Referral ❏ Survival Skills RN ❏ Diabetic Self-Mgmt Class ❏ Ophthalmology ❏ ETT ❏ OTHER

6. Laboratory tests: One week before appointment
❏ Chem panel ❏ HgA1c ❏ Lipids ❏ Microalb-UCr ❏ TSH ❏ CK ❏ OTHER:

7. Patient s/w and d/w Dr.
8. Follow-up: RTC

Time IN:_____
Time OUT:_____

DIABETES DRUG THERAPY MANAGEMENT PROTOCOL

Submitted by: Debra Lopez

Revised: July 2006

PURPOSE

This DTM protocol is done to comply with the pharmacy and medical practice acts regarding drug therapy management by a pharmacist-underwritten protocol of a physician. The procedures, protocols, practices, and other items contained within these documents are intended to be helpful reminders for the pharmacists and physicians of this institution. In no instance should the contents of these documents be considered standards of professional practice or rules of conduct or for the benefit of any third party. The documents herein are guidelines only and allow professional discretion and deviation where the individual health care provider deems variation appropriate as allowed by law.

The individual physicians authorized to prescribe drugs and responsible for the delegation of DTM in the Diabetes Clinic are:_____

The clinical pharmacists who are authorized to prescribe drugs under the physician-initiated protocol and who will carry out the DTM as delegated are _____, and his/her current resident.

In accordance with the incorporated treatment guidelines, the pharmacist may provide care for patients at Blackstock Family Practice under the physician-initiated protocol to include:
- Assesses patients' therapeutic needs as specified per physician consult. Disease states/ailments include, but are not limited to, DM, HTN, hyperlipidemia, smoking cessation, and obesity.
- Evaluates pharmacological and non-pharmacological treatment regimens
- Orders, interprets, and conducts all pertinent laboratory studies
- Initiates and adjusts drugs in accordance with attached pharmacological privileges
- Provides patient education regarding their disease state(s), pharmacological, and non-pharmacological therapy
- Documents patient visits, patient care, and treatment decisions in the medical record. The referring physician will have access to such medical records. The referring physician will also be copied on visit dictations.
- Consults with the referring physician and other members of the health care team, as appropriate, to include ancillary services (e.g., podiatry, dietary, social work, physical therapy, occupational therapy)
- Obtains authorization from the physician for deviations from the protocol
- The schedule for physician review and status reports to the physician is based on each individual patient. The services provided to the patient by the pharmacist will be copied to or provided to the physician after each clinic visit and on an as-needed basis.
- This protocol does not delegate diagnosis to the clinical pharmacist.
- The clinical pharmacist may use the attached treatment guidelines for DTM for DM and associated CAD risk factors, which include, but are not limited to, hyperlipidemia, HTN, smoking cessation, and obesity. The following Texas Diabetes Council algorithms have been attached for references to be used by the clinical pharmacists.

Clinical Pharmacist Drug Therapy Management Protocol

Level of Privileges
- Independent—No routine MD consultation required
    - Vitamins, multivitamins
    - Glucometers and supplies
    - Vaccines
    - OTCs
- MD consultation required for initiating therapy Independent for renewing and adjusting
    - Oral hypoglycemics
    - Noninsulin injectables
    - Insulin
    - Antihypertensives
    - Antihyperlipidemics
    - Anticoagulants
- Independent for renewal only
    - Antianxiety agents, antidepressants
    - Non-narcotic analgesics/anti-inflammatories
    - Urinary antispasmodics
    - Vaginal products
    - Misc. genitourinary agents
    - Misc. GI (antacids, ulcer drugs, antidiarrheals)
    - Progestins, estrogens, contraceptives
    - Misc. cardiovascular
    - Antihistamines
- Systemic and topical nasal products
    - Cough/cold/allergy
    - Antiasthmatic
    - Dermatologic
    - Migraine products
    - Antianginal
    - Thyroid
- MD consultation required
    - Anticonvulsants
    - Antiemetics
    - Anti-infectives/antibiotics
    - Antiparkinsonian
    - Stimulants/anti-obesity/anorexiants
    - Antipsychotics, hypnotics
    - Digestive aids
    - Psychotherapeutics and neurologics
    - Neuromuscular agents
    - Musculoskeletal therapy agents
    - Antimyasthenic agents
    - Analgesics–narcotic
    - Pressors
    - Antiarrhythmics

This Drug Therapy Management protocol was formulated and approved by:

_____
Physician/Date   Medical Director

_____
Physician/Date

_____
Physician/Date

_____
Physician/Date

Requesting Practitioners

_____
Pharm.D./Date

_____
Pharm.D./Date

DIABETES DISEASE MANAGEMENT PROTOCOL

Submitted by: Rosalyn Padiyara, Jennifer D'Souza, Amie Brooks, and Rami Rihani

Created 2006

The Dreyer Medical Clinic Health Management and Therapeutics Committee (HM&T) promotes the use of the Intermountain Healthcare (IHC) "Management of Adult Diabetes Mellitus Care Process Model" (CPM) by all PCPs.

The HM&T Committee has also approved the CPM as the reference protocol for activities performed by Clinical Pharmacists in the Diabetes Health Management Department. The IHC CPM is used with permission from Intermountain Healthcare. Copyright 2005, Intermountain Healthcare. The table below summarizes the IHC CPM.

Prepared by Intermountain Healthcare Clinical Education, Salt Lake City, Utah

Dreyer Medical Clinic—Goals in the Treatment of Adult Diabetes

Measure	Goal
HgA1c (test at least twice yearly)	< 7.0%
BP (check at each office visit)	< 130/80 mm Hg
LDL cholesterol (test annually)	< 100 mg/dL
Triglycerides (test annually)	< 150 mg/dL
Foot examination (perform at least annually)	Normal
Urine microalbumin-creatinine ratio (test at least annually)	< 30
Dilated eye examination (check annually)	Normal

Prepared by Dreyer Medical Clinic, Aurora, Illinois

General Principles in the Management of Adult Diabetes

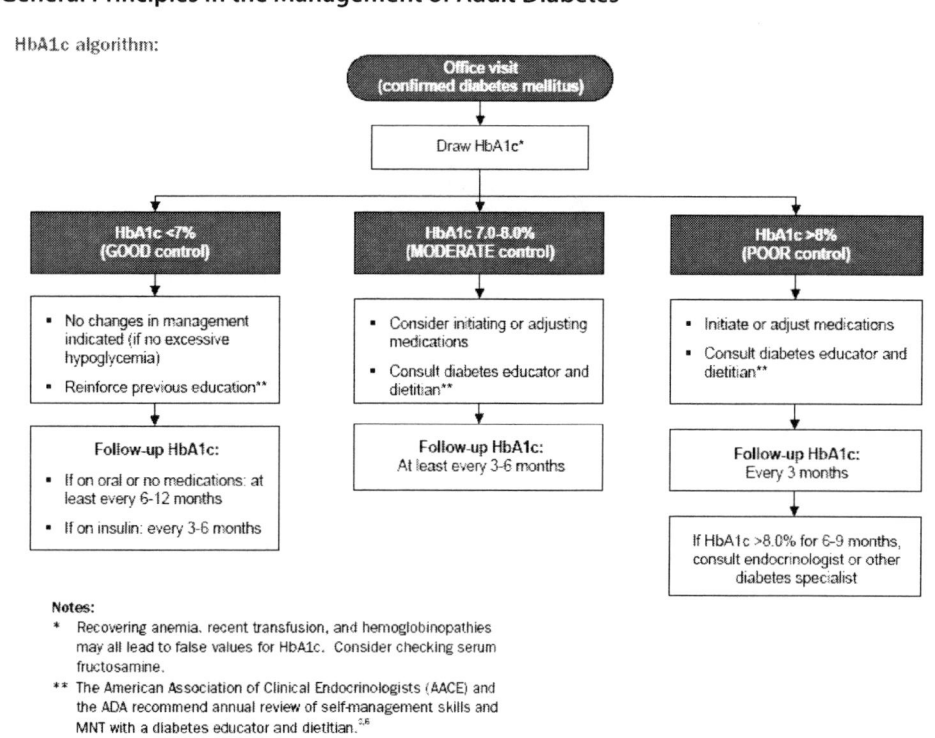

HbA1c algorithm:

Office visit (confirmed diabetes mellitus) → Draw HbA1c*

HbA1c <7% (GOOD control)
- No changes in management indicated (if no excessive hypoglycemia)
- Reinforce previous education**

Follow-up HbA1c:
- If on oral or no medications: at least every 6-12 months
- If on insulin: every 3-6 months

HbA1c 7.0-8.0% (MODERATE control)
- Consider initiating or adjusting medications
- Consult diabetes educator and dietitian**

Follow-up HbA1c: At least every 3-6 months

HbA1c >8% (POOR control)
- Initiate or adjust medications
- Consult diabetes educator and dietitian**

Follow-up HbA1c: Every 3 months

If HbA1c >8.0% for 6-9 months, consult endocrinologist or other diabetes specialist

Notes:
* Recovering anemia, recent transfusion, and hemoglobinopathies may all lead to false values for HbA1c. Consider checking serum fructosamine.
** The American Association of Clinical Endocrinologists (AACE) and the ADA recommend annual review of self-management skills and MNT with a diabetes educator and dietitian.[2,6]

Prepared by Intermountain Healthcare Clinical Education, Salt Lake City, Utah

Oral Therapy
- Initiation, addition, or modification of oral therapy is be based on individual patient characteristics (e.g., allergies, weight, preference, compliance with therapy, insurance coverage), laboratory results (e.g., HgA1c, FPG), and self-monitored blood glucose readings.
- The follow-up interval is based on patient achievement of goals, characteristics of prescribed drugs, and patient capabilities.

Oral Agent(s) plus Insulin
- If blood glucose is not controlled, long-acting insulin may be added to oral therapy.
- Together with standard dosing of long-acting insulin, the Treat-to-Target Weekly Titration Schedule for basal insulin in combination with oral therapy will be used for individuals with DM having an HgA1c of 7.5–10%.

Treat-to-Target Weekly Titration Schedule
1. Start with 10 U daily.
2. Titrate weekly based on SMBG values from the preceding two days, as shown in the table below.

Mean of SMBG Values from Preceding 2 Days (mg/dL)	Increase of Insulin Dosage (U/day)
≥ 180	+8
140–180	+6
120–140	+4
100–120	+2

Copyright © 2003 American Diabetes Association. From Diabetes Care®, Vol. 26;3000–86.
Reprinted with permission from the American Diabetes Association.

Basic Insulin/Physiologic Insulin Therapy
- Basic insulin regimens will be used for patients with type 2 DM not achieving goals on oral therapy.
- Basic insulin regimens are not appropriate for use in patients with type 1 DM unless they are not capable of following the more complex physiologic insulin regimens.
- Physiologic insulin regimens will be used for all capable type 1 patients and are appropriate for type 2 patients who do not achieve goals on basic insulin regimens.
- Initial total daily insulin dose will be 30–60% less than the predicted insulin need, 1.1 µ/kg for obese patients, and 0.55 µ/kg for nonobese patients. The total dose will be divided into half long acting and half short acting, which is further divided by the number of major meals.
- For capable patients, the "1,500–2,200 rule" can be used to help calculate correction doses and to determine the insulin-carbohydrate ratio.

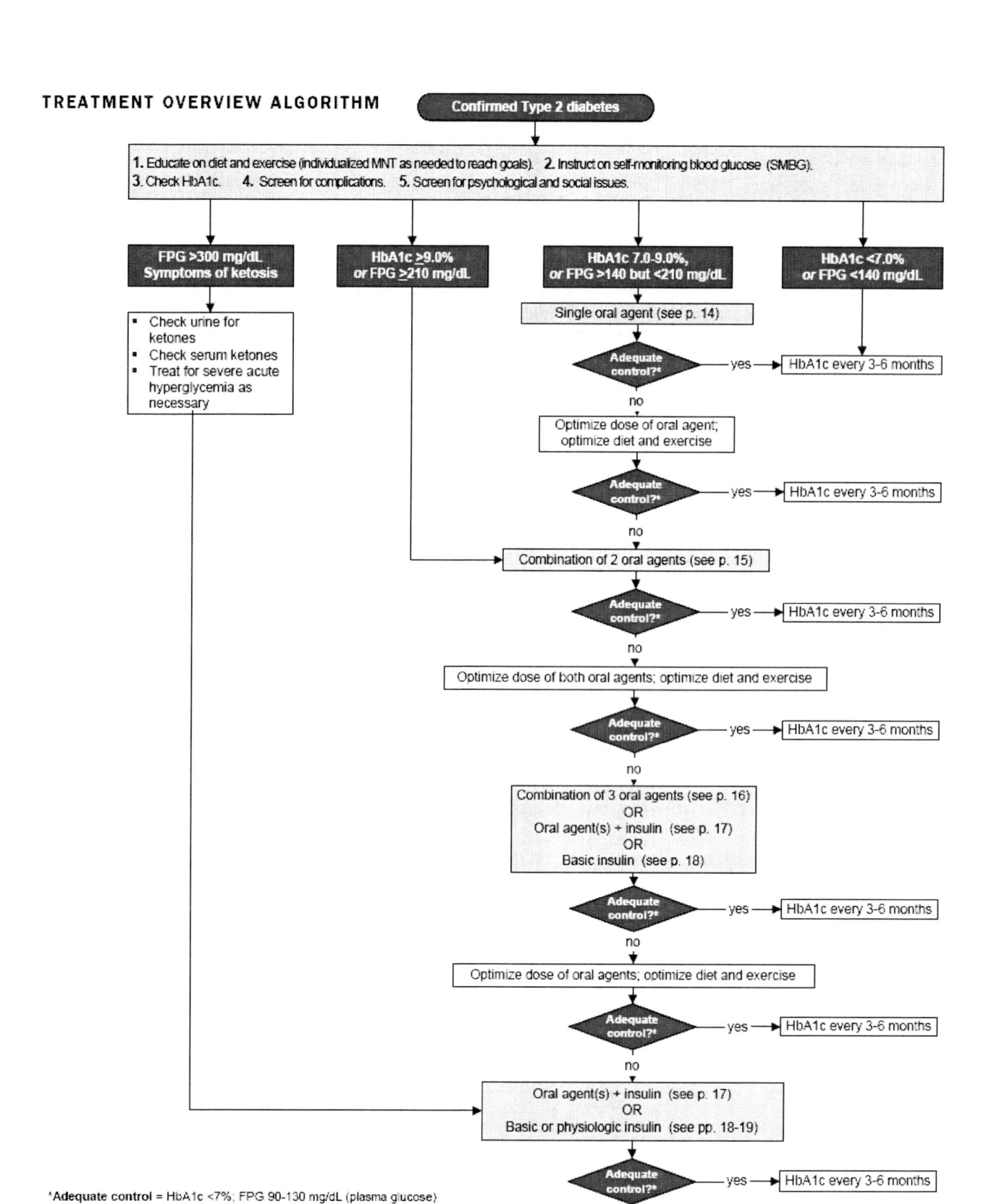

TREATMENT OVERVIEW ALGORITHM

Confirmed Type 2 diabetes

1. Educate on diet and exercise (individualized MNT as needed to reach goals). 2. Instruct on self-monitoring blood glucose (SMBG). 3. Check HbA1c. 4. Screen for complications. 5. Screen for psychological and social issues.

FPG >300 mg/dL — Symptoms of ketosis
- Check urine for ketones
- Check serum ketones
- Treat for severe acute hyperglycemia as necessary

HbA1c ≥9.0% or FPG ≥210 mg/dL → Combination of 2 oral agents (see p. 15)

HbA1c 7.0–9.0%, or FPG >140 but <210 mg/dL → Single oral agent (see p. 14)

HbA1c <7.0% or FPG <140 mg/dL → HbA1c every 3–6 months

Single oral agent (see p. 14)
- Adequate control?* — yes → HbA1c every 3–6 months
- no → Optimize dose of oral agent; optimize diet and exercise
  - Adequate control?* — yes → HbA1c every 3–6 months
  - no → Combination of 2 oral agents (see p. 15)
    - Adequate control?* — yes → HbA1c every 3–6 months
    - no → Optimize dose of both oral agents; optimize diet and exercise
      - Adequate control?* — yes → HbA1c every 3–6 months
      - no → Combination of 3 oral agents (see p. 16) OR Oral agent(s) + insulin (see p. 17) OR Basic insulin (see p. 18)
        - Adequate control?* — yes → HbA1c every 3–6 months
        - no → Optimize dose of oral agents; optimize diet and exercise
          - Adequate control?* — yes → HbA1c every 3–6 months
          - no → Oral agent(s) + insulin (see p. 17) OR Basic or physiologic insulin (see pp. 18–19)
            - Adequate control?* — yes → HbA1c every 3–6 months
            - no → Physiologic insulin (see pp. 18–19)

*Adequate control = HbA1c <7%; FPG 90–130 mg/dL (plasma glucose)

If FPG is normal, but HbA1c level is high, consider postprandial (PP) PG monitoring. PPG actually correlates better with HbA1c than FPG does.

Prepared by Intermountain Healthcare Clinical Education, Salt Lake City, Utah

Management of Hyperlipidemia in Individuals with DM

- The choice of agent will be dictated by the percent change in lipid value needed to achieve goals, formulary coverage, costs, and drug interactions.
- All combination therapy will be confirmed with the PCP if initiated by clinical pharmacists, with the exception of statin plus ezetimibe.

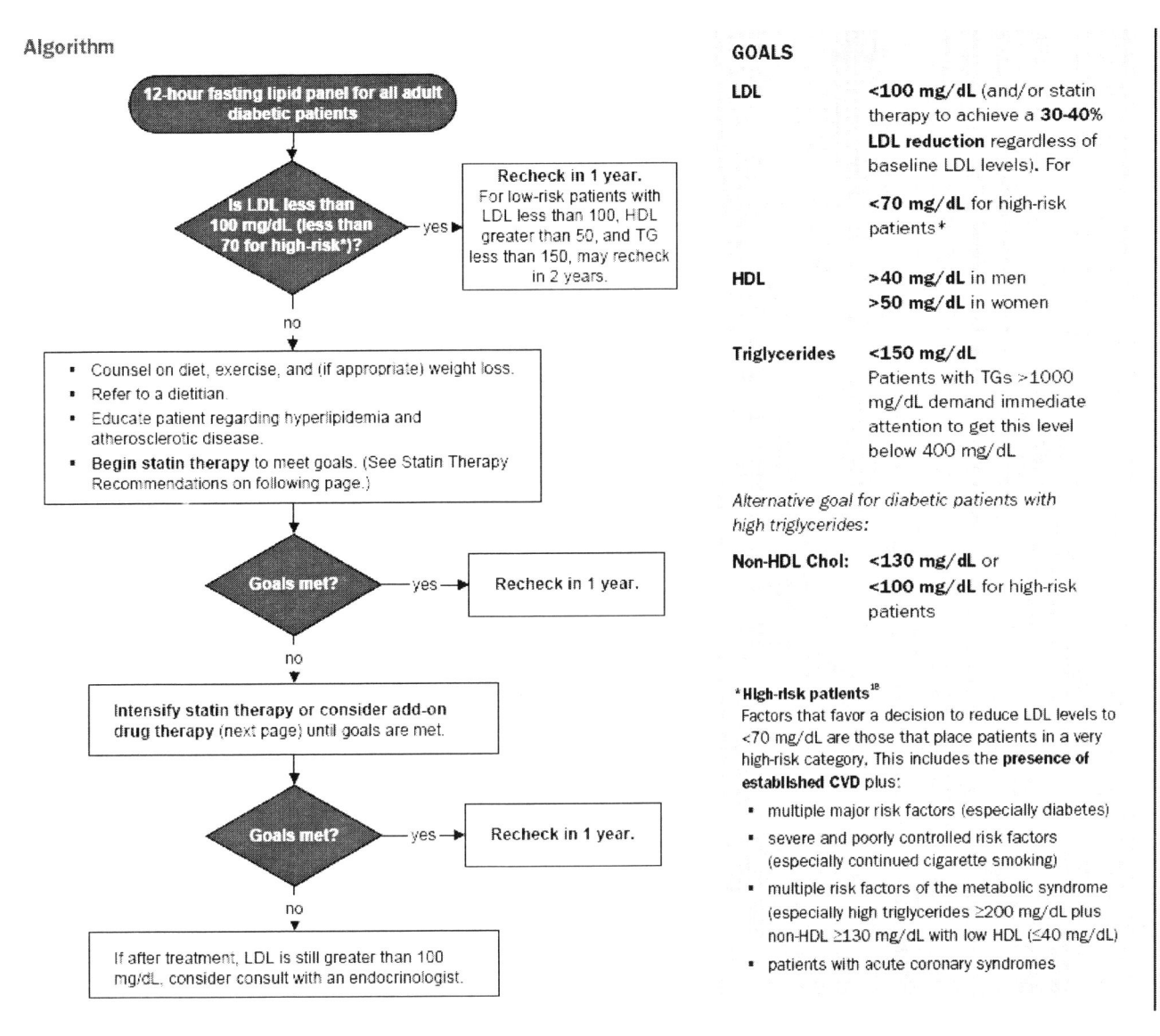

Algorithm

```
   ┌──────────────────────────────────────┐
   │ 12-hour fasting lipid panel for all adult │
   │           diabetic patients          │
   └──────────────────┬───────────────────┘
                      ▼
            ┌──────────────────┐       ┌────────────────────────────┐
            │  Is LDL less than │       │ Recheck in 1 year.         │
            │  100 mg/dL (less than │─yes▶│ For low-risk patients with │
            │  70 for high-risk*)? │     │ LDL less than 100, HDL     │
            └──────────┬───────┘       │ greater than 50, and TG    │
                       │               │ less than 150, may recheck │
                       no              │ in 2 years.                │
                       ▼               └────────────────────────────┘
   ┌──────────────────────────────────────┐
   │ • Counsel on diet, exercise, and (if appropriate) weight loss. │
   │ • Refer to a dietitian.              │
   │ • Educate patient regarding hyperlipidemia and │
   │   atherosclerotic disease.           │
   │ • Begin statin therapy to meet goals. (See Statin Therapy │
   │   Recommendations on following page.) │
   └──────────────────┬───────────────────┘
                      ▼
            ┌──────────────────┐
            │   Goals met?     │─yes─▶ Recheck in 1 year.
            └──────────┬───────┘
                       no
                       ▼
   ┌──────────────────────────────────────┐
   │ Intensify statin therapy or consider add-on │
   │ drug therapy (next page) until goals are met. │
   └──────────────────┬───────────────────┘
                      ▼
            ┌──────────────────┐
            │   Goals met?     │─yes─▶ Recheck in 1 year.
            └──────────┬───────┘
                       no
                       ▼
   ┌──────────────────────────────────────┐
   │ If after treatment, LDL is still greater than 100 │
   │ mg/dL, consider consult with an endocrinologist. │
   └──────────────────────────────────────┘
```

GOALS

LDL   **<100 mg/dL** (and/or statin therapy to achieve a **30-40% LDL reduction** regardless of baseline LDL levels). For

<70 mg/dL for high-risk patients*

HDL   **>40 mg/dL** in men
           >50 mg/dL in women

Triglycerides   **<150 mg/dL**
Patients with TGs >1000 mg/dL demand immediate attention to get this level below 400 mg/dL

Alternative goal for diabetic patients with high triglycerides:

Non-HDL Chol: **<130 mg/dL** or
                   <100 mg/dL for high-risk patients

*High-risk patients[18]

Factors that favor a decision to reduce LDL levels to <70 mg/dL are those that place patients in a very high-risk category. This includes the **presence of established CVD** plus:

- multiple major risk factors (especially diabetes)
- severe and poorly controlled risk factors (especially continued cigarette smoking)
- multiple risk factors of the metabolic syndrome (especially high triglycerides ≥200 mg/dL plus non-HDL ≥130 mg/dL with low HDL (≤40 mg/dL)
- patients with acute coronary syndromes

Prepared by Intermountain Healthcare Clinical Education, Salt Lake City, Utah

Management of HTN

- BP GOAL < 130/80 mm Hg
- Aggressive treatment of BP to less than 130/80 mm Hg greatly reduces cardiovascular risk in individuals with DM—an effect that is equal to or greater than the effect of glucose control.
- BP control has also been shown to decrease the risk of microvascular complications of DM (e.g., retinopathy, neuropathy).
- Most patients need more than one drug to control BP to this level. Adequate BP control is more important than the specific agent(s) used.

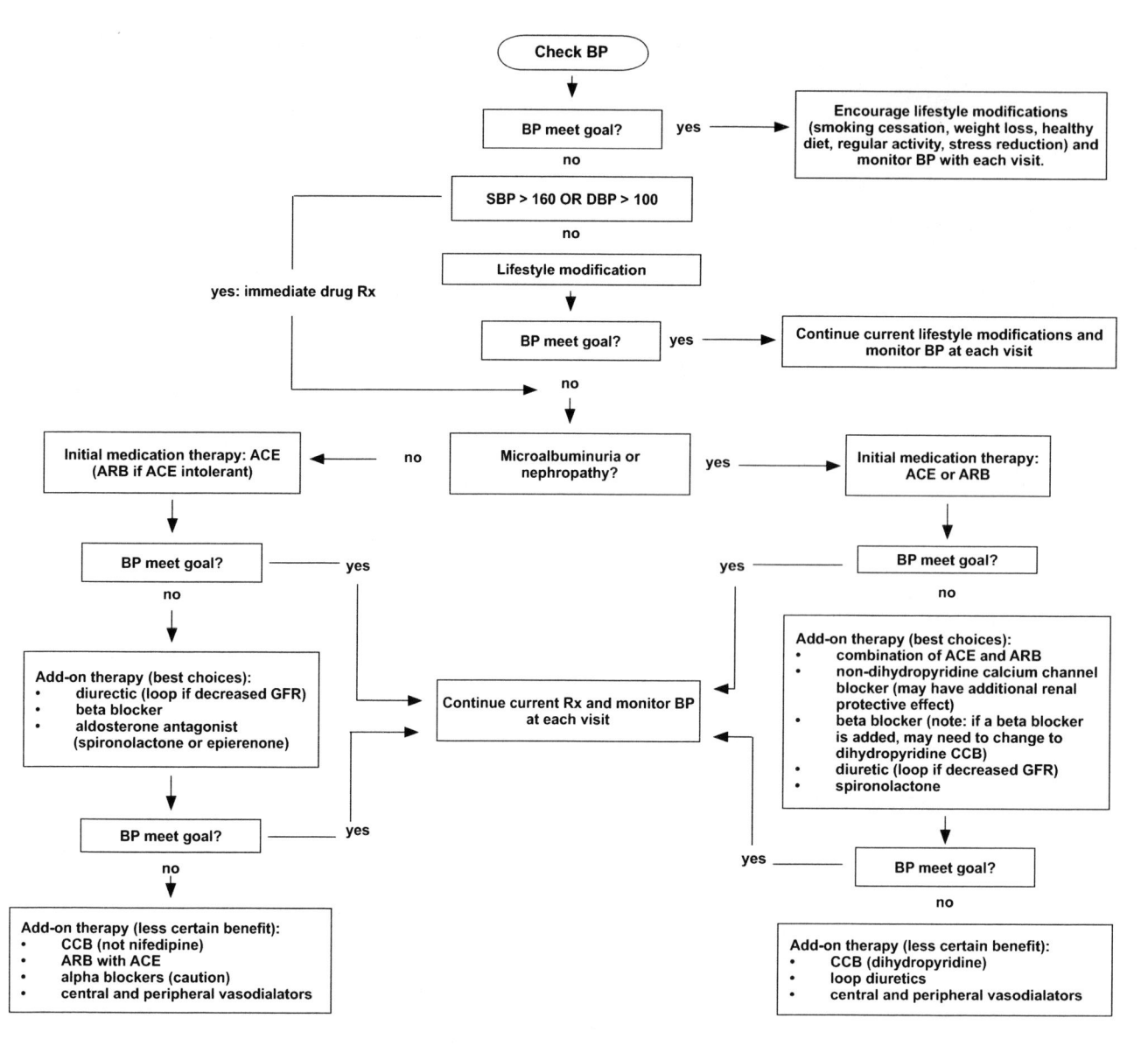

```
Check BP
    ↓
BP meet goal? --yes--> Encourage lifestyle modifications
    no                 (smoking cessation, weight loss, healthy
    ↓                  diet, regular activity, stress reduction) and
SBP > 160 OR DBP > 100     monitor BP with each visit.
    no
    ↓
Lifestyle modification
    ↓
BP meet goal? --yes--> Continue current lifestyle modifications and
    no                  monitor BP at each visit
    ↓
Microalbuminuria or nephropathy?
  no ←              → yes
  ↓                    ↓
Initial medication    Initial medication therapy:
therapy: ACE          ACE or ARB
(ARB if ACE intolerant)
  ↓                    ↓
BP meet goal?         BP meet goal?
  no                    no

Add-on therapy        Add-on therapy (best choices):
(best choices):       • combination of ACE and ARB
• diuretic (loop      • non-dihydropyridine calcium channel
  if decreased GFR)     blocker (may have additional renal
• beta blocker          protective effect)
• aldosterone         • beta blocker (note: if a beta blocker
  antagonist            is added, may need to change to
  (spironolactone       dihydropyridine CCB)
  or epierenone)      • diuretic (loop if decreased GFR)
                      • spironolactone
  ↓                    ↓
BP meet goal?         BP meet goal?
  no                    no

Add-on therapy        Add-on therapy (less certain benefit):
(less certain         • CCB (dihydropyridine)
benefit):             • loop diuretics
• CCB (not            • central and peripheral vasodialators
  nifedipine)
• ARB with ACE
• alpha blockers
  (caution)
• central and peripheral
  vasodialators

Continue current Rx and monitor BP at each visit
```

Prepared by Intermountain Healthcare Clinical Education, Salt Lake City, Utah

References

1. All algorithms have been used with permission from Intermountain Healthcare. Copyright 2005, Intermountain Healthcare.
2. Riddle MC, Rosentock J, Gerich J (on behalf of the Insulin Glargine 4002 Study Investigators). The Treat-to-Target Trial: randomized addition of glargine or human NPH insulin to oral therapy of type 2 diabetic patients. Diabetes Care 2003;26:3080–6.
3. American Diabetes Association. Standards of medical care in diabetes. Diabetes Care 2005;28:S4–S36.

Dreyer Medical Clinic: Personal Diabetes Record

Parameter	Goal	My Value (date)	My Value (date)	My Value (date)
HgA1c	Less than 7%			
Total cholesterol	Less than 200			
LDL "bad" cholesterol	Less than 100			
HDL "good" cholesterol	Greater than 45			
Triglycerides	Less than 150			
BP	Less than 130/80 mm Hg			
Aspirin?	Patients with diabetes should take one daily	Yes No	Yes No	Yes No
Annual foot examination?	All patients should have annual foot examinations	Yes Date No	Yes Date No	Yes Date No
Annual eye examination?	All patients should have annual eye examinations	YES Date No	Yes Date No	Yes Date No
Urine protein	Microalbumin (−)			

Prepared by Dreyer Medical Clinic, Aurora, Illinois

Dreyer Medical Clinic: Drug Record

Name	Dose	How often?	What's it for?

Prepared by Dreyer Medical Clinic, Aurora, Illinois

Dreyer Medical Clinic—Insulin Sensitivity Factor (ISF)

Your ISF = _____ Your target blood glucose = 100_____

What is ISF?
The ISF is the *estimated* number of points your blood glucose should drop with each unit of fast-acting insulin (Humalog, Novolog, or Apidra).

How to use your ISF:
1. Check your blood glucose before a meal.
2. Subtract your target blood glucose.*
3. Divide by your ISF.
4. This is the number of insulin units (fast acting) needed to "correct" your current blood glucose.
5. Add meal dose as assigned.

Meal dose:
1. Take 1 U of insulin for every _____ grams of carbohydrate in your planned meal.
2. If you do not know the # of carbohydrates, take:
   a. _____ units for a small meal, or
   b. _____ units for a large meal

Example:
ISF = 25; target = 100
1. Blood glucose = 250
2. 250 − 100 = 150
3. 150/25 = 6
4. 6 U to correct blood glucose

The ISF works "best" when combined with additional insulin based on the meal you are going to consume.
Please call me if you have questions: (123)123-1234
*If your blood glucose is below your target before a meal, take the meal dose ONLY.

Dreyer Medical Clinic: Lantus Dosing Titration Schedule
1. Increase Lantus (glargine) dose every (_____) according to the scale below. (Example: Every Wednesday, titrate your Lantus).
2. On Wednesday, take the average of your fasting blood glucose readings in the morning and see where it falls on the schedule below (#3).
3. Lantus Titration Schedule
   - If values are consistently ≥ 200, increase Lantus dose by 10 U.
   - If 180–200, increase dose by 8 U.
   - If 140–180, increase dose by 6 U.
   - If 120–140, increase dose by 4 U.
   - If 100–120, increase dose by 2 U.

   Example: If your blood glucose values averaged around 200, then increase your current Lantus dosage by 10 U. Follow this same procedure every Wednesday.
4. Stop increasing your Lantus dose IF:
   - You have any glucose readings less than 60
   - OR
   - You have any three readings that are less than 100 within 1 week
5. Call me with any questions!

Reference
1. Riddle MC, Rosenstock J, Gerich J (on behalf of the Insulin Glargine 4002 Study investigators). The Treat-to-Target Trial. Diabetes Care 2003;26:3080–6.

Prepared by Dreyer Medical Clinic, Aurora, Illinois

DEPO-PROVERA® CONTRACEPTION PROTOCOL

Submitted by: Ila Harris

Revised: 2006

First Injection

The patient must first be educated on all options for birth control, including adverse drug reactions. Depo-Provera® may only be given at or after a physician visit. It must be ordered by a physician and documented on the Depo-Provera® flow sheet.

First Depo-Provera® Injection Given ONLY

- Within the first 5 days of onset of a normal menstrual period (regular; no abnormal bleeding)*
- Within 5 days after a confirmed elective abortion
- To women who have taken oral contraceptives for more than 1 month without interruption*
- To women who have used the birth control patch or ring correctly for more than 1 month
- To women having Implanon® removed simultaneously
- Within the first 5 days postpartum if not breastfeeding
- Within 6 weeks postpartum if *exclusively* breastfeeding* (after negative urine pregnancy test ONLY if more than 2 weeks postpartum)
- After miscarriage, within 5 days after tissue is passed if it is known when the tissue was passed
- If patient is postpartum (not breastfeeding), postabortion, or postmiscarriage and more than 5 days but less than 4 weeks have elapsed AND the woman has NOT had vaginal intercourse
- If none of the above apply, Depo-Provera® will NOT be given, and the patient will be asked to return within 5 days of the onset of her next menses.
- The Depo-Provera® shingle (portion for first injection) should be filled out, signed, and dated by the patient and nursing staff.
- The patient should be instructed to use additional contraception (e.g., condom, female condom, diaphragm, cervical cap) for 10 days after the injection. The patient should be offered a 10-day supply of condoms.

  * *A urine pregnancy test must first be done and must be negative.*

Subsequent Injections

- Patients should be instructed to allow 84 days between injections. Acceptable range is 77 to 90 days between injections. If 90 or fewer days have elapsed, they do not need to fill out shingle.
- The nursing staff should complete, sign, and date the **nursing staff** portion of the shingle.
- For late injections, *both* boxes in the top section OR *all three* boxes in the bottom section MUST be checked.
- For the *second* injection (even if on time), a urine pregnancy test should be done. Depo-Provera® should be given only after a negative urine pregnancy test.

If more than 90 days have elapsed between injections

- The patient should complete the appropriate section (top or bottom) of the patient portion of the **subsequent injections** shingle and sign and date it.
- If the patient indicates that she has NOT had unprotected intercourse in the past 2 weeks, Depo-Provera® may be given after a negative serum pregnancy test.
- If she HAS had unprotected intercourse in the previous 2 weeks, the injection should NOT be given that day. The patient should be told to abstain or use an additional form of contraception (e.g., condom, female condom, diaphragm, cervical cap) for 2 weeks and then return to clinic. A pregnancy test is not necessary.
- At the return visit, a serum pregnancy test should be done. The patient should be asked if she has had unprotected intercourse in the past 2 weeks. If yes, repeat step 2. If no, Depo-Provera® may be given that day after a negative serum pregnancy test.
- The patient should be instructed to use additional contraception for 10 days after the injection. The patient should be offered a 10-day supply of condoms.
- If it has been more than 1 year since the last injection was due, it should be treated as a first injection, and the protocol for the first injection should be followed.
- Depo-Provera® may decrease bone mass and increase risk of osteoporosis later in life. Patients must be educated to take adequate calcium and vitamin D. Use for longer than 2 years is only recommended if other options are not possible or desired.

Patients must have a periodic examination/Pap test. A physician must reorder Depo-Provera® annually and document it on the Depo-Provera® flow sheet.

First Depo-Provera® Injection

Nursing staff
- One of the statements in the patient section applies, physician has verified, and urine pregnancy test (if required) is negative. Depo-Provera® (150 mg intramuscularly) may be given today.
- Patient had a miscarriage, and a physician has verified that the tissue has passed within 5 days. Depo-Provera® may be given today.
- None of the statements in the patient section are checked OR the urine pregnancy test is positive, Depo-Provera® may NOT be given today. Patient was told to return for first shot within 5 days of the start of her next period.
- If * in patient section, urine pregnancy test must be done: • Positive; • Negative

_____   _____
Nursing staff signature   Date

Patient
Please check which one of the following is true:
- My period is regular, and it started less than 5 days ago. (Date last period started: _____)*
- I had an elective abortion 5 or fewer days ago. (Date of abortion: _____)
- I am currently taking birth control pills, and have been for more than 1 month without missing any pills.*
- I am currently using the birth control patch or ring, and have been using it correctly for more than 1 month.
- I am having Implanon® removed today.
- I gave birth 5 or less days ago and I am not breastfeeding. (Date of birth: _____)
- I gave birth in the past 6 weeks and I am breastfeeding only [no other supplements]. (Date of birth: _____)*
- I gave birth or had a miscarriage or abortion less than 4 weeks ago, but more than 5 days ago, and have NOT had vaginal intercourse.
- I had a miscarriage in the past 5 days.
- None of the above apply.
- If given a Depo-Provera® shot today, I agree to use other contraception (e.g., condom, female condom, diaphragm, cervical cap) or not have vaginal intercourse for the next 10 days.

_____   _____
Patient signature   Date

Subsequent Depo-Provera injections (other than initial)

Nursing staff: Today's date: _____ Date of last injection: _____ Days between injections: _____
It has been 90 days or less since the last injection
- Depo-Provera® injection (150 mg IM) may be given
- Urine pregnancy test should be done only if second injection

More than 90 days has elapsed between injections
- Have patient fill in section. Serum pregnancy test should be done only if Depo-Provera® given today.
- Serum pregnancy test results: • Positive OR • Negative OR • Not done
- Depo-Provera® injection (150 mg IM) may be given only if patient has NOT had unprotected intercourse in the previous 2 weeks and serum pregnancy test is negative

_____   _____
Nursing staff signature   Date

Patient (fill out only if more than 90 days between shots)
- I have NOT had vaginal intercourse in the past 2 weeks OR I HAVE had vaginal intercourse in the past 2 weeks but used another form of contraception (e.g., condom that didn't break or leak, female condom, diaphragm, cervical cap) AND
- If given a Depo-Provera® shot, I agree to use other contraception (e.g., condom, female condom, diaphragm, cervical cap) or not have vaginal intercourse for the next 10 days.

_____   _____
Patient signature   Date
                                        OR
_____
- I HAVE had vaginal intercourse without using other contraception (e.g., condom, female condom, diaphragm, cervical cap) in the previous 2 weeks AND
- I understand that I could be pregnant and therefore I will not get the shot today, AND
- I will abstain from vaginal intercourse OR I will use additional contraception (e.g., condom, female condom, diaphragm, cervical cap) for the next 2 weeks and then return to the clinic.

_____   _____
Patient signature   Date

Medroxyprogesterone (Depo-Provera®) Patient Information

How it works: Medroxyprogesterone is an injectable form of birth control that is given every 12 weeks. It works by preventing the ovaries from releasing an egg (ovulation), thickening the cervical mucus to prevent sperm from joining an egg, and altering the lining of the uterus. An injection is given every 12 weeks at the clinic.

Effectiveness: Of every one thousand women who use it correctly and consistently, only three will become pregnant during the first year of use. Three in one hundred women will become pregnant with typical use.

Dosing: An injection of 150 mg of medroxyprogesterone is given every 12 weeks at the clinic.

Adverse Effects
- Missed/abnormal menstrual cycles
    - Periods may be irregular the first few months, and some women experience unusual bleeding or spotting.
    - Commonly, after 6 to 12 months, periods become lighter and fewer, and bleeding may stop altogether.
- Weight gain
- Average weight gain is 5 pounds in the first year; may have additional weight gain in subsequent years
- Decreased bone mass; increased risk of osteoporosis later in life
    - Taking adequate calcium and vitamin D is recommended.
    - Use for longer than 2 years is only recommended if other options are not possible or desired.
- Slow return to fertility
    - On average, the time to conceive is 10 months from the last injection.
- Dizziness, headache, and fatigue
- Abnormal hair growth
- Depression
- Breast tenderness and bloating

Important Points
- Do not massage the area where shot was given immediately after the injection.
- Depo-Provera® does NOT protect against sexually transmitted infections (STIs). Use other methods (such as condoms) to protect against STIs.
- Depo-Provera® is not effective right away. Use a backup method of contraception (such as condoms) for 10 days after receiving your first injection.
- Get adequate CALCIUM, either from your diet or from supplements, to prevent bone loss. You should get 1,000–1,200 mg/day of calcium and at least 400 IU of vitamin D. Ask your doctor if you are getting enough. In addition, exercising and refraining from smoking can help.
- Return in 12 weeks (maximum 90 days). If you are late for your injection, use backup contraceptive methods (such as a condom) until you are able to come in. If you know you will not be able to come back in 12 weeks, come back earlier rather than later.

DEPO-PROVERA® INJECTION PROTOCOL

Submitted by: Kelly Ragucci

Created: 2001

First Injection

Injection is to be given if
- Within the first 5 days of menses*
- Currently taking oral contraceptives for more than 1 month without interruption*
- Within the first 5 days postpartum (whether breastfeeding or not)
- Within 5 days after a confirmed elective abortion
- Having Norplant® (in place for 5 years or less) removed simultaneously
- After miscarriage, within 5 days after tissue is passed
- *Postpartum, postabortion, or postmiscarriage and more than 5 days but less than 4 weeks have elapsed, AND the woman has not had vaginal intercourse*

*A negative urine pregnancy test must be confirmed.

If none of the above applies, the patient should be asked if she has had unprotected intercourse in the past 2 weeks:
- If no, complete a urine pregnancy test and give the injection if the result is negative.
- If yes, complete a urine pregnancy test and give the injection if the result is negative, after having the patient sign the consent form.
- All patients should be educated on potential adverse effects and what to expect.
- If injection is not given within first 5 days of menses, patients should be instructed to use an additional form of contraception (e.g., condom, female condom, diaphragm, cervical cap) for 7 days after the first injection.

Subsequent Injections

- Patients should be instructed to return to the clinic 84 days after the last injection; however, the acceptable range is 77 to 90 days.
- If less than 90 days have elapsed between injections
  - The patient will be given the injection with appropriate education and counseling.
- If more than 90 days have elapsed between injections
  - The patient will be asked if she has had unprotected intercourse in the past 2 weeks
    - If no, complete a urine pregnancy test and give the injection if the result is negative.
    - If yes, complete a urine pregnancy test and give the injection if the result is negative, after the patient signs the consent form.

Prepared by Medical University of South Carolina, Charleston, South Carolina

Depo-Provera® Patient Consent Form

I HAVE had unprotected intercourse in the past 2 weeks AND I understand that I could be pregnant, even though my urine pregnancy test was negative today. I agree to be given the Depo-Provera® injection.

_____   _____
Patient signature   *Date*

EMERGENCY CONTRACEPTION POLICY

Submitted by: Ila Harris

Revised: July 2006

Policy

To provide emergency contraception (Plan B®) to patients who meet the designated criteria.

Procedure

To receive emergency contraception, the patient must be a current patient of the clinic. If a new patient desires emergency contraception, she must come in to be seen by a physician. Patients may request emergency contraception on the telephone or through an appointment. The following eligibility criteria and procedures will be used.

Telephone Call Requests

Any patient calling to request emergency contraception will be directed to a nurse. During the telephone call, the nurse will perform the following activities

1. Ask the patient to answer all of the questions on the attached questionnaire. If the patient refuses to answer the questions, she will not be eligible to receive emergency contraception over the telephone and may need to come in for an appointment.
2. If the patient fits all of the requirements for emergency contraception eligibility (eligibility criteria listed below), the nurse will educate the patient using the patient education material (points 1–11) on how emergency contraception works, possible adverse effects, efficacy, and potential effects on a fetus.
3. If a patient is using oral contraception, education should also be provided on previous points.
4. Verify patient understanding of education provided
5. A prescription for Plan B should be called into a pharmacy. Per protocol, the directions for Plan B should be, "Take two tablets by mouth now," and the prescribing physician will be the medical director of the clinic.
6. The patient will be instructed to make a follow-up appointment to be seen by a physician within 2 weeks.
7. If the nurse has any questions or concerns, he or she should consult the precepting physician.

Appointment Requests and In-Clinic Procedure

- If the patient has come to the clinic to receive emergency contraception, she should be seen by a physician willing to provide the prescription. If the appointment is with a physician not willing to prescribe it, then the patient will be seen by another physician who is willing to prescribe it, or by a nurse (a level 1 office visit is charged), and the telephone protocol will be followed.
- The patient will be given the questionnaire to fill out completely and sign (see attachment). If the patient refuses to answer the questions, she will not be eligible to receive emergency contraception. A urine pregnancy test MUST be done if her menses was 4 or more weeks ago or if she has other acts of unprotected intercourse since her last period (other than the act in the past 120 hours).
- If the patient fits the requirement for eligibility, she will be educated on how emergency contraception works, possible adverse effects, efficacy, and potential effects on a fetus. If a patient is using oral contraception, education should also be provided on points 12 and 13. (See attached patient education sheet.)
- The patient education sheet will be provided to the patient after verbal education. A physician or nurse should verify patient understanding.
- The patient should receive education by a physician regarding nonemergency contraceptive methods. If the patient is being seen by a nurse, the patient should be directed to an available physician (same day or a future appointment within 2 weeks) for a visit to discuss nonemergency contraceptive methods.
- If patient is eligible for emergency contraception, the provider seeing the patient will provide her with a prescription for Plan B® with the directions, "Take two tablets by mouth now." If the nurse sees the patient, the nurse will call in the prescription with the same instructions per protocol under the medical director.
- If the patient has received emergency contraception three times during the past year, she must see a physician only. It is up to the physician's discretion whether or not to prescribe emergency contraception.

Eligibility Criteria (Questions Asked by the Nurse/Health Care Provider)

1. Have you had unprotected intercourse during the past 120 hours (5 days)?*
   - If YES, this is acceptable.
   - If NO and time is greater than 120 hours, patient is NOT eligible.
2. Was the intercourse a consensual act?
   - If YES, this is acceptable.
   - If NO, patient should be sent to the emergency department for further evaluation and consultation.
3. When was the first day of your last menstrual period?*
4. Is this less than 4 weeks ago?*
   - If YES (less than 4 weeks ago), this is acceptable.
   - If NO, ask the next question.
5. If NO, have you had unprotected intercourse (other than the act within the past 120 hours) since your last period.
   - If NO (the patient has NOT had unprotected intercourse other than the act within the past 120 hours), this is acceptable.
   - If YES (the patient HAS had unprotected intercourse in the past 4 weeks in addition to the act within the past 120 hours), the patient should be warned that she may already be pregnant. Emergency contraception will not be effective and will not be given over the telephone because pregnancy must first be ruled out. The patient should come in for an appointment and a urine pregnancy test.
6. Was the last period normal in length and timing?*
   - If YES, this is acceptable.
   - If NO and patient has any abnormal bleeding, pregnancy and/or other disorders must be ruled out. The patient cannot receive emergency contraception over the telephone and should be instructed to schedule an appointment.
7. Have you ever used emergency contraception before?
   - If NO, this is acceptable.
   - If YES and it has been less than three times during the past year, the patient may be given emergency contraception, but she will be unable to receive a repeat prescription until she is seen for contraception counseling.
   - If YES and patient has received emergency contraception three times during the past year, the prescription will not be given over the telephone. Patients desiring emergency contraception must come in and see a physician. It is up the physician's discretion whether or not to prescribe emergency contraception.
8. Are you currently using birth control pills, patches, or a ring?
   - If NO, this is acceptable.
   - If YES, are you currently in need of emergency contraception because of missed doses, interacting drugs, or improper use?
     - Improper Patch Use: If the patch has been off for more than 24 hours or if a new patch was not applied within 48 hours of patch change date.
     - Improper Ring Use: If the ring has been out for more than 3 hours or if it was left in place longer than 4 weeks.
     - If YES, this is acceptable, but the patient should be educated on the applicable points (12–15) from the patient education sheet.

Patient must answer yes to questions 1, 3, and 4 to receive an emergency contraception prescription. If she does not answer yes to these questions, she can be offered an appointment for a urine pregnancy test and possibly receive emergency contraception.

A Patient Will Not Be Eligible for Emergency Contraception If Any of the Following Apply

1. She may be pregnant (last menses 4 or more weeks ago and the patient had unprotected intercourse outside the past 120 hours; irregular menses) or knows she is pregnant.
2. She had unprotected intercourse greater than 120 hours ago.
3. The patient has unexplained vaginal bleeding.

Patient Education for Plan B®

1. Plan B® can be taken up to 120 hours after unprotected intercourse.
2. Plan B® comes in a package with two tablets. We recommend taking BOTH tablets at the same time, immediately.
3. The most common adverse effects with Plan B® are nausea, abdominal pain, headache, dizziness, fatigue, breast tenderness, and menstrual changes (earlier, later, heavier, or lighter).
4. If you vomit within 1 hour of taking either dose, contact our health care professional to discuss whether to repeat that dose.
5. In clinical trials, Plan B® (levonorgestrel 0.75 mg) was found to be 84–89% effective at preventing pregnancy when taken within 72 hours (3 days). It is 63% effective at preventing pregnancy when taken 72 to 120 hours (3 to 5 days) later. It is not 100% effective to prevent pregnancy.
6. If your period is more than 1 week later than expected after taking Plan B®, you may be pregnant. Plan B® can delay or result in other changes in the menstrual cycle.
7. Plan B® may work by inhibiting ovulation (pre-

venting the egg from leaving the ovary), interfering with fertilization (preventing the sperm from meeting the egg), or inhibiting implantation (preventing a fertilized egg from attaching to the uterus). It will not be effective after implantation has occurred.

8. If you are already pregnant or if you become pregnant, Plan B® has not been shown to cause harm to a developing fetus.
9. Plan B® should not be used as a regular birth control method.
10. Plan B® will not protect you from HIV or other STIs.
11. If you experience severe lower abdominal pain, you must consult a health care professional because this may be a sign of an ectopic pregnancy, which is a serious and dangerous medical problem.
12. If you are requesting emergency contraception because of improper use of contraceptive pills, patch, or ring, refer to the patient information that was provided to you or ask your provider or pharmacist how to restart.
13. If you have been taking interacting drugs (antibiotics, St. John's Wort, etc.), you should use backup contraception (e.g., condom) throughout the treatment with the interacting drug and for 1 week after stopping the interacting drug.

GERIATRIC ASSESSMENT CLINIC

Submitted by: Michael E. Ernst

Created: 2002

Description

The clinical pharmacist is an integral member of a multidisciplinary team responsible for the assessment, treatment, and follow-up of ambulatory geriatric patients. As a member of this team, the clinical pharmacist works with a board-certified geriatrician, geriatric fellow, geriatric advanced nurse practitioner, and social worker to directly optimize the care of geriatric patients. The specific role of the clinical pharmacist is to evaluate drug appropriateness, including efficacy, toxicity, and cost-effectiveness, and to optimize therapy through rational drug therapy recommendations for the geriatric patient.

Objectives

The geriatric clinical pharmacist should be able to
- Discuss the pathophysiology and pharmacotherapeutic management of acute and chronic diseases commonly encountered in geriatric populations, such as Alzheimer's dementia, vascular dementia, urinary tract infections, major depressive disorder, hypothyroidism, CHF, COPD, insomnia, osteoporosis, HTN, and diabetes, with the geriatric patient and/or caregiver
- Conduct patient medical and drug histories
- Discuss medical, social, behavioral, and pharmacotherapeutic aspects of geriatric patient care with the geriatric team
- Provide evidence based drug information to the geriatric team or geriatric patient and/or caregiver in a timely manner
- Consider age-related changes in the absorption, distribution, metabolism, and excretion of drugs and their effects on drug therapy initiation, efficacy, discontinuation, and adverse effects in elderly patients
- Provide follow-up for drug adjustments either by follow-up clinic visit or telephone
- Use the information gained from the patient, the patient's caregiver, and the medical record to
  - Provide appropriate patient counseling to the geriatric patient, and/or their primary caregiver, for new and existing drugs
  - Identify and resolve polypharmacy issues
  - Make appropriate drug therapy recommendations for initial dosing of drugs, monitoring guidelines, and follow-up
  - Identify the goal of therapy for each problem
  - Recommend appropriate preventive health therapies and screenings for geriatric patients, such as pneumococcal and influenza immunizations and osteoporosis prevention and treatment

OUTPATIENT GERIATRIC CARE

Submitted by: Karen Pater and Kristen Felice

Created: November 2006

Introduction

Drug and drug-related problems have significant medical and safety consequences for the elderly and economically affect the health care system. A 1997 study evaluating ADEs in the elderly population found that 35% of ambulatory older adults experience ADEs and 29% require health care services for the management of ADEs. The cost of drug-related problems has been calculated to be more than $75 billion in the ambulatory care setting. In addition, if drug-related problems were ranked by cause of death, they would be the fifth leading cause of death in the United States. Given that the elderly population makes up about 12% of the population in the United States and that this figure is expected to rise as the generation of baby boomers reaches geriatric age, efforts to appropriately care for the aging population should be of interest to all health care providers.

The clinical pharmacist is one of many providers in an ambulatory care geriatrics clinic. An ideal clinic setting will implement a multidisciplinary approach, with care provided by board-certified geriatricians, psychiatrists, geriatric advanced nurse practitioners, physician assistants, nursing staff, social workers, and pharmacists. Clinical pharmacists often practice in clinical settings focused on geriatric populations (e.g., general or FM practices). Regardless of the setting, the clinical geriatric pharmacist is a valuable addition to the team, serving as the drug expert and providing consultation with the other health care professionals in the service.

The role of the clinical geriatric pharmacist is to evaluate drug appropriateness and optimize therapy through rational drug selection for the geriatric patient. This guide will provide insight on the different aspects of care that can be provided by a clinical geriatric pharmacist in the outpatient setting.

The clinical geriatric pharmacist should be able to
- Understand age-related changes in the pharmacokinetics and pharmacodynamics of the elderly population and how these changes affect outcomes of drug therapy
- Discuss the pathophysiology and pharmacotherapeutic management of acute and chronic disease states specific to the geriatric population with the patient and/or caregiver
- Provide evidence-based drug information to members of the geriatric team and to patients and their caregivers
- Conduct thorough drug reviews with patients and evaluate for drug adherence and appropriateness
- Identify and resolve polypharmacy issues
- Make appropriate drug therapy recommendations for the initiation of drugs including monitoring and proper follow-up
- Recommend appropriate preventive health strategies and screenings for geriatric patients
- Provide patient education on proper drug use and indications, disease management, home monitoring, and non-pharmacological therapy
- Assist patients with the process of obtaining drugs through the use of Medicare Part D, other third-party insurers, or use of drug assistance programs based on patients' individual needs

Clinic Flow

Referral Process

Patients should be referred to the clinical geriatric pharmacist when drug-related problems are identified by providers. In addition, patients may be referred for continuing assessment of chronic disease states such as DM, HTN, and CHF, specifically when new drug therapies are being considered.

Clinic Visits

Individual Sessions

Patients should expect to spend between 30 and 45 minutes with the pharmacist on an initial visit. This will allow time to obtain all required medical, social, and drug therapy histories necessary to fully assess the appropriateness of drug use. An example of an Initial Visit Form is provided in Appendix A. This form can be modified to meet the needs of specific clinics. It is helpful if patients are prescreened by the pharmacist before physician visits so that the provider has complete and accurate information regarding drug use.

Follow-up visits will be decided on by the pharmacist and referring provider, and time allotments will vary depending on the reason for visits. In general, patients monitored at a Geriatrics Clinic will be seen quarterly—and more often if the need arises. The pharmacist, therefore, can see patients either in conjunction with physician visits or in between visits if necessary.

Group Sessions

Often, there are opportunities to see patients in a group setting, with meetings focused on specific topics for the session. This approach should be considered in large practices so that patient education can be disseminated more efficiently. This also allows patients an opportunity to interact with other patients who may have similar disease states and similar drug-related questions.

Regardless of the type of session used in the clinic, all patients should be provided with a drug calendar at the conclusion of the visit. Examples of a drug calendar are provided in Appendix B.

Innovative Opportunities

In addition to the routine care of geriatric patients in the outpatient setting, clinical pharmacists may be in the position to offer unique services specific to the geriatric population. One such role could be in maintaining records regarding preventive health strategies and screenings for patients. Examples of the Preventive Health Flow Sheet are provided in Appendix C.

Pharmacists can also be instrumental in providing the following types of services, depending on the specific clinic's need and availability of other providers on the geriatric team.

- Participate in initial evaluation of depression and dementia by administering geriatric depression scales and MMSEs
- Conduct balance testing before and after initiation of new drug therapies
- Conduct peripheral arterial disease screenings in all patients presenting for new visits to the Geriatric Clinic through the use of a handheld Doppler device to calculate ankle/brachial index
- Provide in-depth Blood Glucose Monitoring Reports to providers through the use of available software for patient-specific glucometers
- Implement policies and procedures related to the distribution of drug samples
- Operate a "Flu Vaccine Clinic" during influenza season

Regardless of the specific clinical setting, the clinical geriatric pharmacist is an instrumental part of the geriatric team. The opportunities in this specific patient population are endless, and this guide offers ideas and tools for implementing geriatric care in the outpatient setting.

References

1. Hanlon JT, Schmader KE, Koronkowski MJ, et al. Adverse drug events in high risk older outpatients. J Am Geriatr Soc 1997;45:945–8.
2. Bootman JL, Harrison DL, Cox E. The health care cost of drug-related morbidity and mortality in nursing facilities. Arch Intern Med 1997;157:2089–96.
3. Lazarou J, Pomeranz BH, Corey PN. Incidence of adverse drug reaction in hospitalized patients: A meta-analysis of prospective studies. JAMA 1998;279:1200–5.
4. U.S. Census 2000. Available at *www.census.gov/main*. Accessed June 2008.

Appendix A—Geriatric Clinical Pharmacy

Initial Visit Form

Name _____ MR # _____
Insurance _____ Pharmacy _____ # _____

PMH (check applicable boxes)

	Alzheimer's disease
	Arthritis
	CAD
	CHF
	COPD
	Dementia
	Depression
	DM
	Gout
	HTN
	Hyperlipidemia
	Hypothyroidism
	Osteoporosis
	Renal insufficiency

Health Maintenance (date)

Bone density test	
Mammogram	
PSA	
Pneumoccoal vaccine	
Influenza vaccine	
Colonoscopy	

Social

Living situation	
Ethanol	
Tobacco	
Illicits	

Allergy/Intolerance Reaction

Drug	Dose and Schedule	Indication	Adverse Drug Reaction?

Compliance Assessment _____
_____
_____

Appendix B—DRUG CALENDAR

For Jane Doe

Drug (generic and/or brand name)	9:00 A.M.	3:00 P.M.	9:00 P.M.
Enalapril 5-mg tablet Take 1 tablet by mouth daily Used for: high blood pressure	1		
Aspirin EC (enteric coated) 81-mg tablet Take 1 tablet by mouth daily Used for: heart protection	1		
Colace 100-mg capsule Take 1 tablet by mouth twice daily Used for: prevention of constipation	1		1
Simvastatin 20-mg tablet Take 1 tablet by mouth daily Used for: cholesterol			1
Aricept 10-mg tablet Take 1 tablet by mouth at bedtime Used for: memory			1
Calcium citrate plus D 500 mg Take 1 tablet by mouth 3 times daily Used for: calcium supplement for bones	1	1	1
Fosamax 70 mg Take 1 tablet weekly Used for: bone strength	Take 1 tablet weekly		

Appendix C—Geriatric Care Preventive Health Flow Sheet

Test/Vaccination	Previous	2006	2007	2008	2009
Mammogram					
Colonoscopy					
PSA or Pap smear					
DEXA scan					
Pneumovax					
Tetanus					
Influenza vaccine					
Zoster vaccine					

Notes:

Geriatric Evaluation

Test	Previous	2006	2007	2008	2009
MMSE/Minicog					
GDS					
BOMC					
ADL					
IADL					
Get up and go					
FallTrak					
Bladder scan					
ABI					

ABI = ankle/brachial index; ADL = activities of daily living; BOMC = blessed orientation-memory-concentration; DEXA = dual energy x-ray absorptiometry; GDS = geriatric depression scale; IADL = instrumental activities of daily living; MMSE = mini-mental status examination; PSA = prostate-specific antigen.

SENIORS CLINIC REFILL PROTOCOL

Submitted by: Sunny Linnebur

Created: August 2001

Purpose and Objectives
- Expedite patient services by authorizing refills on maintenance drugs
- Reduce PCP refill prescription load and time spent on record review
- Increase PCP time for clinical duties
- Review prescription profiles for drug-related problems
- Monitor for cost-effective therapy

Duties and Responsibilities
- Record refill messages from voice mail and obtain patient charts
- Review the medical record for appropriateness of drug therapy
- Contact the patient to obtain additional information
- Complete appropriate documentation (telephone refill encounter form)
- Refill according to protocol guidelines
- Call in all noncontrolled prescriptions to the pharmacy
- Forward chart for provider signature
- Obtain prior review by PCP for narcotic prescriptions to be written and left at front desk for patient pickup
- Maintain narcotic refill documentation

Refill Process
- Patient requests refills by voice mail
- Paper charts are pulled or the EMR is retrieved if no paper chart is available.
- Chart is reviewed, and the prescription refill is renewed or denied based on protocol.
- PCP authorization is requested if necessary.
- Charts not meeting protocol will be delivered to the patient's PCP for approval or denial of refill request.
- Refill will be authorized as indicated by protocol or provider.
- Prescription will be called in to the patient's pharmacy (excluding Class II drugs).
- Patients will be notified if refills are not authorized or if an appointment must be made.

Time Frame
- Calls received Monday–Thursday by 4:00 P.M. will be processed within 48 hours.
- Calls received on Friday–Sunday will be processed the following Monday.

Refill Authorization Protocol

Patient Type	Noncontrolled Substance	Controlled Substance, Nonnarcotic	Controlled Substance, Narcotic
Seen within 3–6 months	6 months	1 month	No refill without PCP approval
Seen within 6–12 months	3 months	1 month	No refill without PCP approval
Seen after 12 months	1 month plus appointment	No refill plus appointment	No refill plus appointment

Pharmacy Intern will page or e-mail physician if prescription is urgent.

No ACUTE drugs will be approved without PCP approval.

Antibiotics will not be refilled unless the chart clearly indicates that therapy is to be continued for longer than the standard 7–21 days.

Drug	Laboratory Results	Time Frame of Laboratory Results
Warfarin	INR	1 month
	Hemoglobin/Hematocrit	12 months
Diuretics, ACEIs, potassium replacements, NSAIDs	Chemistry panel	6 months
Oral hypoglycemics, insulin	FBS, HgA1c	6 months
Metformin	SCr	6 months
TZDs also	LFTs	Every 2 months for first year; then every 6 months
Lipid-modifying agents	FLP / LFTs	6 months
Digoxin, theophylline, antiarrythmics, lithium	Serum concentrations	6 months
Anticonvulsants	LFTs	
Thyroid replacements	TSH	12 months
Vitamin B_{12}	Serum B_{12}	None
Hormone replacement	Mammogram	12 months

FAMILY MEDICINE REFILL PROTOCOL

Submitted by: Andrea Wessell

Revised: March 2002

Purpose and Objectives
- Expedite patient services by authorizing refills on maintenance drugs
- Reduce PCP refill prescription load and time spent on record review
- Increase PCP time for clinical duties

Duties and Responsibilities
- Record refill messages from voice mail and review patient charts
- Contact the patient to obtain additional information if needed
- Refill according to protocol guidelines
- Obtain review by PCP for narcotic prescriptions to be written and left at front desk for patient pickup
- Call in all noncontrolled prescriptions to the pharmacy
- Complete appropriate documentation (progress note and update drug list in chart)

Refill Process
- Patient requests refills by voice mail.
- Chart is reviewed, and prescription refill is renewed or denied based on protocol.
- PCP authorization is requested if necessary.
- Requests not meeting protocol will be sent to the patient's PCP for approval or denial of refill request.
- Refill will be authorized as indicated by protocol or provider.
- Urgent refill requests will be approved by PCP if available or by another provider in same group.
- Prescription will be called in to the patient's pharmacy (excluding Class II drugs).
- Patients will be notified if refills are not authorized or if an appointment must be made.

Time Frame
- Calls received Monday–Friday by 4:00 P.M. will be processed within 24 hours.
- Calls received Friday–Sunday will be processed the following Monday.

MUSC FMC Refill Authorization Protocol

1. Maintenance Drugs

Patient Type	Noncontrolled Substance	Controlled Substance, Nonnarcotic	Controlled Substance, Narcotic
Seen within 3–6 months	6 months	1 month	No refill without PCP approval
Seen within 6–12 months	3 months	1 month	No refill without PCP approval
Seen after 12 months	1 month plus appt	No refill plus appt	No refill plus appt

If Rx is <u>urgent</u>, nursing staff will contact PCP or provider in group for refill.

No acute drugs will be approved without PCP approval.

<u>Antibiotics</u> will not be refilled unless it clearly indicates in chart that therapy is to be continued for longer than the standard 7–21 days.

2. Drugs with Laboratory Monitoring Requirements

Drug	Laboratory Results	Time Frame of Laboratory Results
Warfarin (Coumadin®)	INR Hemoglobin/hematocrit	1 month 12 months
ACEIs ARBs Diuretics Potassium replacements NSAIDs	Chemistry panel	6 months
Oral hypoglycemics, insulin	FBS, HgA1c	6 months
Metformin	FBS, HgA1c, SCr	6 months
TZDs	FBS, HgA1c, LFTs	Every 2 months for first year; then every 6 months
Lipid-modifying agents	Fasting lipid panel LFTs	6 months
Digoxin, theophylline, lithium, valproic acid Anticonvulsants	Serum concentrations LFTs	6 months
Thyroid replacements	TSH	12 months
Hormone replacement	Mammogram	12 months

Refill Protocol—Sample Drug List

ACEIs	Benazepril (Lotensin®)
	Captopril (Capoten®)
	Enalapril (Vasotec®)
	Lisinopril (Prinivil®, Zestril®)
	Ramipril (Altace®)
	Lotensin HCT® with HCTZ
	Capozide® with HCTZ
	Vaseretic® with HCTZ
	Prinizide® with HCTZ
	Zestoretic® with HCTZ
	Lotrel®—Benazepril plus amlodipine
ARBs	Candesartan (Atacand®)
	Irbesartan (Avapro®)
	Losartan (Cozaar®)
	Valsartan (Diovan®)
	Olmesartan (Benicar®)
	Avalide®—Irbesartan plus HCTZ
	Hyzaar®—Losartan plus HCTZ
	Diovan HCT®—Valsartan plus HCTZ
Diuretics	Aldactone® (spironolactone)
	Chlorthalidone
	Diuril® (chlorothiazide)
	Hydrochlorothiazide
	Hydrodiuril® (HCTZ)
	Lozol® (indapamide)
	Zaroxyln® (metolazone)
	Bumex® (bumetadine)
	Demadex® (torsemide)
	Ethacrynic acid
	Lasix® (furosemide)
	Aldactazide®—Spironolactone plus HCTZ
	Maxzide®—Triamterence plus HCTZ
Potassium replacements	Klor-Con®, Kdur®, MicroK®, others (potassium chloride)

Oral hypoglycemics	Diabinese® (chlorpropamide)
	Glucotrol®, Glucotrol XL® (glipizide)
	Amaryl® (glimepiride)
	Micronase®, Diabeta® (glyburide)
	Precose® (acarbose)
	Glyset® (miglitol)
	Prandin® (repaglinide)
	Starlix® (nateglinide)
Metformin	Glucophage®, Glucophage XR®
	Glucovance® (metformin plus glyburide)
TZDs	Actos® (pioglitazone)
	Avandia® (rosiglitazone)

Lipid-lowering agents	Niaspan® (niacin)
	Mevacor® (lovastatin)
	Zocor® (simvastatin)
	Lipitor® (atorvastatin)
	Lopid® (gemfibrozil)
	Questran® (cholestyramine)
	Colestid® (colestipol)
	Welchol® (colesevelam)

Thyroid replacements	Synthroid®, Levoxyl®, Levothroid®, others (levothyroxine)

REFILL CLINIC POLICIES AND PROCEDURES
Submitted by: Debra Lopez

Created: December 2006

Purpose
- To provide a pharmacy refill service for physicians on vacation/leave, residents on an out-of-town elective/rotation, and/or a predetermined situation that has been approved by the pharmacy clinic

Objectives
- Expedite patient services by authorizing refills on maintenance drugs
- Reduce PCP/resident refill prescription load and time spent on record review
- Increase PCP/resident time for clinical duties
- Review prescription profiles for drug-related problems

Eligibility Criteria
- Age 18 years and older
- Chronic drugs (does not include controlled substances)
- Controlled disease states
- Uncontrolled disease states or laboratory values needed

Refill Process
- Physician submits Pharmacy Refill Service Request Form to Tina Comeaux, and a copy will go to the pharmacy clinic.
- Patients and pharmacies request refills by voice mail or fax.
- Medical records personnel obtain requests and pull charts.
- Medical records personnel will route charts to pharmacy. Pharmacy clinic will determine eligibility for pharmacy refill authorization. Charts for patients not eligible for pharmacy refill authorization will be delivered to the patient's PCP for approval or denial of refill request.
- Pharmacist reviews chart, orders appropriate laboratory tests, and renews or denies prescription refill.
- Pharmacist completes appropriate documentation in chart.
- Refill approvals are sent to patient's nurse. Nurse is responsible for faxing or calling in authorized refill to the pharmacy.
- If patients need a scheduled appointment, the chart will be routed to the scheduler.
- Nurse forwards chart to PCP for review of authorized or denied refill.

Authorization Protocol

Controlled disease state and visit within past 3–6 months	6 months
Controlled disease state and visit within past 6–12 months	3 months
Controlled disease state and visit within past 12 months	1 month plus appt
Uncontrolled disease state or laboratory tests needed	1 month plus appt

Time Frame
A. Requests received on Mondays, Wednesdays, and Fridays by 3:00 P.M. will be processed on the same day. Requests received after 3:00 P.M. on Mondays, Wednesdays, and Fridays will be processed within 48 hours.
B. Requests submitted on Tuesdays and Thursdays will be processed the next day.

This refill protocol was formulated and approved by:
Physician:_____Date:_____

Pharmacy Refill Service Request
I, _____, request refill authority to clinical pharmacists under pharmacy refill protocol while I am away. I understand the pharmacists may authorize refills for my patients. As stated in the guidelines, monitoring laboratory results may be ordered. I will be notified of drugs that have been reviewed. If any changes are necessary, I will note them and return them to the refill authorization pharmacist.

Clinician Signature: _____
Dates of request:_____
Today's Date: _____
Pharmacist Signature:_____

DRUG REFILLS POLICY

Submitted by: Sarah Westberg

Created: August 2006

St. Mary's Duluth Clinic Health System Policy and Procedure

Using the following protocols, nurses may refill a patient's drug for 1 year from the date of the patient's last appointment with his or her Primary Provider Team when the condition for the drug was evaluated and the appropriate laboratory work was completed. If a patient is noted not to have a follow-up provider appointment per the table below, please schedule. If the patient is requesting a drug refill for a drug not included in the chart below, it should be referred to the provider.

If a patient's laboratory results are not up-to-date, nurse will schedule/order laboratory tests, schedule follow-up provider appointment per table below, and refill drug for 3 months. Laboratory tests should be ordered with a note stating, "Laboratory orders per refill protocol." This will alert the providers when they see the results in their in-basket. If laboratory tests return normal, nurse may refill for a 3-month supply plus 1 year of refills.

1. If laboratory work has been completed and is abnormal, refills will occur per Primary Provider's discretion.
2. If a patient has not been seen in 1 year or longer, refill for 3 months and schedule an appointment within 1 month.
3. If a patient is not reestablished with a PCP, nurse should schedule an appointment and refill drug for 3 months.
4. If drug is not on the patient's Drug List in EpiCare or there is a dose discrepancy, <u>nurse</u> should call patient and determine dose, how long he or she has been on the drug, and who prescribed it. Then, with all the information, send the provider a prescription refill note with the most appropriate order placed in Epic for Provider approval. ALWAYS attempt to give the provider a choice to approve or deny.
5. Providers should respond to refill requests by routing to the group
6. All denied medication refills are to be routed to notify the patient and the pharmacy.

ALL SCHEDULED MEDICATIONS— CHECK FOR DRUG CONTRACT— SUPERSEDES MEDICATION REFILL PROTOCOL

All controlled substances (Classes II–IV) should be forwarded to the prescriber for refill authorization unless they have indicated in the "Sig" field of the drug order that it can be refilled monthly (Classes III and IV only).

Generic Drugs

- Okay to substitute generic equivalent for any brand name drugs unless originally prescribed as dispense as written

"Lost" Drug Requests

- Okay to refill all <u>nonscheduled</u> drugs per protocol

Coumadin, Jantoven, and Warfarin

- Coumadin, Jantoven, and warfarin will be <u>refilled</u> by the anticoagulation nurses.
- Refill criteria to be met
  - INR current per Anticoagulation Management Protocol or Appointment made for Visit.
  - Yearly examination with provider
- If patient meets refill criteria, warfarin nurse is to refill a 3-month prescription—Adjust Daily Dosing per Anticoagulation Monitoring. Dispensed amount not to exceed 10 more tablets per month than patient actually dosed, to allow for AC "Bumps."
- If INR is overdue and patient is unable to be reached, may refill for 2 weeks and continue attempts to reach the patient. Follow late patient protocol.
- If patient is noncompliant with setting up INR visit after 3 months, additional refills will be routed to the PCP.

Prepared by St Mary's Medical Center, Duluth, Minnesota

Drug	Office Visit Within	Laboratory Work Required	Refill Authorization (from date of last office visit where condition was assessed)	Other Comments
Allergy				
Antihistamines: Claritin (loratidine), Allegra (fexofenadine), Zyrtec (cetirizine), Clarinex (desloratadine), Atarax/Vistaril (hydroxyzine)	1 year		1 year	
Nasal steroids: Flonase (fluticasone), Nasonex (mometasone), Rhinocort (budesonide), Nasacort AQ (triamcinolone)	1 year		1 year	
Nasal antihistamine: Astelin (azelastine)	1 year		1 year	
Epipen (epinephrine)	1 year		1 year	
Allergy eye drops: Patanol (olopatadine), Zaditor (ketotifen)	1 year		1 year	
Anticoagulants and antiplatelets				
Coumadin (warfarin, Jantoven)		INR per anticoagulation management protocol or appt made for visit Yearly examination with provider		To be refilled by anticoagulation nurses
Ticlid (ticlopidine), Trental (pentoxifylline), Plavix (clopidogrel)	1 year	Ticlid: CBC biweekly for first 3 months of therapy; Trental and Plavix: no laboratory tests needed	1 year	
Aggrenox (dipyridamole and aspirin) or Persantine (dipyridamole)	1 year		1 year	
Antipsychotics				
Zyprexa (olanzapine), Seroquel (quetiapine), Risperdal (risperdone)	1 year	Yearly glucose and weight	1 year	Should be refilled under the original prescribing provider, unless PCP has taken over the prescribing
Clozaril (clozapine)		Weekly WBC for first 6 months; then biweekly WBC		Laboratory tests need to be completed through prescribing provider
Prolixin (fluphenazine), Mellaril (thioridazine)	6 months	Fluphenazine: CBC, ALT or AST, BUN, and SCr every 6 months Thioridazine: CBC and ALT or AST every 6 months	6 months	Should be refilled under the original prescribing provider, unless PCP has taken over the prescribing
Haldol (haloperidol), Navane (thiothixene)	1 year		1 year	
Anxiolytics				
Benzodiazepines: Ativan (lorazepam), Xanax (alprazolam), Valium (diazepam), Klonopin (clonazepam), Prosom (estazolam), Serax (oxazepam), Restoril (temazepam)	6 months		6 months	Schedule IV Should be forwarded to prescriber, unless Sig field indicates "refill monthly." Then, it can be refilled five times within 6 months from date of issue Telephone orders are acceptable
Buspar (buspirone)	6 months		6 months	
Asthma/COPD				
Bronchodilators: Ventolin (albuterol), Combivent (albuterol/ipratropium), Atrovent (ipratropium), Maxair (pirbuterol), Serevent (salmeterol), Foradil (formoterol), Spiriva (tiotropium)	1 year		1 year	Monitor for frequent refills because asthma/COPD may not be controlled; patient should then be seen
Steroid inhalers: Azmacort (triamcinolone), Aerobid (flunisolide), Flovent (fluticasone), Pulmicort (budesonide), Vanceril (beclomethasone)	1 year		1 year	
Leukotriene modifiers: Accolate (zafirlukast), Singulair (montelukast)	1 year		1 year	
Combination Products: Advair (salmeterol/fluticasone)	1 year		1 year	
Theophylline	1 year	Yearly theophylline value	1 year	
Anti-arrhythmics				
Procanbid (procainamide), Rhythmol (propafenone), Betapace (sotalol), Norpace (disopyramide), Mexitil (mexiletine), Tambocor (flecainide), Tikosyn (dofetilide)	1 year Dofetilide 3 months	Flecainide: if dose > 200 mg/day, monitor trough values Dofetilide: ECG and SCr every 3 months	1 year Dofetilide only: 3 months	Should be by original prescriber unless PCP has taken over the prescribing; EKG periodically for all

Drug	Office Visit Within	Laboratory Work Required	Refill Authorization (from date of last office visit where condition was assessed)	Other Comments
Attention deficit hyperactivity disorder				
Strattera (atomoxetine)	1 year		1 year	Patient should have received follow-up with prescriber within first 12 weeks of therapy
Benign prostatic hyperplasia				
α₁-Blockers: Cardura (doxazosin), Minipress (prazosin), Hytrin (terazosin), Flomax (tamsulosin), Proscar (finasteride)	1 year		1 year	
Cardiovascular				
Amiodarone: (Cordarone, Pacerone)	6 months	Every 6 months: liver panel, TSH, and free T4, ophthalmologic examination; yearly chest x-ray (CXR) and EKG	6 months	If no EKG or no CXR, nurse schedule office visit with EKG/CXR first
Digoxin (Lanoxin, Digitek)	1 year	Annual digitalis value	1 year	
Long-acting nitrates: Isordil (isosorbide dinitrate), Imdur (isosorbide mononitrate)	1 year		1 year	
Nitroglycerin (Nitrostat, Nitroquick)	1 year		1 year	Patient should refill every 6 months to maintain drugs' effectiveness
Cholesterol				
Fibrates: Lopid (gemfibrozil), Tricor/Lipofen/Lofibra (fenofibrate)	1 year	Yearly fasting lipid profile and AST or ALT	1 year	
Niacin (Niaspan)	1 year	Yearly fasting lipid profile and AST or ALT	1 year	
Bile acid sequestrants: Questran (cholestyramine), Colestid (colestipol), Welchol (colesevelam)	1 year	Yearly fasting lipid profile and AST or ALT	1 year	
Statins: Lipitor (atorvastatin), Pravachol (pravastatin), Zocor (simvastatin), Mevacor (lovastatin), Lescol (fluvastatin)	1 year	Yearly fasting lipid profile and AST or ALT	1 year	
Dementia				
Acetylcholinesterase inhibitors: Aricept (donepezil), Razadyne (galantamine), Exelon (rivastigmine)	1 year		1 year	
Namenda (memantine)	1 year		1 year	
Depression				
SSRIs: Prozac (fluoxetine), Paxil (paroxetine), Zoloft (sertraline), Celexa (citalopram), Lexapro (escitalopram)	6 months	Nurse to assess for appropriate use	6 months	If pt has not been seen within 6 months, nurse should schedule appt and refill for 3 months
TCAs: Elavil (amitriptyline), Norpramin (desipramine), Tofranil (imipramine), Sinequan (doxepin), Pamelor (nortriptyline)	6 months	Nurse to assess for appropriate use	6 months	If pt has not been seen within 6 months, nurse should schedule appt and refill for 3 months
Miscellaneous: Wellbutrin (bupropion), Serzone (nefazodone), Desyrel (trazodone), Effexor (venlafaxine), Remeron (mirtazapine), Cymbalta (duloxetine)	6 months	Nurse to assess for appropriate use	6 months	If pt has not been seen within 6 months, nurse should schedule appt and refill for 3 months
Dermatology				
Acne antibiotics: topical and oral clindamycin, erythromycin, tetracycline, minocycline	1 year		1 year	
Retin-A, Differin, Azelex, (tretinoin)	1 year		1 year	
Steroid topical creams: Aristocort, Kenalog (triamcinolone), Elocon (mometasone), Aclovate (alclometasone), Temovate (clobetasol), DesOwen (desonide)	1 year		1 year	Refill for 1 year for chronic problems such as psoriasis and eczema
High-potency steroid creams: Cyclocort (amcinonide), Halog (halcinonide), Lidex (fluocinonide), Topicort (desoximetasone)	6 months		6 months	
Metrogel/Metrocream/Metrolotion (Metronidazole)	1 year		1 year	
Diabetes				
Diabetic supplies: lancets, test strips, syringes, glucometers, etc.	6 months		6 months	
All insulins	6 months	Every 6 months: HgA1c	6 months	

Drug	Office Visit Within	Laboratory Work Required	Refill Authorization (from date of last office visit where condition was assessed)	Other Comments
Biguanides: Glucophage, Glucophage XR, Glucovance (metformin)	6 months	Every 6 months: HgA1c, Cr, and ALT or AST	6 months	
Sulfonylureas: Glucotrol (glipizide), Micronase/Diabeta (glyburide), Amaryl (glimepiride)	6 months	Every 6 months: HgA1c	6 months	
TZDs: Actos (pioglitazone), Avandia (rosiglitazone)	6 months	Every 6 months: HgA1c, and ALT or AST	6 months	
Byetta (exenatide), Smylin (pramlintide)	6 months	Every 6 months: HgA1c	6 months	
Combination products: Glucovance (glyburide/metformin), Avandamet (rosiglitazone/metformin)	6 months	See individual complaints	6 months	
Erectile dysfunction				
Phosphodiasterase inhibitors: Viagra (sildenafil), Levitra (vardenafil), Cialis (tadalafil)	1 year		1 year	Patient should not be taking nitrates with these drugs
Gastrointestinal				
H₂-blockers: Zantac (ranitidine), Pepcid (famotidine), tagament (cimetidine), Axid (nizatidine)	1 year		1 year	
Inflammatory bowel disease: mesalamine (Asacol, Pentasa, Rowasa)	1 year	Annually: BUN, Cr	1 year	
Azulfidine (sulfasalazine)	6 months	Every 6 months: CBC, AST or ALT, Cr, K+	6 months	
Zelnorm (tegeserod)	1 year		1 year	
Proton pump inhibitors: Prilosec (omeprazole), Prevacid (lansoprazole), Nexium (esomeprazole), Aciphex (rabeprazole), Protonix (pantoprazole)	1 year		1 year	
Reglan (metoclopramide)	1 year		1 year	
Gout				
Colchicine	1 year		1 year	8-mg total dose per acute attack and 3-day interval between doses
Zyloprim (allopurinol)	1 year	Yearly Cr	1 year	
Hair growth	1 year			
5α reductase inhibitor; Propecia (finasteride)	1 year		1 year	
Headache/Migraine	1 year			
Serotonin agonists: Imitrex (sumatriptan), Maxalt (rizatriptan), Zomig (zolmitriptan), Amerge (naratriptan), Axert (almotriptan)	1 year		1 year	
Other acute migraine: Cafergot (ergotamine and caffeine), Midrin (acetaminophen/isometheptene/dichloralphenazone)	1 year		1 year	
Prophylactic therapy: β-blockers: Inderal (propranolol), Tenormin (atenolol), Lopressor (metoprolol)	1 year		1 year	
Herpes treatment				
Zovirax (acyclovir) oral or topical, Famvir (famciclovir), Valtrex (valcyclovir)	1 year		1 year	Patient must be seen if pregnant with vaginal herpes outbreak. Must have documented diagnosis
Hormone replacement: women				
Estrogen: Premarin, Estratest, Estrace, Ogen, Cenestin, Estinyl, Estratab, Menest, Gynodiol	1 year	Yearly mammogram (unless younger than 40 years)	1 year	If no mammogram in the past 1 year, nurse to schedule mammogram and refill for 3 months
Combination estrogen/progestin: Prempro, Premphase, Femhrt, Ortho-Prefest, Activella	1 year	Yearly mammogram (unless younger than 40 years)	1 year	If no mammogram in the past 1 year, nurse to schedule mammogram and refill for 3 months

Drug	Office Visit Within	Laboratory Work Required	Refill Authorization (from date of last office visit where condition was assessed)	Other Comments
Progestin: Provera (medroxyprogesterone), Prometrium	1 year	Yearly mammogram (unless younger than 40 years)	1 year	If no mammogram in the past 1 year, nurse to schedule mammogram and refill for 3 months
Transdermal estrogen: Estraderm, Climara, Vivelle, Alora, Esclim, Fempatch, Menostar Combipatch (combination of estrogen and progesterone), Estrasorb	1 year	Yearly mammogram (unless younger than 40 years)	1 year	If no mammogram in the past 1 year, nurse to schedule mammogram and refill for 3 months
Vaginal estrogen: Premarin vaginal cream, Estrace vaginal cream, EstroGel, Vagifem, Estring, Femring	1 year	Yearly mammogram (unless younger than 40 years)	1 year	If no mammogram in the past 1 year, nurse to schedule mammogram and refill for 3 months
Hormone replacement: men				
Testosterone (Androgel, testosterone patches)	1 year	Yearly PSA and hemoglobin	1 year	
Hormonal contraceptives				
NuvaRing	1 year	Annual PAP	1 year	If no PAP in the past 1 year, nurse to schedule PAP and refill for 3 months
Ortho-Evra	1 year	Annual PAP	1 year	If no PAP in the past 1 year, nurse to schedule PAP and refill for 3 months
All oral contraceptives	1 year	Annual Pap	1 year	If no PAP in the past 1 year, nurse to schedule PAP and refill for 3 months
Hypertension				
ACEIs: Accupril (quinapril), Monopril (fosinopril), Lotensin (benzapril), Altace (ramipril), Mavik (trandolapril), Univasc (moexepril), Zestril/Prinivil (lisinopril), Vasotec (enalapril), Capoten (captopril)	1 year	Yearly K+ and Cr	1 year	
ARBs: Avapro (irbesartan), Cozaar (losartan) Diovan (valsartan), Atacand (candesartan)	1 year	Yearly K+ and Cr	1 year	
α/β-Blockers: Trandate (labetalol)	1 year		1 year	
β-Blockers: Tenormin (atenolol), Lopressor (metoprolol tartrate), Toprol XL (metoprolol succinate), Inderal (propranolol), Zebeta (bisoprolol)	1 year		1 year	
β-Blocker with ISA: pindolol, Sectral (acebutolol)	1 year		1 year	
Calcium channel blockers: Cardizem/Dilacor/Tiazac (diltiazem), Calan/Covera/Verelan (verapamil), Procardia/Adalat (nifedipine), Norvasc (amlodipine)	1 year		1 year	
Central-acting antiadrenergics: Catapress (clonidine), Aldomet (methyldopa)	1 year		1 year	
Vasodilators: Minoxidil	1 year		1 year	
Diuretics: Lasix (furosemide), Bumex (bumetanide), Demadex (torsemide), Dyazide/Maxzide (triamterene/HCTZ), Zaroxlyn (metoalazone)	1 year	Yearly K+ and Na+	1 year	Repeat K+ in 1–2 weeks after a change in diuretic dose or after the addition of a diuretic
Diuretics: HCTZ, chlorothiazide	1 year	Yearly K+	1 year	Repeat K+ap in 1–2 weeks after a change in diuretic dose or after the addition of a diuretic
Aldactone (spironolactone)	1 year	Yearly K+	1 year	
α₁-Agonist: Guanfacine (Tenex)	1 year		1 year	
Combination products: Prinzide/Zestoretic (Lisinopril/HCTZ), Capozide (captopril/HCTZ), Lotrel (amlodipine/benazepril), Tenoretic (atenolol/chlorthalidone), Uniretic (moexipril/HCTZ), Diovan HCT (valsartan/HCTZ), Accuretic (quinapril/HCTZ, Atacand HCT (candesartan/HCTZ), Hyzaar (losartan/HCTZ), Ziac (bisoprolol/HCTZ)	1 year	See individual complaints	1 year	
Hypothyroid				
Levothyroxine (Levothroid, Synthroid, Cytomel	1 year	Yearly TSH	1 year	
Mood stabilizer				

Drug	Office Visit Within	Laboratory Work Required	Refill Authorization (from date of last office visit where condition was assessed)	Other Comments
Lithium	6 months	Yearly lithium value, Cr, CBC, EKG. Every 6 months: TSH	6 months	
Osteoarthritis				
NSAIDs: Naprosyn (naproxen), Motrin/Advil (ibuprofen), Indocin (indomethacin), Sulindac (clinoril), Feldene (piroxicam), Lodine (etolodac), Nalfon (fenoprofen), Amgesic (salsalate), Relafen (nabumetone), Trilisate (choline magnesium trisalicylate)	1 year	Yearly K+, Na+, Cr, CBC, U/A, and AST or ALT	1 year	
COX-2 inhibitors: Celebrex (celecoxib)	1 year	Yearly K+, Na+, Cr, CBC, U/A, and AST or ALT	1 year	
Osteoporosis				
Bisphosphonates: Actonel (risedronate), Fosamax (alendronate), Boniva (ibandronate)	1 year		1 year	
Miacalcin nasal spray (calcitonin)	1 year		1 year	
Evista (raloxifene)	1 year		1 year	
Pain				
Schedule II controlled substances (Percocet [oxycodone/APAP], Oxycontin [oxycodone], MSContin [morphine], methadone, Dilaudid [hydromorphone])				Refer to provider
Vicodin, Lortab (hydrocodone/APAP)				Schedule III. Should be forwarded to prescriber unless Sig field indicates "refill monthly"; then, it can be refilled five times within 6 months from date of issue; telephone orders acceptable
Darvocet (propoxyphene/APAP)				Schedule III. Should be forwarded to prescriber unless Sig field indicates "refill monthly"; then, it can be refilled five times within 6 months from date of issue; telephone orders acceptable
NSAIDs: Naprosyn (naproxen), Motrin/Advil (ibuprofen), Indocin (indomethacin), Sulindac (clinoril), Feldene (piroxicam), Lodine (etolodac), Nalfon (fenoprofen), Amgesic (salsalate), Relafen (nabumetone), Trilisate (choline magnesium trisalicylate)	1 year	Yearly K+, Na+, Cr, CBC, U/A, and AST or ALT	1 year	
Arthrotec (diclofenac and misoprostol)	1 year	Yearly K+, Na+, Cr, CBC, U/A, and AST or ALT	1 year	
COX-2 inhibitors: Celebrex (celecoxib)	1 year	Yearly K+, Na+, Cr, CBC, U/A, and AST or ALT	1 year	
Ultram (tramadol)	6 months		6 months	Not a controlled substance but may be addictive
Neurontin (gabapentin), Lyrica (pregabalin)	1 year		1 year	
TCAs: Elavil (amitriptyline), Norpramin (desipramine), Tofranil (imipramine), Sinequan (doxepin), Pamelor (nortriptyline)	6 months		6 months	
Muscle relaxants: Flexeril (cyclobenzaprine), Robaxin (methocarbamol), Skelaxin (metaxall), Soma (carisprodol)	6 months	Nurse to assess for appropriate use	6 months	If pt has not been seen within 6 months, nurse should schedule appt and refill for 1 month
Pancreatic enzymes				
Pancrelipase (Creon, Pancrease, Viokase)	1 year		1 year	
Parkinson's				
Sinemet (carbidopa/levodopa), Stalevo (levodopa/carbidopa/entacapone)	1 year	Sinemet: Annual CBC and AST or ALT (AST preferred)	1 year	
Comtan (entacapone)	1 year		1 year	
Cogentin (benztropine), Permax (pergolide), Mirapex (pramipexole), Parlodel (bromocriptine)	1 year		1 year	

Drug	Office Visit Within	Laboratory Work Required	Refill Authorization (from date of last office visit where condition was assessed)	Other Comments
Kidney failure	1 year			
Phosphate binder: Renagel (Sevelamer), Phoslo (Calcium acetate), Fosrenol (Lanthanum)	1 year	Calcium, phosphate, bicarbonate, and chloride values yearly	1 year	
Restless leg syndrome	1 year			
Requip (ropinirole)	1 year		1 year	
Rheumatoid arthritis	1 year			
Methotrexate	1 year			Refer to ordering rheumatologist
Arava (leflunomide)	1 year			Refer to ordering rheumatologist
Imuran (azathioprine)	1 year			Refer to ordering rheumatologist
Plaquenil (hydroxychloroquine)	1 year			Refer to ordering rheumatologist
Seizures	1 year			
Depakote (valproic acid)	1 year	Yearly valproic acid value, ALT or AST, and platelet count	2 years	
Dilantin (phenytoin)	1 year	Yearly AST or ALT and dilantin value	1 year	
Neurontin (gabapentin), Lyrica (pregabalin)	1 year		1 year	
Lamictal (lamotrigine)	1 year		1 year	Patient should be seen immediately if a rash develops
Phenobarbitol	1 year	Annual CBC, ALT, phenobarbital value	1 year	
Topamax (topiramate)	1 year	Blood bicarbonate yearly	1 year	
Tegretol (carbamazepine)	1 year	Yearly CBC, AST or ALT, TSH, and carbamazepine concentration	1 year	Patient should be educated on the need for yearly eye examinations
Sleep				
Ambien (zolpidem), Sonata (zaleplon), Lunesta (eszopiclI)	6 months		6 months	Schedule IV Should be forwarded to prescriber unless Sig field indicates "refill monthly"; then, it can be refilled five times within 6 months from date of issue; telephone orders acceptable
Rozerem (ramelteon)	1 year		1 year	
Incontinence				
Detrol (tolteridine), Ditropan (oxybutynin), Sanctura (trospium), Vesicare (solifenacine), Enablex (darifenecin)	1 year		1 year	Refer to provider if pt has glaucoma
Miscellaneous				
Prednisone	6 months		6 months	If long-term prednisone therapy: if pt has not been seen within 6 months, nurse should schedule appt and refill for 3 months
Dental (SBE prophylaxis)			As-needed dental appt	Amoxicillin 2 g 1 hour before procedure; if allergic to PCN, give clindamycin 600 mg
Iron supplement	1 year	At least annually: iron studies, CBC	1 year	
Potassium	1 year	Annual K+	1 year	Repeat K+ in 1–2 weeks after a change in dose or in diuretic

Vitamins

- **Vitamin E:** Has an anticoagulant effect. Okay to use with 325 mg of ASA daily, but for patients who take higher-dose NSAIDs, Plavix, Coumadin, Heparin, or Lovenox, it is not recommended. Dose should be no higher than 400 U/day. Literature illustrates no cardiovascular benefit, and there may actually be some cardiovascular harm, with vitamin E. In addition, it has not been proved to help with memory.
- **Vitamin C:** Increases iron absorption. Good to use if patient is iron-deficient. Not appropriate for anyone suffering from iron overload (e.g., hemochromatosis)
- **Vitamin K:** Not appropriate for anyone taking Coumadin
- **Iron:** Not appropriate for anyone with iron overload (i.e., hemochromatosis)
- **Thyroid drugs:** Iron, calcium, and fiber can interfere with thyroid replacement drugs, as can meals. Recommend taking thyroid drugs on empty stomach in morning
- **Vitamin D:** 400–800 U/day. Higher doses for patients who do not go outdoors and get sunlight. May cause hypercalcemia if taken with too much calcium, especially with older women on thiazide diuretics (HCTZs)
- **Calcium:** 1,200–1,500 mg/day in two or three doses, to be taken with meals, for osteoporosis prevention and treatment. Need vitamin D to be absorbed. Calcium carbonate less expensive, only slightly less well absorbed than calcium citrate. <u>Patients taking proton pump inhibitors may not be able to adequately absorb calcium carbonate (gastric acid is needed to be absorbed), so calcium citrate should be recommended.</u>
- **Megavitamin doses:** We do not recommend megavitamin doses. We recommend the standard recommended daily allowance (RDA) doses on a typical multivitamin bottle.
- **Brand:** There is no good evidence to suggest that one brand is better than another. We suggest an RDA-approved generic brand.

IMMUNIZATION PROTOCOL AND SURVEYS
Submitted by: Melissa Blair

Created: 2000

Trained pharmacists of the FM Pharmacy, acting as agents for the undersigned physician, according to and in compliance with the South Carolina Pharmacy Practice Act, may administer the immunizations listed below to adult FM patients on the premises of the FM Pharmacy for a fee
- Influenza vaccine
- Pneumococcal vaccine
- Other vaccines may be added to or deleted from this list by written supplementary instruction from the undersigned.

While immunizing, pharmacists must maintain perpetual records of all immunizations administered. For FM patients, this will be done according to standard fashion in the EMR Practice Partner. Before immunization, vaccine candidates will be questioned regarding previous adverse events after immunization, food or drug allergies, and current health. All vaccine candidates will be informed of the specific benefits and risks of the vaccine offered and will be observed for adverse events for a suitable period after immunization. If an anaphylactic reaction occurs, the emergency policies and procedures of the FMC will be followed.

As authorizing physician, I will review, on a quarterly basis, the activities of the pharmacists administering vaccines under this protocol. Authorization will be valid until one year from the date indicated below, unless revoked in writing or unless extended in writing.

Physician Name:_____

Physician Signature:_____

Medical License Number:_____

Date: _____

Patient Name	Date Given	Site Given	Vaccine Given	Lot #	Expiration Date	Manufacturer	Physician Sent Info? (FM pt—note written) (other—letter written)	RPh

Flu Shot Checkoff Sheet

Before Visit
____Run prescription through pharmacy computer system. If working off protocol, create prescription and run through system.
____Make sure patient understands and is willing to pay $10.00 for flu shot (unless patient is on Medicaid, which will be processed through the computer).

At Visit
____Patients **must** get copy of Vaccine Information Statement and go over it to make sure they do not have questions.
____Ask about egg allergies and previous reaction(s) to flu shot.
____Review probable adverse events after getting shot.
____Give shot.

Documentation—For Family Medicine Patients
____Fill out Pharmacy Immunization Contact Sheet.
____Open immunization section in Practice Partner.
____Edit note.
____Click on Qtext on top toolbar. Type in abbreviation for desired immunization. Example: FLU
____Tab through rest of spaces and fill in information.
____If patient is older than 65 years, go to Health Maintenance; be sure to put an X in the Flu box.

Documentation—For Nonfamily Medicine Patients
____Fill out Pharmacy Immunization Contact Sheet.
____Fill out letter to physician and fax/mail to office.

Supplies Needed for Immunizations
- Alcohol wipes
- Gauze pads 1 × 1 inch
- Band-Aids
- Sharps containers
- Gloves
- Three-milliliter syringes—23 gauge, 1-inch needles

Immunization Letter

Date: _____

Dear Dr._____,

Your patient,_____, received immunization against influenza at the Family Medicine Pharmacy on _____. The vaccine was administered by _____.

Please feel free to call us at if you have any questions.

Sincerely,

Health Professional Immunization Survey

The clinical pharmacists in this clinic are trying to expand their role. In doing so, we ask that you provide us with your opinion of our new role as adult immunizers. Thanks for your time.

1. I am comfortable with clinical pharmacists providing adult immunizations in clinic.
   ❏ Strongly agree ❏ Agree ❏ Undecided ❏ Disagree ❏ Strongly disagree
2. It is appropriate for clinical pharmacists to provide adult immunizations.
   ❏ Strongly agree ❏ Agree ❏ Undecided ❏ Disagree ❏ Strongly disagree
3. Documentation for the immunizations provided by the clinical pharmacist is appropriate.
   ❏ Strongly agree ❏ Agree ❏ Undecided ❏ Disagree ❏ Strongly disagree
4. Clinical pharmacists providing adult immunizations have given me more time to spend in other areas of my practice.
   ❏ Strongly agree ❏ Agree ❏ Undecided ❏ Disagree ❏ Strongly disagree
5. Adult immunizations are a good service for pharmacists to provide.
   ❏ Strongly agree ❏ Agree ❏ Undecided ❏ Disagree ❏ Strongly disagree
6. Trained pharmacists should be providing adult immunizations in local pharmacies.
   ❏ Strongly agree ❏ Agree ❏ Undecided ❏ Disagree ❏ Strongly disagree
7. Please designate the professional category that is most applicable to you:
   ____Licensed Practical Nurse (LPN)
   ____Midlevel Provider (PA or NP)
   ____Patient Care Assistant (PCA)
   ____Physician
   ____Registered Nurse

Immunization Patient Survey

"Hello, my name is _____ and I am calling from the Family Medicine Center. Is _____ available?"
If not, ask when would be a good time to call back._____

"You received a flu shot/pneumonia shot from us within the past couple of months, and we would like to ask you a couple of questions. This should not take more than three minutes of your time."

Please listen to the following statements and state the answer that best represents your answer. Thank you.

1. The person who gave me my flu shot provided me with appropriate information regarding the immunization.
   ❏ Strongly agree   ❏ Agree   ❏ Undecided   ❏ Disagree   ❏ Strongly disagree
2. I felt comfortable with the person who gave me my flu shot.
   ❏ Strongly agree   ❏ Agree   ❏ Undecided   ❏ Disagree   ❏ Strongly disagree
3. I would like that person to provide flu shots at the Family Medicine Center next year.
   ❏ Strongly agree   ❏ Agree   ❏ Undecided   ❏ Disagree   ❏ Strongly disagree
4. What was the professional degree of the person who gave you your flu shot?
   ❏ PA   ❏ Nurse   ❏ Pharmacist   ❏ Medical Assistant   ❏ Nurse's Aid
5. Nurses are qualified to give immunizations.
   ❏ Strongly agree   ❏ Agree   ❏ Undecided   ❏ Disagree   ❏ Strongly disagree
6. Pharmacists are qualified to give immunizations.
   ❏ Strongly agree   ❏ Agree   ❏ Undecided   ❏ Disagree   ❏ Strongly disagree
7. Physician assistants are qualified to give immunizations.
   ❏ Strongly agree   ❏ Agree   ❏ Undecided   ❏ Disagree   ❏ Strongly disagree
8. Medical assistants are qualified to give immunizations.
   ❏ Strongly agree   ❏ Agree   ❏ Undecided   ❏ Disagree   ❏ Strongly disagree
9. Nurses' aids are qualified to give immunizations.
   ❏ Strongly agree   ❏ Agree   ❏ Undecided   ❏ Disagree   ❏ Strongly disagree
10. Pharmacists are now allowed to give immunizations. Would you feel comfortable getting an immunization from a pharmacist at a community pharmacy?
    ❏ Yes
    ❏ No, why?_____

Gender: ❏ Male
          ❏ Female
Age:_____

Race: ❏ Caucasian
          ❏ African American

Time Spent:_____minutes

HEALTH FAIR SCREENING FORM

Submitted by: Pamela Stamm

Created: 2005

Name:_____ *[Health Fair Location Here]*

Health Screening Results   *[Name of Pharmacy/Sponsor/School Here]*

Screening Test	Results	Assessment/Recommendations
Body composition analysis Wt (lb) BMI (kg/m^2) Body fat (%)		☐ Normal (18.5–24.9) BMI ☐ Overweight (25–29.9) ☐ Obese ≥ 30 Recommendations ☐ Reduce weight by 5–10% through calorie reduction and exercise to reduce obesity-related health risks (with physician's approval) ☐ Maintain current weight
Blood pressure		If not on treatment ☐ Normal (≤ 120/80 mm Hg) ☐ Elevated (> 120/80 to 139/89 mm Hg) ☐ Elevated, may need treatment (≥ 140/90 mm Hg) If on treatment ☐ Goal (< 140/90 mm Hg or < 130/80 mm Hg with diabetes) ☐ Elevated Recommendations ☐ Reduce salt intake to < 2,400 mg/day ☐ Reduce weight (as stated above) ☐ Increase exercise with physician's approval toward a minimum goal of 30 minutes most days (i.e., 5) per week ☐ See physician for blood pressure check ☐ Consider daily enteric-coated aspirin, discuss with physician

Osteoporosis screening
Stiffness index (young adult)
 	
T-score (young adult)
 	
Stiffness index (age matched)
 	
Z-score (age matched)
		☐ Normal T-score
		☐ T-score suggests possible reduced bone density
		Recommendations
		☐ Optimize calcium intake through diet or supplementation with calcium to total ☐ 1000-1,200 mg/day or ☐ 1,500 mg/day. Individual doses of calcium should be < 500 mg (50% RDA) and spread throughout the day
		  ☐ Consider calcium carbonate; take with food
		  ☐ Consider calcium citrate; may be taken with or without food
		☐ Optimize vitamin D intake through supplementation to total ☐ 200 IU or ☐ 400–800 IU or ☐ 600–800 IU
		☐ Consider multivitamin for women
		☐ Increase weight-bearing exercise with physician's approval toward a minimum goal of 30–45 minutes for 3–4 days per week
		☐ Share results with physician
		☐ Recommend DEXA scan for further evaluation

Cholesterol TC (mg/dL) HDL (mg/dL) TC/HDL ratio (mg/dL) Non-HDL (mg/dL) Framingham CHD risk (10-year risk of heart attack/death)		☐ HDL cholesterol is ☐ low (< 40) or ☐ acceptable or ☐ > 60 (protective) ☐ Non-HDL (LDL and VLDL) cholesterol is ☐ acceptable or ☐ elevated Recommendations ☐ Increase aerobic exercise with physician's approval toward a minimum goal of 30 minutes most days (e.g., 5) per week ☐ Reduce saturated fats (non-lean red meats, fried foods, high-fat dairy), slowly increase fiber toward 25–30 g per day, reduce cholesterol from diet to < 200 mg/day ☐ Add plant stanols to diet (Benecol products, Take Control spreads) and use per instructions on container ☐ Share results with physician
Blood glucose (mg/dL) Ate ____ hours ago		☐ Normal postprandial (≤ 140 mg/dL) ☐ Possibly elevated postprandial (≥ 140 mg/dL) Recommendations ☐ See dietary and exercise recommendations marked above ☐ Reduce intake of refined sugars (low fiber [< 5 g/serving] cereal, white bread, candy) and starchy foods, russet potatoes, corn, white rice, grits ☐ Share results with physician

Prepared by Harrison School of Pharmacy, Auburn University, Auburn, Alabama

INDIGENT CARE PROGRAM
Submitted by: Dave Hachey
Revised: October 2003

We have streamlined a patient assistance program for about 180 patients, and it has worked well because (1) there is continuity of care without breaks in therapy and (2) it is not time-consuming.
A few points to help things along

1. Drug directory. Make a formulary that makes it easy to obtain drugs. In this case, have one or two ACEIs/PPIs/statins that are easy to obtain from one or two companies. Use the drug directory to help choose programs. (Note: Astra-Zeneca has a new combined program.)
2. Time-saving. When a physician "refers" a patient to us, we have the physician sign the form at that time for that patient's drug. We have the patient sign the form, and for the most part, we fill out most of the form. Patients (for the most part) tend fill out forms erroneously; when that occurs, the forms are then sent back, and we have to start all over again. Use the "intake form" so that there is a face sheet on each patient. Make folders for each patient.
3. When the drug comes in, log it in ("date arrived" file) and dispense it to the patient. When he or she comes to pick it up, we have him/her sign another form and write his/her name in a calendar about one month from the day it is picked up. Then, when that week comes, we fill out the rest of the form and place it in the documents box with the signature field highlighted. After the patient signs it, it is ready to go.
4. Prefilled forms. Have the folders of forms already filled out with an address and telephone number, etc., so that you can just fill out the pertinent information. I have attached our form for Pfizer. Just put it on letterhead. It works. It may be a little frustrating getting things up and running, but it will soon flow.

Drug Class	Drug	Company
ACEIs	Accupril	Pfizer-Parke Davis
	Monopril	Bristol Meyers Squibb (BMS)
	Prinivil/Vasotec	Merck
	Zestril	Astra-Zeneca
	Lotensin	Novartis
Antidepressants	Celexa/Lexapro	Forest
	Effexor XR	Wyeth-Ayerst
	Prozac	Lilly
	Zoloft	Pfizer-PD
Anti-epileptics/mood stabilizers	Dilantin/Neurontin	Pfizer-PD
	Depakote	Abbott
	Tegretol	Novartis
Anti-inflammatories	Vioxx	Merck
Antipsychotics	Zyprexa	Lilly
	Seroquel	Astra-Zeneca
ARBs	Atacand (and HCT)	Astra-Zeneca
	Cozaar/Hyzaar	Merck
	Avapro/Avalide	BMS
	Diovan	Novartis
Asthma/COPD	Proventil	Schering
	Singulair	Merck
	Atrovent/Combivent	Boehringer
	Asthmacort	Aventis
β-Blockers	Toprol XL	Astra-Zeneca
	Inderal LA	Wyeth-Ayerst

Prepared by Idaho State University.

Drug Class	Drug	Company
CCBs	Tiazac	Forest
	Norvasc	Pfizer-PD
	Procardia XL	Pfizer-PD
	Cardizem	Aventis
	Covera-HS	Pharmacia
Diabetes	Actos	Takeda
	Avandia	GlaxoSmithKline
	Glucophage	BMS
	Glucotrol XL	Pfizer-PD
	Insulin	Lilly
Estrogens/Osteoporosis	Premarin	Wyeth-Ayerst
	Fosamax	Merck
PPIs	Prilosec/Nexium	Astra-Zeneca
	Prevacid	TAP
	Protonix	Wyeth-Ayerst
Statins/Fibrates	Lipitor	Pfizer-PD
	Pravachol	BMS
	Zocor/Mevacor	Merck
	Tricor	Abbott
Miscellaneous	Cordorone	Wyeth-Ayerst
	Coumadin	BMS
	Plavix	BMS

	Information Needed			
Company	Income documentation	Written Prescription	Mail or Fax	Reapplication
Abbott	Tax return yearly Medicaid denial letter	No	Fax (847) 937-9826	Call company and they will send 3-month's supply
Astra-Zeneca	No	No	Mail	Call company every 3 months (800) 698-0085
Aventis	Tax return yearly or pay stub and the like	Yes	Mail	New form
Boehringer	Tax return or 4506 form	No	Mail	Company sends reapplication envelope
BMS	No	No	Fax (800) 736-1611	Send 6-month's supply first time; then call every 3 months (800) 736-0003 (option 2-2-4)
Forest	No	Yes	Mail	New form
GlaxoSmithKline	Tax return or recent pay stub (year-to-date earnings)	Yes—Company must be called; after enrolling, give patient coupon and prescription	Mail (once income is received and form is signed)	Call
Lilly (non-Zyprexa)	No	No	Mail	New application every 4 months
Lilly (Zyprexa)				
Merck	No	No	Mail	Patient calls every 3 months after initial application
Novartis	Yes	Yes	Mail	Company sends reapplication envelope
Ortho-McNeil	Yes—once yearly	Yes	Mail	Fill out new application
Pfizer-PD	Yes—Tax return or 4506 form if did not file taxes (once yearly)	Yes	Mail	New application every 3 months
Schering	Yes	No	Mail	Fill out specific reorder forms and fax
Takeda	Yes (*and HIPPA)	Yes	Fax	Company sends reapplication envelope
TAP	No	No	Fax	New application each time and fax it (sends only 60 days)
Wyeth-Ayerst	No (*HIPPA)	No	Mail	New application every 3 months

Last Name	First Name	DOB	SSN	
Address	City Zip	Ph1	Doctor	
Patient: Spouse: Total household monthly income	Patient: Spouse: Income source	Dependents	(Y / N) Insurance	Drug allergies

Drug (dose and frequency)	Company Name	Date Request Sent	Date Arrived	Special Attention
Med: Dose: Sig:				
Med: Dose: Sig:				
Med: Dose: Sig:				
Med: Dose: Sig:				
Med: Dose: Sig:				

Date Arrived	Name and Phl	Called	Drug	Signature	Date Picked up	Forms to fill out?
1)				X		Have pt sign: We call: 3 mo/6 mo
2)				X		Have pt sign: We call: 3 mo/6 mo
3)				X		Have pt sign: We call: 3 mo/6 mo
4)				X		Have pt sign: We call: 3 mo/6 mo
5)				X		Have pt sign: We call: 3 mo/6 mo
6)				X		Have pt sign: We call: 3 mo/6 mo
7)				X		Have pt sign: We call: 3 mo/6 mo
8)				X		Have pt sign: We call: 3 mo/6 mo

Pocatello Family Medicine
465 Memorial Drive
C/O Jim Sharp
Pocatello, ID 83209

Date:_____

Pfizer Patient Assistance Program
P.O. Box 230970
Centreville, VA 20120

To Whom It May Concern:

My patient is in need of a 90-day supply of drug from Pfizer as indicated below. They are financially unable to pay for their drugs at this time (fall well below the poverty level) and have no type of insurance to cover drug. Enclosed is a prescription for a 90-day supply, and it would be greatly appreciated at this time if you could assist my patient by supplying the following drug(s) to our office, which we will dispense to them.

    Patient:_____
    Drug:_____
    Sincerely,

    DEA #:_____

PHARMACEUTICAL REPRESENTATIVE POLICY AND PROCEDURE

Submitted by: Steve Smith

Revised: October 2000

So You Are New to the WW Knight Family Practice Center

The Toledo Hospital Family Practice Residency is made up of seven attending physicians and eighteen Family Practice residents. There are six residents in each of the three years.

Guidelines for Interacting with Our Program

We accept a limited supply of selected drug samples. If you would be so kind as to tell our receptionist which products you have, she can tell you if we need any samples. Please stop by during the hours of 9:00 A.M. to 4:00 P.M. so that we can get an attending physician's signature for you.

If you need to witness the physician's signature, we will not be able to accommodate this need. If you need a signature from a specific physician, we will not be able to meet this need. In this case, please request that your company assign you to all of our faculty physicians so that you can accept the signature from whichever attending physician is available to sign.

We have display times on Monday and Wednesday from 11:50 A.M. to 1:15 P.M. You can meet and discuss your products with both attending and resident physicians at this time. These should be scheduled in advance by calling _____.

We also have "Drug Lunch" day on Thursdays from 12:00 P.M. (*meridies,* or noon) to 12:30 P.M. We ask that you provide a modest lunch for 25 to 30 persons. You will have about 15 minutes to present your product information to the group. These should be scheduled in advance by calling _____. Because we need to make other lunch arrangements if you cannot make a scheduled "Drug Lunch," please call Jennifer *as soon as you know* that you need to cancel.

We hold our staff to high standards for appropriate interaction with vendors of medical products. If you ever have questions about our practices, please contact our _____.

Dear Pharmaceutical Representative:

We greatly appreciate samples of drugs because they assist us in starting new drugs and help patients who cannot afford all of their drugs.
- Because of time and space limitations, we are implementing new processes on how we handle samples
  - We do not accept all samples. Please ask the receptionist because she will know what we need.
  - We are not publishing a formulary of what samples we accept because it will change as needed.
  - If you need to witness the physician signature, we will not be able to meet that need.
  - If you need to have the signature of a specific physician, we will not be able to meet that need.
  - In the past, Steve Smith contacted you when we needed samples. Please stop by the office to see if we need samples rather than wait for a telephone call.

Physicians who will sign for samples are:

_____

_____

Please have your company add all of these to your physician list because we cannot guarantee who will be available to sign for samples at any given time.

Should you have any questions about our process, please contact _____.

INTERACTIONS WITH PHARMACEUTICAL AND PROPRIETARY COMPANIES—POLICY AND PROCEDURE

Submitted by: Lisa Edgerton

Revised: December 2006

Principles of Pharmacotherapeutics

1. The primary purpose of the clinical services at the Coastal Family Medicine Center (CFMC) is to provide high-quality care for patients.
2. An important educational goal for residents and faculty is the acquisition of basic and advanced knowledge of pharmacotherapeutics, as well as the ability to critically evaluate new information about drugs. Residents and faculty should select therapeutic options based on their patients' best interest, including patient need, treatment efficacy, and cost. Residents and faculty should learn to use unbiased, published reviews of therapeutic options as the primary basis for drug choice and be able to evaluate commercially sponsored programs for their scientific accuracy and integrity.
3. It is the responsibility of faculty to ensure an educational curriculum for residents that assists residents in their acquisition of pharmacotherapeutic knowledge.
4. The CFMC and the New Hanover Regional Medical Center Residency in FM strictly adhere to the Accreditation Council for Graduate Medical Education (ACGME), "Principles to Guide the Relationship Between Graduate Medical Education and Industry."

Faculty

1. Faculty should model behavior consistent with the ethical guidelines developed by responsible professional organizations (e.g., AMA, AAFP), which discuss appropriate relationships between clinicians and pharmaceutical and other proprietary companies.
2. To promote high-quality resident education, faculty members are encouraged to avoid any appearance of conflict of interest. Consistent with this objective, faculty should disclose to peers and residents general financial or other relationships between a faculty member and pharmaceutical companies.
3. Faculty may not accept honoraria directly from pharmaceutical or other proprietary companies for speaking at CFMC residency–associated/sponsored educational meetings. Faculty may, however, use their own discretion regarding involvement in non–CFMC-associated educational meetings and programs.
4. Faculty may serve as consultants to pharmaceutical or proprietary companies for clearly defined professional services.
5. Faculty, residents, and the Department should participate in pharmaceutical company–sponsored research only if the research is scientifically valid, would be justifiable even if company funding were not available, results are not subject to censorship, and sponsoring company is publicly identified.
6. Department resources, including staff time, should not be used to support proprietary-sponsored activities that occur independently of the educational structure of the Department.

Educational Conferences and Activities

1. The Department assumes full responsibility for the content and activities of educational conferences.
2. Pharmaceutical and other proprietary companies may support departmental activities through unrestricted educational grants to the Department. The Department will publicly acknowledge all contributions to any educational fund.

Gifts

1. The Department follows in principle the AMA guide on gifts to physicians by industry.
2. Pharmaceutical or proprietary companies may donate educational materials, such as books, to the residency program for distribution to residents.
3. Proprietary companies should not distribute personal gifts or promotional items directly to faculty, residents, or staff.

Prepared by Coastal Family Medicine Center, Wilmington, North Carolina

Pharmacotherapeutic Knowledge and Detailing

1. Interactions with medical service respresentatives (MSRs) may serve a useful function to faculty and residents by increasing their knowledge of drug formulations.
2. All MSRs should check in at the receptionist desk located on the first floor of the CFMC. A faculty physician will be available at both the start of morning clinic between 8:00 and 8:30 A.M. and at the start of afternoon clinic between 1:00 and 1:30 P.M. to speak with the MSRs. The front desk should notify the CFMC faculty member who precepts for that clinic. If no preceptor faculty member is available, the front desk should contact another faculty physician in the building. If no physician faculty is available, check with the CFMC Pharm.D. or Behavioral Medicine Faculty or to make an appointment and return at another time.
3. In accordance with the University of North Carolina Hospital policy, MSRs will not be allowed in any patient care areas or on the second floor of the CFMC, except by prior invitation of a clinician.
4. The CFMC does not control resident activities outside working hours; nonetheless, residents should be aware of the potential marketing intent of outside activities such as proprietary-sponsored social or sporting activities.
5. All MSRs should make official contact within the CFMC through the CFMC Pharm.D. or the Behavioral Medicine faculty if the Pharm.D. is unavailable. An appointment may be scheduled with the CFMC Pharm.D. by contacting the administrative assistant at (910) 343-1122.
6. MSRs are invited to discuss their drugs/products with the faculty, residents, and staff at one of our noon conferences or other educational programs. An MSR should reserve a date in advance by contacting the administrative assistant. MSRs will be permitted to present their drugs/products to the faculty and residents as a group for a 10- to 15-minute period between 12:15 and 12:30 P.M. during CFMC Thursday lunch meetings. MSRs who do not respect our noon conference schedule may be asked to terminate their presentation.

Samples

1. The decision to accept samples is entirely at the discretion of the CFMC faculty. MSRs wishing to leave samples should leave them directly with a CFMC faculty member, including the Pharm.D. or Behavioral Medicine faculty, before the conference/program they are sponsoring or during a scheduled appointment. If a physician's signature is required by the MSR, it may be obtained by any CFMC faculty.
2. **As stated above, no MSR will be permitted in the patient care areas on the first floor of the CFMC.**
3. Because our storage space for drug samples is limited, the Department reserves the right to refuse samples that may not suit our patients' needs or for which we have no available space.
4. When samples are received, they must be logged into the Sample Log-in Book located near the sample closet. The lot number and expiration date of the drug must be recorded on the appropriate page in the Log-in Book.
5. Whenever samples are removed from the sample closet for a patient (or an employee), the patient's name, dispensing date, prescribing physician, drug dispensed, quantity dispensed, lot number, and expiration date must be entered in the sample sign-out logbook located near the sample closet. This bound logbook contains carbonless copy duplications of all samples dispensed from the CFMC (see example attached). The top white copy is intended to be given directly to the patient with instructions on how to take the drug prescribed.
6. In accordance with state and federal laws, all samples distributed from the CFMC must be labeled with the patient's name, date, amount dispensed, prescriber's name, and directions for use. This information must also be documented on the drug list in the computerized patient record.
7. Sample drugs are to be used only for patients of the CFMC.

Coastal Family Medicine
2523 Delaney Avenue, Wilmington, NC 28403 (910) 763-5522

Patient Name/Sticker:_____
Date_____

SAMPLE DRUG DIRECTIONS FOR USE

Drug & Strength	Quantity	Directions

This is Not a Prescription

| Lot #: | Do Not Use After: |

Patient Counseling Provided   ☐ YES ☐ NO

*Signature:*_____
per:_____

POLICY STATEMENT ON MEDICAL SERVICE REPRESENTATIVES

Submitted by: Eric Jackson

Revised: February 2005

Purpose

The purpose of this policy statement is to provide guidelines governing the activities of MSRs and the use of drug samples in the Asylum Hill Family Practice Center. Although recognizing the legitimate service and educational roles of these individuals to our faculty, residents, and staff, the Therapeutics Committee has developed the following guidelines to provide structure and order to the MSR activities in the office.

In the initial Therapeutics Committee meeting with each MSR, the representative will be provided with an explanation of the concept of a "Drug Sample Formulary." In addition, the committee will describe the type of information required for evaluation of new drugs being considered for addition to the sample cabinet.

Guidelines for MSR Activities

1. Appointments for meetings with the Therapeutics Committee are made by the academic secretary of the office at 714-6520. Appointments may be scheduled for Tuesday mornings from 9:15 to 9:30 A.M. and from 9:30 to 9:45 A.M. The following are acceptable reasons for meeting with the committee
   - To discuss or present information on recently released drugs or new uses of older products. Each MSR will provide the committee with monograph packets (including bibliography and reprints of comparative drug trials) for new drugs released as soon as such information is available to health care practitioners.
   - To inform the department of pharmaceutical company–supported CME programs and other educational materials (e.g., live presentations, films and tapes, books)
   - To provide the department with patient education material that is not product oriented
2. At a scheduled meeting, the MSR must check in with the academic secretary, who will notify a committee member that the drug representative has arrived.
3. Each MSR is asked to provide the committee with a business card. These cards will be kept in a file in alphabetic order by company name to facilitate our contacting a drug representative, should the need arise.
4. As described in item 1 above, MSRs may meet with the committee on Tuesday mornings between 9:15 and 9:45 A.M. Representatives are not allowed to be in the office detailing their products at other times.
5. Samples of controlled drugs (Schedules II–V) are strictly prohibited.
6. The name, strength, quantity, expiration date, and lot number of all approved drug samples must be recorded by the MSR on the "Sample Drug Log" form, which is located on the academic secretary's bulletin board.
7. When giving drug samples to patients, the provider must document this activity in the EMR, enter required information on the "Drug Sample Dispensing Record," and write in the date, patient name, physician name, and directions for use on the preprinted labels for affixing to the drug sample package.
8. The department has a policy prohibiting the acceptance of gifts from pharmaceutical representatives unless the item has modest value and supports patient care. Examples of acceptable gifts are pregnancy dating devices, EKG calipers, and unbiased textbooks or pocket guides.
9. The department also has a policy that limits the use of drug samples to patients only. Samples are not for the personal use of faculty, residents, staff, or their family members.
10. Office visitation privileges for MSRs are considered a courtesy. Such privileges may be revoked by the Therapeutics Committee for violations of any of the above guidelines.

Prepared by Asylum Hill Family Practice Center, Hartford, Connecticut

Sample Rx Labels

Asylum Hill Family Practice Center 99 Woodland Street, Hartford, CT Date: _____ (860) 714-4212 Patient:_____ Physician: _____ Directions:_____	Asylum Hill Family Practice Center 99 Woodland Street, Hartford, CT Date: _____ (860) 714-4212 Patient:_____ Physician: _____ Directions:_____
Asylum Hill Family Practice Center 99 Woodland Street, Hartford, CT Date: _____ (860) 714-4212 Patient:_____ Physician: _____ Directions:_____	Asylum Hill Family Practice Center 99 Woodland Street, Hartford, CT Date: _____ (860) 714-4212 Patient:_____ Physician: _____ Directions:_____
Asylum Hill Family Practice Center 99 Woodland Street, Hartford, CT Date: _____ (860) 714-4212 Patient:_____ Physician: _____ Directions:_____	Asylum Hill Family Practice Center 99 Woodland Street, Hartford, CT Date: _____ (860) 714-4212 Patient:_____ Physician: _____ Directions:_____
Asylum Hill Family Practice Center 99 Woodland Street, Hartford, CT Date: _____ (860) 714-4212 Patient:_____ Physician: _____ Directions:_____	Asylum Hill Family Practice Center 99 Woodland Street, Hartford, CT Date: _____ (860) 714-4212 Patient:_____ Physician: _____ Directions:_____
Asylum Hill Family Practice Center 99 Woodland Street, Hartford, CT Date: _____ (860) 714-4212 Patient:_____ Physician: _____ Directions:_____	Asylum Hill Family Practice Center 99 Woodland Street, Hartford, CT Date: _____ (860) 714-4212 Patient:_____ Physician: _____ Directions:_____
Asylum Hill Family Practice Center 99 Woodland Street, Hartford, CT Date: _____ (860) 714-4212 Patient:_____ Physician: _____ Directions:_____	Asylum Hill Family Practice Center 99 Woodland Street, Hartford, CT Date: _____ (860) 714-4212 Patient:_____ Physician: _____ Directions:_____
Asylum Hill Family Practice Center 99 Woodland Street, Hartford, CT Date: _____ (860) 714-4212 Patient:_____ Physician: _____ Directions:_____	Asylum Hill Family Practice Center 99 Woodland Street, Hartford, CT Date: _____ (860) 714-4212 Patient:_____ Physician: _____ Directions:_____
Asylum Hill Family Practice Center 99 Woodland Street, Hartford, CT Date: _____ (860) 714-4212 Patient:_____ Physician: _____ Directions:_____	Asylum Hill Family Practice Center 99 Woodland Street, Hartford, CT Date: _____ (860) 714-4212 Patient:_____ Physician: _____ Directions:_____

Prepared by Asylum Hill Family Practice Center, Hartford, Connecticut

Sample Drug Dispensing Record

ALWAYS CHECK THE EXPIRATION DATE!!!!!

Date	Patient Name	Medical Record #	Physician or Nurse Practitioner	Drug	Strength	Quantity	Lot #/ Expiration Date	Recorder Signature

Sample Drug Log-in

Date	Company	Drug Generic/Brand	Strength	Size	Lot #	Expir Date	Qty	Medical Service Representative	Clinic Rep	Prescription Drug Y/N

*Samples that do not require a prescription for dispensing (OTCs) need not be labeled for dispensing. Instructions are printed on the manufacturer's package.

Prepared by Asylum Hill Family Practice Center, Hartford, Connecticut

EDUCATION

THERAPEUTICS FOR FAMILY PRACTICE RESIDENTS

Submitted by: Eric Jackson

Revised: June 2006

Pharmacotherapeutics Core Curriculum (two-year cycle)

1. Antihypertensive Agents
2. Type 2 DM
3. HF
4. Asthma
5. Principles of Pain Management
6. NSAIDs and COX2 Inhibitors
7. Anti-anginal Agents
8. Coughs and Colds (antihistamines, decongestants, expectorants, and cough suppressants)
9. Lipid-Lowering Agents
10. Anti-anxiety Agents, Hypnotics
11. Antipsychotic Agents, Antidepressants, and Lithium
12. Anticonvulsants
13. Drugs Used for Upper GI Disorders (peptic ulcer disease and GERD)
14. Antidiarrheal Agents, Laxatives, and Cathartics
15. Clinical Pharmacokinetics and Therapeutic Drug Monitoring
16. Treatment of Vaginitis
17. Antibiotics for Common Ambulatory Infections
18. Treatment of Hyperuricemia and Gout
19. Treatment of Migraine Headache
20. Contraception
21. HIV/AIDS Update

Geriatrics Core Curriculum

1. Geriatric Pharmacology and Pharmacokinetics
2. Herbal Products/Dietary Supplement Use

Evidence-Based Medicine/Critical Appraisal of Literature

1. Information Mastery: Eight-part series taught as part of the longitudinal Psychosocial Medicine Rotation for second-year residents
2. Departmental Journal Club
3. Information Resources for Herbal Products and Dietary Supplements

Therapeutics Committee

1. Drug Sample Cabinet Formulary
2. Policies Regulating Medical Service Representative Activity at Asylum Hill Family Practice Center

PHARMACOTHERAPY ROTATION FOR FAMILY PRACTICE RESIDENTS

Submitted by: Ila Mehra Harris

Revised: 2006

Goals and Objectives

This is an elective rotation for FM physician residents. The goal of the pharmacotherapy rotation is to teach residents the principles of rational drug therapy evaluation, prescribing, and monitoring. This rotation may last 2 to 4 weeks.

At the completion of this rotation, the resident will be able to

1. Conduct a complete drug history and evaluation
2. Effectively review patient charts to evaluate drug therapy
3. Evaluate a patient's drug therapy with respect to indications, efficacy, toxicity, and convenience/compliance and cost
4. Select and use cost-effective drug therapy
5. Monitor a patient's drug therapy appropriately for efficacy and toxicity
6. Select and use appropriate drug information resources, including electronic and online references
7. Understand the principles of conducting a Medline search
8. Identify, prevent, and educate patients about common adverse effects of drugs
9. Understand the principles of basic biostatistics and literature evaluation
10. Critically review drug therapy literature
11. Select the most appropriate patient-specific drug therapy for common disorders in primary care
12. Effectively educate a patient about his/her drugs
13. Educate a patient on smoking cessation
14. Correctly evaluate and adjust a patient's warfarin therapy based on his/her INR
15. Understand and use patient assistance programs for patients who cannot afford their drugs

Activities

1. Chart review and discussion with focus on drug therapy
2. Interview patients for drug evaluation
3. Educate patients on drug therapy for common disorders such as asthma, DM, contraception, and smoking cessation
4. Selecting cost-effective drug therapy
5. Evaluate and adjust patient's warfarin
6. See patients for smoking cessation, select appropriate therapy, and discuss behavioral modification
7. See patients for asthma and DM education and follow-up drug adjustments
8. See patients for drug therapy management
9. Review and discuss a journal article
10. Search for information using a variety of drug information sources
11. Topic discussions on drug therapy for common conditions seen in primary care. Specific topics selected by residents. Potential topics include
    - HTN
    - Dyslipidemia
    - CHF
    - DM
    - Peptic ulcer disease/GERD
    - Asthma
    - COPD
    - Anticoagulation
    - Depression
    - Contraception
    - STIs
    - Drugs in pregnancy and lactation
    - Osteoporosis
    - Osteoarthritis
    - Gout
    - Anticoagulation
    - Smoking cessation

DRUG FOCUSED HOME VISIT—GOALS AND OBJECTIVES

Submitted by: Lisa Edgerton

Revised: December 2006

Goals

To provide the FM resident the tools and skills necessary to appreciate patient challenges in adhering to drugs as prescribed and to recognize potential drug-related events in a home environment

Objectives

To effectively evaluate patient drug regimens by identifying potential and actual drug-related problems, resolving actual drug-related problems, and preventing potential drug-related problems

Expectations and Strategies

1. Each first-year resident will identify one patient appropriate for a home drug visit. Appropriate home visits include patients on multiple drugs; patients whose adherence or compliance is uncertain, possibly because of physical disability or lack of understanding; patients whose caregivers request a better understanding of the home environment; and patients who are homebound.
2. Obtain permission from patient to complete home drug visit, provide directions to home, and set up an appropriate time window for visit
3. Advise patient and/or patient's family that a team of two interns and one Pharm.D. will be present during the home visit
4. Obtain pertinent vital signs during the home visit when indicated
5. Ask to see all drugs in the home
6. Ask the patient and caregiver specific questions about each drug, including dosage, frequency, and indication
7. Identify any drug-related problems, including untreated conditions, improper drug selection, failure to receive drug, overdose, ADRs, drug interactions, and drug use without indication
8. Document the home visit encounter in the electronic medical record indicating changes in therapy, refills approved, and follow-up appointment where indicated

Outcome

The completion of a drug home visit is to ensure the FM resident understands the daily challenges that a patient undergoes to adhere to a drug regimen.

Reference

1. American Society of Hospital Pharmacists. ASHP statement on pharmaceutical care. Am J Hosp Pharm 1993;50:1720–3.

JOURNAL CLUB PRESENTATION—GOALS AND OBJECTIVES

Submitted by: Lisa Edgerton

Revised: December 2006

Goals

To provide the FM resident the skills and tools to effectively evaluate and analyze clinical trials and apply study results to outcomes that matter to patients

Objectives

To effectively evaluate the methodologic design, validity, results, and outcomes of landmark journal article

Expectations and Strategies

1. Each second- and third-year family practice resident will select a landmark journal article and present one article yearly in Jeopardy format during the Coastal Family Medicine (CFM) Conference Series.
2. For each article, 17 questions and answers written in Jeopardy format must be submitted to Lisa Edgerton, Pharm.D., one week before presentation. The submitted questions will then be reviewed and inserted in a PowerPoint Jeopardy template.
3. Moderate question and answer session, clarifying any points of discrepancy
4. Discuss the limitations of the trial design
5. Summarize information learned from article analysis

Outcome

The presentation and coordination of a journal club to CFM residents, students, and faculty in Jeopardy format to ensure the understanding and applicability of evidence-based literature to patient care and to observe how this literature compares with current or standard practice

FAMILY PRACTICE RESIDENCY PROGRAM JOURNAL CLUB

Submitted by: Eric Jackson

Revised: February 2007

Presentation Format

1. Begin by giving the reason you selected your topic, preferably in the form of a focused clinical question. At a minimum, briefly describe your patient or the issue addressed by the paper. In doing this you should cover **relevance** (common problem, patient-oriented outcome).
2. Background: **very briefly** describe current state of knowledge about the question or issue.
3. Methods, study design, and validity: (details depend on type of study—therapeutic intervention, diagnosis, or prognosis). **See appropriate Information Mastery Worksheet**
   - Setting (hospital, ambulatory, emergency department, primary care vs. specialty clinic)
   - Patient population—are they similar enough to our patients or practice to allow us to generalize the results?
   - Briefly describe or list inclusion and exclusion criteria
   - Intervention and control (therapeutics article); description of tests and diagnostic standards (diagnosis)
   - Primary or main outcome measures
   - Statistics—were appropriate tests used (nominal, ordinal, interval data)?
     - Nominal or categorical data—descriptive statistics
     - Ordinal—Chi square (exact tests)
     - Interval/Ratio (continuous)—t-test (two means), ANOVA (three or more means)
4. Primary or main results
5. Authors' conclusion(s): Are they justified by the results?
6. Discussion
7. Your conclusion/bottom line/recommendation to audience
   - Are the results clinically as well as statistically significant?
   - Will the results of this study affect or change your practice?

Miscellaneous Items/ Issues to Address

1. Is there an attempt to imply causation when the results suggest only an association?
2. Does either the author or funding source present an opportunity for bias?
3. Helpful to provide a handout or use visual aids—key tables or figures from the article

Prepared by Family Medicine Center at Asylum Hill, Hartford, Connecticut

JOURNAL CLUB PREPARATION EVALUATION

Resident:_____

Faculty: _____

Date:_____

Formulation of a Focused Clinical Question

Asks an answerable clinical question with these four elements:
- Patient or problem
- Intervention
- Comparison intervention (if necessary)
- Outcome(s)—preferably patient (rather than disease) oriented
    - ❏ Exceptional
    - ❏ Very Good
    - ❏ Acceptable
    - ❏ Marginal

Effectiveness of Literature Search

Searching for the best evidence using bibliographic databases, POEM (Patient-Oriented Evidence that Matters) bulletin boards and related surveys of the literature, references of recent systematic reviews, etc.

- ❏ Exceptional
- ❏ Very Good
- ❏ Acceptable
- ❏ Marginal

Critical Appraisal of the Evidence

Assessing relevance (common problem and important outcome) and validity (methods/statistics) of the article

- ❏ Exceptional
- ❏ Very Good
- ❏ Acceptable
- ❏ Marginal

Applying Evidence to Patient Care

Assessing the clinical relevance and significance of the article

- ❏ Exceptional
- ❏ Very Good
- ❏ Acceptable
- ❏ Marginal

Comments and/or Suggestions

_____
_____
_____
_____
_____
_____
_____
_____
_____
_____
_____
_____

Prepared by Family Medicine Center at Asylum Hill, Hartford, Connecticut

JOURNAL CLUB SESSION EVALUATION

Session: Journal Club

Presenter: _____

Date: _____

Content Informative

❏ Exceptional
❏ Very Good
❏ Acceptable
❏ Marginal

Presentation Effective in Achieving the Session's Goals

❏ Exceptional
❏ Very Good
❏ Acceptable
❏ Marginal

Presentation Enjoyable

❏ Exceptional
❏ Very Good
❏ Acceptable
❏ Marginal

Overall Quality of the Session

❏ Exceptional
❏ Very Good
❏ Acceptable
❏ Marginal

Comments and/or Suggestions

_____
_____
_____
_____
_____
_____
_____
_____
_____
_____
_____

Prepared by Family Medicine Center at Asylum Hill, Hartford, Connecticut

THERE'S NO SUCH THING AS A FREE LUNCH

Submitted by: Eric Jackson

Revised: January 2005

Objectives

At the completion of this presentation, the attendee will be able to
1. Describe criteria established by the AMA and American College of Physicians that define or describe an appropriate relationship between physicians and the pharmaceutical industry
2. Describe components of the ACCP Position Statement on Pharmacists and the Pharmaceutical Industry: Guidelines for Ethical Interactions
3. Appreciate and describe the difference between drug information and pharmaceutical marketing
4. Describe the effects on physician prescribing of gift giving and marketing by drug companies

When to Accept and When Not to Accept Gifts

A Quick Ethics Quiz

1. Is it appropriate for the chair of the Connecticut House of Representative's Environmental Protection Committee to be lavishly entertained by one of the "Dirty 6" power generating plants?

2. Is it appropriate for a pharmaceutical company to provide an evening dinner meeting at a four-star restaurant for all members (residents and faculty) of a family practice residency program?

3. Is it appropriate for a pharmaceutical company to provide a pizza lunch for a noon core conference?

4. A maker of medical diagnostic equipment is offering to compensate you for your time and travel expenses to attend a seminar focusing on the company's newest technology. Should you accept the compensation and take part?

5. You are attending a national medical association meeting. A pharmaceutical company is sponsoring an evening educational program in the hotel where the meeting is taking place. You and your spouse (not a physician) are invited. Should the two of you attend the program?

6. A manufacturer of medical supplies has allowed you to accumulate "points" by attending several educational/promotional meetings, and now the company says you may use those points to choose a gift from a catalog of education options. Should you take the gift?

Brief List of References

1. Wazana A. Physicians and the pharmaceutical industry: Is a gift ever just a gift? JAMA 2000;283:373–80.
2. No Free Lunch Web site: http://www.nofreelunch.org/. Accessed June 2008.
3. Coyle SL. Physician-industry relations. Part 1. Individual physicians. Ann Intern Med 2002;136:396–402.
4. Coyle SL. Physician-industry relations. Part 2. Organizational issues. Ann Intern Med 2002;136:403–6.
5. ACCP Position Statement. Pharmacists and the pharmaceutical industry: guidelines for ethical interactions. http://www.accp.com/position/Guidelines_for_Ethical_Interactions.pdf (Accessed July 2008)
6. Haines ST, Dumo P. Relationship between the pharmaceutical industry and pharmacy practitioners: undue influence? Am J Health Syst Pharm 2002;59:1871–4.
7. American Society of Hospital Pharmacists. ASHP guidelines on pharmacists' relationships with industry. Am J Hosp Pharm 1992;49:154. (This guideline was reviewed in 2001 by the Council on Legal and Public Affairs and by the ASHP Board of Directors and was still found to be appropriate.)

ADVANCED PRACTICE EXPERIENCE IN PRIMARY CARE/FAMILY PRACTICE

Submitted by: Pamela Stamm

Revised: June 2003

Course Description

Advanced practice experience in providing pharmaceutical care to patients as they initially access the health care system

Background

Relation to Pharmaceutical Care
This rotation provides the Pharm.D. student experience in establishing caring relationships with patients in an ambulatory clinic setting. As the student identifies actual and potential patient-specific drug-related problems, he/she will collaborate with PCPs and other members of the health care team to resolve and/or prevent them.

Practice Description

This practice experience will occur at the Columbus Regional Family Practice Residency Program where the instructor's practice is based. In this setting, the student will have the opportunity to interface with medical residents who are learning to become Family Physicians. The student will have the opportunity to learn from health care providers and to teach health care providers about rational pharmacotherapy. These opportunities will occur during conferences, patient discussions during and outside of patient visits, and through providing direct care to patients.

Outcomes and Goals

A checked box indicates focused evaluations will occur during the rotation.

- **Communication Abilities**—The student shall read, write, speak, listen, and use media to communicate.

  1. Effectively communicate, verbally and in writing (e.g., consultations, progress notes, drug information responses) with other health care professionals (e.g., pharmacists, physicians, nurses) about therapeutic plans, other patient care needs, and health care issues
  2. Articulate and support drug therapy recommendations
  3. Write patient care notes/documents that
     - Are accurate and logical, yet contain only pertinent information
     - Provide complete drug therapy directions (dosage, route, frequency, duration, monitoring parameters, and time of follow-up)
     - Use correct terminology, spelling, and grammar
  4. Effectively communicate patient and/or drug self-management information to patients and health professionals
  5. Deliver appropriate and effective patient counseling skills
  6. Formulate and deliver programs for health care consumers that center on disease prevention and wellness promotion (i.e., smoking cessation, exercise, nutrition, immunizations, and weight reduction)
  7. Prepare and present an educational program to a group of health care professionals or patients in an effective manner

- **Thinking Abilities**—The student shall acquire, comprehend, apply, synthesize, and evaluate information. The student shall integrate these abilities to identify, resolve, and prevent problems and make appropriate decisions.

  1. Provide concise, applicable, and timely responses to requests for drug information from health care professionals and patients. Specifically, the student shall
     - Perceive, assess, and evaluate drug information needs
     - Apply a systematic approach to solve drug information questions
     - Demonstrate efficient literature search strategies
     - Select and use the most appropriate references and cite only pertinent references
     - Interpret and synthesize information from multiple sources into a concise written or verbal presentation
  2. Compare and contrast new information that is encountered during daily rotation activities with prior knowledge to assess its value and refine one's personal understanding
  3. Critically analyze and evaluate biomedical literature and use evidence to optimize patient care

Prepared by Harrison School of Pharmacy, Auburn University, Auburn, Alabama

- **Professional Ethics and Identity**—The student shall behave ethically. The student shall accept the responsibilities embodied in the principles of pharmaceutical care.

  1. Make appropriate ethical and legal decisions
  2. Accept responsibility and provide patient-centered care
  3. Maintain excellence in personal practice
  4. Exhibit a professional demeanor
  5. Conduct direct patient care activities using a consistent approach that reflects the philosophy of primary care as well as pharmacy practice

- **Social Interaction, Citizenship, and Leadership**—The student shall demonstrate appropriate interpersonal and intergroup behaviors.

  1. Display appropriate interpersonal behaviors
  2. Display appropriate team behaviors

- **Self-Learning Abilities**—The student shall continuously assess his/her learning needs and develop the ability to respond appropriately.

  1. Display independent personal learning aptitude
  2. Self-assess pharmacotherapy/practice responsibilities and develop improved approaches to pharmacotherapy and other aspects of practice
  3. Recognize self-limitations (e.g., prejudices, assumptions, bias)
  4. Assess one's own abilities independently
  5. Consider strengths and weaknesses when developing a personal learning plan
  6. Implement and successfully complete personal learning plans
  7. Respond appropriately to constructive feedback
  8. Identify areas for new practice opportunities and/or new professional roles and use self-directed learning skills to initiate or implement them

- **Patient Assessment**—The student shall contribute to the database of information about the patient by (a) performing a drug history, review of systems, and physical assessment; (b) requesting laboratory tests; and (c) assessing medical, sociobehavioral, and economic status.

  1. Perform an accurate and effective drug history/patient interview
  2. Perform an accurate and effective sociobehavioral assessment
  3. Perform relevant and accurate physical assessment procedures
  4. Develop functional patient databases by gathering and generating relevant information

- **Drug Therapy Assessment**—The student shall assess the appropriateness of patient's drug therapy, including consideration of the chemical, pharmaceutical, pharmacokinetic, and pharmacological characteristics of the administered drugs.

  1. Assess each acute and chronic medical problem
  2. Identify the following drug-related problems
     - Drug therapy is needed for untreated indications
     - Patient is receiving a drug that has no indication, and/or there is therapeutic duplication
     - There is a better choice of drug based on factors such as patient/disease characteristics, formulary, and cost
     - Drug therapy needs optimization (population- and patient-specific pharmacokinetic and pharmacodynamic data indicate a drug regimen is not optimized)
     - Drug nonadherence
     - Drug-induced disease/medical conditions
     - Sociobehavioral and economic barriers to effective drug therapy
     - ADRs that are substantiated by laboratory, tests, and physical findings
     - Routes of administration that are the best, safest, and most cost-effective
     - Drug interactions that are substantiated with pharmacokinetic/dynamic and compatibility information
  3. Identify and evaluate each drug-related problem
  4. Prioritize drug-related problem list

- **Develop, Implement, and Monitor Drug Therapy Plans**—The student shall develop a therapeutic plan for the patient, which includes appropriate monitoring to address any problem identified.

  1. Establish desired therapeutic outcomes
  2. Consider drug and nondrug therapy alternatives
  3. Develop drug therapy plans that are patient-specific, comprehensive, logical, practical, consider current evidence-based medicine recommendations, include strategies for prevention, and include patient education
  4. Establish a plan for therapeutic drug monitoring that includes accurate documentation of population and patient-specific guidelines, dosage history/administration times, monitoring guidelines, and daily SOAP notes/plans
  5. Develop and implement the pharmacotherapeutic plan promptly, efficiently, accurately, and effectively
  6. Use an effective patient monitoring system (use monitoring forms)
  7. Monitor the patient and follow up at appropriate intervals

8. Revise drug therapy plans on a continuing basis
9. Ensure continuity of pharmaceutical care to and from the acute and ambulatory care settings

- **Pharmacotherapy Decision-Making**—The student shall demonstrate the ability to make pharmacotherapy decisions. (Pharmacotherapy decisions determine what, why, where, and how drug therapy is provided. The making of pharmacotherapy decisions is the foremost expression of the professional knowledge, responsibility, and authority of pharmacists.) The intent of a decision is to maximize the patient's response to drug therapy and prevent or resolve a drug-related problem(s) to ensure positive outcomes.

    1. Pursue the role of drug therapy practitioner over that of drug therapy advisor
    2. Participate in pharmacotherapy decision-making by:
        - Identifying opportunities for decision-making
        - Proactively engaging decision-making opportunities
        - Formulating decision rationale that is the result of rigorous inquiry, scientific reasoning, and evidence
        - Pursuing the highest levels of decision-making
        - Seeking *independence* in *making* decisions and *accepting* personal responsibility for the outcomes to patients resulting from one's decisions
        - Personally enacting decisions

Rotation Activities

Orientation to Family Practice Program

During the first day of the rotation, the student will be oriented to the family practice program and clinic. Pertinent policies and procedures will be reviewed. The student should

1. Tour the site and meet the staff. The instructor will explain the staff member's duties to the student and the student's responsibilities to the staff as a pharmacy student
    - Give phone number list
    - Give code list
    - Doors between Family Practice Clinic (FPC) and faculty offices lock at about 5:00 P.M. If the preceptor is out of office for the afternoon, be sure to take your bags and books to clinic with you. If you forget, call 1430 to reach a person who will let you into the faculty area.
2. The student and instructor should discuss rotation-specific policies and procedures. Specific discussion points include
    - Confidentiality
    - Appropriate dress
    - Lines of authority
    - Available drug information resources
    - Concept of "work time"– free time to work on projects or patients. You may work in the mailroom or library. Check with the preceptor before leaving the building.
3. Learn about the instructor's practice philosophy regarding professional responsibilities and pharmaceutical care
4. Learn how to access computer and library resources that have password security/limited access to the public
5. Review specific devices, physical assessment procedures, and patient education commonly performed in the FPC
    - Glucometer
    - Camit Pro
    - Inhaler technique
    - Asthma Outcomes Study
    - BP technique and other vital signs
    - Targeted physical examination

Daily Responsibilities

1. Establish rapport with a medical resident and work together during the resident's clinic. Specifically, collaborate with the resident during each patient's clinic visit by assisting with drug histories, answering drug information questions, identifying and solving drug-related problems, and/or providing patient education. The student's specific contributions will be dependent on the resident and clinic. The student is expected to be assertive and self-directed in establishing a working relationship with the resident and identifying the most effective ways to contribute to patient care.
2. Independently develop a patient database, assess drug therapy, and develop a pharmacotherapy plan for assigned patients that are encountered in clinic. The instructor will observe patient assessment and drug history skills using the "Snapshot" forms provided by the Department of Experiential Education as well as the instructor's own forms. The student is expected to prepare a SOAP note summarizing all findings when:
    - An intervention is made and the student is the primary caregiver
    - A drug history is taken
    - The preceptor and student are providing direct patient care
    - The student contacts a patient at home (e.g., Coumadin follow-up)
    - The student is conducting Indigent Trust Fund screenings
3. Provide answers to drug information questions that

arise during clinic. <u>Drug information responses</u> that cannot be located in a reputable source must be reviewed with the instructor before communication with other health care practitioners. Formal drug information responses should be placed in your learning portfolio; otherwise, include them on your intervention sheet.

4. Give one informal <u>Journal Article</u> Presentation to your instructor. Prepare a printed handout as described in the rotation manual for each journal club. A copy of the presentation and instructor evaluation form should be placed in your learning portfolio. The instructor may assign additional literature analysis learning experiences as part of a weekly journal club.

5. Give a formal Pharmacy <u>Grand Rounds</u> Patient Presentation to clinical pharmacists and staff in the Department of Pharmacy. The student is responsible for selecting the date for the presentation, getting approval of that date from the preceptor, and signing up for the presentation on the Pharmacy Conference Room door during the <u>first week</u> of the rotation. A copy of the presentation and faculty evaluation forms should be placed in your learning portfolio. The instructor will hold informal meetings to discuss patients one to three times each week. The student will be responsible for keeping a notebook of patient data obtained for two purposes: (1) to serve as a reference during patient discussions, and (2) to serve as a reminder, after identifying patients, to follow up with the patient at his/her next appointment.

6. Document all patient care activities in your portfolio using the Columbus Regional Department of Pharmacy Intervention Form (copy in rotation binder) and as stated in the Advanced Practice Experience Manual. The instructor will assess entries such as SOAP notes and interventions several times weekly and formally evaluate all entries at the end of the rotation. Make a tick mark by the diseases encountered in the FPC on the Problem List. Make copies of the form provided in your rotation manual.

7. The instructor may require the completion of an independent self-directed project. Examples include writing a "New Drug Update" to be distributed to the Family Practice Residents as a learning tool to keep them abreast of new drugs. An example is provided in your rotation manual. The sheet is limited to one page front and back. The <u>rough draft due date</u> is the last day of the first month for students on Primary Care I and II at this site.

8. Perform self-assessments by
   - Completing self-evaluation before midpoint and final evaluations with instructor
   - Corroborating midpoint and final rotation self-assessment ratings with those of the instructor
   - Performing a self-assessment of each document placed in the learning portfolio
   - Writing a reflective self-evaluation at the end of the rotation

9. Demonstrate use of a core library of journals, reference books, and databases that comprise your personal library

10. <u>Weekly patient presentation:</u> Give a weekly patient presentation that includes data gathering, a complete patient assessment of therapy, and a management plan. When one student is on rotation, each student will select and present a different patient each week. When two or more students are on rotation, the students will rotate the selection of the patient so that only one patient is discussed formally each week. Each student will be responsible for formally writing this patient up in a SOAP note referencing recommendations back to guidelines and/or the primary literature. Students may not collaborate on this assignment. The goal is to compare each student's assessment and plan and discuss the patient's medical and sociobehavioral problems. An example is provided in the rotation manual. Keep in mind for this assignment that all disease states and all drug therapies are fair game for discussion. It is suggested that you select simple patients with one or two medical problems at the beginning of the rotation and move to more complex patients at the end of rotation. You can expect to be asked any of the following for each drug the patient is taking
    - Mechanism of action
    - Clinically relevant differences among drugs within a class
    - Therapeutic use and indications
    - Contraindications
    - Available dosage forms (e.g., patch, injection, implant, oral tablet)
    - Relative costs among agents
    - Appropriate dosing for adults (including the most appropriate route of administration and effect of organ dysfunction)
    - Clinically relevant adverse reactions
    - Significant pharmacokinetic and pharmacodynamic parameters
    - Clinically significant drug interactions (e.g., drug–drug, drug–food, drug–disease)
    - Appropriate monitoring guidelines to assess efficacy and toxicity

11. For each patient evaluation, students will identify <u>all</u> of the applicable "Drug-Related Problems" listed below and formulate a plan that addresses the problem with appropriate recommendations that are evidence-based and use appropriate materials and resources

Untreated Indications—Patient has a medical problem that requires drug therapy, but is not receiving a drug for that indication.

Improper Drug Selection—There is an indication for a drug, but patient is receiving the wrong drug.

Subtherapeutic Drug Selection—Patient has a medical problem that is being treated with an insufficient dose of the correct drug.

Failure to Receive Drugs—Patient has a medical problem because they are not receiving a drug for pharmaceutical, psychological, sociological, or economical reasons.

Overdose—Patient has a medical problem that is being treated with too much of the correct drug (toxicity).

ADR—Patient has a medical problem caused by an adverse effect of a drug.

Drug Interactions—Patient has an actual or potential medical problem because of a drug–drug, drug–disease, or drug–food interaction.

Drug Use without Indication—Patient is taking a drug for no medically apparent indication.

Cost/Compliance—Patient is receiving a drug that has an alternative agent that would be more cost-effective and/or potentially would improve compliance.

12. In addition, you will be asked questions that you did not expect; however, keep in mind that this session is to drive you to reach deeper, so the instructor will try to push your knowledge base.

13. You can expect to take home three or four learning issues for each case. These should be answered and returned to the preceptor before the next scheduled Bar and Grill.

Typical Rotation Schedule

(*Each rotation schedule will vary somewhat and will be provided on the first day of the rotation and updated periodically throughout the rotation*)

Times	Monday	Tuesday	Wednesday	Thursday	Friday	Weekends
8–9 A.M.	Appt. reminders and no-shows/ work time	Grand Rounds	Pharmacotherapy clinic/ Coumadin follow-ups/see patients with a specific resident	Work Time	Work time/Journal Club/weekly patient presentation/topic discussions	Read on diseases commonly seen in FP; work on assigned tasks
9–10 A.M.		Pharmacotherapy clinic				
10–11 A.M.						
11–12 noon				11:30–12:30: Pharmacy Grand Rounds (first and third Thursday)		
12–1 P.M.	Attend Family Practice Conferences as designated on official schedule and Pharmacy Grand Rounds on the first and third Thursday.					
1–2 P.M.	Pharmacotherapy Clinic/Coumadin follow-up/see patients with a specific resident	Coumadin telephone follow-ups/ work time when finished	Pharmacotherapy Clinic/ Coumadin follow-up/see patients with a specific resident	Pharmacotherapy Clinic/participate in Rheumatology Clinic/see patients with a specific resident	Appt reminders and reschedule no-shows/ work time	
2–3 P.M.						
3–4 P.M.					Weekly wrap-up with preceptor	
4–5:30 P.M.						
Evenings: Expect to leave the FPC around 5:30 P.M. EST. At home, you should read about diseases and therapy seen in clinic each day and work on assigned tasks.						
Clinic Days: Your responsibilities in clinic will vary from day to day depending on the number of students and residents on rotation. You can expect to see two to four patients per full Pharmacotherapy clinic day by the end of four weeks. One-half day each week you will spend seeing patients with a resident. The SOAP notes for morning patients are due before leaving the FPC each evening to facilitate timely posting in charts. SOAP notes for afternoon patients are due the next morning at 8:30 A.M.						

Textbooks

- The student is expected to build a personal library that has text resources. The following list outlines topics of resources to be included in the personal library; the student is expected to select a specific text or reference that covers the stated topic
  - Pharmacotherapy Book/Reference
  - General Drug Information Reference (required for clinic time)
  - General Medicine Book/Reference
  - Physical Assessment Book/Reference
  - Laboratory Interpretation Book/Reference
  - Pharmacokinetics Book/Reference
  - Adverse Drug Reaction Book/Reference
- The student is expected to be self-directed in obtaining drug literature pertinent to patient care issues. The student is expected to have Internet access to use the university and Ovid resources and conduct Web searches. Some Medline databases are available free of charge from the National Library of Medicine.
- The instructor may assign additional readings based on specific patient care issues or conferences.
- Students are expected to check their e-mail and have Internet access on a daily basis. E-mail should be reserved for when clinic duties and SOAP notes are complete, before hours, after hours, or during lunch.
- Students must possess a beeper so that other health care professionals and the instructor can reach them within the FPC.

Grading and Assessment Procedures

Course Requirements and Grading Criteria:

Performance Based on Instructor's
Daily Observations.................................60%
- The midpoint evaluation will be weighted 10%, and the final evaluation will be weighted 50% of this section grade. If, for some reason, a formal midpoint evaluation is not conducted, then the final examination will be worth 60%.

Written Assignments..............................20%
Progress/SOAP notes (5%)
- New Drug Update/Project (5%)

Verbal Communication Skills....................20%
Journal Club (5%)
- Grand Rounds (10%)
- Daily Patient Presentations (5%)
- Weekly Patient Presentations (5%)

Participation in all rotation activities...........S/U
- The student is required to spend a minimum of 40 hours per week at the rotation site. The student is expected to be prompt in attending all rotation activities.

- **Absence:** (unexcused or without prior authorization) from any rotation activities and late assignments will be deemed unsatisfactory, and a failing grade may be submitted irrespective of other grades.
- **Tardiness:** A student will receive a verbal warning for tardiness to the rotation, including early morning grand rounds. For each occurrence afterward, the student can be expected to have 5% deducted from his/her final grade.

Assessment System

This rotation is part of an abilities-based outcomes curriculum. The ***Auburn University School of Pharmacy, Advanced Practice Experience Manual*** provides specific details and policies about how students are assessed during rotations.

Policies

Specific policies pertaining to all Advanced Practice Experience rotations are found in the ***Auburn University School of Pharmacy, Advanced Practice Experience Manual.***

Attendance

Students are required to be at the rotation site a minimum of 40 hours per week. As a professional, the student is expected to stay beyond the usual work hours when patient care still needs to be completed.

Special Needs

It is the policy of the Auburn University to provide accessibility to its programs and activities and reasonable accommodation for persons defined as having disabilities under Section 504 of the Rehabilitation Act of 1973, as amended, and the American with Disabilities Act of 1990.

Students should contact the Program for Students with Disabilities, 1244 Haley Center, 334-844-2096 (Voice/TT), and must receive this approval before individual instructors grant any special circumstances.

Students with defined special needs should see the Director of Experiential Education at the beginning of the P4 Year so that accommodations can be scheduled. Students should also see the site instructor to make specific accommodations.

I am open to suggestions/critique at any time. Please feel free to discuss your specific wants or needs with me regarding this experience. Your grade will not suffer. I want the rotation to be both interesting and valuable to you. Do not hesitate to contact me regarding any matter.

Welcome to Family Practice!

FAMILY MEDICINE INPATIENT ROTATION

Submitted by: Kelly Ragucci and Andrea Wessell

Revised: December 2006

Preceptors:_____
Office:_____
Pager:_____
E-Mail:_____

Rotation Goals and Objectives

1. Increase knowledge of commonly encountered disease states requiring admittance to an FM inpatient service
   - Present and discuss selected therapeutic topics to faculty on a scheduled basis (five per month)
   - Understand pathophysiology and treatment of disease states encountered on daily attending rounds
2. Develop skills necessary to promote optimal and rational drug therapy
   - Obtain patient-specific information necessary to develop a therapeutic and monitoring plan
   - Perform drug histories on admitted patients
   - Monitor and evaluate drug therapy for all service patients and make recommendations to optimize pharmaceutical outcomes
   - Recognize drug–drug and drug–disease interactions
   - Recommend dosage adjustments for patient with impaired renal and hepatic function
   - Provide alternative therapies in case of patient failure or intolerance
   - Present and discuss patients with faculty on a daily basis
   - Prepare and present at weekly Internal Medicine Pharm.D. student case presentations (once weekly)
3. Optimize skills necessary to communicate effectively with patients and other health care professionals
   - Answer drug information questions on request, using appropriate resources
   - Provide formal in-service presentations to the team on drug therapy–related topics as requested
   - Provide discharge drug counseling to patients, particularly those receiving multiple drugs, those who are nonadherent, and those who were started on new drugs while in the hospital
   - Document patient counseling in patient charts
4. Understand the importance of continuity of care among treatment sites
   - Provide continuity between hospital and ambulatory sites through written and verbal procedures
   - Determine which patients need pharmacy follow-up after discharge

During this rotation, students are required to attend:

- FM morning report—Tuesdays and Thursdays, 8:00 A.M. FM Large Classroom (*attend based on team attendance)
- Daily attending rounds—8:30 A.M. FM Large Classroom or MUH
- Resident Interactive Teaching Experience (RITE)—Fridays, 12:00–1:00 P.M., COP 302A
- Internal Medicine student case presentations—Fridays, 2:00–4:00 P.M., COP Student Lounge

Evaluation

1. Students will be given a verbal midpoint and written final evaluation by the preceptor(s).
2. Students will perform self-evaluations and bring them to the midpoint and final evaluation.
3. An evaluation of the preceptor and rotation site is to be completed at the end of the rotation.
4. Grades will be determined as follows
   - Daily activities and case presentations—70% (see description of case presentations)
   - Topic discussions—30% (see grading scale)
   - Case Presentations (grade incorporated into general evaluation)

Expectations

1. Be prepared to give a patient case presentation in SOAP format.
2. Identify all the patient's problems.
3. Create a complete **pharmacy problem list** by prioritizing the patient's problems.
4. Identify the subjective and objective signs/symptoms for each problem.
5. Assess the status of each problem on patient's admission.
6. Discuss your plan for each problem for this hospi-

talization. Be sure to list the important monitoring guidelines for each problem.
7. During case presentations, be prepared to discuss how your plan would change if the patient did not respond or had significant toxicities to initial therapy. To do this, you will of course need to know the adequate therapeutic response to each problem, as well as the important toxicities of the therapies you plan to recommend.

Topic Discussions (Five topics per month)
References
- Good references to use include
  - Primary
    - Journal articles with original data
  - Tertiary
    - American Family Physician (ejournal)
    - Dipiro et al., Pharmacotherapy: A Pathophysiologic Approach
    - Micromedex
    - MD Consult
    - Sanford Guide to Antimicrobial Therapy
    - Medical dictionaries
    - Package inserts
    - Other online journals and textbooks
    - Class notes
  - Evidence-Based Guidelines
    - National Guidelines Clearinghouse, www.guidelines.gov (Accessed June 2008)
    - Guidelines published on subjects by pertinent and reputable associations. Examples:
      - NHLBI guidelines for disease states pertaining to heart, lung, or blood disorders
      - CHEST guidelines for acute treatment of stroke, DVT, atrial fibrillation
      - ADA guidelines for acute treatment of DKA

Grading scale for references used
1. Used only notes from class
2. Used tertiary references only
3. Used multiple sources, mostly tertiary references
4. Used multiple sources, including primary literature, evidence-based guidelines, and tertiary references when appropriate

Pathophysiology
A good discussion of the pathophysiology of a disease state should include mechanisms of the given disorder as well as
- Risk factors
- Signs/symptoms
- Diagnostic criteria
- Morbidities and mortality

Grading Scale for Pathophysiology
1. Unable to explain basic pathophysiology
2. Able to explain basic pathophysiology
3. Pathophysiology is explained with good mastery but is incomplete
4. Pathophysiology is explained with thorough understanding

Treatment
A successful discussion of treatments should include drugs (first line, alternative, and controversial), dosages, and duration of therapy. In addition, drugs used to manage adverse effects and toxicities of primary therapies should be discussed. Special instructions for specific patients (e.g., kidney and/or liver insufficiency) should be presented. Pharmacology, major adverse effects, cost-effectiveness, and drug interactions should be included for each drug.

Grading Scale for Treatment
1. Unable to explain treatment or treatment is inappropriate
2. Explains drug of choice (primary treatment), unable to give alternatives
3. Able to discuss primary and alternative treatments and discuss therapeutic controversies
4. Able to discuss primary and alternative treatments, discuss therapeutic controversies, and apply information to patient-specific situations

Monitoring
The discussion of monitoring should include monitoring guidelines for therapeutic success, failure, and toxicity where appropriate. These may include patient assessment and laboratory values.

Grading Scale for Monitoring
1. Unable to explain monitoring or monitoring is inappropriate
2. Able to explain basic monitoring guidelines (what and why)
3. Able to explain monitoring guidelines (what, why, and how often) in detail
4. Able to develop a monitoring plan for a specific patient situation

Ideas for Topic Discussions
(Top 5 to be ranked by the learner)
- Urosepsis/urinary tract infection
- CHF Exacerbation
- Pneumonia
- Sickle Cell Disease
- Asthma/COPD Exacerbations
- Angina/MI
- Atrial Fibrillation
- Thromboembolism (DVT/PE)
- DKA/hyperosmolar hyperglycemic nonketotic coma
- Management of Stroke

DIABETES FOR A DAY EXERCISE

Submitted by: Debra Lopez

Revised: December 2006

Breakfast

1. You are on 12 U of NPH and 10 U of lispro insulin in addition to the following regular sliding scale

Blood Glucose Concentration	Lispro Insulin Dose
< 100 mg/dL	Give regularly scheduled dose
101–140 mg/dL	Add 2 U of regular (Reg)
141–160 mg/dL	Add 4 U of Reg
161–200 mg/dL	Add 6 U of Reg
201–250 mg/dL	Add 8 U of Reg
> 250 mg/dL	Add 10 U of Reg, check urine for ketones (not included in kit)

2. Perform your prebreakfast blood glucose test and then add 140 mg/dL to your reading.
3. Use the sliding scale for insulin above to determine the appropriate amount of lispro to be added to the current regimen.
4. You are now ready to mix and inject. Draw up using saline; however, do not inject more than 5 U.
5. Record your results in the following table

Actual blood glucose value?
Simulated blood glucose value?
Sliding scale used?
Total insulin in syringe?

Prelunch

1. You are a 53-year-old person with type 2 DM and osteoarthritis.
2. Your current prelunch regimen is 5 U of lispro with a correction factor/insulin sensitivity factor of 30 mg/dL and an insulin-to-carbohydrate (CHO) ratio of 1:15. Your target blood glucose is less than 180 mg/dL.
3. For your prelunch blood test and injection, use the paper tape included in the kit, and tape your middle knuckle on each finger and thumb before performing your blood glucose test.
4. Add 70 mg/dL to your glucose result.

5. Keep the tape on to perform injection. Draw up using saline; however, do not inject more than 5 U. Record your results in the following table

Actual blood glucose value?
Simulated blood glucose value?
How much insulin did you need to correct for?
How much insulin did you add for CHO counting?
Total insulin in syringe?

Predinner

1. You have type 2 DM with retinopathy.
2. Your predinner schedule consists of 7 U of lispro. You never count CHO, but you do use a correction factor/insulin sensitivity factor of 25 mg/dL. Your target blood glucose is less than 180 mg/dL.
3. For your predinner test/injection, apply a thin film of Vaseline to the outside lenses of the safety glasses included in your kit. Wear these glasses while performing your blood glucose test.
4. Add 140 mg/dL to your glucose result.
5. Keep glasses on to perform the injection. Draw up using saline; however, do not inject more than 5 U. Record your results in the following table

Actual blood glucose value?
How much insulin did you need to correct for?
Total insulin in syringe?

INSULIN PRACTICE QUESTIONS AND KEY

Submitted by: Debra Lopez

Revised: December 2006

Answers

1. Initiate patient on an insulin regimen at 0.5 U/kg/day to include lispro and glargine in three injections total per day (one injection of glargine and two injections of lispro). Patient has no history of insulin use. (Wt = 200 lb) (1 point)
   91 kg × 0.5 U/kg/day = 45 U/day
   Basal = 10 U of glargine
   Bolus = 40% of total daily dose (TDD); 45 × 0.4 = 18 U divided by two meals
   9 U prebreakfast, 9 U predinner, and 10 U of glargine at bedtime (can choose any two of three meals)
   *Remember that your TDD when initiating glargine will not add up to what you initially came up with because glargine is initiated at on 10 U/day. TDD really helps determine your bolus amount.

2. Patient on humulin 70/30, 40 U every morning and 20 U every night. Switch patient to two injections of Humalog Mix 75/25. What would be the appropriate regimen? (Wt = 187 lb) (1 point)
   40 U 75/25 prebreakfast and 20 U 75/25 predinner (stays the same)

3. Patient on humulin 70/30, 50 U every morning and 25 U every night. Switch patient to glargine and lispro with four injections total per day (one injection of glargine and three injections of lispro) (1 point)
   50 + 25 = 75 U total 75 × 0.7 = 53 U of NPH and 75 × 0.3 = 22 U of Reg
   7 U of lispro prebreakfast, prelunch, and predinner (1:1 ratio with Reg and lispro) and 42 U of glargine at bedtime
   ALTERNATIVELY, 80-80 Rule: 80% of 42=34 U/3 = 11 U premeals and 42 U of glargine at bedtime

4a. Patient with type 1 DM wants to start on two injections initially. Recommend an initial starting dosage at 0.5 U/kg/day using NPH and Reg. Do not use a premixed formulation (Wt = 148 lb) (1 point)
   67 kg × 0.5 U/kg/day = 34 U/day
   14 U of NPH and 7 U of Reg prebreakfast and 7 U of NPH and Reg predinner
   OR 2/3 (2:30 A.M.), 1/3 (11 P.M.) method= 15–16 U of NPH and 8 U of Reg prebreakfast and 5 U of NPH and 5 U of Reg predinner

4b. After one week of injections and good glycemic control, patient is ready to start three injections total per day. Recommend a regimen using glargine and lispro (1 point).
   7 U of lispro prebreakfast, 7 U of lispro predinner, and 16 or 17 U of glargine at bedtime
   ALTERNATIVELY, 80-80 Rule: 80% of 17 = 14 U/2 = 7 U premeals (same thing)

4c. After one week of injections and good glycemic control, patient is ready to start four injections total per day. The patient also should be switched from glargine to detemir. Recommend a regimen using detemir and lispro (1 point).
   5 U of lispro prebreakfast, 5 U prelunch, 5 U of lispro predinner, and 16–17 U of detemir at bedtime

5. Patient naïve to insulin needs to start an insulin regimen using Humalog Mix 75/25, two injections total per day. What would be the appropriate regimen using 0.5 U/kg/day? (Wt = 194 lb) (1 point)
   88 kg × 0.5 U/kg/day = 44 U/day
   26 U prebreakfast (60% of TDD) and 18 U predinner (40% of TDD)
   OR 44 × 2/3 = 29 U in the morning and 44 × 1/3 = 15 U at night
   OR 29 U prebreakfast (2/3 of TDD) and 15 U predinner (1/3 of TDD)

6. Patient on 11 U of NPH and 5 U of Reg every morning and 5 U of NPH and 5 U of Reg every night. Switch to three injections total per day with one glargine and two aspart. (1 point)
   16 U total of NPH/day × 0.8 = 13 U of glargine
   5 U of lispro prebreakfast, 5 U of lispro predinner, and 13 U of glargine at bedtime
   ALTERNATIVELY, 80-80 Rule: 80% of 13 = 10 U/2 = 5 U premeals (same thing)

7. Patient on 20 U of NPH at bedtime and oral agents every morning. Switch patient to three injections total per day of glargine and lispro using 0.5 U/kg/day (one injection of glargine and two injections of lispro) (Wt = 229 lb) (1 point)
   104 kg × 0.5 U/kg/day = 52 U/day
   Bolus = 40% × 52 = 20 U
   10 U of lispro prebreakfast, 10 U of lispro predinner, and 20 U of glargine at bedtime
   OR 80-80 rule= 80% of 20=16 U/2 = 8 U premeals

8. Patient on 5 U of NPH and 5 U of lispro every morning and 5 U of NPH and 5 U of lispro every night. Rearrange patient's regimen to a more appropriate regimen using the same type of insulin and the same total units per day. (1 point)
   20 U total/day 8 U of NPH and 4 U of lispro every morning and 4 U of NPH/lispro every night
   OR 2/3—1/3 method = 9 U of NPH and 4 U of lispro every morning and 3 U of NPH/lispro every night

9. Patient on once-daily insulin therapy using 30 U of detemir. Switch patient to NPH. (1 point)
   30 U of NPH (can distribute even further to 20 U in morning and 10 U at night or 18 U in morning and 12 U at night)

10. Patient on 30 U of glargine and 5 U of aspart premeals (four injections total). If switching patient from glargine to two injections of NPH, how much total NPH would be given? (1 point)
    30 U of glargine × 20% = 6 + 30 = 36 or 38 U of NPH

PATTERN MANAGEMENT PROBLEMS AND KEY

Submitted by: Debra Lopez

Revised: December 2006

Answer

Current regimen is
   20 U NPH/8 U of Reg prebreakfast
   8 U of Reg prelunch and predinner
   10 U of NPH at bedtime

Prebreakfast	Prelunch	Predinner	Bedtime
99	112	200	240
120	118	250	100
116	122	300	130
118	140	189	200
84	99	192	95
93	97	205	114

AVG 222

Which set of values would you target first? Which insulin would you adjust to change those target values, and by how much?
(Target predinner by increasing prelunch Reg or prebreakfast NPH by 1–3 U)

Current regimen is
   20 U NPH/8 U of Reg prebreakfast
   8 U of Reg prelunch and predinner
   10 U of NPH at bedtime

Prebreakfast	Prelunch	Predinner	Bedtime
200	112	99	240
250	118	120	100
300	122	116	130
189	140	118	200
192	99	84	95
205	97	93	114

AVG 222

Assuming no somogyi, which set of values would you target first? Which insulin would you adjust to change those target values, and by how much?
(Target prebreakfast by increasing bedtime NPH by 1–3 U; could also switch to glargine using 24 U).

Current regimen is
   20 U NPH/8 U of Reg prebreakfast
   8 U of Reg prelunch and predinner
   10 U of NPH at bedtime

Prebreakfast	Prelunch	Predinner	Bedtime
200	112	99	240
250	118	120	100
300	122	116	130
189	140	118	200
192	99	84	95
205	97	93	114

AVG 222

Assuming the patient has somogyi, which set of values would you target first? Which insulin would you adjust to change those target values, and by how much?
(Target prebreakfast and decrease bedtime NPH by 1–3 U or move NPH to dinner.)

Current regimen is
20 U NPH/8 U of Reg prebreakfast
8 U of Reg prelunch and predinner
10 U of NPH at bedtime

Prebreakfast	Prelunch	Predinner	Bedtime
200	54	99	240
250	118	120	100
300	66	116	130
189	62	118	200
192	98	84	95
205	76	93	114

AVG 79

Which set of values would you target first? Which insulin would you adjust to change those target values, and by how much?
(Target prelunch by decreasing prebreakfast Reg by 1–3 U)

Current regimen is
20 U of NPH/8 U of Reg prebreakfast
8 U prelunch and predinner
10 U of NPH at bedtime

Prebreakfast	Prelunch	Predinner	Bedtime
240	112	99	200
100	118	120	250
130	122	116	300
200	140	118	189
95	99	84	192
114	97	93	205

AVG 222

Which set of values would you target first? Which insulin would you adjust to change those target values, and by how much?
(Target bedtime by increasing predinner Reg by 1–3 U)

Current regimen is
5 U of lispro premeals
20 U of glargine at bedtime

Prebreakfast	Postprandial Breakfast	Postprandial Lunch	Postprandial Dinner	Bedtime
112	118	200	99	240
118	94	250	120	100
122	156	300	116	130
140	76	189	118	200
99	180	192	84	95
97	140	205	93	114

AVG 222

Which set of values would you target first, which insulin would you adjust to change those target values and by how much?
(Target postprandial lunch by increasing prelunch lispro by 1–3 U)

Current regimen is
5 U of lispro premeals
20 U of glargine at bedtime

Prebreakfast	Postprandial Breakfast	Postprandial Lunch	Postprandial Dinner	Bedtime
200	118	112	99	240
250	94	118	120	100
300	156	122	116	130
189	76	140	118	200
192	180	99	84	95
205	140	97	93	114

AVG 222

Which set of values would you target first? Which insulin would you adjust to change those target values, and by how much?
(Target prebreakfast by increasing glargine by 6 U)

Current regimen is
5 U of lispro premeals
20 U of glargine at bedtime

Prebreakfast	Postprandial Breakfast	Postprandial Lunch	Postprandial Dinner	Bedtime
118	200	112	99	240
94	250	118	120	100
156	300	122	116	130
76	189	140	118	200
180	192	99	84	95
140	205	97	93	114

AVG 222

Which set of values would you target first? Which insulin would you adjust to change those target values, and by how much?
(Target postprandial breakfast by increasing prebreakfast lispro by 1–3 U)

Current regimen is
7 U of aspart and 12 U of NPH prebreakfast
5 U of aspart prelunch
9 U of aspart and 10 U of NPH predinner

Prebreakfast	Postprandial Breakfast	Postprandial Lunch	Postprandial Dinner	Bedtime
200	240	112	99	118
250	100	118	120	94
300	130	122	116	156
189	200	140	118	76
192	95	99	84	180
205	114	97	93	140

AVG 222

Which set of values would you target first? Which insulin would you adjust to change those target values, and by how much?
(Target prebreakfast by increasing predinner NPH by 1–3 U [moving NPH to bedtime might be an option if patient is willing to do 4 injections instead of 3]; if converting to glargine use 18 U at bedtime.)

Current regimen is
7 U of aspart and 12 U of NPH prebreakfast
5 U of aspart prelunch
9 U of aspart and 10 U of NPH predinner

Prebreakfast	Postprandial Breakfast	Postprandial Lunch	Postprandial Dinner	Bedtime
99	240	112	54	118
120	100	118	118	94
116	130	122	66	156
118	200	140	62	76
84	95	99	98	180
93	114	97	76	140

AVG 79

Which set of values would you target first? Which insulin would you adjust to change those target values, and by how much?
(Target postprandial dinner by decreasing predinner aspart by 1–3 U)

BONUS:
Current regimen is
5 U of lispro premeals
20 U of glargine at bedtime

Prebreakfast	Postprandial Breakfast	Postprandial Lunch	Postprandial Dinner	Bedtime
118	240	112	99	200
94	100	118	120	250
156	130	122	116	300
76	200	140	118	189
180	95	99	84	192
140	114	97	93	205

What could be causing the bedtime highs?
(Bedtime snack)

What would be the next step?
(Adding lispro prebedtime snack) (Amount could be determined by the number of carbohydrate servings.)

AMBULATORY CARE CLERKSHIP ROTATION PRE- AND POST-TEST AND ANSWER KEY

Submitted by: Deanna McDanel, Erin Newkirk, and Beth Bryles Phillips

Created: June 2005

NAME:_____
Rotation Cycle_____
Rotation Dates_____

Answer

HTN (17 points)

1. Based on the JNC 7 guidelines, list the BP classifications and specified ranges of adults eighteen years or older (4 points; 0.5 point for classification and 0.5 point for range).
   Normal: < 120/80 mm Hg (1 point)
   Pre-HTN: 120–139/80–89 mm Hg (1 point)
   Stage 1: 140–159/90–99 mm Hg (1 point)
   Stage 2: ≥ 160/100 mm Hg (1 point)

2. List appropriate lifestyle modifications for the management for HTN (5 points: 1 point each)
   Weight reduction
   DASH diet
   Sodium reduction
   Physical activity
   Moderation of alcohol (or cigarette smoking cessation)

3. What laboratory monitoring is appropriate for ACEIs and HCTZ, and when should this be completed after starting therapy? (4 points)
   Laboratory values: baseline SCr/BUN, potassium ± sodium (2 points for laboratory values; 0.5 each)
   Monitoring: baseline, repeat one to two weeks from initiation, two to four weeks from dose increase (2 points for follow-up)

4. List at least two absolute and two relative contraindications for β-blocker therapy (4 points: 2 points for absolute, 2 points for relative)
   Absolute (any two of the following): severe bradycardia (HR < 50–60 beats/minute), high-degree (second or third) atrioventricular block, sick sinus syndrome, severe LV failure (decompensated), vasospastic angina, hypotension
   Relative (any two of the following): asthma, COPD, severe depression, PVD, insulin-dependent DM

Hyperlipidemia (19 points)

1. Separately list the five CHD risk factors (be specific) and at least four CHD risk equivalents. (9 points)
   Cardiovascular Risk Factors: (5 points, 1 point each: okay if miss some specifics)
   Age (> 45 for men, > 55 for women) [0.5 point if just list "age"]
   Cigarette smoking
   FH of premature CHD (< 55 for men; < 65 for women) [0.5 point if just list "Family History"]
   HDL < 40 mg/dL
   HTN
   Cardiovascular Risk Equivalents (4 points; any 4 of the following; no points for CHD, CAD, or MI)
   Abdominal aortic aneurysm
   Angina
   Carotid artery disease
   Stroke of carotid origin
   TIA
   50% obstruction of carotid artery
   Peripheral arterial disease
   Intermittent claudication
   DM
   > 20% Framingham score

2. List the LDL target goals (risk classification) for patients depending on their cardiovascular risk (4 points: 0.5 point for each classification/risk factors and 0.5 point for each goal)
   LDL Goal:
   Low Risk: 0–1 Risk Factor—Goal LDL < 160 mg/dL
   Moderately High Risk: 2+ Risk Factors—Goal LDL < 130 mg/dL [Option: If 10-year risk 10–20% LDL goal of < 100 mg/dL]
   High Risk: CHD or CHD Risk Equivalents (or 10-year risk > 20%)—Goal LDL < 100 mg/dL [Option of less than 70 mg/dL]
   Very High Risk: CHD plus multiple major risk factors (especially DM), severe/poorly controlled risk factors (smoking), metabolic syndrome, acute coronary syndrome—Goal LDL < 70 mg/dL

3. List the potential ADRs associated with statin therapy and the appropriate monitoring for efficacy and toxicity of these agents. (6 points: 3 points each)
    ADRs (3 points, any three of the following): myopathy, myalgia, muscle weakness; nausea/vomiting; signs of liver dysfunction; rhabdomyolysis
    Monitoring (3 points; one for ALT, one for lipid test, one for CK; 0.5 point each if only list laboratory results but not specifics). ALT at baseline, twelve weeks, with any dosage increase, and then every six to twelve months (may vary based on statin patient is taking). CK at baseline and if muscle signs/symptoms; repeat fasting lipid panel eight to twelve weeks after initiation of therapy, every six to twelve months if stable

DM (11 points)
1. What are the contraindications for the use of metformin? (3 points)
    Stage 3 and 4 HF (1 point; 0.5 pt if just say CHF)
    Renal insufficiency SCr > 1.4 for females, SCr > 1.5 for males (1 point; 0.5 point if just say renal diagnosis)
    1 point if one of the following:
    Active liver disease
    Alcohol abuse
    Contrast dye
    History of metabolic acidosis (at risk of lactic acidosis or prior lactic acidosis)

2. What are the goal values for blood glucose and HgA1c concentrations for patients with DM? Be specific (4 points: 1 point each)
    Fasting: 90–130 mg/dL
    Postprandial: < 180 mg/dL
    Bedtime: 110–150 mg/dL
    HgA1c: < 7.0%

3. List the complications associated with DM and ways to prevent the complications (4 points plus bonus points).
    [0.5 point each complication, 0.5 point each prevention measure]
    Retinopathy — yearly eye examination (1 point)
    Nephropathy — yearly microalbumin, strict BP control, ACEI/ARB (1 point)
    Neuropathy — check feet daily (1 point)
    CAD — aspirin 81 mg daily (1 point)

    Bonus 0.5 points for each of the following:
    Dental — Every six months if dentate, every twelve months if edentate (+ 0.5 point)
    Vaccines — yearly influenza vaccine,
    pneumococcal (+0.5 point)
    Infections/wound healing — strict blood glucose control (+0.5 point)

Anticoagulation (13 points)
1. List five drug–drug interactions (be specific) with warfarin and their corresponding effect on the INR (5 points—0.5 point for each drug interaction; 0.5 for corresponding effect)
    Examples:
    Bactrim—Increase (Inc) INRRifampin—Decrease (Dec) INR
    Cipro—Inc INRCarbamazepine, rifampin, phenytoin—Dec INR
    Vitamins/Herbals—Inc or Dec INRAmiodarone—Inc INR
    Aspirin—Inc bleeding (may Inc INR) Not NSAIDs or alcohol
    Azole antifungals—Inc INRVitamin K 0.5

2. What are three potential causes of a subtherapeutic INR? (3 points; 1 point each; only 0.5 point if not specific)
    Missed dose
    Increased dietary vitamin K intake/initiation of MVI/Viactiv chew/Ensure
    Drug interaction
    Hypothyroid
    Increased activity level/weight gain (0.5 point)

3. What are five potential causes of a supratherapeutic INR (5 points, 1 point each; only 0.5 point if not specific)?
    Extra dose
    Decreased dietary vitamin K intake/decrease or discontinuation of MVI/Viactiv chew/Ensure
    Drug interaction
    Binge drinking
    Hyperthyroidism
    Fever/Illness
    Diarrhea
    HF exacerbation
    Weight/Exercise decrease (0.5 point)

ANTICOAGULATION PHARMACIST CREDENTIALING EXAMINATION AND CERTIFICATION

Submitted by: Christopher Lamar

Revised: July 2004

All questions are multiple choice. There is only one correct answer for each question. There are fifty questions, and a score of 75% is required to pass the examination. Any questions about the examination are referred to the anticoagulation clinic manager. All therapeutic decisions follow the 1998 American College of Chest Physicians guidelines and the Cherokee Indian Hospital Anticoagulation Service Policy and Procedures.

Please circle only one answer per question.

Section One—Clot Formation

1. Clotting is initiated by all of the following except
   A. Epithelial injury
   B. Altered bloodflow
   C. Hypercoagulability
   D. High concentrations of vitamin K
   E. Platelet activation

2. Activated platelets may result in
   A. Vasoconstriction
   B. Aggregation
   C. Initiation of coagulation cascade
   D. Stimulation of fibroblast and smooth muscle cell proliferation
   E. All of the above

3. Factors associated with vasoconstriction include all of the following except
   A. Serotonin
   B. Adenosine diphosphate
   C. Thromboxane A2
   D. Platelet factor 4
   E. Platelet factor 3

4. All of the following are true statements about vitamin K except
   A. It is a fat-soluble vitamin
   B. Requires pancreatic and biliary secretions for absorption
   C. Is bound to albumin
   D. Is stored in the liver
   E. Is found naturally in many green leafy vegetables

Section Two—Warfarin Pharmacology and Dosing

5. The goal of warfarin therapy is to?
   A. Dissolve clots without the adverse effects of bleeding occurring
   B. Eliminate vitamin K while reducing complications of bleeding disorders
   C. Limit thrombus extension and to prevent thrombosis while minimizing bleeding complications
   D. Dissolve blood clots that may exist secondary to antiphospholipid antibodies
   E. Make patients come in every month to get money for the hospital

6. Warfarin affects which of the following clotting factors?
   A. 2, 7, 9, 10
   B. 5, 8
   C. 2, 9, 10, 11, 12
   D. A and B
   E. None of the above

7. Warfarin
   A. Breaks up clots
   B. Prevents clot formation by preventing the reduction of vitamin K
   C. Prevents clot formation by directly binding to clotting factors
   D. Stimulates antithrombin III
   E. None of the above

8. With regard to warfarin therapy, clotting factors decline in what order?
   A. 2, 7, 9, 10, protein C
   B. 5, 8, protein C, 9, 7, 10, 2
   C. 7, protein C, 9, 10, 2
   D. 2, 10, protein C, 8, 5
   E. Protein C, 2, 10, 7, 9

9. With high warfarin doses
   A. Clotting factors are eliminated.
   B. Clotting factors continue to be activated at about 20% of normal.
   C. Anticoagulant effects occur more quickly.
   D. All of the above
   E. None of the above

10. NADPH-dependent reductase offers an alternative method for what to occur?
    A. Inhibition of warfarin
    B. Activation of clotting factors
    C. Anticoagulation
    D. All of the above
    E. None of the above

11. Increased concentrations of warfarin may be found in which subgroups of patients?
    A. Acidodic
    B. Elderly
    C. Low albumin
    D. B and C
    E. All of the above

12. Warfarin effects will continue for how long after discontinuation of therapy (multiple-dose therapy)?
    A. Months
    B. One day
    C. Four to five days
    D. Two to three weeks
    E. Effects will stop instantly.

13. Which statement is false concerning larger loading doses of warfarin?
    A. Loading doses will increase the INR faster.
    B. Loading doses could result in faster anticoagulation.
    C. Loading doses can result in hypercoagulable states.
    D. Loading doses deplete factor and protein C more quickly.
    E. Loading doses are not recommended.

14. As patients get older, average maintenance doses of warfarin tend to
    A. Get larger
    B. Get smaller
    C. Become harder to maintain goal INRs
    D. Become easier to maintain goal INRs
    E. None of the above

15. When taking a social history, what factors are important with regard to warfarin therapy?
    A. Alcohol intake
    B. Diet
    C. OTC drug use
    D. Transportation to the hospital
    E. All of the above

Section Three—Adverse Reactions Associated with Warfarin

16. The risk of bleeding while taking warfarin is greatest when?
    A. During the first six to twelve months of therapy
    B. If there is a history of bleeding
    C. If there is renal insufficiency
    D. A and B
    E. All of the above

17. Which of the following statements regarding warfarin skin necrosis is false?
    A. Generally occurs 3 to 8 days after initiation of therapy
    B. May be fatal
    C. Associated with a rapid decline in protein C
    D. Can be prevented with large loading doses of warfarin
    E. Associated with thrombosis of venules in subcutaneous fat

18. Warfarin may be expected to cause
    A. Discoloration of stools
    B. Discoloration of urine
    C. Alopecia
    D. A and B
    E. B and C

19. Warfarin therapy is contraindicated in
    A. Pregnancy
    B. Liver disease
    C. Uncontrolled HTN (SBP more than 180 mm Hg; DBP more than 100 mm Hg)
    D. Arterial aneurysm
    E. All of the above

20. What are the common symptoms of occult bleeding?
    A. Abdominal pain, nausea, headache, and lower extremity weakness
    B. Lightheadedness, pallor, tachycardia, and fainting
    C. Vision changes, muscle aches, and jaundice
    D. Dry mouth, hot flashes, and vision changes
    E. Nausea and vomiting

21. Which statements are true about administration of vitamin K?
    A. Oral and intravenous administration provides predictable and reliable results, whereas subcutaneous administration is often variable and unpredictable.

B. High doses of vitamin K can result in difficulty when resuming warfarin therapy.
C. After high doses of vitamin K are given, heparin therapy is often required to maintain anticoagulation.
D. IV vitamin K can result in anaphylactic reactions.
E. All of the above are true.

Section Four—Warfarin Drug Interactions

22. Increasing synthroid dosage in a patient on warfarin could result in
    A. Increased INR due to increased metabolism of clotting factors
    B. Increased INR due to increased metabolism of warfarin
    C. Decreased INR due to increased metabolism of clotting factors
    D. Decreased INR due to increased metabolism of warfarin
    E. None of the above

The addition of the following drugs will increase (A), decrease (B), or have no change (C) on the INR

23. Allopurinol_____
24. Simvastatin_____
25. Bactrim_____
26. Antacids_____
27. Carbamazepine_____
28. Digoxin_____
29. Phytonadione_____
30. Erythromycin_____

31. A patient is recently started on Rifampin and Isoniazid therapy for presumed TB. What will happen to the INR?
    A. Rifampin will increase the INR
    B. Isoniazid will decrease the INR
    C. Isoniazid will increase the INR
    D. Neither drug will affect the INR
    E. A and B

32. When should a patient just started on rifampin and isoniazid therapy return for a follow-up INR?
    A. 3 to 4 weeks
    B. 1 day
    C. 4 to 7 days
    D. 1 to 2 months
    E. 1 year

Section Five—Laboratory Results

33. The INR is affected by
    A. Drugs
    B. Diet
    C. Social life
    D. Disease states
    E. All of the above

34. A higher International Sensitivity Index (ISI) value can result in a _____ INR?
    A. Less accurate
    B. Increased
    C. Decreased
    D. Unchanged
    E. More accurate

35. Warfarin therapy can prolong the:
    A. aPTT
    B. PT
    C. INR
    D. B and C
    E. All of the above

Section Six—Indications for Warfarin Therapy

Please complete the following table

Indication	Goal INR	Duration
36. DVT of proximal vein	_____	_____
37. DVT of calf vein	_____	_____
38. Recurrent DVT	_____	_____
39. Atrial Fibrillation	_____	_____
40. Tissue Heart Valve	_____	_____
41. Mechanical Heart Valve Replacement	_____	_____
42. Cardiomyopathy	_____	_____
43. Porcine Heart Valve Replacement	_____	_____

Section Seven—Heparin Therapy

44. The initial bolus dose for heparin therapy in the treatment of DVT using the weight-based nomogram is
    A. 40 U/kg
    B. 5,000 U
    C. 1,000 U
    D. 80 U/kg
    E. 100 U/kg

45. The initial heparin infusion for the treatment of DVT using the weight-based nomogram is
    A. 18 U/kg/hour
    B. 80 U/kg/hour
    C. 100 U/kg/hour
    D. 1,250 U/hour
    E. 5,000 U/hour

46. After initiating heparin therapy using the weight-based nomogram, when should the aPTT be checked?
    A. In 6 hours
    B. In 12 hours
    C. The next morning
    D. In 2 hours
    E. In 24 hours

47. After making an infusion adjustment using the weight-based nomogram, when should the aPTT be rechecked?
    A. In 6 hours
    B. In 12 hours
    C. The next morning
    D. In 2 hours
    E. In 24 hours

48. Which of the following statements about standard concentrations of heparin at CIH is false?
    A. The final concentration is 50 U/mL.
    B. Either 5 mL from a 5,000 U/mL 10-mL vial or 2.5 mL from a 10,000 U/mL 4-mL vial can be used.
    C. 500 mL of dextrose is the standard solution to mix heparin.
    D. 100 mL of 0.9% saline is the standard solution to mix heparin.
    E. Heparin can be double concentrated (100 U/mL) in 0.9% saline if requested.

Section Eight—Cases

Mr. Jones is an 81-year-old Indian man with a medical history of Alzheimer's-type dementia, atrial fibrillation (for 25 years), and Parkinson's disease. Current drugs include donepezil 1 tablet daily, sinemet 25/100 CR 3 times daily, lansoprazole 15 mg daily, and warfarin 3 mg daily. His INR today is 1.4. He states that he takes his warfarin as instructed, one tablet daily. He also claims to have fallen four times during the past week but says he has not cut himself.

49. Which one of the following is the next logical step in Mr. Jones' therapy?
    A. Tell Mr. Jones that he should be taking 1½ purple tablets every day and that he will need to take them this way to keep his INR in the goal range.
    B. Give Mr. Jones 1 extra 2-mg tablet now to help increase his INR, and have him return in 1 week to recheck his INR while on 2 mg daily.
    C. Refer Mr. Jones back to his primary provider because he is not a good warfarin candidate.
    D. Kick Mr. Jones out of the hospital for not taking his drug as he should.
    E. Ask Mr. Jones about his eating habits before adjusting his warfarin dose.

Mrs. Smith is a 30-year-old woman with a history of idiopathic thrombosis in her left leg, which resulted in a DVT of her left calf 3 months ago. After a thorough workup, Mrs. Smith was found to have a deficiency of protein C (determined before anticoagulation therapy). She has been on warfarin for 3 months now with her goal INR obtained at each visit. Her INR today, however, is 1.6, and she states that she has been staying at her friend's house for the past 6 days and that her friend is a vegetarian. She is now living at home.

50. What is the next logical step in Mrs. Smith's therapy?
    A. Discontinue warfarin therapy because Mrs. Smith's indication for warfarin is a DVT, which occurred in her calf.
    B. Continue warfarin therapy for DVT for at least 6 months.
    C. Discontinue warfarin therapy at next "in range" INR.
    D. Continue warfarin therapy because she has protein C deficiency.
    E. None of the above

51. Which of the following is the best recommendation for her low INR with regard to warfarin therapy?
    A. Nothing, because warfarin is being discontinued.
    B. Increase dose by 10% and recheck in 1 week.
    C. Continue current dose and recheck in 1 week.
    D. Increase dose by 10% and recheck in 1 month.
    E. Decrease dose by 10% in expectation that INR will increase.

Mr. Clark has been coming in for his INRs for 3 months. He takes warfarin 5 mg daily for atrial fibrillation. His INR fluctuates between 1.1 and 4.0. His dosage has not changed, and he is coming in every 1 to 2 weeks to have his INR reevaluated.

52. Which of the following questions are important to ask Mr. Clark?
    A. Are you taking your warfarin every day and at the same time?
    B. Are you eating consistently? Can you tell me what you are eating?
    C. Are you drinking alcohol?
    D. Are you taking any new drugs?
    E. All of the above are important questions to ask Mr. Clark.

53. Mr. Clark confides that he is drinking what he calls "a little bit"; which of the following are true concerning alcohol and warfarin therapy?
    A. Chronic alcohol may increase the metabolism of warfarin.
    B. Chronic alcohol may lower the INR.
    C. Binge drinking may decrease the metabolism of warfarin.
    D. Binge drinking may increase the INR.
    E. All of the above are true.

54. Mr. Wolfe states that his "little bit of drinking" consists of about one six pack per day and going out to the bar for a couple of shots of tequila with his buddies on the weekend. He is also complaining of abdominal pain and states that he needs something for his stomach. What risks does Mr. Wolfe have?
    A. Mr. Wolfe may have an addiction to alcohol.
    B. His abdominal pain may be due to liver damage.
    C. His stomach pain may be due to GI ulceration.
    D. Mr. Smith may not be a good candidate right now for warfarin therapy.
    E. All of the above.

55. What questions would you want to ask Mr. Wolfe?
    A. Are you having any maroon-colored or black tarry stools?
    B. Why do you drink tequila instead of whiskey?
    C. Have you been coughing up or throwing up blood?
    D. A and B
    E. A and C

56. What is the next logical step in Mr. Wolfe's therapy?
    A. Contact Mr. Wolfe's primary provider to determine what is best for Mr. Wolfe.
    B. Stop warfarin therapy.
    C. Order CBC, LFTs, amylase, and lipase, and start Mr. Wolfe on lansoprazole and tell him to come back next week.
    D. Call the police.
    E. Quit your job.

57. Mrs. Teesateskie is a 48-year-old Indian woman with a history of two DVTs in her right leg. A work-up was done; however, no deficiencies in protein C, protein S, or other clotting factors were found. Her current warfarin dosage is 4 mg/day. Past INRs are as follows:

    | 1/19 | 2.2 | on 4 mg per day |
    | 2/14 | 1.8 | on 4 mg per day |
    | 3/17 | 2.4 | on 4 mg per day |
    | Today | 2.6 | on 4 mg per day |

    What is the next logical step in Mrs. Teesateskie's therapy?
    A. Decrease warfarin 5 mg and follow up in 2 weeks.
    B. Increase warfarin dosage to 5 mg/day and follow up in 2 weeks.
    C. Continue current dose and follow up in 2 weeks.
    D. Continue current dose and follow up in 1 month.

58. Mr. Walkingstick, a 48-year-old man, has just received a diagnosis of atrial fibrillation and been started on warfarin therapy. His primary provider does not plan on cardioversion. How long will Mr. Walkingstick be on warfarin?
    A. One year
    B. Three months
    C. Six months
    D. Indefinitely

59. What is Mr. Walkingstick's goal INR?
    A. 1.5–2.5
    B. 2–3
    C. 2.5–3.5

60. Mr. Walkingstick was recently started on warfarin, and his IRN results are as follows:

    | 3/10 | 3.3on | 5 mg daily |
    | 3/17 | 1.7on | 2.5 mg daily |
    | 3/24 | 1.6on | 2.5 mg daily |
    | 3/31 | 1.8on | 2.5 mg daily |

    Which of the following plans is the most logical step in Mr. Walkingstick's anticoagulation therapy?
    A. Change warfarin dosage to 5 mg daily.
    B. Change warfarin dosage to 3 mg Monday, Wednesday, and Friday; take 2 mg on the other days.
    C. Change warfarin dosage to 3 mg daily.
    D. Give 2 mg extra today and then change to 5 mg daily.
    E. Continue warfarin 2.5 mg daily.

PHARMACIST COMPETENCIES— ANTICOAGULATION

Submitted by: Jessica Starr

Created: June 2005

Learning Objectives

1. Understand the pathophysiology of thromboembolic disorders
2. Identify and evaluate the signs and symptoms of a thromboembolism and risk factors for the development of a thromboembolism
3. Develop a comprehensive understanding of the pharmacology of warfarin therapy, including
   - Mechanism of action
   - Pharmacokinetics
   - Pharmacodynamics
4. Identify the major indications for warfarin therapy.
   - Prevention of venous thromboembolism
   - Treatment of a venous thromboembolism
   - Atrial fibrillation
   - Valvular heart disease
5. Identify the following for each of the major indications for warfarin therapy
   - The optimal therapeutic range and target INR
   - The appropriate length of therapy
6. Design an appropriate plan for the initiation and maintenance of warfarin therapy for an individual patient including
   - Frequency of monitoring
   - Dose adjusting warfarin when appropriate
   - Reversal of anticoagulation with vitamin K when indicated
7. Develop an understanding of the instruments and laboratory analyses used to monitor anticoagulation intensity.
   - Point-of-care monitors
   - PT
   - INR
8. Identify the risk factors for anticoagulation-induced bleeding and understand how to manage these patients appropriately.
9. Describe the major adverse events associated with warfarin therapy and explain how to detect, evaluate, and manage these events.
10. Identify and accommodate major drug–drug, drug–herb, drug–food, and drug–disease interactions of warfarin.
11. Understand how to appropriately manage oral anticoagulation in patients undergoing invasive procedures (bridge therapy).

Required References

1. Ansell J, Hirsh J, Dalen J, et al. The pharmacology and management of the vitamin K antagonists. Chest 2004;126:204S–33S. Erratum in: Chest 2005;127:415–6.
2. Dunn AS, Turpie AG. Perioperative management of patients receiving oral anticoagulants. *Arch Intern Med* 2003;163:901–8.
3. Eisen GM, Baron TH, Dominitz JA, et al. Guideline on the management of anticoagulation and antiplatelet therapy for endoscopic procedures. Gastrointest Endosc 2002;55:775–9.
4. Geerts WH, Pineo GF, Heit JA, et al. Prevention of venous thromboembolism. Chest 2004;126:338S–400S.
5. Haines ST, Racine E, Zeolla M. Venous thromboembolism. In: Dipiro JT, Talbert RL, Yee GC, eds. Pharmacotherapy. New York: McGraw-Hill, 2002:337–43.
6. Heck AM, DeWitt BA, Lukes AL. Potential interactions between alternative therapies and warfarin. AJHP 2000;57:1221–7.
7. Buller HR, Agnelli G, Hull RD, et al. Antithrombotic therapy for venous thromboembolic disease. Chest 2004;126:401S–28S.
8. Kehoe WA. Anticoagulation and dental procedures. Pharm Lett 1998;14:141006.
9. Salem DN, Stein PD, Al-Ahmad A, et al. Antithrombotic therapy in valvular heart disease—native and prosthetic. Chest 2004;126:457S–82S.
10. Sherman JJ. Monitoring patients in an anticoagulation clinic: Practical considerations. http://www.uspharmacist.com/oldformat.asp?url=newlook/files/feat/anticoagulation.htm. Accessed June 2008.
11. Singer DE, Albers GW, Dalen JE, et al. Antithrombotic therapy in atrial fibrillation. Chest 2004;126:429S–456S.

Additional References

1. Hirsh J, Fuster V, Ansell J, Halperin JL, American Heart Association, American College of Cardiology Foundation. American Heart Association/American College of Cardiology Foundation Guide to warfarin therapy. Circulation 2003;107:1692–711.
2. Kearon C, Hirsh J. Management of anticoagulation before and after elective surgery. N Engl J Med 1997;336:1506–11.

WRITTEN COMPETENCY ASSESSMENT

1. Which of the following physiologic factors promotes an antithrombotic effect in the body?
   a. Platelets
   b. Prothrombin
   c. Slow rate of bloodflow
   d. Protein C

2. Which of the following is a symptom of a DVT?
   a. Leg warmth
   b. Constriction of superficial veins
   c. Neck vein distension
   d. Fever

3. Which of the following is a symptom of a PE?
   a. Bradycardia
   b. Slow, labored breathing
   c. Shortness of breath
   d. HTN

4. Which of the following is true regarding the signs and symptoms associated with a VTE?
   a. Patients with a VTE commonly develop very specific signs and symptoms.
   b. Patients are commonly diagnosed based on signs and symptoms alone.
   c. The signs and symptoms associated with a VTE are nonspecific and often absent.
   d. VTEs are always asymptomatic, and diagnosis is made by means of objective tests only.

5. Which of the following is a risk factor for the formation of a VTE?
   a. Young age
   b. Malignancy
   c. An excess of protein C or S
   d. Minor surgery lasting less than 30 minutes

6. Which of the following clotting factors is inhibited by warfarin?
   a. III
   b. V
   c. VI
   d. IX

7. Warfarin produces its anticoagulant effect by which of the following mechanisms?
   a. Directly inhibiting circulating clotting factors
   b. Directly inhibiting the conversion of fibrinogen to fibrin
   c. Preventing the formation of clotting factors by depleting concentrations of vitamin K
   d. Preventing the formation of clotting factors by increasing concentrations of vitamin K

8. The time required for warfarin to achieve its antithrombotic effect is dependent on
   a. The time it takes for warfarin to reach peak plasma concentrations
   b. The elimination half-lives of the clotting factors it depletes
   c. The time required for warfarin to reach steady-state concentration
   d. The length of time it takes for warfarin to stop the production of clotting factors in the liver

9. Warfarin typically achieves its antithrombotic effect after treatment for
   a. 6 hours
   b. 2 days
   c. 10 days
   d. 21 days

10. The intensity of warfarin's anticoagulation is best monitored by which of the following laboratory tests?
    a. PT
    b. INR
    c. aPTT
    d. Anti-factor Xa

11. Potential limitations of monitoring anticoagulation therapy by PT include which of the following?
    a. The PT responds to a reduction in only two of the four clotting factors, thereby making it an inaccurate assessment of anticoagulation intensity.
    b. Prolonged and less prolonged PTs generally result from the use of a more or less responsive thromboplastin reagent.
    c. The PT must be standardized with a reagent called ISI, which is expensive and not practical to use.
    d. The PT reflects only a reduction in clotting factor IX, which makes it an inaccurate assessment of anticoagulation intensity during the first week of therapy.

12. Which of the following is true regarding point-of-care monitors to measure anticoagulation intensity with warfarin therapy?
    a. The point-of-care monitor is the most accurate way to monitor anticoagulation.
    b. The whole-blood fingerstick sample must be drawn in a glass capillary tube to ensure enough blood to place on the test cartridge.
    c. Point-of-care machines eliminate the need for thromboplastin reagents and thus remove the variability between different central laboratories.

d. Point-of-care monitors provide expedient PT/INR values, so the clinician can evaluate the result and make appropriate recommendations during the patient's clinic visit.

13. Which of the following mechanisms will potentiate the antithrombotic effects of warfarin
    a. Hepatic dysfunction
    b. High concentrations of circulating vitamin K
    c. Induction of CYP 2C9 enzyme
    d. Good nutritional status

14. When warfarin therapy is initiated in most patient populations (i.e., young healthy adults), an appropriate dosage is
    a. 1 mg/day
    b. 2 mg/day
    c. 5 mg/day
    d. 15 mg/day

15. If rapid anticoagulation is required (patient has an acute DVT) at the time of warfarin administration, heparin or LMWH should be overlapped with warfarin until which of the following occurs
    a. There have been 2 days of overlap and the INR is stable.
    b. The INR is within the therapeutic range and stable, and there have been 5 days of overlap.
    c. There have been 5 days of overlap.
    d. The INR has been within the therapeutic range for at least 3 days.

16. When initiating warfarin therapy, the INR should be monitored
    a. Every 12 hours until a stable dose response has been achieved
    b. Every day until a stable dose response has been achieved
    c. Every few days until a stable dose response has been achieved
    d. Every few weeks until a stable dose response has been achieved

17. Once the INR response is stabilized, the frequency of INR monitoring should be:
    a. Every week
    b. Every 2 weeks
    c. Every 4 weeks
    d. Every 6 weeks

18. When a patient has an INR outside the desired therapeutic range for an unknown reason, the most appropriate way to manage the patient is
    a. Start monitoring the INR every day
    b. Adjust the daily dose of warfarin up or down by increments of 5–20%
    c. Adjust the weekly dose of warfarin up or down in increments of 5–20%
    d. Hold the next dose of warfarin and then adjust the daily dose of warfarin up or down by increments of 5–30%

19. When a patient has an INR outside the desired therapeutic range and vitamin K is going to be administered, you should
    a. Use 15 mg of vitamin K orally to quickly lower the INR into the therapeutic range
    b. Rapidly infuse 10 mg of vitamin K intravenously to lower the INR quickly into the therapeutic range
    c. Use 2.5 mg of vitamin K orally to quickly lower the INR into the therapeutic range
    d. Slowly infuse 20 mg of vitamin K intravenously to lower the INR into the therapeutic range without causing anaphylaxis

20. A 43-year-old white woman comes into the clinic today to have her INR checked, and it is 4.2. She is currently taking 5 mg of warfarin every day for a first-episode idiopathic DVT she had six weeks ago. She has been stable on this dose of warfarin since it was initiated six weeks ago. She has had no changes in her diet, and she has not recently started any new drugs or OTCs. She is not actively bleeding. Which of the following is the best way to manage this patient?
    a. Hold the next dose of warfarin, give 2.5 mg of vitamin K orally, and resume therapy with a dosage of 4 mg/day
    b. Hold the next dose of warfarin and resume therapy at 5 mg on Monday, Wednesday, Friday, Saturday, and Sunday and 2.5 mg on Tuesday and Thursday
    c. Decrease the dosage of warfarin to 4 mg on Mondays, Wednesdays, Fridays, Saturdays, and Sundays and 3 mg on Tuesdays and Thursdays
    d. Hold the next dose of warfarin, give 2.5 mg of vitamin K orally, and resume therapy with 5 mg on Mondays, Wednesdays, Fridays, Saturdays, and Sundays and 2.5 mg on Tuesdays and Thursdays

21. A 43-year-old white woman comes into the clinic today to have her INR checked, and it is 4.2. She is currently taking 5 mg of warfarin every day for a first-episode idiopathic DVT she had 6 weeks ago. She has been stable on this dosage of warfarin since it was initiated 6 weeks ago. She has had no changes in her diet, and she has not recently started any new drugs or OTCs. She is not actively bleeding. You adjust the dose of her warfarin appropriately. This patient should follow up in the Pharmacotherapy Clinic to have her INR checked in:
    a. 3 days
    b. 5 days
    c. 2 weeks
    d. 3 weeks

22. A 43-year-old white woman comes to the clinic today to have her INR checked, and it is 4.2. She is currently taking 5 mg of warfarin every day for a first-episode idiopathic DVT she had 6 weeks ago. She has been stable on this dosage of warfarin since it was initiated 6 weeks ago. She has had no changes in her diet, and she has not recently started any new drugs or OTCs. She is not actively bleeding. Which one of the following is the target INR for this patient?

    a. 1.5 (range of 1–2)
    b. 2.0 (range of 1.5–2.5)
    c. 2.5 (range of 2–3)
    d. 3.0 (range of 2.5–3.5)

23. A 55-year-old African American man comes to the clinic today to have his INR checked, and it is 1.6. He is currently taking 7.5 mg of warfarin every day for atrial fibrillation and a bileaflet mechanical heart valve in the mitral position. He has been stable on this dosage of warfarin for a couple of months. He has had no changes in his diet, and he has not recently started any new drugs or OTCs. He is not actively bleeding. He has 5-mg tablets. Which of the following is the best way to manage this patient's drug therapy?

    a. Increase the dosage to 7.5 mg on Mondays, Wednesdays, Fridays, and Saturdays and 10 mg on Tuesdays, Thursdays, and Sundays
    b. Overlap patient with heparin/LMWH and increase dosage to 7.5 mg on Mondays, Wednesdays, Fridays, and Saturdays and 10 mg on Tuesdays, Thursdays, and Sundays
    c. Overlap patient with heparin/LMWH, and increase the dosage to 10 mg on Mondays, Wednesdays, Fridays, Saturdays, and Sundays and 7.5 mg on Tuesdays and Thursdays
    d. Give patient a one-time bolus dose of 10 mg of warfarin and increase the dose to 10 mg on Mondays, Wednesdays, Fridays, Saturdays, and Sundays and 7.5 mg on Tuesdays and Thursdays

24. A 55-year-old African American man comes to the clinic today to have his INR checked, and it is 1.6. He is currently taking 7.5 mg of warfarin every day for atrial fibrillation and a bileaflet mechanical heart valve in the mitral position. He has been stable on this dose of warfarin for 2 months. He has had no changes in his diet, and he has not recently started any new drugs or OTCs. He is not actively bleeding. You adjust the dose of his warfarin appropriately. This patient should follow up in the Pharmacotherapy Clinic to have his INR checked in

    a. 5 days
    b. 1 week
    c. 2 weeks
    d. 6 weeks

25. A 55-year-old African American man comes to the clinic today to have his INR checked, and it is 1.6. He is currently taking 7.5 mg of warfarin every day for atrial fibrillation and a bileaflet mechanical heart valve in the mitral position. He has been stable on this dosage of warfarin for 2 months. He has not had any changes in his diet, and he has not recently started any new drugs or OTCs. He is not actively bleeding. Which one of the following is the target INR for this patient?

    a. 1.5 (range of 1–2)
    b. 2.0 (range of 1.5–2.5)
    c. 2.5 (range of 2–3)
    d. 3.0 (range of 2.5–3.5)

26. A 48-year-old white woman comes to the clinic today to have her INR checked, and it is 3.4. She is currently taking 5 mg of warfarin on Mondays, Wednesdays, and Fridays and 7.5 mg on Tuesdays, Thursdays, Saturdays, and Sundays for a PE she had 3 months ago. Her last INR 4 weeks ago was 2.5. She has had no changes in her diet, and she has not recently started any new drugs or OTCs. She is not actively bleeding. Which of the following methods is best to manage this patient's therapy?

    a. Because the patient is not actively bleeding and there has been no change in diet or drugs, continue current regimen and have the patient come back to the clinic in 1 week to have her INR redrawn.
    b. Decrease the dosage to 5 mg on Mondays, Wednesdays, Fridays, and Saturdays and 7.5 mg on Tuesdays, Thursdays, and Sundays
    c. Decrease the dosage to 5 mg every day except for Mondays and Fridays and give 7.5 mg on Mondays and Fridays
    d. Decrease the dosage to 5 mg/day

27. A 37-year-old African American woman is currently taking 7.5 mg of warfarin daily for a DVT she had 2 months ago. Her last INR, 4 weeks ago, was 1.9. Today, her INR is 1.5. Which of the following is the most appropriate method for managing this patient's treatment?

    a. Increase the dosage to 7.5 mg on Tuesdays, Wednesdays, Thursdays, Saturdays, and Sundays and 11.25 mg on Mondays and Fridays
    b. Increase the dosage to 11.25 mg every day
    c. Increase the dosage to 11.25 mg on Sundays and 7.5 mg on Mondays, Tuesdays, Wednesdays, Thursdays, Fridays, and Saturdays
    d. It is not appropriate to increase the dose at this time. Have the patient come back to the clinic in 2 weeks to have her INR rechecked

28. Which of the following is the most appropriate way to administer vitamin K to a patient who is actively bleeding and whose INR is between 5 and 9?

    a. Give a 10-mg dose of vitamin K orally
    b. Give a 2.5-mg dose of vitamin K orally
    c. Give a 2-mg dose of vitamin K IV
    d. Vitamin K should never be used in a patient with an INR of 9 or less.

29. A patient calls your clinical complaining of bloody stools for about 3 days. She says that, at first, it was just a few streaks of blood, but it has become heavy.

Today, she saw a clot. She currently takes 7.5 mg of warfarin every day for a first-episode idiopathic DVT she had 2 months ago. She has been stable on this dosage of warfarin since it was initiated. She has not had any changes in her diet, nor has she recently started any new drugs or OTCs. Which of the following is the best recommendation to make?

a. Tell her to come to your clinic to have her INR checked.
b. Tell her to call you back in 2 days if the problem has not resolved.
c. Tell her to stop taking her warfarin until the problem resolves.
d. Tell her to go to the emergency department.

30. A patient with a first-episode DVT or PE with reversible risk factors should be treated with warfarin for which of the following periods

a. 6 weeks
b. 3 months
c. 6 months
d. 12 months

31. A patient with a first-episode idiopathic DVT or PE should be treated with warfarin for which of the following periods

a. 6 weeks
b. At least 3 to 6 months
c. At least 6 to 12 months
d. Indefinitely

32. A patient with a first-episode DVT or PE and documented antiphospholipid antibody syndrome should be treated for which of the following periods

a. Three months of therapy is recommended, and six months of therapy is suggested.
b. Six months of therapy is recommended, and twelve months of therapy is suggested.
c. Twelve months of therapy is recommended, and indefinite therapy is suggested.
d. You should always treat a patient indefinitely.

33. A 58-year-old white man currently takes 5 mg of warfarin every day for a first-episode idiopathic DVT he had 2 months ago. He has been stable on this dosage of warfarin since it was initiated. Currently, his INR is 2.4. He is scheduled to have his gallbladder removed in 1 week. Which of the following is the most appropriate way to manage this patient's therapy?

a. Reduce the dosage of warfarin by 50% (2.5 mg daily) and monitor closely for bleeding postoperatively.
b. Stop warfarin therapy on the day before surgery and then reinitiate it once surgery is completed.
c. Stop warfarin therapy 4 days before surgery. Initiate subcutaneous heparin or subcutaneous LMWH 2 days before surgery. Discontinue heparin or LMWH 12 hours before surgery. Reinitiate warfarin therapy once the surgery is over and overlap with heparin or LMWH.
d. Stop warfarin therapy 4 days before surgery. Initiate subcutaneous heparin or subcutaneous LMWH 2 days before surgery. Discontinue heparin or LMWH 12 hours before surgery. Reinitiate warfarin therapy once the surgery is over.

34. A patient with two or more episodes of documented DVT or PE should be treated for

a. 3 months
b. At least 6 months
c. 12 months
d. Indefinitely

35. A 64-year-old African American woman with persistent atrial fibrillation presents to the pharmacy with a prescription for warfarin 5 mg orally daily. Her atrial fibrillation is rate controlled with metoprolol. She has a medical history significant for HTN, DM, and CHF. Which of the following risk factors alone is not an indication for treatment of atrial fibrillation with warfarin?

a. Age (64 years)
b. HTN
c. DM
d. CHF

36. A 29-year-old African American man comes to your clinic today to have his INR checked, and it is 1.5. He currently takes 5 mg of warfarin every day. He has been stable on this dosage for a couple of months. On questioning the patient, you discover that he has incorporated spinach into his diet. He claims that he likes to eat about three servings of spinach per week. Which of the following is the most appropriate way to manage this patient's therapy?

a. Tell the patient that he must stop eating spinach and have him come back to the clinic in 2 weeks to recheck his INR.
b. Adjust the dosage of his warfarin accordingly, and tell him that he must stop eating spinach. Have him come back to the clinic in 2 weeks to recheck his INR.
c. Tell the patient that he can eat spinach as long as he eats it in consistent amounts each week. Adjust the dosage of his warfarin accordingly and have him come back to the clinic in 2 weeks to recheck his INR.
d. Tell the patient that he can eat spinach as long as he eats it every day in consistent amounts. Adjust the dosage of his warfarin accordingly and have him come back to the clinic in 2 weeks to recheck his INR.

37. A patient calls your clinical claiming that she has had a bad cold for about 4 days. Today, she blew her nose twice, and both times, she saw streaks of blood in her tissue. She is currently taking 5 mg of warfarin every day for rate-controlled atrial fibrillation. Which one of the following recommendations is best to make?

a. Tell her to come to your clinic to have her INR checked.
b. Tell her to call you back if her nose continues to bleed or if the bleeding becomes excessive.
c. Tell her to stop taking her warfarin until the problem resolves.
d. Tell her to go to the emergency department.

38. A 33-year-old white woman calls your clinic today to inform you that she is having a dental procedure (multiple extractions) performed in 2 weeks and is worried about taking her warfarin while she is getting the procedure done. Which of the following advice is best to give her?
    a. Dental procedures can cause significant bleeding, and she needs to stop warfarin therapy about 4 days before the procedure to allow her INR to return to normal. She should resume therapy with warfarin once the procedure is over.
    b. Dental procedures can cause significant bleeding, and she needs to stop warfarin therapy about 2 days before the procedure to allow her INR to return to normal. She should resume therapy with warfarin once the procedure is over.
    c. Dental procedures can cause significant bleeding, and she needs to stop warfarin therapy about 2 days before the procedure to allow her INR to return to normal. She should take lovenox injections while she is off warfarin to be appropriately anticoagulated. She should resume therapy with warfarin once the procedure is over.
    d. Although a dental procedure may cause some bleeding, it is not necessary to stop warfarin therapy before the procedure.

39. Indicate the effect each of the following would have on a patient's INR:
    a. Metronidazole
        1. Increase
        2. Decrease
    b. Synthroid
        1. Increase
        2. Decrease
    c. Fluconazole
        1. Increase
        2. Decrease
    d. Spinach
        1. Increase
        2. Decrease
    e. Amiodarone
        1. Increase
        2. Decrease
    f. Rifampin
        1. Increase
        2. Decrease
    g. Nafcillin
        1. Increase
        2. Decrease
    h. Hepatic dysfunction
        1. Increase
        2. Decrease
    i. Ginseng
        1. Increase
        2. Decrease
    j. Vitamin E
        1. Increase
        2. Decrease
    k. Coenzyme Q10
        1. Increase
        2. Decrease

40. A 43-year-old white woman comes to your pharmacy today with a prescription for amiodarone. She currently takes 5 mg of warfarin every day for a first-episode idiopathic DVT she had 6 weeks ago. She has been stable on this dosage of warfarin since it was initiated 6 weeks ago. Which of the following is the best way to manage this patient's drug therapy?
    a. Decrease the dosage to 4 mg every day
    b. Increase the dosage to 7.5 mg every day
    c. Decrease the dosage to 5 mg on Mondays, Wednesdays, Fridays, and Saturdays and 3 mg on Tuesdays, Thursdays, and Sundays
    d. Decrease the dosage to 2.5 mg every day

41. Which of the following is true regarding warfarin-induced skin necrosis?
    a. It is caused by the thrombosis of capillaries in the subcutaneous fat.
    b. There is an association between protein S deficiency and warfarin-induced skin necrosis.
    c. It most commonly occurs after the patient has been on warfarin for an extended period.

42. A 62-year-old white woman comes to your clinic today to have her INR checked, and it is 3.3 (goal INR of 2–3). She currently takes 7.5 mg of warfarin every day. She has been stable on this dosage for about 2 months. On questioning the patient, you discover that she has been taking metronidazole 500 mg orally 3 times daily. She is on day 6 of a 14-day course of therapy. Which of the following is the best way to manage this patient's situation?
    a. Call the patient's physician and have him or her change the drug to an antibiotic that will not interact with warfarin.
    b. Tell the patient to take 5 mg of warfarin while she is taking the metronidazole and, once her course of metronidazole is over, go back to 7.5 mg daily. Have her follow up in your clinic in 4 weeks.
    c. Do not make any changes at this time. Have the patient follow up in your clinic in 2 weeks.
    d. Do not make any changes at this time. Have the patient follow up in your clinic the day after she stops taking metronidazole therapy.

43. A 48-year-old African American woman comes to your clinic today to have her INR checked, and it is 3.1 (goal 2–3). She is currently taking 5 mg of warfarin on Mondays, Wednesdays, and Fridays and 7.5 mg on Tuesdays, Thursdays, Saturdays, and Sundays for a DVT she had 5 months ago. Her last INR 4 weeks ago was 2.8. She has had no changes in her diet, and she

has not recently started any new drugs or OTCs. She is not actively bleeding. Which of the following is the best way to manage this patient's drug regimen?

a. Because the patient is not actively bleeding and there has been no change to diet or drugs, continue current regimen and have patient come back to the clinic in 4 weeks to have INR redrawn.
b. Decrease the dose to 5 mg on Mondays, Wednesdays, Fridays, and Saturdays and 7.5 mg on Tuesdays, Thursdays, and Sundays.
c. Decrease the dose to 5 mg on every day except for Sunday, and give 7.5 mg on Sunday.
d. Decrease the dose to 5 mg every day.

44. A 25-year-old white man comes to the clinic today to have his INR checked, and it is 6.3 (goal 2–3). He is currently taking 5 mg of warfarin for a PE he had 3 months ago. He has had no changes in his diet, and he has not recently started any new drugs or OTCs. He is not actively bleeding or at risk of bleeding. Which of the following is the best way to manage this patient's therapy?

a. Tell the patient to hold the next two doses of warfarin and then take 5 mg on Mondays, Tuesdays, Wednesdays, Thursdays, Fridays, and Saturdays and 2.5 mg on Sunday. Have the patient follow up in 2 weeks.
b. Decrease the dosage of warfarin to 5 mg on Mondays, Wednesdays, Fridays, Saturdays, and Sundays and 2.5 mg on Tuesdays and Thursdays. Have the patient follow up in the clinic in 1 week.
c. Tell the patient to hold the next two doses of warfarin and then take 5 mg on Mondays, Wednesdays, Fridays, Saturdays, and Sundays and 2.5 mg on Tuesdays and Thursdays. Have the patient follow up in the clinic in 2 weeks.
d. Tell the patient to hold the next 2 doses of warfarin and then take 5 mg on Mondays, Wednesdays, Fridays, and Saturdays, and 2.5 mg on Tuesdays, Thursdays, and Sundays. Have the patient follow up in the clinic in 1 week.

45. A 38-year-old African American man comes to the clinic today to have his INR checked, and it is 9.5 (goal 2–3). He is currently taking 5 mg of warfarin for a DVT he had 6 months ago. He has had no changes in his diet, and he has not recently started any new drugs or OTCs. He is not actively bleeding. Which of the following is the best way to manage this patient's therapy?

a. Tell the patient to hold the next two doses of warfarin and then take 5 mg on Mondays, Wednesdays, Fridays, Saturdays, and Sundays and 2.5 mg on Tuesdays and Thursdays. Have the patient follow up in the clinic in 1 week.
b. Administer 2.5 mg of vitamin K orally. Hold the warfarin for the next 3 days and then decrease the dosage of warfarin to 5 mg on Mondays, Wednesdays, Fridays, Saturdays, and Sundays and 2.5 mg on Tuesdays and Thursdays. Have the patient follow up in the clinic in 1 week.
c. Administer 2.5 mg of vitamin K orally. Hold the warfarin and have the patient come back to the clinic to recheck his INR. Continue to hold warfarin until the INR is within the therapeutic range. Once INR is within range, decrease the dosage of warfarin to 5 mg on Mondays, Wednesdays, Fridays, and Saturdays and 2.5 mg on Tuesdays, Thursdays, and Sundays. Have the patient follow up in the clinic in 1 week.
d. Administer 2.5 mg of vitamin K orally. Hold the warfarin and have the patient come back to the clinic to recheck his INR. Continue to hold warfarin until the INR is within the therapeutic range. Once the INR is within range, decrease the dosage of warfarin to 5 mg on Mondays, Wednesdays, Fridays, Saturdays, and Sundays and 2.5 mg on Tuesdays and Thursdays. Have the patient follow up in the clinic in 1 week.

46. A 54-year-old white woman, currently being treated with warfarin for a DVT she had 3 months ago, calls your clinic today to inform you that she is having a percutaneous endoscopic gastrostomy tube placed in 3 weeks and is worried about taking her warfarin while she is having the procedure. Which of the following recommendations is best?

a. Endoscopic procedures can cause significant bleeding, and she needs to stop warfarin therapy about 5 days before the procedure to allow her INR to return to normal. She should resume therapy with warfarin once the procedure is over.
b. Endoscopic procedures can cause significant bleeding, and she needs to stop warfarin therapy about 5 days before the procedure to allow her INR to return to normal. She should begin enoxaparin (Lovenox) injections the same day she stops warfarin therapy to stay anticoagulated. She should resume therapy with warfarin once the procedure is over.
c. Endoscopic procedures can cause significant bleeding, and she should stop warfarin therapy about 2 days before the procedure to allow her INR to return to normal. She should take enoxaparin (Lovenox) injections while she is off warfarin to be appropriately anticoagulated. She should resume therapy with warfarin once the procedure is over.
d. Although endoscopic procedures may cause some bleeding, it is not necessary to stop warfarin therapy before the procedure.

PHARMACIST COMPETENCIES— SMOKING CESSATION

Submitted by: Jessica Starr

Created: June 2005

Learning Objectives

1. Compare and contrast both the health consequences of tobacco use and the benefits of cessation
2. Develop a general understanding of the pharmacology of nicotine use and dependence
3. Understand the Transtheoretical Model of Change and the ways in which it applies to smoking cessation
4. Describe how to use the National Cancer Institute's 5 A's when counseling patients on smoking cessation
5. Explain the importance of behavioral modifications in smoking cessation
6. Construct a smoking cessation plan using individually tailored interventions
7. Identify the advantages, disadvantages, and differences of the pharmacological aids for smoking cessation

References

1. Benowitz N, Dempsey D. Pharmacotherapy for smoking cessation during pregnancy. Nicotine Tob Res 2004;6:S189–S202.
2. Berger B, Braxton Lloyd K, Hudmon KS. The pharmacist's role in smoking cessation. Part 1. US Pharm 2001;May:57–64.
3. Berger B, Braxton Lloyd K, Hudmon KS. The pharmacist's role in smoking cessation. Part 2. US Pharm 2001;July:56–62.
4. Berger B. Change is a multistep process. US Pharm 1999;Oct:68–77.
5. Fagerstrom KF. The epidemiology of smoking, health consequences and benefits of cessation. Drugs 2002;62:1–9.
6. Fiore MC, Bailey WC, Cohen SJ, et al. A clinical practice guideline for treating tobacco use and dependence. A U.S. Public Health Service Report. JAMA 2000;283:3244–54.
7. Hughes JR, Shiffman S, Callas P, Zhang J. A meta-analysis of the efficacy of over-the-counter nicotine replacement. Tob Control 2003;12:21–7.
8. Joseph AM, Fu SS. Safety issues in pharmacotherapy for smoking in patients with cardiovascular disease. Prog Cardiovasc Dis 2003;45:429–41.
9. Sweeney CT, Fant RV, Fagerstrom KO, McGovern JF, Henningfield JE. Combination nicotine replacement therapy for smoking cessation: rationale, efficacy and tolerability. CNS Drugs 2001;15:453–67.
10. Velicer WF, Prochaska JO, Fava JL, Norman GJ, Redding CA. Smoking cessation and stress management: applications of the transtheoretical model of behavior change. Homeostasis 1998;38:216–33.
11. University of California, San Francisco. Rx for change: Clinician-assisted tobacco cessation. Available at http://rxforchange.ucsf.edu/. Accessed June 1, 2008.

Written Competency Examination

1. Which of the following is a symptom of nicotine withdrawal?
   A. HTN
   B. Decreased appetite
   C. Difficulty concentrating
   D. Bradycardia

2. Cigarette smoking substantially increases the risk of which of the following
   A. Stroke
   B. Respiratory track infections
   C. Spontaneous abortion
   D. Prostate cancer

3. The pharmacological properties of nicotine include
   A. Peripheral vasodilatation
   B. Stimulation of ganglionic adrenergic receptors
   C. Catecholamine release by the adrenal medulla
   D. Respiratory depression

4. Which of the following best reflects the symptoms associated with nicotine withdrawal?
   A. Symptoms usually start to occur about one week after cessation, reach a peak within the first month, and subside after about three months. The craving for nicotine may last for a year.
   B. Symptoms usually start to occur about one week after cessation, reach a peak within the first month, and subside after about three months. The craving for nicotine may never completely go away.
   C. Symptoms usually occur within hours of cessation, reach a peak within the first week, and then subside for several weeks. The craving for nicotine may last for a year.
   D. Symptoms usually occur within hours of cessation, reach a peak within the first week, and then subside for several weeks. The craving for nicotine may never completely go away.

5. According to the U.S. Public Health Service—Clinical Practice Guideline, the 5A's intervention is only effective in patients who
   A. Have expressed a desire to quit
   B. Are offered this intervention routinely and consistently at every visit
   C. Need to learn relapse prevention
   D. Have suffered medical complications from smoking

6. R.B., a 32-year-old white man, presents to the clinic today with a severe productive cough, shortness of breath, and increased temperature for 3 days and receives a diagnosis of acute bronchitis. He has received two previous diagnoses of acute bronchitis. He has smoked two packs of cigarettes/day for 8 years. He tried to quit last year using the patch but was only able to remain abstinent for 2 days. Which of the following is the best intervention for R.B. today?
   A. Nothing. R.B.'s failure to quit smoking on his first attempt indicates that he will be unable to quit in the future.
   B. See that R.B. receives appropriate treatment for his acute bronchitis today and offer him smoking cessation counseling at a subsequent visit.
   C. See that R.B. receives appropriate treatment for his acute bronchitis today and ask him if he is willing to quit at this time.
   D. It is inappropriate to continue to discuss R.B.'s smoking habit because he is already aware of the health implications from the media.

7. All patients should be offered pharmacotherapy to aid in smoking cessation, except under special circumstances. Which of the following populations would you consider giving special consideration?
   A. Elderly patients
   B. Patients smoking fewer than 10 cigarettes/day
   C. Women of childbearing age
   D. Patients with asthma or COPD

8. When assisting a patient who is ready to quit smoking, which of the following is the most appropriate recommendation?
   A. Discuss smoking triggers and the ways in which the patient will successfully overcome them.
   B. Encourage the patient to smoke only if the urge gets really bad.
   C. Encourage the patient to cut out the least favorite cigarettes of the day first and then gradually work up to eliminating the favorite cigarette of the day.
   D. Recommend that the patient set up a 2-week taper that gradually cuts back on the number of cigarettes the patient is smoking before the quit date.

9. Which of the following interventions should be implemented in all smokers who present to your clinic?
   A. Advise the patient to quit smoking.
   B. Set a quit date for the patient.
   C. Help the patient pick a pharmaceutical aid to facilitate in the quitting process.
   D. Develop a comprehensive quit plan for the patient.

10. When helping patients in the preparation stage create a smoking cessation quit plan, which of the following should be done?
    A. Set up a 2-week taper that gradually cuts back on the number of cigarettes the patient is smoking before the quit date.
    B. Set up a 4-week taper that gradually cuts back on the number of cigarettes the patient is smoking before the quit date.
    C. Set a quit date within 2 weeks.
    D. Set a quit date within 4 weeks.

11. M.R., a 28-year-old white woman, presents to your clinic today for anticoagulation follow-up. She has a 10 pack-year history of smoking. You advise her to quit smoking and assess her readiness to quit. She states that she is willing to quit within the next 30 days. Which of the following is the best action for you to take at this time?
    A. Help her identify the rewards of quitting.
    B. Help her identify the negative consequences of smoking.
    C. Reinforce why quitting is personally relevant.
    D. Help her identify events that increase the risk of smoking or relapse.

12. M.T. is a 45-year-old white woman who has a 30 pack-year history of smoking. She comes to ask for your help with quitting smoking. She has been going to night school and states that she thinks she will be able to quit smoking in about 2 months when her final examinations are over. Which one of the following stages of change is M.T. in?
    A. Precontemplation
    B. Contemplation
    C. Preparation
    D. Action

13. M.T., a 45-year-old white woman, comes to you today for your help with smoking cessation. She thinks she will be able to quit smoking in about 2 months when her final examinations are over. Which of the following is the best thing you can do for M.T. at this point?
    A. Set patient-specific goals and remove barriers to change.
    B. Develop a plan of action and praise the patient for readiness to quit smoking.
    C. Discuss with the patient what she anticipates to be the greatest obstacles to overcome and what she perceives as the benefits of smoking cessation.
    D. Develop discrepancies (pros and cons) by asking the patient what she likes and dislikes about smoking.

14. M.T., a 45-year-old white woman, has been working with you for the past month on setting up a smoking cessation plan. She is in the preparation stage, and a quit date has been set. She is currently smoking 20 cigarettes/day. She wants your help in picking a pharmacological product to aid her in this process. She has not previously tried any products. Which one of the following products do you recommend?
    A. Nicotine patch 14 mg/day for 6 weeks and then 7 mg/day for 2 weeks
    B. Bupropion (Zyban) 150 mg orally every 12 hours for 12 weeks
    C. Nicotine gum 2 mg every 1 to 2 hours for the first 6 weeks and then every 2 to 4 hours for the next 3 weeks; finally, every 4 to 8 hours for the last 2 weeks
    D. Nicotine nasal spray 1 dose every 15 minutes for a maximum of 80 doses in 1 day for 12 weeks

15. M.T. is a 45-year-old white woman who has smoked 2 packs per day for 5 years. She is in the preparation stage, and a quit date has been set. Follow-up care must be arranged. Which of the following is the best follow-up plan for M.T.?
    A. Tell her to call your office if she has any questions.
    B. Schedule a follow-up visit in 1 month to check on her quit status.
    C. Arrange a follow-up visit within 1 week after her quit date.
    D. Give her a pamphlet about the benefits of quitting smoking.

16. S.F. comes to you today because she started using the nicotine patch about a week ago and is having trouble sleeping at night. She wakes up often during the night because of abnormal and vivid dreams. Which one of the following actions do you recommend?
    A. Tell her to take the patch off before she goes to bed at night and then apply a new patch each morning.
    B. Discontinue the patch because vivid dreams and night awakenings are an adverse effect of the patch that will not go away.
    C. Initiate bupropion (Zyban) because it will help with the dreams and night awakenings and facilitate the smoking cessation process.
    D. Tell her to wear the patch only at night and to use another form of nicotine replacement during the day (gum, lozenge, inhaler, or nasal spray).

17. B.A. used to smoke 15 cigarettes per day but has been using the nicotine patch 21 mg/day for several weeks to aid in smoking cessation. He claims that he has not had a cigarette since his quit date but that sometimes, the "cravings are really bad." He wants to

start nicotine gum in addition to the patch to help with the cravings. Which of the following is the best advice to give him?
- A. He cannot take two forms of nicotine replacement at the same time. If he needs a product to help with the cravings, then he should discontinue the patch and start using the gum.
- B. Decrease the dosage of the patch to 7 mg/day and start nicotine gum at a dosage of 2 mg every 1 to 2 hours.
- C. Decrease the dosage of the patch to 14 mg/day and start nicotine gum at a dosage of 4 mg every 1 to 2 hours.
- **D. Start nicotine gum at a dose of 2 mg whenever he craves a cigarette.**

18. C.S., a 54-year-old white woman, is hesitant to quit smoking because she is worried that she will gain weight. Her husband quit smoking cold turkey 2 years ago and gained 20 pounds. She wants to know if there is any pharmacological product that will prevent her from gaining weight. Which one of the following is best to tell her?
    - A. All nicotine replacement therapies prevent weight gain.
    - B. Bupropion (Zyban) has been shown to prevent weight gain.
    - C. Nicotine gum has been shown to prevent weight gain.
    - **D. Nicotine gum and bupropion (Zyban) have been shown to delay, but not prevent, weight gain.**

19. C.B., a 32-year-old African American man, has a 15 pack-year history of smoking. He comes to you today because he is ready to quit smoking. His son recently received a diagnosis of asthma, and he states that now is finally the time to quit. He has tried quitting a couple of times in the past without success. Which one of the following stages of change is C.B. in?
    - A. Precontemplation
    - B. Contemplation
    - **C. Preparation**
    - D. Action

20. C.B., a 32-year-old African American man, has a son who recently received a diagnosis of asthma, and he has come to you today because he is finally ready to quit smoking. He has tried quitting in the past without luck but has decided that now is the time. Which one of the following is the best intervention for C.B. today?
    - **A. Help the patient set goals and remove barriers to change.**
    - B. Recommend that the patient buy a pack of nicotine gum and starting chewing tomorrow.
    - C. Discuss with the patient what he anticipates to be the greatest obstacles to overcome and what he perceives as the benefits.
    - D. Develop discrepancies by asking the patient what he likes and dislikes about smoking.

21. C.B., a 32-year-old African American man, is ready to stop smoking. After thoroughly discussing all pharmacological treatment options, you decide that bupropion (Zyban) is the most appropriate option for C.B. at this time. Which one of the following recommendations is best to help C.B. take his drug?
    - A. Start bupropion (Zyban) on your quit date at a dosage of 150 mg daily for 3 days and then increase the dosage to 150 mg twice daily. Allow at least 8 hours between doses and avoid taking them at bedtime to minimize insomnia.
    - B. Start bupropion (Zyban) on your quit date at a dosage of 150 mg twice daily. Allow at least 12 hours between doses and avoid taking them at bedtime to minimize insomnia.
    - C. Start bupropion (Zyban) 3 days before your quit date at a dosage of 150 mg daily for 3 days. On your quit date, increase the dosage to 150 mg twice daily. Allow at least 8 hours between doses and avoid taking at bedtime to minimize insomnia.
    - **D. Start bupropion (Zyban) while you are still smoking and set a quit date 1 to 2 weeks after the initiation of therapy. Start at a dosage of 150 mg daily for 3 days; then, increase the dosage to 150 mg twice daily. Allow at least 8 hours between doses and avoid taking at bedtime to minimize insomnia.**

22. C.B., a 32-year-old African American man, has been taking bupropion (Zyban) for several weeks now and claims that he has not had a cigarette since his quit date but that sometimes, the "cravings are really bad." He wants to start nicotine gum in addition to the bupropion (Zyban) to help with the cravings. Which one of the following is the best advice to give him?
    - **A. Bupropion (Zyban) can be used safely with the nicotine gum and other forms of nicotine replacement therapy.**
    - B. Nicotine replacement therapy cannot be given in combination with bupropion (Zyban).
    - C. Only the nicotine patch can be given in combination with bupropion (Zyban).
    - D. The gum can be given in combination, but you must use only half of the recommended dose.

23. B.A., 45-year-old white woman, has been taking bupropion (Zyban) for 9 weeks and is not able to abstain from smoking completely. She reports that she cheats all the time. Which of the following is the best recommendation for B.A.?
    - A. Increase the dosage of bupropion (Zyban) to 150

mg orally 3 times daily and reassess in 4 weeks.

B. Discontinue the bupropion (Zyban). Patients who have not made significant progress after 7 weeks usually will not be able to achieve total abstinence.

C. Continue bupropion (Zyban) for a total of 12 weeks and then reassess. Many patients require prolonged duration of therapy before they are able to achieve complete abstinence.

D. Recommend adding the nicotine patch 21 mg in addition to the bupropion (Zyban) and reassess in 4 weeks. Patients commonly need an additional form of nicotine replacement therapy before they are able to achieve total abstinence.

24. N.W., a 46-year-old white man, wants to start using the nicotine inhaler because he thinks he will need a product that mimics the hand-to-mouth ritual of smoking. How do you counsel this patient to use this product?

A. Use the inhaler only when you are craving a cigarette. Puff on the inhaler until the craving goes away. Take quick, short puffs to prevent inhalation into the lungs. Do not use more than 4 cartridges per day.

B. Use the inhaler only when you are craving a cigarette. Puff on the inhaler continuously for 20 minutes and then dispose of it. Take quick, short puffs to prevent inhalation into the lungs. Do not use more than 6 cartridges per day.

C. Use at least 6 cartridges per day. Puff on the inhaler continuously for 20 minutes and then dispose of it. Take quick, short puffs to prevent inhalation into the lungs. Do not use more than 16 cartridges per day.

D. Use at least 6 cartridges per day. Puff on the inhaler continuously for 20 minutes and then dispose of it. Inhale with deep puffs to achieve adequate concentrations into the lungs. Do not use more than 16 cartridges per day.

25. A 28-year-old African American woman presents to your clinic today for help with smoking cessation. She recently bought nicotine gum but claims that it made her so nauseated she could not take it. She wants your help in choosing a product that will not make her so sick. Which one of the following should you tell her?

A. Most nicotine replacement therapies make you sick, so the best you can recommend is a lower dose of the gum.

B. Try chewing the gum immediately after you are finished eating to help minimize GI tract upset.

C. This is how to properly use nicotine gum; call me if you are still experiencing nausea after proper use.

D. Get a prescription for promethazine to take with the gum to help with the nausea.

26. M.J., a 29-year-old white man, has been working with you for the past month to set up a smoking cessation plan. He is in the preparation stage, and a quit date has been set. You decide that the best product for M.J. at this time is nicotine gum. Which of the following represents the best way to counsel M.J. on its use?

A. Chew each piece slowly and consistently. Once the tingling sensation goes away, spit out the piece of gum. Chew a new piece every 1 to 2 hours for the first 6 weeks of therapy. Do not eat or drink for the 15 minutes before or during use.

B. Chew each piece slowly and then park between cheek and gum when tingling sensation begins. Resume chewing when tingling fades, and repeat process until the tingling does not return. Chew a new piece every 1 to 2 hours for the first 6 weeks of therapy. Do not eat or drink for the 15 minutes before or during use.

C. Chew each piece slowly and then park between cheek and gum when tingling sensation begins. Once tingling sensation goes away, spit out the gum. Chew a new piece every 15 minutes for the first 6 weeks of therapy. Do not eat or drink for the 30 minutes before or during use.

D. Chew each piece slowly and then park between cheek and gum when tingling sensation begins. Resume chewing when tingling fades, and repeat process until the tingling does not return. Chew a new piece every 30 minutes for the first 6 weeks of therapy. Do not eat or drink for the 30 minutes before or during use.

27. A 43-year-old African American man with a medical history significant for HTN and DM presents to your clinic today to talk with you about pharmacological aids to help him quit smoking. He heard from a friend that nicotine replacement therapy should not be used in patients with high BP or other types of cardiovascular disease. Which of the following responses is best?

A. His friend is correct; patients with cardiovascular disease should not use any type of nicotine replacement therapy. Help him find an alternative to aid in smoking cessation.

B. He can use nicotine replacement therapy but only at half of the recommended dose. Help him pick an appropriate product.

C. He can use nicotine replacement therapy but only if his BP is tightly controlled. Help him pick an appropriate product and encourage him to come to you weekly while he takes the nicotine replacement therapy to get his BP checked.

D. Nicotine replacement therapy is safe in patients with cardiovascular disease, particularly the patch. Help him pick an appropriate product.

28. J.S., a 26-year-old white woman, has been coming to you for about 8 months for help with smoking cessation. Her quit date was about 6½ months ago, and she has had great success using both bupropion (Zyban) and the nicotine inhaler. She is concerned because she heard that she should not continue to use her smoking cessation products long term, and she is worried that she will start smoking again if she has to stop using them. Which of the following recommendations should you make?
    A. She can continue taking the bupropion (Zyban) but must discontinue the inhaler.
    B. She can continue taking both drugs long term; however, she should only use the inhaler when she really needs it.
    C. She can continue using the inhaler when she really needs it, but she should stop the bupropion (Zyban). If she relapses, then she can try another 3 months of Zyban.
    D. She must discontinue both drugs. If she starts smoking again, then she can set another quit date and try a different pharmaceutical aid.

SELECTED REFERENCES

Clinical Services

Pharmacists in Primary/Ambulatory Care

Ables AZ, Baughman OL III. The clinical pharmacist as a preceptor in a family practice residency training program. Fam Med 2002;34:658–62.

Adler DA, Bungay KM, Wilson IB, et al. The impact of a pharmacist intervention on 6-month outcomes in depressed primary care patients. Gen Hosp Psychiatry 2004;26:199–209.

Alsuwaidan S, Malone DC, Billups SJ, Carter BL for the IMPROVE Investigators. Characteristics of ambulatory care clinics and pharmacists in Veterans Affairs medical centers. Am J Health Syst Pharm 1998;555:68–72.

American College of Clinical Pharmacy White Paper. Establishing and evaluating clinical pharmacy services in primary care. Pharmacotherapy 1994;14:743–58.

American Society of Health-System Pharmacists. Statement on the pharmacist's role in primary care. Am J Health Syst Pharm 2000;56:1665–7.

Amruso NA. Ability of clinical pharmacists in a community pharmacy setting to manage anticoagulation therapy. J Am Pharm Assoc 2004;44:467–71.

Anastasio GD, Dutro MP, Parent LS. Applying family medicine concepts to prescribing [Letter]. Fam Med 1986;18:259.

Anastasio GD, Sigmon JL. Prescription-writing errors [Letter]. J Fam Pract 1990;30:108.

Anastasio GD, White TR, Fries JC. Computerized prescription inventory program for the education of residents (PIPER). J Fam Pract 1986;23:598–600.

Armour CL, Taylor SJ, Hourihan F, et al. Implementation and evaluation of Australian pharmacists' diabetes care services. J Am Pharm Assoc 2004;44:455–66.

Baumgartner RP, Land MJ, Hauser LD. Rural health care: opportunity for innovative pharmacy services. Am J Hosp Pharm 1972;29:94–400.

Beaucage K, Lachance-demers H, Ngo TT, et al. Telephone follow-up of patients receiving antibiotic prescriptions from community pharmacies. Am J Health Syst Pharm 2006;63:557–63.

Beck JK, Dries TJ, Cooke EC. Development of an interdisciplinary, telephone-based care program. Am J Health Syst Pharm 1998;55:453–7.

Blake EW, Blair MM, Couchenour RL. Perceptions of pharmacists as providers of immunizations for adult patients. Pharmacotherapy 2003;23:248–54.

Blakey SA, Hixson-Wallace JA. Clinical and economic effects of pharmacy services in a geriatric ambulatory clinic. Pharmacotherapy 1999;20:1198–203.

Bogden PE, Abbott RD, Williamson P, et al. Comparing standard care with a physician and pharmacist team approach for uncontrolled hypertension. J Gen Intern Med 1998;12:740–5.

Bond CA, Monson R. Sustained improvement in drug documentation, compliance, and disease control: A four-year analysis of an ambulatory care model. Arch Intern Med 1984;144:1159–62.

Borenstein JE, Graber G, Saltiel E, et al. Physician-pharmacist comanagement of hypertension: A randomized, comparative trial. Pharmacotherapy 2003;23:209–16.

Borgsdorf LR, Miano JS, Knapp KK. Pharmacist-managed drug review in a managed care system. Am J Hosp Pharm 1994;51:772–7.

Brown CA, Bailey JH, Lee J, et al. The pharmacist-physician relationship in the detection of ambulatory drug errors. Am J Med Sci 2006;331:22–4.

Brown D, Helling DK, Jones ME. Evaluation of clinical pharmacist consultations in a family practice office. AJHP 1979;36:912–5.

Brown JM, Helling DK, Alexander MM, Burmeister LF. Comparative evaluation of clinical pharmacists and physicians in the management of drug-related telephone calls in family practice offices. Am J Hosp Pharm 1982;39:437–43.

Bucci KK, Frey KA. A description of a pharmacotherapy curriculum in a university-based family medicine program. Ann Pharmacother 1992;26:991–4.

Bucci KK, Frey KA. Involvement of pharmacy faculty in the development of policies for pharmaceutical sales representatives. J Fam Pract 1992;34:49–52.

Bucci KK, Weart CW, Carson DS, Shaughnessy AF. Ambulatory care pharmacy services at the Family Medicine Center of the Medical University of South Carolina. Top Hosp Pharm Manage 1988;8:11–8.

Bungay KM, Adler DA, Rogers WH, et al. Description of a clinical pharmacist intervention administered to primary care patients with depression. Gen Hosp Psychiatry 2004;26:210–8.

Capoccia KL, Boudreau DM, Blough DK, et al. Randomized trial of pharmacist interventions to improve depression care and outcomes in primary care. Am J Health Syst Pharm 2004;61:364–72.

Carmichael JM, O'Connell MB, Devine B, et al. Collaborative drug therapy management by pharmacists. ACCP Position Statement. Pharmacotherapy 1997;17:1050–61.

Caro JJ, Lee K. Pharmacoeconomic evaluation of a pharmacist-managed hypertension clinic. Hypertens Rep 2002;4:418.

Carter BL, Helling DK. Ambulatory care pharmacy services: The incomplete agenda. Ann Pharmacother 1992;26:701–7.

Carter BL, Helling DK. Ambulatory care pharmacy services: Has the agenda changed? Ann Pharmacother 2000;34:772–86.

Carter BL, Helling DK, Jones ME, et al. Evaluation of family physician prescribing: Influence of the clinical pharmacist. Drug Intell Clin Pharm 1984;18:817–21.

Carter BL, Helling DK, Jones ME, Friedman RL, Ellsworth A. Multicenter study of family physician prescribing. J Fam Pract 1984;19:497–501.

Carter BL, Zillich AJ, Elliott WJ. How pharmacists can assist physicians with controlling blood pressure. J Clin Hypertens 2003;5:31–7.

Cassidy IB, Keith MR, Coffey EL, Noyes MA. Impact of pharmacist-operated general medicine chronic care refill clinics on practitioner time and quality of care. Ann Pharmacother 1996;30:745–51.

Catizone C, Mrtek RG. Office-based pharmacy in the United States: The development of a practice alternative. Am Pharm 1984;24:24–32.

Chabot I, Moisan J, Gregoire JP, et al. Pharmacist intervention program for control of hypertension. Ann Pharmacother 2003;37:1186–93.

Chen J, Britten N. Strong medicine: An analysis of pharmacist consultations in primary care. Fam Pract 2000;17:480–3.

Chi J. Documentation in patient records is key when physicians sue pharmacists. Hosp Pharm Rep 1991;48:37–8.

Chiquette E, Amato MG, Bussey HI. Comparison of an anticoagulation clinic with usual medical care. Arch Intern Med 1998;158:1641–7.

Chisholm MA, Mulloy LL, Jagadeesan M, et al. Impact of clinical pharmacy services on renal transplant patients' compliance with immunosuppressive drugs. Clin Transplant 2001;15:330–6.

Chisolm MA, Mulloy LL, Jagadeesan M, et al. Effect of clinical pharmacy services on the blood pressure of African-American renal transplant patients. Ethn Dis 2002;12:392–7.

Chrischilles EA, Helling DK, Aschoff CR. Effect of clinical pharmacy services of the quality of family practice physicians prescribing and drug costs. Ann Pharmacother 1989;23:417–21.

Chrischilles EA, Helling DK, Rowland CR. Model for cost-benefit analysis of clinical pharmacy in family practice. AJHP 1982;39:992–8.

Chrischilles EA, Helling DK, Rowland CR. Clinical pharmacy services in family practice: Cost-benefit analysis I: physician time and quality of care. Drug Intell Clin Pharm 1984;18:333–41.

Chrischilles EA, Helling DK, Rowland CR. Clinical pharmacy services in family practice: Cost-benefit analysis II: Referrals, appointment compliance, and costs. Drug Intell Clin Pharm 1984;18:436–41.

Chrischilles EA, Helling DK, Rowland CR. Cost-benefit analysis of clinical pharmacy services in three Iowa family practice offices. J Clin Hosp Pharm 1985;10:59–66.

Cioffi ST, Caron MF, Kalus JS, et al. Glycosylated hemoglobin, cardiovascular, and renal outcomes in a pharmacist-managed clinic. Ann Pharmacother 2004;38:771–5.

Clifford RM, Davis WA, Batty KT, et al. Effect of a pharmaceutical care program on vascular risk factors in type 2 diabetes: The Fremantle diabetes study. Diabetes Care 2005;28:771–6.

Coast-Senior EA, Kroner BA, Kelley CL, et al. Management of patients with type 2 diabetes by pharmacists in primary care clinics. Ann Pharmacother 1998;32:636–41.

Connelly DP, Rich EC, Curley SP, Kelly JT. Knowledge resource preferences of family physicians. J Fam Pract 1990;30:353–9.

Corey G. Clinical pharmacy in family practice [Letter]. J Fam Pract 1990;31:670–2.

Cranor CW, Buntin BA, Christensen DB. The Asheville project: Long-term clinical and economic outcomes of a community pharmacy diabetes care program. J Am Pharm Assoc 2003;43:173–84.

Curtiss FR. Clinical pharmacist intervention in a primary care medical group reduces financial losses [Comment]. J Manage Care Pharm 2004;10:355.

D'Achille KM, Swanson LN, Hill WT Jr. Pharmacist-managed patient assessment and drug refill clinic. Am J Hosp Pharm 1978;35:66–70.

D'Angelo AC. The family pharmacist [Editorial]. Drug Intell Clin Pharm 1979;13:347.

Davidson MB, Karlan VJ, Hair TL. Effect of a pharmacist-managed diabetes care program in a free medical clinic. Am J Med Qual 2000;15:137–42.

Davis RE, Crigler WH, Martin H. Pharmacy and family practice: Concept, roles and fees. Drug Intell Clin Pharm 1977;11:616–21.

Dent LA, Scott, JG, Lewis E. Pharmacist-managed tobacco cessation program in Veteran's Health Administration community-based outpatient clinic. J Am Pharm Assoc 2004;44:700–15.

Dickerson LM, Denham AM, Lynch T. The state of clinical pharmacy practice in family practice residency programs. Fam Med 2002;34:653–7.

Dunham DM, Stewart RD, Laucka PV. Low-density-lipoprotein cholesterol in patients treated by a lipid clinic versus a primary care clinic. Am J Health Syst Pharm 2000;57:2285–6.

Ellis SL, Carter BL, Malone DC, et al. Clinical and economic impact of ambulatory care clinical pharmacists in management of dyslipidemia in older adults: The IMPROVE study. Pharmacotherapy 2000;20:1508–16.

Emmerton L, Shaw J, Kheir N. Asthma management by New Zealand pharmacists: A pharmaceutical care demonstration project. J Clin Pharm Ther 2003;28:395–402.

Erikson SH. Closing the sample closet. Fam Pract Manag 1995;43–7.

Ernst ME, Brandt KB. Evaluation of 4 years of clinical pharmacist anticoagulation case management in a rural, private physician office. J Am Pharm Assoc 2003;43:630–6.

Finley PR, Rens HR, Pont JT, et al. Impact of a collaborative care model on depression in a primary care setting: a randomized controlled trial. Pharmacotherapy 2003;23:1175–85.

Forstrom MJ, Ried LD, Stergachis AS, et al. Effect of a clinical pharmacist program on the cost of hypertension treatment in an HMO family practice clinic. Drug Intell Clin Pharm 1990;24:304–9.

Galt KA. Cost avoidance, acceptance and outcomes associated with a pharmacotherapy consult clinic in a Veterans Affairs Medical Center. Pharmacotherapy 1998;18:1103–11.

Garrett DG, Bluml BM. Patient self-management program for diabetes: First-year clinical, humanistic, and economic outcomes. J Am Pharm Assoc 2005;45:130–7.

Gattis WA, Hasselblad V, Whellan DJ, et al. Reduction in heart failure events by the addition of a clinical pharmacist to the heart failure management team; results of the PHARM study. Arch Intern Med 1999;159:1939–45.

Geber J, Parra D, Beckey NP, et al. Optimizing drug therapy in patients with cardiovascular disease: The impact of pharmacist-managed pharmacotherapy clinics in a primary care setting. Pharmacotherapy 2002;22:738–47.

Geyman JP. Clinical pharmacy in family practice. J Fam Pract 1980;10:21–2.

Gourley DR, Gourley GA, Solomon DK, et al. Part 1. Development, implementation, and evaluation of a multicenter pharmaceutical care outcomes study. J Am Pharm Assoc 1998;38:567–73.

Gourley GA, Portner TS, Gourley DR, et al. Part 3. Humanistic outcomes in the hypertension and COPD arms of a multicenter outcomes study. J Am Pharm Assoc 1998;38:586–97.

Grace KA, McPherson MI, Burstein AH. Diabetes care and cost of pharmacotherapy versus medical services. Am J Health Syst Pharm 1998;55(suppl 4):S27–9.

Grainger-Roussear TJ, Miralles MA, et al. Therapeutic outcomes monitoring: Application of pharmaceutical care guidelines to community pharmacy. J Am Pharm Assoc 1997;37:647–61.

Grindrod KA, Patel P, Martin JE. What interventions should pharmacists employ to impact health practitioners' prescribing practices? Ann Pharmacother 2006;40:1546–57.

Gums J. Recent advances: Ambulatory care and family medicine. Ann Pharmacother 1995;29:716–8.

Hammond RW, Schwartz AH, Campbell MJ, et al. Collaborative drug therapy management by pharmacists—2003. Pharmacotherapy 2003;23:1210–25.

Hanlon JT, Andolsek KM, Clapp-Channing NE, Gehlbach SH. Drug prescribing in a family medicine residency program with a pharmacotherapeutics curriculum. J Med Educ 1986;61:64–7.

Hanlon JT, Weinberger M, Samsa GP, et al. A randomized, controlled trial of a clinical pharmacist intervention to improve inappropriate prescribing in elderly patients with polypharmacy. Am J Med 1996;100:428–37.

Hatoum HT, Witte KW, Hutchinson RA. Patient care contributions of clinical pharmacists in four ambulatory care clinics. Hosp Pharm 1992;27:203–6, 208–9.

Hawkins DW, Fiedler FP, Douglas H, Eschbach RC. Evaluation of a clinical pharmacist in caring for hypertensive and diabetic patients. Am J Hosp Pharm 1979;36:1321–5.

Haxby DG, Weart CW, Goodman BW. Family practice physicians' perceptions of the usefulness of drug therapy recommendations from clinical pharmacists. Am J Hosp Pharm 1988;45:824–7.

Helling DK, Hepler CD, Jones ME. Effect of direct clinical pharmaceutical services on patients' perceptions of health care quality. Am J Hosp Pharm 1979;36:325–9.

Hobson RJ, Sewell GJ. Supplementary prescribing by pharmacists in England. Am J Health Syst Pharm 2006;63:244–53.

Holsclaw SL, Olson KL, Hornak R, et al. Assessment of patient satisfaction with telephone and mail interventions provided by a clinical pharmacy risk reduction service. J Manage Care Pharm 2005;11:403–9.

Howell RR, Jones KW. Prescription-writing errors and markers: The value of knowing the diagnosis. Fam Med 1993;25:104–6.

Hume AL. Sources of influence on the prescribing practices of residents in family medicine [Letter]. Drug Intell Clin Pharm 1991;25:102–3.

Isetts BJ, Brown LM, Schondelmeyer SW, et al. Quality assessment of a collaborative approach for decreasing drug-related morbidity and achieving therapeutic goals. Arch Intern Med 2003;163:1813–20.

Ives TJ, Parry JL, Gwyther RE. Serum drug level utilization review in a family medicine residency program. J Fam Pract 1984;19:507–12.

Jaber LA, Halapy H, Fernet M, et al. Evaluation of a pharmaceutical care model on diabetes management. Ann Pharmacother 1996;30:238–43.

Jackson AB, Humphries TL, Nelson KM, et al. Clinical pharmacy travel medicine services: A new frontier. Ann Pharmacother 2004;38:2160–5.

Jackson EA. The role of pharmacists in family practice residency programs [Comment]. Fam Med 2002;34:692–3.

Jackson MJ, Drechsler-Martell CR, Jackson EA. Family practice residents' prescribing patterns. Drug Intell Clin Pharm 1985;19:205–9.

Johnson JA, Bootman JL. Drug-related morbidity and mortality: A cost-of-illness model. Arch Intern Med 1995;155:1949–56.

Johnston TS, Heffron WA. Clinical pharmacy in family practice residency programs. J Fam Pract 1981;13:91–4.

Jones RA, Lopez LM, Beall DG. Cost-effective implementation of clinical pharmacy services in an ambulatory care clinic. Hosp Pharm 1991;26:778–82.

Joy MS, DeHart RM, Gilmartin C, et al. Clinical pharmacists as multidisciplinary health care providers in the management of CKD: A joint opinion by the nephrology and ambulatory care practice and research networks of the American College of Clinical Pharmacy [Editorial]. Am J Kidney Dis 2005;45:1105–18.

Juhl RP, Perry PJ, Norwood GJ, Martin LR. The family practitioner-clinical pharmacist group practice: A model clinic. Drug Intell Clin Pharm 1974;8:572–5.

Kahn RF, Spadaro DC, Price RD. Pharmacy teaching for family practice residents. Fam Med 1985;27:24–5.

Kalister H, Newman RD, Read L, et al. Pharmacy-based evaluation and treatment of minor illnesses in a culturally diverse pediatric clinic. Arch Pediatr Adolesc Med 1999;153:731–5.

Karig AW, James JD. Educating the doctor of pharmacy student in the family practice setting. Drug Intell Clin Pharm 1978;12:36–9.

Kiel PJ, McCord AD. Pharmacist impact on clinical outcomes in a diabetes disease management program via collaborative practice. Ann Pharmacother 2005;39:1828–32.

Kiel PJ, McCord AD. Collaborative practice agreement for diabetes management [Letter]. Am J Health Syst Pharm 2006;63:209–10.

Klockars SJ, Blair MM, Ragucci K. Survey of clinical pharmacy services in a family medicine clinic [Letter]. Am J Health Syst Pharm 2003;60:485–6.

Knoell DL, Pierson JF, Marsh CB, et al. Measurement of outcomes in adults receiving pharmaceutical care in a comprehensive asthma outpatient clinic. Pharmacotherapy 1998;18:1365–74.

Knowlton CH, Zarus SA, Voltis O. Pharmacy-based therapeutic drug monitoring. Am Pharm 1993;33:57–64.

Koechelar JA, Sfeir TL, Wilson B. Outcome-focused counseling program for quality assurance in ambulatory care. Am J Hosp Pharm 1990;47:2020–2.

Koffler AB, See S, Mumford J, et al. Implementing and evaluating a pharmacy consult service within a family medicine residency program. Am J Health Syst Pharm 2002;59:1200–4.

Lai LL, Sorkin AL. Cost-benefit analysis of pharmaceutical care in a Medicaid population: from a budgetary perspective. J Manage Care Pharm 1998;4:303–8.

Leal S, Glover JJ, Herrier RN, et al. Improving quality of care in diabetes through a comprehensive pharmacist-based disease management program. Diabetes Care 2004;27:2983–4.

Leal S, Soto M. Pharmacists disease state management through a collaborative practice model. J Health Care Poor Underserved 2005;16:220–4.

Lee JK, Grace KA, Taylor AJ. Effect of a pharmacy care program on drug adherence and persistence, blood pressure, and low-density lipoprotein cholesterol. JAMA 2006;296:2563–71.

Letassy NA, Armor BL, Britton M, Farmer K. Pharmacist-managed diabetes service in a family medicine practice improves patient outcomes. Diabetes Trends 2003;15:21–32.

Libby EA, Laub JJ. Economic and clinical impact of a pharmacy-based antihypertensive replacement program in primary care. Am J Health Syst Pharm 1997;54:2079–83.

Lobas NH, Lepinski PW, Abramowitz PW. Effects of pharmaceutical care on drug cost and quality of patient care in an ambulatory care clinic. AJHP 1992;49:1681–8.

Love DW, Hodge NA, Foley WA. The clinical pharmacist in a family practice residency program. J Fam Pract 1980;10:67–72.

Ludy JA, Gagnon JP, Caiola SM. The patient-pharmacist interaction in two ambulatory settings: Its relationship to patient satisfaction and drug misuse. Drug Intell Clin Pharm 1977;11:81–9.

Luzier AB, Forrest A, Feuerstein SG, et al. Containment of heart failure hospitalizations and cost by angiotensin-converting enzyme inhibitor dosage optimization. Am J Cardiol 2000;86:519–23.

Madaras-Kelly KJ, Hannah EL, Bateman K, et al. Experience with a clinical decision support system in community pharmacies to recommend narrow-spectrum antimicrobials, nonantimicrobial prescriptions, and OTC products to decrease broad-spectrum antimicrobial use. J Manag Care Pharm 2006;12:390–7.

Mason JD, Colley CA. Effectiveness of an ambulatory care clinical pharmacist: A controlled trial. Annals Pharmacother 1993;27:555–9.

McCord AD. Clinical impact of a pharmacist-managed diabetes mellitus drug therapy management service. Pharmacotherapy 2006;26:248–53.

McKenney JM, Witherspoon JM, Pierpaoli PG. Initial experiences with pharmacy clinic in a hospital-based group medical practice. Am J Hosp Pharm 1981;38:1154–8.

McKenney JM, Wyant SL, Atkins D, et al. Drug therapy assessments by pharmacists. Am J Hosp Pharm 1980;37:824–8.

Meyer SK, Brittan JC, Destache C, et al. A pharmacy fellowship in a family practice training program. Fam Med 1986;18:394–6.

Monson R, Bond CA, Schuna A. Role of the clinical pharmacist in improving drug therapy: Clinical pharmacists in outpatient therapy. Arch Intern Med 1981;141:1441–4.

Morello CM, Zadvorny EB, Cording MA, et al. Development and clinical outcomes of pharmacist-managed diabetes care clinics. Am J Health Syst Pharm 2006;63:1325–31.

Muller BA, McDanel DL. Enhancing quality and safety through physician-pharmacist collaboration [Letter]. Am J Health Syst Pharm 2006;63:996–7.

Nelson AA, Beno CE, Davis RE. Task and cost analysis of integrated clinical pharmacy services in private family practice centers. J Fam Pract 1983;16:111–6.

Nelson AA, Meinhold JM, Hutchinson RA. Changes in physicians' attitudes toward pharmacists as drug information consultants following implementation of clinical pharmaceutical services. Am J Hosp Pharm 1978;35:1201–6.

Nichol A, Downs GE. The pharmacist as physician extender in family medicine office practice. J Am Pharm Assoc 2006;46:77–83.

Odegard PS, Goo A, Hummel J, et al. Caring for poorly controlled diabetes mellitus: A randomized pharmacist intervention. Ann Pharmacother 2005;39:433–40.

Olson KL, Rasmussen J, Sandhoff BG, et al. Lipid management in patients with coronary artery disease by a clinical pharmacy service in a group model health maintenance organization. Arch Intern Med 2005;165:49–54.

Pauley TR, Magee MJ, Cury JD. Pharmacist-managed, physician-directed asthma management program reduces emergency department visits. Ann Pharmacother 1005;29:5–9.

Perry PJ, Hurley SC. Activities of the clinical pharmacist practicing in the office of a family practitioner. Drug Intell Clin Pharm 1975;9:129–33.

Pickard AS, Hung SY. An update on evidence of clinical pharmacy services' impact on health-related quality of life. Ann Pharmacother 2006;40:1623–34.

Ragucci KR, Fermo JD, Wessell AM, et al. Effectiveness of pharmacist-administered diabetes mellitus education and management services. Pharmacotherapy 2005;25:1809–16.

Rapoport A, Akbik H. Pharmacist-managed pain clinic at a Veterans Affairs medical center. Am J Health Syst Pharm 2004;61:1341–3.

Rehring TF, Stolcpart RS, Sandhoff BG, et al. Effect of a clinical pharmacy service on lipid control in patients with peripheral arterial disease. J Vasc Surg 2006;43:1205–10.

Reid F, Murray P, Storrie M. Implementation of a pharmacist-led clinic for hypertensive patients in primary care—a pilot study. Pharm World Sci 2005;27:202.

Reilly V, Cavanagh M. The clinical and economic impact of a secondary heart disease prevention clinic jointly implemented by a practice nurse and pharmacist. Pharm World Sci 2003;25:294–8.

Rickles NM, Svarstad BL, Statz-Paynter JL, et al. Pharmacist telemonitoring of antidepressant use: Effects on pharmacist-patient collaboration. J Am Pharm Assoc 2005;45:344–53.

Robinson JD, Curry W, Dallman JJ, et al. Antibiotic prescribing in a family medicine residency program. J Fam Pract 1982;15:111–7.

Robinson JD, Stewart RB, Curry RW. The pharmacist as a member of the primary care team: Experience in a university-based program. Postgrad Med 1982;71:97–103.

Roth MT, Andrus MR, Westman EC. Outcomes from an outpatient smoking-cessation clinic. Pharmacotherapy 2005;25:279–88.

Rothman R, Malone R, Bryant B, et al. Pharmacist-led, primary care-based disease management improves hemoglobin A1c in high-risk patients with diabetes. Am J Med Qual 2003;18:51–8.

Sadik A, Yousif M, McElnay JC. Pharmaceutical care of patients with heart failure. Br J Clin Pharmacol 2005;60:183–93.

Saini B, Krass I, Armour C. Development, implementation, and evaluation of a community pharmacy-based asthma care model. Ann Pharmacotherapy 2004;38:1954–60.

Sarrafizadeh M, Waite NM, Hobson EH, et al. Pharmacist-facilitated enrollment in drug assistance programs in a private ambulatory care clinic. Am J Health Syst Pharm 2004;61:1816–20.

Schneider EF, Weart CW, Carson DS. Family medicine clinical pharmacy: The South Carolina experience. J Pharm Pract 1992;5:31–6.

Schumock GT, Butler MG, Meek PD, et al. Evidence of economic benefit of clinical pharmacy services: 1996–2000. Pharmacotherapy 2003;23:113–32.

Scott DM, Boyd ST, Stephan M, et al. Outcomes of pharmacist-managed diabetes care services in a community health center. Am J Health Syst Pharm 2006;63:2116–22.

Sellors J, Kaczorowski J, Sellors C, et al. A randomized controlled trial of a pharmacist consultation program for family physicians and their elderly patients. CMAJ 2003;169:17–22.

Shah S, Dowell J, Greene S. Evaluation of clinical pharmacy services in a hematology/oncology outpatient setting. Ann Pharmacother 2006;40:1527–33.

Shaughnessy AF, D'Amico F. Long-term experience with a program to improve prescription-writing skills. Fam Med 1994;26:168–71.

Shaughnesy AF, D'Amico F, Nickel RO. Improving prescription-writing skills in a family practice residency. Ann Pharmacother 1991;25:17–21.

Shaughnessy AF, Hume AL. Clinical pharmacists in family practice residency programs. J Fam Pract 1990;31:305–9.

Shaughnessy AF, Nickel RO. Prescription-writing patterns and errors in a family medicine residency program. J Fam Pract 1989;29:290–5.

Shojania KG, Ranji SR, McDonald KM, et al. Effects of quality improvement strategies for type 2 diabetes on glycemic control: A meta-regression analysis. JAMA 2006;296:427–40.

Siegel D, Lopez J, Meier J, et al. Academic detailing to improve antihypertensive prescribing patterns. Am J Hypertens 2003;16:508–11.

Singh-Franco D, Li L, Hannah S, et al. Role of clinical pharmacists in a heart failure clinic. Hosp Pharm 2005;40:890–6.

Snella KA, Sachdev GP. A primer for developing pharmacist-managed clinics in the outpatient setting. Pharmacotherapy 2003;23:1153–66.

Solomon DK, Portner TS, Bass GE, et al. Part 2. Clinical and economic outcomes in the hypertension and COPD arms of a multicenter outcomes study. J Am Pharm Assoc 1998;38:574–85.

Sookaneknun P, Richards RM, Sanguansermsri J, et al. Pharmacist involvement in primary care improves hypertensive patient clinical outcomes. Ann Pharmacother 2004;38:2023–8.

Sramek JJ, Tornatore FL. The family pharmacist [Letter]. Drug Intell Clin Pharm 1977;11:369.

Steyer TE, Ragucci KR, Pearson WS, et al. The role of pharmacists in the delivery of influenza vaccinations. Vaccine 2004;22:1001–6.

Thompson JF, McGhan WF, Ruffalo RL, et al. Clinical pharmacists prescribing drug therapy in a geriatric setting: Outcome of a trial. J Am Geriatrics Soc 1984;32:154–9.

Till LT, Voris JC, Horst JB. Assessment of clinical pharmacist management of lipid-lowering therapy in a primary care setting. J Manage Care Pharm 2003;9:269–73.

Vivian EM. Improving blood pressure control in a pharmacist-managed hypertension clinic. Pharmacotherapy 2002;22:1533–40.

Walker S, Willey CW. Impact on drug costs and utilization of a clinical pharmacist in a multisite primary care medical group. J Manag Care Pharm 2004;10:345–54.

Walton T, Holloway KP, Knauss MD. Pharmacist-managed anemia program in an outpatient hemodialysis population. Hosp Pharm 2005;40:1051–6.

Weinberger M, Murray MD, Marrero DG, et al. Effectiveness of pharmacist care for patients with reactive airways disease: A randomized controlled trial. JAMA 2002;288:1594–602.

Weitzel KW, Presley DN, Showalter ML, et al. Pharmacist-managed headache clinic. Am J Health Syst Pharm 2004;61:2548–50.

White EV. A family pharmacist takes a critical look at the report of the study commission on pharmacy. Drug Intell Clin Pharm 1977;11:94–101.

Willey ML, Chagan L, Sisca TS, et al. A pharmacist-managed anticoagulation clinic: Six-year assessment of patient outcomes. Am J Health Syst Pharm 2003;60:1033–7.

Witt DM, Sadler MA, Shanahan RL, et al. Effect of a centralized clinical pharmacy anticoagulation service on the outcomes of anticoagulation therapy. Chest 2005;127:1515–22.

Yanchick J. Implementation of a pharmacist run drug therapy monitoring clinic in the primary care setting. Am J Health Syst Pharm 2000;57(suppl 4):S30–4.

Zillich AJ, Doucette WR, Carter BL, et al. Development and initial validation of an instrument to measure physician-pharmacist collaboration from the physician perspective. Value Health 2005;8:59–66.

Zillich AJ, Ryan M, Adams A, et al. Effectiveness of a pharmacist-based smoking-cessation program and its impact on quality of life. Pharmacotherapy 2002;22:759–65.

Zillich AJ, Sutherland JM, Kumbera PA, et al. Hypertension outcomes through blood pressure monitoring and evaluation by pharmacists (HOME study). J Gen Intern Med 2005;20:1091–6.

EDUCATION

Users' Guides to Medical Literature Series (http://www.cche.net/usersguides/main.asp)

Barratt A, Irwig L, Glasziou P, et al. Users' guides to the medical literature. XVII. How to use guidelines and recommendations about screening. JAMA 1999;281:2029–34.

Bucher HC, Guyatt GH, Cook DJ, et al. Users' guides to the medical literature. XIX. Applying clinical trial results. A. How to use an article measuring the effect of an intervention on surrogate end points. JAMA 1999;282:771–8.

Dans AL, Dans LF, Guyatt GH, et al. Users' guides to the medical literature. XIV. How to decide on the applicability of clinical trial results to your patient. JAMA 1998;279:545–9.

Drummond MF, Richardson WS, O'Brien BJ, et al. Users' guides to the medical literature. XIII. How to use an article on economic analysis of clinical practice. A. Are the results of the study valid? JAMA 1997;277:1552–7.

Giacomini MK, Cook DJ. Users' guides to the medical literature. XXIII. Qualitative research in health care. A. Are the results of the study valid? JAMA 2000;284:357–62.

Giacomini MK, Cook DJ. Users' guides to the medical literature. XXIII. Qualitative research in health care. B. What are the results and how do they help me care for my patients? JAMA 2000;284:478–82.

Guyatt GH, Sackett DL, Cook DJ. Users' guides to the medical literature. II. How to use an article about therapy or prevention. A. Are the results of the study valid? JAMA 1993;270:2598–601.

Guyatt GH, Sackett DL, Cook DJ. Users' guides to the medical literature. II. How to use an article about therapy or prevention. B. What were the results and will they help me in caring for my patients? JAMA 1994;271:59–63.

Guyatt GH, Sackett DL, Sinclair JC, et al. Users' guides to the medical literature. IX. A method for grading health care recommendations. JAMA 1995;274:1800–4.

Guyatt GH, Naylor CD, Juniper E, et al. Users' guides to the medical literature. XII. How to use articles about health-related quality of life. JAMA 1997;277:1232–7.

Guyatt GH, Sinclair J, Cook DJ, et al. Users' guides to the medical literature. XVI. How to use a treatment recommendation. JAMA 1999;281:1836–43.

Guyatt GH, Haynes RB, Jaeschke RZ, et al. Users' guides to the medical literature. XXV. Evidence-based medicine: Principles for applying the users' guides to patient care. JAMA 2000;284:1290–6.

Hayward RSA, Wilson MC, Tunis SR, et al. Users' guides to the medical literature. VIII. How to use clinical practice guidelines. A. Are the recommendations valid? JAMA 1995;274:570–4.

Hunt DL, Jaeschke R, McKibbon KA. Users' guides to the medical literature. XXI. Using electronic health information resources in evidence-based practice. JAMA 2000;283:1875–9.

Jaeschke R, Guyatt GH, Sackett DL. Users' guides to the medical literature. III. How to use an article about a diagnostic test. A. Are the results of the study valid? JAMA 1994;271:389–91.

Jaeschke R, Guyatt GH, Sackett DL. Users' guides to the medical literature. III. How to use an article about a diagnostic test. B. What are the results and will they help me in caring for my patients? JAMA 1994;271:703–7.

Laupacis A, Wells G, Richardson S, et al. Users' guides to the medical literature. V. How to use an article about prognosis. JAMA 1994;272:234–7.

Levine M, Walter S, Lee I, et al. Users' guides to the medical literature. IV. How to use an article about harm. JAMA 1994;271:1615–9.

McAlister FA, Laupacis A, Wells GA, et al. Users' guides to the medical literature. XIX. Applying clinical trial results. B. Guidelines for determining whether a drug is exerting (more than) a class effect. JAMA 1999;282:1371–7.

McAlister FA, Straus SE, Guyatt GH, et al. Users' guides to the medical literature. XX. Integrating research evidence with the care of the individual patient. JAMA 2000;283:2829–36.

McGinn TG, Guyatt GH, Wyer PC, et al. Users' guides to the medical literature. XXII. How to use articles about clinical decision rules. JAMA 2000;284:79–84.

Naylor CD, Guyatt GH. Users' guides to the medical literature. X. How to use an article reporting variations in the outcomes of health services. JAMA 1996;274:554–8.

Naylor CD, Guyatt GH. Users' guides to the medical literature. XI. How to use an article about a clinical utilization review. JAMA 1996;275:1435–9.

O'Brien BJ, Heyland D, Richardson WS, et al. Users' guides to the medical literature. XIII. How to use an article on economic analysis of clinical practice. B. What are the results and will they help me in caring for my patients? JAMA 1997;277:1802–6.

Oxman AD, Sackett DL, Guyatt GH. Users' guides to the medical literature. I. How to get started. JAMA 1993;270:2093–5.

Oxman AD, Cook DI, Guyatt GH. Users' guides to the medical literature. VI. How to use an overview. JAMA 1994;272:136–71.

Randolph AG, Haynes, RB, Wyatt JC, et al. Users' guides to the medical literature. XVIII. How to use an article evaluating the clinical impact of a computer-based clinical decision support system. JAMA 1999;282:67–74.

Richardson WS, Detsky AS. Users' guides to the medical literature. VII. How to use a clinical decision analysis A. Are the results of the study valid? JAMA 1994;273:1292–6.

Richardson WS, Detsky AS. Users' guides to the medical literature. VII. How to use a clinical decision analysis B. What are the results and will they help me in caring for my patients? JAMA 1995;273:1610–3.

Richardson WS, Wilson MC, Guyatt GH, et al. Users' guides to the medical literature. XV. How to use an article about disease probability for differential diagnosis. JAMA 1999;281:1214–9.

Richardson WS, Wilson MC, Williams JW Jr, et al. Users' guides to the medical literature. XXIV. How to use an article on the clinical manifestations of disease. JAMA 2000;284:869–75.

Wilson MC, Hayward RSA, Tunis SR, et al. Users' guides to the medical literature. VIII. How to use clinical practice guidelines. B. What are the recommendations and will they help you in caring for your patients? JAMA 1995;274:1630–2.

Annals of Emergency Medicine Stats Series

Gaddis ML, Gaddis GM. Introduction to biostatistics. Part 1. Basic concepts. Ann Emerg Med 1990;19:86–9.

Gaddis ML, Gaddis GM. Introduction to biostatistics. Part 2. Descriptive statistics. Ann Emerg Med 1990;19:309–15.

Gaddis ML, Gaddis GM. Introduction to biostatistics. Part 3. Sensitivity, specificity, predictive value, and hypothesis testing. Ann Emerg Med 1990;19:591–7.

Gaddis ML, Gaddis GM. Introduction to biostatistics. Part 4. Statistical inference techniques in hypothesis testing. Ann Emerg Med 1990;19:820–5.

Gaddis ML, Gaddis GM. Introduction to biostatistics. Part 5. Statistical inference techniques for hypothesis testing with nonparametric data. Ann Emerg Med 1990;19:1054–9.

Gaddis ML, Gaddis GM. Introduction to biostatistics. Part 6. Correlation and regression. Ann Emerg Med 1990;19:1462–8.

Canadian Medical Journal EBM Series (http://www.cmaj.ca/cgi/collection/evidence_based_medicine_series)

Barratt A, Wyer PC, Hatala R, et al. Tips for learners of evidence-based medicine. 1. Relative risk reduction, absolute risk reduction and number needed to treat. CMAJ 2004;171:353–8.

Hatala R, Keitz S, Wyer P, et al. Tips for learners of evidence-based medicine. 4. Assessing heterogeneity of primary studies in systematic reviews and whether to combine their results. CMAJ 2005;172:661–5.

McGinn T, Wyer PC, Newman TB, et al. Tips for learners of evidence-based medicine. 3. Measures of observer variability (kappa statistic). 2004;171:1369–73.

Montori VM, Kleinbart J, Newman TB, et al. Tips for learners of evidence-based medicine. 2. Measures of precision (confidence intervals). CMAJ 2004;171:611–5.

Montori VM, Wyer P, Newman TB, et al. Tips for learners of evidence-based medicine. 5. The effect of spectrum of disease on the performance of diagnostic tests. CMAJ 2005;173:385–90.

Wyer PC, Keitz S, Hatala R, et al. Tips for learning and teaching evidence-based medicine: Introduction to the series [Editorial]. CMAJ 2004;171:347–8.

How to Read a Paper Series (http://www.health.library.mcgill.ca/ebm/greenhalgh.htm)

Greenhalgh T. How to read a paper. The Medline database. BMJ 1997;315:180–3.

Greenhalgh T. How to read a paper. Getting your bearings (deciding what the paper is about). BMJ 1997;315:243–6.

Greenhalgh T. How to read a paper. Assessing the methodological quality of published papers. BMJ 1997;315:305–8.

Greenhalgh T. How to read a paper. Statistics for the non-statistician: different types of data need different statistical tests. BMJ 1997;315:364–6.

Greenhalgh T. How to read a paper. Statistics for the non-statistician II: "significant" relations and their pitfalls. BMJ 1997;315:422–5.

Greenhalgh T. How to read a paper. Papers that report drug trials. BMJ 1997;315:480–3.

Greenhalgh T. How to read a paper. Papers that report diagnostic or screening test. BMJ 1997;315:540–3.

Greenhalgh T. How to read a paper. Papers that tell you what things cost (economic analyses). BMJ 1997;315:496–9.

Greenhalgh T. How to read a paper. Papers that summarize other papers (systematic reviews and meta-analyses). BMJ 1997;315:672–5.

Greenhalgh T. How to read a paper. Papers that go beyond numbers (qualitative research). BMJ 1997;315:740–3.

Information Mastery and EBM

Braitman LE. Confidence intervals assess both clinical significance and statistical significance. Ann Intern Med 1991:114:515–7.

Del Mar C, Glasziou P, Mayer D. Teaching evidence based medicine. BMJ 2004;329:989–90.

Lewis SJ, Orlando BI. The importance and impact of evidence based medicine. J Manag Care Pharm 2004;10:3–5.

Levine M, Ensom MH. Post hoc power analysis: An idea whose time has passed? Pharmacotherapy 2001;21:405–9.

Shaughnessy AF, Slawson DC, Bennett ML. Becoming an information master: A guidebook to the medical information jungle. J Fam Pract 1994;39:489–99.

Shaughnessy AF, Slawson DC, Bennett ML. Separating the wheat from the chaff: Identifying fallacies in pharmaceutical promotion. J Gen Intern Med 1994;9:563–8.

Shaughnessy A, Slawson DC. Are we providing doctors with the training and tools for lifelong learning? BMJ 1999;319:1–3.

Slawson DC, Shaughnessy AF, Bennett ML. Becoming a medical information master: Feeling good about not knowing everything. J Fam Pract 1994;38:505–13.

Sterne JAC, Smith GD. Sifting the evidence—what's wrong with significance tests? BMJ 2001;322:226–31.